Exploring the Edges of Texas

Publication of this book
is generously supported by
a memorial gift in honor of
Mary Frances "Chan" Driscoll,
a founding member of the Advisory Council
of Texas A&M University Press,
by her sons
Henry B. Paup '70 and T. Edgar Paup '74

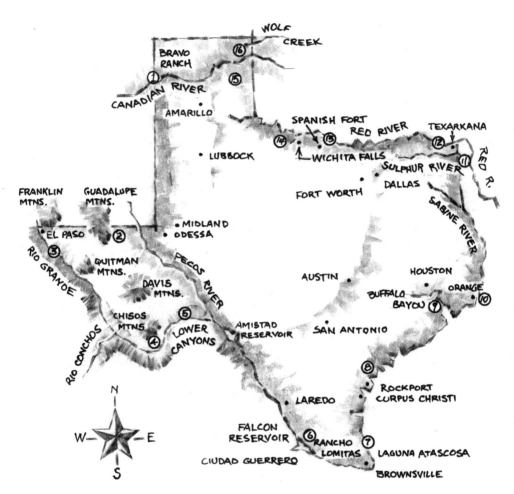

Exploring the Edges of Texas

Walt Davis and Isabel Davis

Drawings by Walt Davis

Texas A&M University Press   College Station

This paper meets the requirements
of ANSI/NISO Z39.48–1992 (Permanence of Paper).
Binding materials have been chosen for durability.

LIBRARY OF CONGRESS CATALOGING-IN-PUBLICATION DATA

Davis, Walt, 1942–
Exploring the edges of Texas / Walt Davis and Isabel Davis ;
drawings by Walt Davis. —
1st ed.
p. cm. —
Includes bibliographical references and index.
ISBN-13: 978-1-60344-153-7 (cloth : alk. paper)
ISBN-10: 1-60344-153-0 (cloth : alk. paper)
1. Texas—Description and travel—Anecdotes.   2. Davis, Walt, 1942– Travel—
Texas—Anecdotes.   3. Davis, Isabel, 1942– Travel—Texas—Anecdotes.
4. Texas—Boundaries—Anecdotes.   5. Automobile travel—Texas—
Anecdotes.   I. Davis, Isabel, 1942– II. Title.
F386.6.D38   2010
917.6404'64—dc22
2009023271

Dedication

For our grandchildren,
Quin Walter, Max Foster, & May Isabel,
with the hope that they will find
wonder and amazement
in the natural world
our generation
leaves behind

Contents

· ·

Acknowledgments

One of the unexpected pleasures of writing this book has been the opportunity to meet and work with so many knowledgeable, generous, and supportive people. Early on, Shannon Davies, natural environment editor for Texas A&M University Press, took us under her editorial wing and helped us mold the manuscript. Later, Thom Lemmons shepherded that manuscript through the many steps necessary to create a well-crafted book. Along the way, the staff at Texas A&M Press offered encouragement and expertise that made our work easier and our book better.

Randy Mallory, photographer, writer, and frequent contributor to *Texas Highways Magazine,* read everything we wrote and made many helpful suggestions. Dr. Fred Tarpley and Carolyn Trezevant—neighbors, friends, and advocates for clarity and proper punctuation—helped immensely, as did Panhandle historian Dr. Fred Rathjen, and Isabel's sister Mary Brown. Authors Jim Ainsworth, Kimberly Willis Holt, Jill Nokes, and Matt White, gave advice when we needed it most. Special thanks go to our critique group in Amarillo: Janda Raker, Joan Sikes, Harry Haines, Diane Neal, Jarrad Neal, Michael Bourne, and Jody Koumalats. George Getschow welcomed two novice writers to the prestigious Mayborn Literary Nonfiction Writers Conference of the Southwest. It was there that Deanne Stillman and William Harper administered tough love during manuscript critiques that improved our writing and deepened our respect for the wordsmith's art.

Traveling frequently into unknown territory, we came to understand the importance of an experienced and trustworthy guide. "Broken Hand" Fitzpatrick was not available, so Alvin Lynn stepped in and led us onto the High Plains along an old Comanchero trail. Dr. Gerald Schultz took us into a prehistoric zoo and brought us back in one piece. Tami Besmehn and her sisters, Terri and Jean, saw us safely through the Lower Canyons of the Rio Grande, and Don Greene escorted us through the wilds of Houston on Buffalo Bayou. Bill Scurlock and Earnest Cook, aided by Bill's boys, Jason and Jacob, led the way down the Sulphur River to the Red. Buddy Hollis introduced us to the natural wonders of Newton County. Jack Loftin braved scorching heat to show us the fossil treasures of Archer County, and Steve West introduced us to the birds and bats of Carlsbad Caverns.

Exploring libraries, archives, and collections that held clues to our story required guides of a different sort. At Harvard University, Lisa Decesare of the Gray Herbarium Library, located letters and reports pertaining to Charles Wright. Walter Kittridge helped us find plant specimens in the Gray Herbarium, and Chuck Schaff let us into the fossil collection at the Museum of Comparative Zoology. At Yale University, Barbara Narendra introduced us to the Texas meteorite, "Red River," in the Peabody Museum of Natural History, and Nancy Lyon served as our guide to the spectacular holdings of the Sterling Library.

Closer to home, Betty Bustos welcomed us into the Panhandle-Plains Museum's archive, and Jeff Indeck and Rolla Shaller did the same for its extensive collection of artifacts and fossils. Staff at the Cornette Library at West Texas A&M University provided access to its holdings and helped us secure the loan of important documents from other institutions. Mary Jarvis, Sidnye Johnson, Pam Wilson, Linda Chenoweth, and Carolyn Ottoson were especially helpful.

Archivist Jim Conrad and special collections assistant Dee Dee Marshall of the Gee Library, Texas A&M University–Commerce, found many useful things for us. Cheri Carew of the Commerce Public Library arranged several interlibrary loans. The staff of the Orange Public Library and Bonnie Smith, Chair of the Newton County Historical Commission, helped us locate and reproduce key documents.

The many people who told their stories, shared the results of their research, and made available their lifetime of experience, provided the heart and soul of this book. Jim and Johnnie Sue McDonald talked to us about ranching on the High Plains. Nancy and Fred Gehlbach passed on lessons learned from years of ecological research, much of it in the Guadalupe Mountains National Park, where rangers Fred Armstrong, Anne Marie Ballou, Gordon Bell, Dave Bieri, and Tom Hartung answered our questions and gave us welcome advice on back-country path finding. Wayne Bartholomew, of Frontera Audubon nature preserve, helped us find people and places in the Lower Rio Grande Valley. Benito Treviño shared his passion for preserving the plants and folk wisdom of the brush country. Mick Castillo told us about resource management in Santa Anna National Wildlife Refuge, and Chris Best put the botanical riches of South Texas into historical and geographical perspective.

John Wallace, at Laguna Atascosa National Wildlife Refuge, introduced us to wildlife biologist Jody Mays, our guide through the mosaic of Gulf Coast habitats. At Rockport, we met volunteer bird guides Polly Freese and Ray Little. In Houston, urban historian Janet K. Wagner and community activist Terry Hershey opened the door to that city's complex relationship with Buffalo Bayou.

Michael Hoke, in Orange, took time out from hurricane preparation to tell us the story of the Shangri La botanical garden. Biographer Ellen W. Rienstra answered our questions about the the Lutcher and Moore Lumber Company and the family histories of its owners.

Meredith and Ethel Edwards told us what it was like to live through a Red River flood. Dee Ann Story and Kathleen Gilmore described their colleague and friend R. King Harris, and provided information about French trading posts near Texarkana. Farther upriver, Robert Fenoglio helped us find the site of the old Tayovaya/Wichita village near Spanish Fort, and Clarice Whiteside escorted us through her father's collection of artifacts in Nocona. Adrian and Cliffy Hill outlined twentieth century changes in the Red River valley that have altered the pattern of people's lives.

In the Panhandle, Harley Goettsche recalled for us his early fossil-hunting days. Harold and Kirk Courson explained how conservation easements work and what it takes to facilitate archeological excavations. Archeologist Scott Brosowske briefed us on the Plains Village culture, and Danny Witt took us on a tour of archeological sites on the LIPS Ranch. Allan and Will Durett welcomed us onto the Spring Creek Ranch, and next door, Jack Shelton and his family granted access to the Bravo. Their hospitality made our visits to their property both productive and enjoyable.

Many people played host during our travels around the state. Eleanor Glazener opened the doors to her weekend home overlooking the Canadian River. Julie Johnson and Don McDonald offered up their adobe guest house near the rim of Palo Duro Canyon. My sister, Patti Hamilton, and her husband, Cla, provided good meals, hot showers, and a warm bed on several occasions. Good friends Mary Ann Cathey and Fred Stoker hosted us in Canyon, and Evelyn Luciani did the same in Marfa. Beth and Larry Francell invited us to a delightful dinner at their historic home in Fort Davis, and across the state in another vintage home, Linda Scurlock fed a hungry band of river-runners twice. On a hot day in August, Marie Loftin open her door to a wilted team of fossil-hunters, plied us with bottomless glasses of iced tea and brought us back to life with a home-cooked meal and fresh apple pie. Hospitality is a tonic to the traveler.

Our list of unsung heroes includes Steve Young, who jump-started our truck when the alternator failed, then helped us change a flat in triple digit heat. The men at Loe's radiator shop in Midland dropped everything to perform an emergency radiator repair, and Lemay's Towing from Texarkana pulled us off a pesky culvert near the Sulphur River. And imagine our surprise, while changing a flat on a backcountry road in the Chisos, when three cyclists appeared out of nowhere, dropped their bikes, and helped us out. Jenny and Mark Aliprandini, and Dan Klepper were not just good Samaritans, they were fellow desert pilgrims.

And, as any author with family ties knows, someone has to take on extra duty to free up time for travel, research, and writing. Isabel's sisters, Sally Evans and Mary Brown, did that for us, and we are grateful. If it takes a village to raise a child, it takes a whole town to produce a book. We are deeply indebted to all who helped along the way.

Preface

· ·

The border of Texas creates one of the most widely recognized shapes in all of geography. That border is longer than the Amazon River. Driving its every twist and turn would be like driving from Miami to Los Angeles by way of New York. Flying from the Swiss Alps to the mountains of Afghanistan would cover no greater distance than a journey along the edge of Texas. This book is the account of such a journey.

Credit Frank X. Tolbert for planting the seed. His *Dallas Morning News* column, "Tolbert's Texas," was a staple in our house when I was growing up in Oak Cliff. It was one of the few items in the newspaper besides the "funnies" that I read regularly. In 1955, five days before my thirteenth birthday, Tolbert left Dallas in a Willis Jeep, accompanied by his nine-year-old son, Frank Jr., to circumnavigate Texas and phone in articles about their adventures. I rode with them, vicariously, and vowed to repeat their feat when I grew up.

Fifty years later, I found a way to keep that promise. My wife, Isabel, and I set out on our own trip around the state. The journey would take us through nine of the ten ecological regions of Texas. We were bound to see some beautiful country, encounter plenty of wildlife, and meet some interesting people along the way. "While we are at it," I suggested, "let's write a book about our experiences." Isabel agreed, and the adventure began.

We divided the border into sixteen segments. In each segment we picked a spot to highlight: national park, stretch of wild river, mountain range, archeological site. Next we looked for a firsthand account of that place written by a previous visitor: artist, explorer, naturalist, paleontologist, archeologist. With these historical touchstones we could compare past and present aspects of the places visited. The result was a plan for a four thousand-mile-long, three-century-deep exploration of the edge of Texas.

Executing the plan required three modifications. If we found an interesting place near the Red River but not on its banks, we included it. If a compelling story unfolded inland from the shore of the Gulf of Mexico, we told it. We agreed that if a place or event occurred in a county impinging on the state line, it was fair game. The border we explored was one county wide (with a few exceptions).

The second modification was more painful. We did not circle the state in a single trip as the Tolberts had. Family obligations made such an extended trip impossible. We drove to the border many times, completed a section or two, and returned to home base. A map of our travels looks more like a spider web the shape of Texas than a single line encircling it.

The last modification had to do with time. We compressed it. If we had to make more than one trip to get the whole story of a place, we combined them into a single narrative. If it made more sense to change the order in which things happened, we did so. Our goal was to tell a true story with the boring parts left out and the confusing parts rearranged.

With our rules of engagement in place, we next defined individual roles. Isabel kept a journal of our travels, headed up the research effort, critiqued drafts, and was the official fact-checker. I served as expedition artist, produced initial drafts, and made final revisions. Traveling we did together.

The "why" of our trip is more difficult to explain than the "what" or the "how." We could combine the skills and experiences of two professional careers into a single project. For me it was the continuation of a life-long love affair with outdoor Texas. I spent thirty years on the staff of the Dallas Museum of Natural History organizing collections, building wildlife dioramas, teaching, and leading field trips. I rafted down the Rio Grande, rappelled into caves, and hiked the deserts and mountains of the Trans-Pecos. I spent the last twelve years of my career as director of the Panhandle-Plains Historical Museum, where I learned to appreciate the history, archeology, and paleontology of the High Plains. This trip around Texas enabled me to revisit some familiar places and also break new ground.

For Isabel it was a chance to do some interesting detective work. She put the research skills of a professional librarian to work ferreting out the letters, journals, diaries, and official reports we needed to reconstruct the stories of the men and women in whose footsteps we walked. Her sleuthing took us to museums, archives, and universities far from Texas.

Another reason for writing this book was born in a university much closer to home. Samuel Wood Geiser was chairman of the biology department at Southern Methodist University for many years and wrote a book entitled *Naturalists of the Frontier*. In it he tells the story of eleven men who made important scientific discoveries in nineteenth century Texas. One, a botanist, walked nearly seven hundred miles from San Antonio to El Paso in 1849 collecting plants for the Harvard herbarium. Another, born in Switzerland, died while collecting fossils near the Red River in 1880.

Reading Geiser's book, we realized that the natural history of Texas was written by people of passion and determination who risked danger and endured hardship in the name of science. A trip around the state gave us a chance to connect their personal stories to the places they explored, to the plants and animals they discovered, and to the fossils and artifacts they unearthed. It also provided us an opportunity to compare Texas then with Texas now and assess the differences.

On a more personal level, our trip gave us an opportunity to examine the strange power natural places have over many people. Isabel and I have been deeply affected by it. As a boy I wandered up and down Ash Creek near our home in Dallas. I came to know its inhabitants well: crawdads, tadpoles, blue jays, and squirrels. On many a Saturday morning, before the family was up, I left the house with a chocolate bar, canteen of water, bird book, and binoculars to explore the farther reaches of my domain. I tasted freedom on those walks and discovered the solitary pleasure of wild places.

Isabel grew up in rural East Texas spending much of her time out-doors. Spring found her picking dewberries, alert for snakes beneath the vines. She spent summer afternoons in the secret shade of a wild grape arbor. Isabel learned where to look for edible plants: sour dock, wild plums, chinquapins, and the lip-numbing bark of the tickle tongue tree. She climbed trees, swam in the creek, and went on family fishing trips to a deep hole in the Neches River called Big Eddy.

Isabel took me there shortly after we married. We unpacked our Volkswagen "bug," pitched our tent, and cooked supper on a Coleman stove. With darkness came a deafening nocturnal chorus of katydids, tree frogs, bull frogs, toads, and chuck-will's-widows. When a great-horned owl hooted nearby, we crouched under a fallen tree, and I imitated the sound of a wounded animal. The owl sailed silently out of the woods and lit on a branch above our heads, barely beyond reach—a wild silhou-ette against a background of stars. The bird brought with it one more manifestation of the power natural places had exerted on each of us since childhood. That night we experienced it together.

In the years that followed, we camped in the Chisos Mountains of Big Bend and chalked up a long list of "lifers," birds neither of us had seen before. We climbed Enchanted Rock by the light of the moon and explored bat caves illuminated by carbide lamps on hard hats. We canoed the Brazos, Trinity, and Guadalupe. We rafted down the Rio Grande. Experiencing such places affected us deeply and reminded us that we are part of something much larger than ourselves—something that began long ago in a time beyond imagining.

Fifty years after Frank X. Tolbert planted an idea in the head of a thirteen-year-old boy, Isabel and I started out on our own circum-navigation of Texas. We had a plan, but the unexpected was a constant companion. That was part of the adventure.

Exploring the Edges of Texas

WALT DAVIS

Prairie Pathfinder

We made our beds under the canopy of the starry heavens,
which shone so luminously that there was more pleasure in tracing
the various constellations than in endeavoring to sleep.

J. W. ABERT,

Gúadal P'a: The Journal of Lieutenant J. W. Abert
from Bent's Fort to St. Louis in 1845

L IEUTENANT ABERT'S mapping expedition was nearing the Texas-New Mexico border on September 3, 1845, when something went wrong. It happened while his men were setting up camp on a patch of prairie beside the Canadian River. Wagons were parked, tents pitched, horses and mules grazed nearby. Suddenly, shouts rang out, and men came running. Abert recorded the incident in his journal: "We were always obliged to burn a place in the prairie, in the center of which the fire is built, some of the people standing by with blankets ready to prevent its spreading too far. In this instance the fire got beyond all control, but fortunately the wind was blowing from our camp and by much exertion the fire was kept from spreading in that direction. The tall reeds which grew so luxuriantly in the valley below us, with a loud crackling noise were . . . swept away by the devouring flame. Soon it reached the trees on the side of the bank and, leaping from bough to bough, quickly despoiled them of their verdant foliage; then, mounting the bluff, was borne rapidly off over the far-spreading prairie."[1]

Jim McDonald, manager of Spring Creek Ranch

As frightening as the fire was to those in harm's way, it had long been a natural occurrence on the Great Plains. Thunderstorms brought precious water but also lightning. A single strike could spark a blaze. Driven by the wind, it might burn for days and scorch hundreds of square miles of prairie. Native Americans often set fires to drive game or confuse enemies. Whatever the cause, fire was a boon to the prairie habitat, enriching the soil and keeping the grassland free of trees. Some fires were so intense they created their own weather, as Lieutenant Abert soon discovered: "About 7 o'clock in the evening it had extended to a great distance and was rapidly advancing in a semicircular form . . . The flames having disturbed the equilibrium of the atmosphere, a countercurrent soon bore back a heavy cloud . . . which advanced until directly over our heads, when a severe thunderstorm broke upon us, illuminated by vivid flashes of lightning . . . The crackling of consuming vegetation and the low murmurings of the whirling eddies of wind which skirted the burning edge deepened the impression of this scene of grand sublimity."[2]

By morning, the conflagration was far away, and U.S. Army Lt. James W. Abert turned his attention to smoke more sinister than sublime. His expedition had entered Comanche-Kiowa country, and signal fires carried news of its arrival onto the plains ahead. From that point on, Abert's guides selected campsites carefully, with an eye toward protection from surprise attack. On September 5, with smoke from the prairie fire still visible behind them, Abert crossed into Texas with four wagons, sixty-three head of horses and mules, and thirty-two men, including eleven Frenchmen and two African-Americans.[3] The young lieutenant had been sent by Capt. John C. Frémont to "make a reconnaissance . . . along the Canadian River."[4]

One hundred-fifty years later, Isabel and I set out on a reconnaissance of our own. We want to see what remains of the world Abert explored. Having read his report and studied his map, we believe his first campsite in Texas was along Mineosa Creek on what is today the Spring Creek Ranch. We intend to find it.

Driving west from Channing on State Highway 767, we pass through some of the most sparsely inhabited real estate in Texas. Oldham County has fewer than two people per square mile, and our highway map shows only five roads in nearly fifteen-hundred square miles. But the wildflower population is immeasurable. Prairie verbena, Indian blanket, pink paintbrush, and purple foxglove bloom in roadside ditches. Scurvy pea and spectacle pod grow there too, beside yellow daisy, chocolate daisy, pink mimosa, and globe mallow.

Trees, however, are scarce—not a single one to be seen as we turn off the highway and drive south toward ranch headquarters. Five miles later, we pull up to a cluster of white houses, sheds, barns, and corrals nestled under the shade of huge cottonwoods watered by the springs that give the ranch its name. Foreman Jim McDonald emerges from a modest frame house and walks out to greet us. He is in his late fifties, straight as a board, and weather-beaten. His wife, Johnnie Sue, is tiny and energetic with short no-nonsense hair and skin seasoned by the same weather that tanned her husband.

When Isabel asks how many hands it takes to run a thirty-six thousand-acre ranch, McDonald answers, "We are it." He says the two of them do 90 percent of the work, from building fence to branding. "Johnnie Sue and I can put in a mile of fence posts before lunch. The other day, with the help of one hired hand, we branded, castrated, and doctored 164 calves in two-and-a-half hours. That's better than a calf a minute."

I explain that we have come looking for the campsite where Lt. Abert's party spent the night beside a stream of clear water winding through a deep ravine.[5] McDonald offers to lead us to a spot overlooking Mineosa Creek, a spring-fed stream closely resembling the one Abert described. Declining an offer to ride with us, he walks over to a battered orange dirt bike, kicks it into action, and roars off in a narrow cloud of dust. Jim McDonald rides the range on a motorcycle rather than a horse. He buys secondhand bikes several at a time, reconditions them, and rides them into the ground. In twenty-five years of ranch work, he has worn out twenty-five bikes. They are less trouble than horses, he believes, and faster. We clock the Honda XR at thirty-five miles per hour on straightaways but nearly run into it when McDonald skids to a halt. Laying down the bike, he steps off the road into a patch of prairie verbena and picks a spray. "Smell this," he says, sticking a fist-full of blue flowers under my nose. "I like the aroma, but sometimes it's so heavy it's nauseating." A few seconds later we are bouncing along after him, eyes fixed on a bike that could stop any minute to smell the flowers.

He finally pulls up on a rise with a sweeping view to the west. We step from the truck into an ageless panorama. "This is just gorgeous," Isabel says turning in a slow circle. "There is not a tree, a building, a telephone pole—nothing but prairie and sky as far as the eye can see." Somewhere in the immensity before us is the place where Abert and his men spent their first night on Texas soil. Finding their campsite will take more time than we anticipated. We decide to come back to this spot later, with our travel trailer, and use it as a base camp for a more thorough exploration.

When the young lieutenant came this way, war with Mexico was in the air. Ambitious military officers could smell it coming, and with it, the opportunity for fame and glory. Eager to understand the lay of the land that might become tomorrow's battlefield, the U.S. Army dispatched its best and brightest pathfinders to map the American Southwest. Conspicuous among them was Capt. John C. Frémont, who was ordered to make his way to Bent's Fort on the Arkansas River, then move south to explore the Canadian.[6] But Frémont had a different idea. He ignored orders, set a course for California, and assigned a junior officer to complete the original mission.

The captain made a curious choice when he picked a replacement. Lt. Abert was just three years out of West Point, where he graduated fifty-fifth in a class of fifty-six. He was the undistinguished member of a distinguished military family. His grandfather, John Abert, came from France with Rochambeau to help win the American Revolution. His father, John James Abert, fought in the War of 1812 and was chief of the Corps of Topographical Engineers when his son was assigned to that branch of service.[7] The young lieutenant did have three talents, however, that would serve him well—he could draw, he could write, and he could delegate.

The first thing he did was give day-to-day control of the expedition to his guide, Thomas "Broken Hand" Fitzpatrick.[8] At forty-six, Fitzpatrick was twenty-one years older than Abert[9] and already a living legend. He was present at the original fur trapper's rendezvous in 1825 and was the brains behind the Rocky Mountain Fur Company. He and Jedediah Smith discovered the South Pass over the Rockies, and Fitzpatrick led the first two wagon trains over it on what became known as the Oregon Trail.[10] Although the guide had never explored the Canadian River country, his experience in wilderness travel and his knack for keeping his charges safe in hostile territory insured the success of Abert's assignment.

Fortunately, the expedition's professional hunter, John Hatcher, did know the territory well. He had lived on the plains with the Kiowa and had been adopted into the tribe. The senior member of the party was octogenarian Caleb Greenwood—a veteran mountain man also adopted by the Kiowa.[11] With the help of these three men, Abert turned a low-profile, high-risk assignment into a career-making success.

After seventeen days of meticulous work in a dangerous place, Abert's party exited the Texas Panhandle, all hands accounted for, mission accomplished. According to historian Frederick Rathjen, the resulting map was "the first trustworthy representation of that vast territory."[12] The accompanying report contained "the best description of the primeval Panhandle . . . replete with observations of the land and its native human, animal, and vegetable occupants."[13]

Isabel and I return to Spring Creek Ranch and park our travel trailer on the knoll overlooking Mineosa Creek. We picture ourselves sitting under the awning in the late afternoon sipping cold beer and drinking in primeval Panhandle scenery. Instead, clouds gather, and the wind picks up. Stalks of yucca blossoms bob back and forth while clumps of stiff grass bend and shiver with each new gust. A cold front drops the temperature ten degrees in thirty minutes, setting off thunderstorms to the west. I park the truck beside the trailer to break the force of the wind, then climb onto the roof with a roll of duct tape to batten down the antenna and kitchen vent clattering in the gale.

Thankfully, the storm passes harmlessly to the south, and we sleep soundly until the alarm buzzes at 6:30 A.M. After a quick breakfast, we pack a lunch, and drive to our morning rendezvous. The foreman of a neighboring ranch to the south has agreed to guide us to a portion of Mineosa Creek that closely fits Abert's description of a coliseum of rock in a tortuous ravine. Cody Mason is a stout, clean-shaven young man wearing a gimme cap from Tavebaugh Veterinary. The even younger cowboy with him, Jason Davis, wears a dirty white Carhart jacket and a blood-spattered felt cowboy hat pulled down tight over his ears.

They look at our map, confer briefly, then climb into a white heavy-duty pickup and head south. We follow, noting that Mason has tied, not one, but two spare tires to the flatbed behind the cab. Fifteen miles and five windmills later, the road shrinks to a double track with grass and scrub mesquite growing in the middle. We finally stop and walk to an overlook with an expansive view of the creek winding back and forth between tight bends beneath hundred-foot cliffs. Davis gathered cattle out of this pasture yesterday and warns us about rattlesnakes. Mason reinforces the message, telling us that some of the larger snakes are "progressive." He explains that some rattlers on this part of the ranch advance rather than retreat when cornered.

Mason and Davis review the landmarks we must follow on our way out. Then they climb back into their truck and leave us to explore on foot. We pack up water and snacks and take a solemn oath to watch where we put our hands and feet from this point on. Less than ten minutes pass before we hear a nerve-rattling buzz. A small diamondback with black bands encircling its tail retreats quickly into a catclaw acacia. We give it wide berth. With eyes riveted to the ground, we carefully explore rocky ledges looking for a way down.

Davis had seen water in the creek recently, but we see only dried mud and sand. A familiar chattering overhead catches our attention, and we risk a glance skyward to see cliff swallows banking and turning above our heads. Water must be near because these birds build nests of fresh mud. Sure enough, at the next overlook we spot pools below and a cattle trail that descends the canyon wall.

The first thing we notice is a plant that shouldn't be here—salt cedar. Sometimes called tamarisk, this invader from Africa and the Middle East is a growing menace in the Southwest. It soaks up precious water by the gallon and leaves native species, especially cottonwood, dying of thirst. Other trees are more familiar—rough-barked, disease-resistant hackberry and delicate soapberry with golden, grape-sized fruit popular with mockingbirds and cedar waxwings. These trees are savvy survivors acclimated to the harsh winters and blistering summers of the High Plains. Hackberry has been around for at least four million years. Its fossilized seeds show up in sedimentary rocks of that vintage.[14]

We notice an even more ominous change from Abert's day. The springs are gone. The Canadian River valley was once famous for its bubbling springs and flowing freshwater creeks. Today, the water level is dropping in the underlying Ogallala aquifer, a buried reservoir the size of Lake Erie that stretches from Texas to South Dakota. Mammoth irrigation wells pump water out faster than rain can replace it, and cities suck it up to meet the needs of urbanites. Some scientists consider the water in the Ogallala "fossil water" and classify it as a non-renewable resource.[15]

Abert reported taking a refreshing bath in a stream near his party's first campsite in Texas. If he were to bathe in Mineosa Creek today, he would not find the clear, cold, spring-fed pool he described in 1845. Instead, he would lie down in a shallow, mud-bottomed puddle of rainwater stained green with algae and pock-marked with cow tracks.

After five hours of looking, however, we cannot pinpoint the location of Abert's campsite. Thirty-three men, camped for a single night a century-and-a-half ago, left few clues. Taking one last look from the rim on the way out, we spy what local archeologist Jack Hughes called a "living artifact." Curly dock is a sturdy plant with twisted leaves and a rust-colored seed head. It grows back year-after-year from a large tuberous root that Plains Indians found delectable. Women dug it up and brought it into camp where cast-off seeds and roots sprouted long after the gatherers had gone. Persistent stands of curly dock frequently mark Native American campsites. Maybe adopted Kiowas Caleb Greenwood and John Hatcher found an old Indian campsite that fit the needs of a weary band of map-makers and stopped here for the night. Without a metal detector and a lot of luck, we may never know.

"What a waste," Isabel laments as we climb back in the truck. "No campsite, and after all that watching and only one snake. I'm glad it wasn't 'progressive.'" Back at the trailer, we notice clouds gathering again in the west. A potent electrical storm bears down on our hilltop campsite as we pack up and leave for home. For the next week, the local weatherman's radar screen is filled with angry red patches indicating "strong thunderstorms with dangerous lightning" all along the Canadian River valley.

It is nearly noon when the waitress at the Eagle Diner in Canyon, Texas, pulls two long tables together near the front window, facing the courthouse square. The bell attached to the door jangles as the first customer arrives. She is part of a group that has been meeting for lunch and conversation since 1985. As the librarian pulls up a chair, the paleontologist comes in, then the archeologists, the museum people, and finally the historian and his wife. Noted for strong opinions freely expressed, members proudly call themselves "curmudgeons." Bring up any question about the history, geology, archeology, or biology of the High Plains, and one of them will have an answer.

Today, Isabel and I take seats next to Alvin Lynn, a retired science teacher and coach who knows more about the historic trails of the Texas Panhandle than anyone else in the state. Lynn is a tall, fit man just turned seventy. Gray hair, clipped short, frames a tanned bare crown. Deep-set, sky-blue eyes echo the faded denim of a well-worn, pearl-buttoned Levi shirt and jeans.

We push aside the silverware, paper napkins, and iced tea glasses, to open up our travel-worn copy of *The Roads of Texas.* We show Lynn the place where we parked our trailer and the spot where we think Abert may have camped. Lynn lays beside our map a photocopy of Lieutenant Abert's official report of his travels and gives us the bad news.

"I don't believe Abert camped on Mineosa creek."

He opens the report to a section entitled *Comanche Country—Flowers on the Plains—Unseen Indians,* and reads: "We continued on the same trail as yesterday until about 8 o'clock, when, finding that we were rapidly diverging from the river, we were forced to leave it and to shape our course almost direct for the Goo-al-pa [the Comanche name for the Canadian River] . . . after a toilsome march of 17 miles, reached the bank, cañoned by bluff escarpment 100 feet high and absolutely impossible of descent. We were obliged to make a retrograde movement, and camped in a deep tortuous ravine where we found a little stream of clear water, in which I had a delightful bath where it made a very abrupt bend back upon itself and seemed enclosed by a coliseum of rocks."[16]

Lynn plots distances and directions on the map before us and pencils in his idea of Abert's route. "I have been to this spot," he says, pointing to the place where the Comanchero trail diverges from the river. "If they left the trail here and went straight to the river, then the 'deep tortuous ravine' they camped in was probably Chisum Canyon, not Mineosa Creek."

Lynn collects a list of clues from Abert's report to help us pinpoint the elusive campsite. The lieutenant records "limestone underlain by new red sandstone . . . huge petrified logs . . . Antelopes . . . shore larks [prairie horned larks] . . . yucca of the plains . . . and cottonwood." One wildflower especially impressed him. "We saw here an abundance of the cardinal flower, *Lobelia cardinalis*. They looked most brilliantly as they glistened in bright scarlet array among the green plants which grew so luxuriantly along the border of the stream as to conceal it in many places entirely."[17]

"Why don't we give it another try?" Lynn suggests. "I'll go with you and take along the metal detector. Maybe we can find some hard evidence of the expedition."

Alvin Lynn slows his four-wheel-drive Chevy pickup as we cross the state line into eastern New Mexico not far from Nara Visa. We are looking for the unmarked entrance to Bravo Ranch, once part of the fabled XIT. Shortly after turning in and crossing back into Texas, we pick up two of the clues we are looking for. A small herd of pronghorns (antelope to Abert) looks up from grazing, assembles in tight formation, courses across the rolling short-grass pasture, then stops and turns to look back. That mistake would have meant fresh meat for supper in Abert's day. Prairie horned larks flush ahead of the truck, fly a short distance, then drop back to earth and disappear. Pronghorns and larks are encouraging signs, but hardly definitive.

"I want to show you something," Lynn says, as the truck rolls to a stop, and he sets the brake. We can see for miles in every direction. Lynn points to the ground where solid rock breaks the surface of the prairie. "Mortar holes," he announces. Oval holes have been worn into the rock where Native American women ground food with stone pestles. The view from their work station is spectacular. Farther on, Lynn drives up to a spring-fed pool all but hidden by prairie grasses and announces that we are parked in the middle of the Comanchero trail that Abert followed out of New Mexico.

We stop again at a likely-looking spot in a rocky ravine. Lynn starts off with shovel at the ready over his left shoulder. With his right hand, he swings a metal detector in rapid arcs over the ground, listening for beeps that signal metal underneath. He turns up a tobacco can, a horseshoe, pieces of barbed wire, an old shotgun shell, and several square nails, but no trace of the Abert expedition. We will have to depend on the clues recorded in Abert's journal to narrow the search. That's when Alvin Lynn's intimate knowledge of the area pays off again.

The lieutenant reported seeing red sandstone for the first time in the ravine where his party camped. According to Lynn there are no significant outcrops of this Permian sandstone west of Chisum Canyon, but many to the east. According to our map, there is a place nearby where the canyon makes "a very abrupt bend back on itself." We decide to drive over and check it out.

From a distance, the first thing we notice is a huge cottonwood tree. Dead limbs litter the ground beneath this ancient monarch. The bark has weathered away, exposing smooth bone-white wood. Cattails border a clear stream that flows between the tree and an encircling cliff. At the base of this "coliseum" of rock is the layer of red sandstone we had hoped to find.

Lynn breaks out his metal detector, while Isabel walks downstream looking for cardinal flowers, and I climb the cliff to survey the scene from above. The place certainly fits Abert's description. There is plenty of room for his expedition's four wagons and sixty-three head of horses and mules. Chunks of petrified wood lie scattered about. Lynn says they are common on this part of the ranch and that larger pieces, the size Abert reported, have been discovered nearby and carted away.

I climb down from the rim to take a closer look at Chisum Spring.

Its clear, cold water is piped into a concrete water trough around which thirsty cows have trampled vegetation. A barbed wire fence surrounds the spring's source to keep the cattle out and creates a protected oasis for grass and weeds. A speck of red catches my eye. Up close I see that it is a small scarlet tube splitting into five petals at the open end—a cardinal flower. It is one of the last blooms on a vigorous plant standing almost four feet tall and covered with spent blossoms. Three other plants are equally large and prolific. Remove the cattle from the equation, and I can easily imagine cardinal flowers thick enough to hide the stream that gives them life—just as Abert described.

Back in the truck, we review the evidence. Pronghorns, larks, cardinal flowers, and even petrified wood, still do not prove we have found the elusive campsite on the prairie. Locating Permian red sandstone strengthens the case. Alvin Lynn's careful analysis of distance and direction of travel, combined with his familiarity with the Comanchero trail, strongly suggest that we have reached our goal, but without hard physical evidence, we cannot be certain. We have, however, seen and experienced the landscape the expedition passed through.

Three days after Abert bathed in a spring-fed stream bordered by cardinal flowers, the lieutenant wrote in his journal: "We all silently drew up in a line along the crest of the bluff, that we might obtain a view of the first band of buffaloes we have seen on the Canadian. Some were quietly feeding on the nutritious vegetation; others lazily reclining on the tender grass, chewing the cud; here and there clouds of dust ascending, from the midst of which the hollow bellowing of bulls was heard, dashing at each other in dread combat. Whilst regaling our eyes with this glad sight, an old voyageur [*sic*] was dispatched in the anticipation of luxuriating on the fat ribs and tender loins; but some of the animals perceiving him, the alarm was instantly given throughout the band, and we saw them all gallop away and disappear behind the hills."[18]

Within forty years, free-ranging herds of bison were gone from the Great Plains and with them a Native American way of life that had evolved over twelve millennia. The invention of barbed wire in 1875 made it possible to subdivide the once boundless plains. Remnants of the old Comanchero trail were incorporated into the one hundred forty thousand–acre Mineosa pasture of the three million acre XIT Ranch. The land has since been subdivided into the Bravo, the Spring Creek, and other smaller operations.

Time left the old trail behind. No modern highway or topographic map mentions it. No historical marker commemorates it or the place where thirty-three men spent a night on the prairie a long time ago. What they saw soon changed forever. What we saw is changing still. But the humbling immensity of grass and sky remain. The bison and the bison hunters are absent from the scene but not the pronghorns. They are still unable to outrun their curiosity. And every year, hidden away in some of the deep torturous ravines where old springs still seep, brazen scarlet trumpets sound the timeless song of rebirth and renewal.

WALT DAVIS

Island in the Desert

. . . .

El Capitan . . . appeared to float above the sea of night.
It soared over the gathering darkness as luminous as if made
of polished tigereye, fire opal and carnelian. It looked like
the beginning of the world or its end as it hung detached
above the blackness of the lower elevations.

HELEN CRUICKSHANK,
A Paradise of Birds, When Spring Comes to Texas

WE LEAVE THE CANADIAN RIVER behind and head south, bound for an "island in the sky" four hundred miles away. Our route takes us through the heart of the old XIT Ranch. Scores of playa lakes dot the landscape. Gray legions of sandhill cranes march in fields of stubble near Muleshoe reservoir. Approaching Andrews, we encounter vast stretches of sand dunes. Some are held in place by stunted groves of scrub oak, while others threaten to cover the highway with slithering ribbons of blowing sand. Here and there drilling rigs bore holes into deeply-buried layers of oil-bearing Permian rock. We are headed to a place where uplift and erosion have exposed that rock to create a mountain range famous among geologists and biologists the world over.

After crossing the Pecos River, we notice a cloud on the western horizon that seems tethered to one place. As we get closer, the pale silhouette of distant mountains appears beneath it. Early Texas geologist George G. Shumard was impressed by this scene back in 1855. He

Fred and Nancy Gehlbach running a transect, Guadalupe Mountains National Park

wrote in his journal, "The Guadalupe Mountains . . . rise abruptly from a gently ascending surface, and attain at the highest point an altitude of nearly three thousand feet above their base and about eight thousand feet above the level of the ocean. . . . To the south the range terminates abruptly in a frightful precipice upwards of two thousand feet high."[1]

Tonight we will park our trailer near the base of that "frightful precipice" in a place Shumard called "The Pinery." He described it as a canyon "upwards of a half a mile wide, and bounded on either side by . . . walls of such extreme height that their summits appear often enveloped in clouds."[2]

The last rays of sunlight glance off the high ridges, and shadows fill the canyon as we arrive, secure the trailer, and heat up leftovers for supper. There are no hookups for water or electricity in Pine Springs Campground, so we will be "boondocking" for the next five days. After supper we play dominoes by candlelight to conserve battery power. At bedtime we step outside and look up into a black dome crossed by a river of stars.

Fifty years ago these remote mountains welcomed a young graduate student and his new bride. Fred Gehlbach had just been handed the opportunity of a lifetime, and wife Nancy joined him for the first of many summers of fieldwork in the Southwest. He was enrolled in the Department of Conservation at the University of Michigan, where department head Stan Cain was his major professor. John F. Kennedy had just been elected president and appointed Stuart Udall secretary of the interior. Udall asked Cain to be undersecretary for parks and wildlife. When land in the Guadalupe Mountains was set aside for a new national park, Cain asked Gehlbach to write an ecological plan for it.

While his major professor worked with Udall in Kennedy's Camelot, Fred and Nancy Gehlbach labored in less regal circumstances. For a while they spread their sleeping bags on the floor of the ticket office at Carlsbad Caverns and showered in the ranger's barracks. One summer their home was an unfurnished stone cabin in McKittrick Canyon. The place was infested with mice and packrats that attracted blood-sucking bugs called *triatomas* known to transmit sleeping sickness. Nancy watched them emerge from the fireplace and stalk across the floor toward increasingly nervous prey. On the night they spotted the fourteenth *triatoma*, the couple abandoned the cabin and slept under a nearby juniper tree.

The work was hard, especially in temperatures that reached as high as 108 degrees. The Gehlbachs laid out 183 transect lines along the eastern front of the Guadalupes, including McKittrick Canyon. Along these transects, which ranged in length from two hundred to six hundred feet, they sampled plants and animals at intervals of fifty feet. By the time they were through, the Gehlbachs knew the Guadalupes, and especially McKittrick Canyon, as well as master gardeners know their own gardens.

Isabel and I decide to hike into McKittrick Canyon to see the Gehlbach's "garden" first hand. Grass and desert shrub cover the rocky ground between widely spaced junipers and oaks as we start up the trail. At the first stream crossing in this 2,000-foot-deep canyon, we notice a sudden change. There is more shade. Oaks and junipers are taller here, and madrones are more common and much larger than those at the canyon's mouth. As we gain elevation, we spot the first bigtooth maples, then chinquapin oaks, and ponderosa pine. The trees are relics of a time when the climate of West Texas was cooler and wetter than today.

Behind us, in a cave on the south side of the canyon, Gehlbach found evidence of that earlier time. Sorting through three-thousand-year-old fossils discovered in Pratt's Cave, he came across the bones of short-horned lizards. The animals no longer live in the canyon, but a small population survives in mountain meadows one thousand feet higher.[3]

In nearby Burnett Cave, the eight thousand-year-old bones of yellow-bellied marmots, long-tailed voles, and bushy-tailed woodrats mingled with the remains of shrub oxen, mountain deer, and camels. The woodrats still live in the mountains of southern New Mexico. The nearest relatives of the marmot and vole live three hundred miles to the north in the Sangre de Cristo Mountains.[4] The oxen, deer, and camels have disappeared entirely[5] from a landscape that has been warming and drying for millennia. From this and other evidence, Gehlbach estimated that the relic habitat of the high Guadalupes has been retreating upslope at the rate of a few inches to a foot per year for the past three thousand years.[6] He compared the increasingly isolated high mountain refuge to an island emerging from a surrounding sea of desert. The metaphor became the title for a book he would write many years later, *Mountain Islands and Desert Seas.*

As we hike farther up the canyon, we find bigtooth maples touched with gold, the first blush of autumn color. Rough-barked, scalloped-leaved chinquapin oaks seem out of place here. We remember them growing in riparian woodlands much farther east. Where water seeps from limestone cliffs, maiden-hair ferns seem to sprout from solid rock. Beside a still pool of clear water, the sun strikes a tall ponderosa pine exuding the warm scent of vanilla.

We take a break at the stone cabin where the Gehlbachs were stalked by blood-sucking bugs. The wilderness hideaway was built by retired geologist Wallace E. Pratt, who donated much of the land for the park. A huge madrone shades the front door and porch. Gehlbach was especially fond of the species, saying, "no other can match its white spike of fragrant April blossoms, its pinkish bark peeling to smooth white, its glossy evergreen leaves, and its picturesque countenance. McKittrick's madrones are the finest I know of in the Borderlands, but their future is in jeopardy. They are being girdled, eaten alive by an overly large mule deer herd."[7]

On the way back to the truck after our ramble through the canyon, we are glad to see that the madrones have survived and seem to be thriving again. Tomorrow I plan to hike into the high country to see another part of Gehlbach's garden—the Bowl—a spectacular temperate island in a desert sea. Isabel decides to visit the miniature oasis of Smith Spring.

❀

The day begins with a cloudless sky and an orange glow along the eastern horizon. A light breeze rustles through the gray oaks as I shoulder my pack and start up the Tejas Trail. The rising sun warms my back, as I set my sights for a place far ahead, where the path disappears over a saddle between two rock outcrops.

There is a sudden snort. A mule deer has seen me and is skulking away, followed by a spotted fawn. Two yearlings snap to attention and trot after the others with an occasional series of stiff-legged hops. Trees grow along the dry streambed, but not on the steep, south-facing slope to the right. By contrast, the north-facing canyon wall is green with juniper and oak.

I reach the saddle earlier than anticipated and take a break to look around. Pickups and trailers down in the campground look like tiny scale models. Beyond them, Highway 182 sweeps out of sight around the shoulder of El Capitan. The Delaware Basin sprawls toward the horizon in a jumble of low hills and winding arroyos. Ahead, the trail is steeper, rockier, and doubles back frequently as it snakes the remaining fourteen hundred feet to the top.

For each foot of elevation gained, if Gehlbach is right, I step back a year in time, for a total of six hundred years so far. The plants and animals at this altitude lived where our trailer is parked around the time Columbus stumbled upon the New World. The upcoming switchbacks will carry me up another two hundred feet into a biological community not seen down in the campground since the Mayans reached their zenith in Central America.

Back on the trail, such thoughts disappear in the face of the heart-thumping reality of the climb. I plant each foot carefully. A twisted ankle here would spoil an otherwise perfect day. Sweat beads up on my forehead. I become aware of my breathing—four steps per breath. I stop to rest at the end of a switchback and discover that there are no others. This is the top. I am well ahead of schedule. I feel like a boy again, alone in the wilderness.

A sign with an arrow points the way to the Bowl, and I immediately enter a different world. Tall trees arch over the trail: Douglas fir, Gambel oak, piñon, and ponderosa pine. A young golden eagle circles slowly above on motionless wings. In sunny patches beside the trail, wildflowers bloom: drooping bluebells and trumpet-like scarlet gilia. A stand of cancer root has passed its prime and withers in a bed of pine straw. Mountain chickadees flit through the branches, and a vigilant Steller's jay stops briefly to give me a stern look and a scolding. A few years ago, fire blackened scores of trees. A mortally wounded ponderosa pine stands beside the trail, split from top to bottom by a recent lightning bolt.

At noon I stop for lunch at the far side of the Bowl, where tall groves of pine and fir alternate with grassy meadows. A fallen tree provides my picnic table and bench. Boots off and socks hung out to dry, I eat lunch barefoot and watch the antics of a pair of acorn woodpeckers perched in dead trees across the meadow. Suddenly, one flies up in a swooping arc, catches something in mid-air, and sails back to its resting place. Not long after, its companion repeats the performance. They seem more like flycatchers than woodpeckers as they "sally forth" for bugs instead of digging them out of dead trees.

After lunch I pack up and start back. At one point, the trail offers a breathtaking view down Pine Canyon, across the dry expanse of the Delaware Basin, to the faint silhouette of the Davis Mountains one hundred miles away. I try to imagine a time when the forest behind me spilled down the canyon at my feet and across the intervening slopes. According to Fred Gehlbach, scattered trees and lush grassland covered the lowlands beyond in a scene reminiscent of East Africa's savannahs.[8]

The trail looks steeper now. A twinge of pain has lodged behind my left knee, and the spring is gone from my step. Loose rocks in the trail are treacherous. I slip on one. Feet shoot forward, and I sit down hard. No harm done, but every step now demands full attention. The trip down takes almost as long as the hike up, but I walk into camp right on time.

Isabel has been to Smith Spring, an idyllic spot with a crystalline pool of water under ancient madrones—a place I clearly recall from a hike there years ago. She wants to know what it was like in the Bowl. I am unable to convey the beauty and wonder of what I have seen and felt today. Such is the price of hiking alone.

❁

We spend our last evening in the Guadalupes thirty-five miles to the north of Pine Springs Campground in Carlsbad Caverns. Local biologist and bird bander Steve West has invited us to join a team studying one of Carlsbad's lesser known inhabitants, the cave swallow. These aerial acrobats feed on insects during the day and roost in the cavern at night. In the spring they lay eggs in mud nests plastered into pockets and ledges in the ceiling of the cave. When the weather turns cold and insects cease to fly, the swallows head south for the winter. We are surprised to find them still in residence this late in the fall.

Visitors are gathering in the amphitheater overlooking the entrance as we arrive. We check in with the park ranger who is readying her microphone for the evening bat flight program. "The crew is already inside," she says. "Just step over the chain and go right on down." Slanting rays from the setting sun warm the limestone ledges encircling the black maw of the entrance. Twittering platoons of cave swallows circle overhead in preparation for group dives into the darkness. We descend steeply out of the sunlight into a twilight zone where the aroma of guano hangs in the still, cool air.

Below, we can make out a figure holding a ten-foot aluminum pole upright. A whisper-thin mist net stretches from his pole to that of his partner farther away. Between them, other figures in twos and threes are busy with something that demands their total attention. A young woman stands up cradling a fluttering bird she has disentangled from the net. She hands it to a man in white T-shirt, jeans, and running shoes.

"This one's already banded," he says, and reads off a number. Then he deftly spreads one wing with thumb and forefinger, lays a small ruler beside it, and calls out "112 millimeters." Another young woman in a safari hat with matching shirt and pants jots down the measurement on a clipboard. "Tail–47," he announces next, then thrusts the bird into an empty bread wrapper, clips it to a hand-held spring scale, and calls out, "weight–35 grams." Absent-mindedly, he reaches into the wrapper, pulls out the bird, and tosses it backwards into the darkness.

"I've been doing this since Jimmy Carter was president," West says with a smile. "The goal for the evening is to band at least twenty-five new birds. That will bring the total for this season up to one thousand." He explains that most of tonight's banding crew are from Carlsbad High School's Chihuahuan Desert Lab. Their teacher says they will get special credit for helping out.

The net is now empty, and West instructs the two "pole men" to raise it back into place. They step apart to stretch the net tight then push it up into the flight path of entering swallows. Our eyes have adjusted to the dim light, and we can see several thin black strings extending from pole to pole. Between them hangs an even thinner net of black thread. Seen against the blue sky, the net is barely visible, but against the darkness of the cave, it disappears completely. Another platoon of swallows circles outside, their wings transparent in the sunlight. Suddenly the group dives *en masse*. Most avoid the trap, but one comes to a sudden stop, the net sags with its weight, and after a brief struggle the bird is held fast. Another rockets in and is caught–then three more. With five birds in the net, West instructs the pole men to bring it down. "Walt," he says, "want to give it a try?"

Isabel and I banded cave swallows in the Texas Hill Country forty years ago. The process is tedious, but must be completed quickly to avoid stressing the captive. My bird has gripped several threads with its feet. One wing and the head are entangled. I turn it over, and something warm and wet squirts into my palm. I wipe it on my jeans. The little swallow rests quietly, while I untangle it. Expressionless black eyes stare back at me, and its heart ticks faintly against my fingers. White throat and belly contrast with the dark iridescence of the head and back. There is a rust-colored patch on its forehead. I pass it to West who holds a tiny metal band in a pair of needle-nosed pliers. One squeeze and the captive has a numbered bracelet no bigger around than a piece of spaghetti. Measure–bag–weigh–release, then on to the next in line.

Isabel takes a turn, frees her bird quickly, and hands it to West. He takes one look: "Here's another banded one, number 1921–50439." It is a female banded on May 26 last year. At the time she weighed twenty-five grams and had a tick over the right eye. Recaptured less than a month later, she had developed a brood patch (a featherless spot on the breast for incubating eggs) and had lost one gram of weight. Today, the tick is gone, and she has gained back the lost gram. According to West, this individual has a bright future. Seventy percent of hatchlings die in the first year, but their chance for survival goes up after that. At two years or older, Isabel's swallow will probably become a regular breeder at Carlsbad. It could live to the ripe old age of eight–with luck, twelve or thirteen. We reach the evening's goal of twenty-five swallows, then catch and band two more–over one thousand birds this season alone whose activities will be tracked for years to come.

While we have been working, the sun has set, and the piece of sky framed by the mouth of the cave has lost it luminosity. West turns to the park ranger assigned to monitor the evening's activities.

"Do you think it's time to wrap it up? I think the bats are beginning to fly."

"Yes," he agrees. "I can see movement down below."

It is the ranger's job to see that bird banding does not interfere with the bats. Consequently, we cannot leave the cave until over a million Mexican freetails have passed over us and out to their nocturnal hunting grounds. West carefully folds the net, stuffs it in a plastic bag, then sees that the other equipment is safely stowed away. We begin to look for comfortable places to wait out the exodus. Some sit cross-legged on the path, others perch on the rock wall, or lean against it, feet outstretched. Conversation continues, softly.

"We are lucky to have this many birds so late in the season," West confides. "Back in the early eighties they were all gone by the middle of October, but now some are still hanging around the first or second week of November. They used to arrive in mid-March. Now we see them as early as the first week of February."

"Why?" I want to know. "How do you account for that?"

"Global warming," he answers, without hesitation. "The swallows depend on flying insects for survival. As the earth warms, winters get shorter and shorter, insects come out sooner and stay active longer. Swallows take advantage of that, and we see the result in our records."

If what he says is right, global warming has enabled cave swallows to lengthen their stay at Carlsbad Caverns by four to six weeks over the past twenty-five years. The warming trend that has driven voles, wood-rats, and short-horned lizards into their mountain retreats continues, but this latest change is measured in tens of years, not thousands. We have more questions, but West has turned his attention to the black hole below us.

I fail to see the bats West and the ranger have spotted. Looking again a few moments later, I finally detect movement—not individual objects in motion, but a current in the darkness itself. A faint sound rises from below—soft, like wind in pines. The smell of guano grows stronger. Suddenly, bats are in the air around us. They fly in a counterclockwise spiral, gaining altitude one orbit at a time. A few flutter past us and are briefly silhouetted against the darkening sky before turning back. The teacher taps Isabel on the shoulder. "You're going to wish you had a hat," she says.

The first squadron of circling bats reaches exit speed and clears the mouth of the cavern, followed by a second, and a third. The air is full of them now spiraling madly a few feet above our heads. Something tiny touches my arm as if a gnat has landed—guano. The wind-in-the-pines sound grows louder accompanied by the leathery noise of wings slapping together in the confusion. We are in a whirlpool of bats—tens of thousands of them—hundreds of thousands. Ten minutes, twenty minutes, half an hour, and still they fly. It is nearly dark before the exodus begins to ebb.

Finally the ranger gives the word, and the team gathers its equipment. Leaving the protection of the rock wall, we turn right onto an exposed switchback, walking against the current of spiraling bats. They circle up out of the darkness, bank into a hard left turn, and come straight at us at eye level, veering suddenly off course to avoid smacking us in the face. For a few anxious moments we are in the center of the maelstrom, but no one is hit, and we continue up the path.

The amphitheater is almost empty when we reach the top. Isabel thanks our host for an unforgettable evening. We exchange cards and promise to stay in touch. As the last bats disappear into the dark sky, and the swallows settle down for the night in the cave, we are left with a puzzle. Have we just witnessed the local effect of global warming—the beginning of a new and immediate problem? Or have we merely seen the most recent extension of climate change that has been going on for millennia?

The puzzle remains unanswered weeks later as we drive up to Fred and Nancy Gehlbach's home tucked away in a patch of woods in the hardscrabble hills west of Waco. He has retired from full-time teaching at Baylor University. They are still a close-knit team and travel widely in the borderland of the southwestern United States and Central America.

Nancy Gehlbach meets us at the front door wearing jeans and a sweatshirt emblazoned with gray wolves. She calls Fred down from his upstairs office. Both, though gray, are slim and fit. They project a youthful exuberance and laugh often. Like many seasoned couples, they are quick to fact check each other and frequently combine forces to remember things that happened fifty years ago.

Nancy Gehlbach recalls a time while she and her husband were camping out in the ticket office at Carlsbad. They were still in their sleeping bags one morning, when they overheard a group gathered outside to watch the bats return to the cave. When a canyon wren belted out its distinctive cascading call, a woman nearby said to her husband, "Well, I didn't know bats could sing." "Oh my goodness yes," her knowledgeable husband responded, "they have a beautiful song."

Hearing that we hiked to Pratt Cabin, Fred Gehlbach tells about finding the first spotted owl nest in Texas not far from that spot. We are able to report that at least six pairs now nest in the Guadalupe backcountry. When the conversation turns to the fossils in Pratt Cave, Gehlbach turns to his wife and says, "Remember, that's where we always saw the bobcat. Practically every time we passed that spot the cat was there."

When we finally get around to describing our experience with Steve West and the cave swallows that come earlier and stay later, I pop the question.

"Why?"

"What is his theory?" Gehlbach counters.

"He says global warming," I respond.

"That's what I would think."

"But your research indicates that warming and drying has been going on for thousands of years in the Southwest. Why isn't this just the continuation of that long-term trend?"

"It is," he says. "It is the continuation of long-term interglacial trends, but it is accelerated by carbon dioxide and the rest of the greenhouse gases. It has accelerated just in the last century."

"What is the evidence?"

"The Intergovernmental Panel on Climate Change has got slightly over a hundred year's worth of evidence. The main analysis of this began in the seventies in the Carter administration and has picked up steam in the last decade or two. The evidence is absolutely conclusive. Now if you want to look at the biological evidence, I could give you a three or four hour lecture on that, because it is horrendous. It is very widespread."

"Give us an example," Isabel suggests.

"The general picture here is our winter birds are coming later, and some of them are not coming at all anymore. They are staying shorter periods of time. That's just the winter birds. Now our nesting birds that spend the winter in the tropics are coming in earlier and staying later, the same thing as the bats in the caves. I've got forty-five years of data on this."

"Butterflies too," Nancy Gehlbach notes. "We had zebra butterflies here just the other day—still had zebras and julias in December, which is just amazing."

Each answer brings more questions, but our time is up and we must go. Time may be up for the forests and meadows of the high Guadalupes as well. If present trends continue, the days of Douglas fir and ponderosa pine in the Bowl may be numbered, and its mountain meadows are likely to disappear. The same trends are affecting mountains twelve hundred miles away in northern Montana's Glacier National Park. Its namesake glaciers numbered 150 in 1919. Now there are less than thirty. By 2030 they will be gone.[9]

The mountain islands of Texas, which have long held biological relics above the reach of an encroaching desert sea, are about to be submerged. Primordial patterns of seasonal change are disappearing. Migration, for some species, may soon be moot. Camped in McKittrick Canyon fifty years ago, a young graduate student and his bride could not fathom the changes about to engulf the place they had come to study.

WALT DAVIS

Walking to El Paso

· ·

Again, the desert closes against the river, and the gritty wastelands
crumble onto its very banks, and nothing lives but creatures of
the dry and hot; and nothing grows but desert plants of thirsty pod,
or wooden stem, or spiny defense.

PAUL HORGAN, *The Great River*

U.S. HIGHWAY 62–180 loses altitude rapidly as it leaves the foothills of the Guadalupes, turns west, and knifes through three miles of snow-white salt flats decorated with yucca, purple-tinged prickly pear, and blackfoot daisies. After crossing fifty miles of desert, the road climbs through the Hueco Mountains, emerges in a field of sand dunes, and carries us across another stretch of flat Chihuahuan Desert to El Paso.

Here, eons ago, the Rio Grande broke through the Franklin Mountains and opened a path to the sea. Native Americans had lived in the area for millennia before Spaniards arrived in the sixteenth century and named the place *El Paso del Norte*. Three hundred years later, a man passed this way whose story has piqued our curiosity and brought us into the rugged mountains and scorching desert that keep the river company. In 1849, Charles Wright walked 673 miles from San Antonio, across the Pecos River, through the Davis and Quitman mountains, and up the Rio Grande to El Paso.[1] We want to understand why a Connecticut Yankee with a degree from Yale and friends at Harvard would do such a thing. What could have been worth the effort and the risk?

Guatemalans walking to Van Horn, foothills of the Quitman Mountains

Charles Wright would not recognize the river we find flowing through El Paso today. Most of its water has been diverted into the irrigation canals and municipal water systems demanded by a burgeoning human population. The mighty Rio Grande, once capable of carving its way through mountains, has shrunk to a sluggish stream, its muddy waters confined in a concrete ditch. Crossing the international bridge between El Paso and Ciudad Juarez, Isabel and I join a river of people that flows between the two cities.

Below us the Rio Grande threads its way through islands of silt, litter, algae, and weeds. The concrete bank on the Mexican side is splashed with spray-painted messages shouting *Alto al Yanki Terrorismo* and *No Mas Bombas al Mundo*. Portraits of Che Guevara and Uncle Sam glare at one another. Nearby, a six-foot peace symbol seems to call for a truce. Three chain link fences stand between the river and El Paso. One is topped with five strands of barbed wire encircled by a coil of razor-edged concertina. Plastic bags caught in the barbs and shredded by the wind look like tattered Tibetan prayer flags fluttering against a bright sky.

Leaving the tumult of both cities behind, we head southeast on State Highway 20 between irrigated fields green with onions and alfalfa. At McNary, we turn onto Ranch Road 192, and miles later come to the end of the pavement. Our map shows a bladed dirt road following the river to a place called Indian Hot Springs. Along the way we hope to find some remnant of the world Wright walked through 150 years ago. Our bug-spattered Silverado bounces along under a blue sky punctuated with summer cumulus. It is one of those rare days when the desert seems to be in a good mood, and a cool breeze lulls us into a false sense of security.

A sign on an access road to the river breaks the spell and warns, "Property of U.S. Government DO NOT TRESPASS International Boundary and Water Commission." A green-and-white border patrol SUV is parked beside the road. We heed the warning and drive on by. To our right a thin line of green betrays the course of the river. To our left the parched Chihuahuan Desert stretches beyond the horizon. On one side, water, foliage, and shade. On the other, searing sunlight, rock, and thorny plants with Spanish names: cholla, opuntia, ocotillo, lechugilla. Charles Wright would recognize this place. We are getting closer to the man and his mission.

In the book box we always carry on the back bench of the truck, sits a well-worn copy of *The Naturalists of the Frontier* by Samuel Wood Geiser. The author pieced together the story of Wright's foray along the Texas border using letters the botanist wrote to Asa Gray, his friend and patron at Harvard. From Geiser we learn that Wright started his trek worried that a carefully planned expedition was coming unraveled at the last minute.

Gray had convinced wealthy friends to cover Wright's travel expenses. He also talked the U.S. Secretary of War into allowing the botanist to accompany a military supply train bound for a new fort on the Rio Grande at Paso del Norte. Gray had secured letters of introduction from Professor Joseph Henry, Secretary of the Smithsonian Institution, and from the U.S. Secretary of State, hoping that support from powerful and influential people would secure safe passage for his botanizing protégé.

That hope evaporated when Wright presented his credentials to General Harney in San Antonio. Harney reluctantly agreed to let Wright accompany the expedition; but, with space in the wagons at a premium, he would not provide a place for Wright, his baggage, or his plant presses. Food would be Wright's problem, not the Army's. After an impassioned plea from Dr. Baker, the expedition's physician and the botanist's new friend, Harney finally agreed to make room for Wright's baggage and presses. But he made it clear that the Harvard botanist would be walk- ing to El Paso and would have to depend on the kindness of individual officers and soldiers for food and water.

Wright did find a group of men (a "mess" in Army lingo) who agreed to share its food with him. But no sooner was one problem solved than another appeared. On the first day out, the expedition slogged through torrential rain along roads already muddy from earlier storms. The second day dawned with a violent thunderstorm. Wright's plant presses and absorbent paper, critical to preserving specimens in the field, were soaked.

From a camp near present-day Castroville, he penned a cry of despair to Gray on the evening of June 2: "You wrote to me [Jan. 17, 1848] of working like a dog . . . then call your situation dog-paradise and mine hog- and ass-paradise combined and you *may* realize my situation–sleep all night if you can in the rain and walk 12–15 miles next day in the mud and then overhall [*sic*] a huge package of soaked plants and dry them by the heat of the clouds . . . I have the pleasing prospect of being dependent for six months on a parcel of men who call me a fool and wish me at the bottom of the sea . . . I am fully resolved that this season will close my botanical travels on horseback or on foot if I can not operate to better advantage. I'll give it up and turn my attention to something else."[2]

Months earlier, in the more civilized environs of Harvard College, Gray and Wright realized that a golden opportunity for science was opening up in the newly annexed state of Texas. No botanist had penetrated as far inland as the desert country west of the Pecos River where dozens of new plant species surely waited to be discovered. Unfortunately, the Mescalero Apache waited too. Annexation meant little to these desert warriors who still controlled the countryside. Citizens of Mexico and the United States moved cautiously in large well-armed groups from stronghold to stronghold. The newest island in this archipelago of safety was the fort at Paso del Norte, and the expedition Wright joined was bringing supplies and men to garrison it.

The wagon train was an impressive sight, snaking slowly along the muddy roads of Central Texas. Six companies of the Third Infantry, led by Maj. Jefferson Van Horne, were on the move. A company of the First Infantry provided protection for a party of forty-niners on their way to the gold fields in California. Colonel Johnston directed a team of engineers and laborers who would widen the trail they were following and make it into a proper military road. Capt. S. W. French, as assistant quartermaster, was in charge of the 275 wagons required to provision both the expedition and the new fort.[3] French shouldered logistical responsibility for a population equivalent to that of a small town on the move through hostile territory. No wonder he did not at first show Wright the attention he thought he deserved. Over time, however, the quartermaster did improve the botanist's living and working conditions, eventually earning Wright's gratitude.

Through June and July, French carefully recorded their progress from one watering place to the next. Wright marched on, dutifully collecting plants as time and circumstance permitted. But on August 2, he suffered an attack of malaria, and the quartermaster found room for the delirious patient aboard one of his overcrowded wagons. When Wright recovered, eleven days later, the expedition had crossed the Pecos River and entered scientifically unexplored territory.

He hit the botanical mother lode in the watered valleys and upland prairies of the Davis Mountains. On August 24 he recorded thirty-eight collecting numbers.[4] His plan was to collect a dozen examples of each species, and he may well have prepared over four hundred specimens that day. By the end of the fifth day, he had found no less than sixteen plants new to science.[5]

The botanist was happy, but the quartermaster was apprehensive. Between the Davis Mountains and the Rio Grande lay a parched stretch of Chihuahuan Desert and the barren Quitman Mountains. French knew that the most dangerous part of their journey lay ahead, and recorded his concern in his official report: "From here to Eagle Springs, a distance of 60 mi., no certain or living water is found . . . Although the precaution was taken to march the train in four divisions, each on consecutive days, yet water was not found sufficient for one-third of the animals: consequently, they had to march 70 miles without water."[6]

Men and animals survived the ordeal, drank deeply at Eagle Springs, then climbed and crossed the Quitmans arriving on the banks of the Rio Grande on September 4, 1849. A week later the wagons rolled to a stop at Coon's Hacienda (El Paso) having traveled 673 miles in 105 days. Along the way Charles Wright walked into botanical history. Asa Gray found seventy-three new species in the collection of dried plants Wright sent back to Harvard. Their scientific descriptions ran to such length that Gray published them in book form, *Plantae Wrightianae,* Part I.[7]

All traces of the military road Charles Wright walked on his way to El Paso have long since disappeared. The Great River is now no bigger than a small creek. In places, two steps take you across without wetting your socks. The broad sand flats and stands of native cane are gone. Salt cedar chokes the channel, drinking up all but a trickle of water. But, looking away from the river, we see what Wright saw a century-and-a-half ago. Recent rains have changed the color of a normally parched landscape to an unaccustomed green. Strawberry cactus and pitaya celebrate the gift of moisture with countless mounds of crimson and fuscia blossoms. Ocotillo blooms so profusely that a scarlet haze seems to hang suspended over the desert floor.

Signs beside the road have been pointing the way to Indian Hot Springs—a traveler's oasis for centuries. It is high noon, and after crunching and jolting along this back country road for two hours, we look forward to a picnic under one of the giant cottonwoods. Topping a knoll we come to a gate. Beyond it we can see a flat place of several acres with scattered interior roads that remind us of a country fairground, but with no one in sight. Everything is painted white: buildings, water tank, airplane hangar, rock walls, even the metal fence posts.

A sign beside the gate reads, "Private Property No Trespassing." The desert oasis is now a private hunting enterprise off-limits to the public.

Disappointed, we decide to drive ahead, rather than turn around and return the way we came. According to our map, the road we have been following will take us into the foothills of the Quitman Mountains, then across the desert to Interstate 10. If Charles Wright could cross these mountains on foot, and if the U.S. Army could haul 275 fully-loaded mule-drawn wagons over them, surely we can get across in a 1995 Chevrolet pickup.

Soon we are crawling in low gear up a rocky one-lane path scraped along a ridge that climbs onto the right shoulder of the Quitmans. Where the track straddles the divide between two dry creeks, boulders, pushed aside by the road builders, have tumbled a hundred feet into the streambed below. Behind us, in the distance, we catch a last glimpse of the green oasis of Indian Hot Springs beside the silver thread of the river with the mountains of Mexico rising beyond. There is no place wide enough to turn around, and we decide to face whatever lies ahead rather than risk backing down what we just came up.

Around the next bend, rocky hills and valleys close in around us, and the road demands total concentration. Tires slip on the loose rock. I watch the temperature gage for signs of overheating and keep an eye on the fuel level. We creep along at ten to fifteen miles an hour, and time seems to stand still. Finally, we seem to be going down more often than up; but, at a deceptively flat arroyo, we meet the most serious obstacle of our crossing. When the stream last flowed, it left a cut-bank on one side that exceeds the clearance of our pickup. We are hours, if not days, from help should we fail to bridge the gap. Having forgotten to pack a shovel, we build a ramp of stones and gravel by hand and gingerly inch the truck across.

Relieved, we drive out onto the desert flats and intersect the road and power line that lead to Interstate 10 and civilization. Giving up on finding shade, we pull off and stop for a late lunch. An immense calm replaces the jarring noise and anxiety of the mountain crossing. From the foothills behind us, ash-colored alluvium spills downslope, freckled with olive-green creosote bushes and scattered clumps of prickly pear.

Ahead of us, the pale blue silhouette of the Eagle Mountains rises out of a dusky haze to mark eastern horizon. Just beyond the road, a bone-dry arroyo winds its way south through the unrelenting sameness of the desert landscape looking for the Rio Grande. Gravel crunches noisily underfoot, as I drop the tailgate and lift out the ice chest and food box. We feel alone in the desert, but we are mistaken.

Two men in jeans and black T-shirts rise up out of nowhere and walk straight toward us. One wears a baseball cap and has a jacket tied around his waist. The other man is smaller and bare-headed. Fear rattles the brain. Thousands of dollars of camera and computer gear lie in plain sight. The keys are in the truck. The men are young and fit, with black hair glistening in the sun. We are not young. Gray hair trumpets the fact; and, without weapons of any kind, we have no way to close the gap.

"*Es muy caliente, no?*" says the taller one without a hat.

"*Si, muy caliente,*" I reply with a forced smile and nervous nod.

"*Este es Tejas?*" he asks.

"*Si,*" I answer. "This is Texas."

Each man carries a small plastic bag with a can of beans in it. The next sentence exceeds our cumulative recall of high school Spanish, but we pick out the word *migra*.

Isabel whispers, "He probably wants to know if we have seen the border patrol."

"*No migra,*" I answer, truth being quicker than wisdom.

Agua is the key word in the next otherwise unintelligible sentence. I retrieve two small bottles of water from the cab of the truck and hand them over. The tall one carries a three-liter Sprite bottle with something of an amber color in it. He takes a generous swig of the new water and pours the rest on top of the mysterious liquid in his own dingy plastic container. Isabel pulls out an unopened gallon jug of water, hands it over, then gets out extra bread and ham for two more sandwiches.

The talkative one thanks us profusely then gives me a white-tailed deer antler indicating to his companion that he should do the same. It is a matched pair. *Van Horn* is the key word in the next question. I pull out a map and, with a combination of finger pointing and arm waving, explain that Van Horn is on the other side of the Eagle Mountains.

Isabel appears with sandwiches, and the talker says something to his companion, who pulls out a wallet and fishes a coin from an inner compartment. It is a Guatemalan quetzal. Having now "paid" us for both the water and the food, the two men strike out cross-country, eating as they walk, swinging a fresh gallon of water and two cans of beans between them. We watch as the desert that coughed them up swallows them again.

Have we stumbled onto something here—a trail, a rendezvous point? There are no markers, no path, no litter. I walk toward a pair of Spanish dagger yucca joined at the base like Siamese twins. With crowns of creamy white blossoms, they are striking exceptions to the sea of uniformity that surrounds them. Nearby I find a cairn of rust-colored rocks and, in its shade, a white-tailed deer antler.

The sun is low in the western sky now, and we want to be off this road and out of the desert before nightfall. Kicking up a cloud of dust that can be seen for miles, we head north scanning the vast sweep of land between us and the Eagle Mountains for a last glimpse of the Guatemalans. Nothing. They have vanished.

Finally, we notice pavement up ahead: not the interstate, but a road that leads to it. We also notice the green trim of a white border patrol SUV parked in the thin shade of an acacia. As we pass, the agent starts his engine, switches on the head-lights, and pulls in behind. When I stop, he walks to the driver's-side window and asks with practiced politeness,

"Are you both U.S. citizens?"

"Yes."

"Is there anyone with you?"

"No."

"Mind if I take a look in the back?"

"Not at all."

The officer glances into the back seat and the bed of the truck, returns to his car and then, rather than resume his spot in the shade, heads back to town.

"He probably wasn't out here on routine patrol," Isabel says. "I think he was waiting specifically for us."

Our foray along the border has been a "subject of interest" to the U.S. Border Patrol.

As the excitement of our trip down the river and over the mountains finally subsides, we take stock of our search for that earlier traveler. What did Charles Wright experience during his journey through the same terrain? What drew him on in spite of dangers far more serious than the ones we faced? We decide that the answers may lay, not where his journey ended, but where it began—in the hallowed halls of Harvard.

✿

A call to the Gray Herbarium and Archive gives us hope. Botanist Walter Kittredge is custodian of the plants Wright collected in Texas, and he will be glad to show them to us. Archivist Lisa Decesare is familiar with the letters Wright wrote to Gray, and she can show us other documents that we may find interesting. Our tour around Texas makes a detour to Cambridge, Massachusetts.

We walk to campus from a nearby bed-and-breakfast, struck by the contrast between Cambridge and the Texas border country we left behind. Trees blot out the sky. Space is at such a premium that a permit is required to park in front of one's own house. Closer to campus, orange plastic safety nets cordon off construction sites where heavy equipment groans forward and beeps back. We shut the door on the noise and confusion when we enter the building that houses the Gray Herbarium and find ourselves in a world of quiet orderliness.

Walter Kittredge meets us in the lobby. His slightly-graying hair is pulled back in a ponytail, and his infectious smile puts us immediately at ease. He explains that the herbarium houses 1,939,914 pressed plant specimens on three floors and a basement. Somewhere in all of that are the plants collected in Texas in 1849. We are looking for a few needles in a multistoried haystack. Walter says, "It's simple. Everything is arranged by family, then geographically, and finally alphabetically, with type specimens in red folders at the end of the family section. Charts on every floor list the cabinets in which families are stored." The botanist volunteers to walk us through the first search.

A few minutes later we gingerly open a red folder and gaze down upon a plant dug from Texas soil a century-and-a-half ago. The yellow blossoms and green leaves have faded to a lifeless gray, and we dare not touch the brittle stems. A paper packet, made from a discarded letter, enfolds a handful of seeds. I wonder if they would sprout if planted. Walter points out a note in Asa Gray's hand—the hurried Spencerian script of a trained penman without a moment to spare.

After a couple of false starts we locate a wild snapdragon (*Cordylanthus wrightii*) collected near the Rio Grande and a four-o'clock (*Allonia corymbosa*) from the foot of the Eagle Mountains, the range the Guatemalans crossed on their way to Van Horn. By the time the herbarium closes for the day, we have located more than a dozen of Wright's Texas plants. We walk back to our bed-and-breakfast satisfied to have seen the fruit of Charles Wright's labors in Texas. Tomorrow we will try to make contact with the man himself, through the letters he exchanged with Asa Gray.

Archivist Lisa Decesare greets us ominously. "I'm afraid I have some bad news," she says after introductions. "Wright's letters for the year 1849 are missing from the collection. They were reported missing in 1984. I'm sorry I didn't check on them before you came all this way." After yesterday's success, the news comes as a deep disappointment. We retreat to a corner of the reading room to consider our options.

The other files we requested are piled on a table before us, and half-heartedly we begin thumbing through them. I find one paper, published in 1987, that quotes the very letters we want to read. Isabel finds another, published in 1992, that does the same. How can this be? Either the authors never saw the letters they quoted, or they had access to documents now deemed inaccessible. Isabel reports the puzzle to Decesare, who finds it as curious as we do. She huddles with the head librarian, asks someone to answer her phone, and disappears. Thirty minutes later she walks through the door, beaming, with a folder in her hand. "I found them," she reports. "They were in an old office used by a previous researcher."

Opening the folder we find travel-worn letters in Wright's own hand. Some were sent from wilderness campsites to San Antonio by horseback, then to Port Lavaca, and by packet to Harvard. Some are firsthand accounts written in the heat of the moment. A few, composed after his return, are more thoughtful reflections on his experience. The letters reveal the human dimension of his extraordinary journey. From one in particular, a complex individual emerges and stands before us.

Early on, Wright struck up a friendship with expedition physician Dr. Baker, an educated man with whom the Yale graduate found cultured companionship. They sang together in the evening and took turns reading the Bible to each other. But the physician had some irritating personality quirks that began to disturb the botanist. Wright complains to Gray that "the Doctor is . . . exceedingly vain. On the Leona he asked me to assist him in coloring his white locks which show below his hat. I was disgusted at the vanity which led him to seek to conceal his age among a parcel of men and in a wilderness."[8]

Wright goes on to describe the downward spiral of their relationship.

> It was not long however before the doctor began to find fault with the cooking more than I thought was necessary in a camp. The tea was too strong or too weak, the rice was *bitter* with smoke, the bread was tough or burnt to a coal, and the coffee was muddy or cold as ice. If anything fell it was *smashed*, if wood was

scarce, "there was not enough to put in a hummingbird's eye." If anything was cooking too slowly there was not a *particle* of fire under it. If anything was broken, I broke it. . . . His remarks on any subject whatever commonly end by "don't you think so" or "is it" or "ain't it" thus he wishes his hearer to endorse his opinion. I would sometimes dissent when an argument would surely spring up which ended by his *silencing* not *embracing* me. I have frequently snored and pretended to be asleep to avoid assenting to his interrogatives after we had gone to bed. . . . At last I was never so well pleased as when he was gone away.[9]

Finally, a trivial disagreement got out of hand, as two educated men far from civilization reached the breaking point. Wright tells Gray how it happened: "Well in descending Devil's river we had some bad road–the mules at a certain place mired and fell. I had gone a little ahead and sat down on a hill-side and a little after the doctor [Baker] came on and took a seat near me–within reach. After some criticism from him on the conduct of the waggon [*sic*] . . . I made the humble observation that 'there was another waggon which had been stalled.' He denied it and as I had been sitting for half an hour watching the efforts of the drivers to extricate their team I could not do otherwise that reassert my former remark. After two or three affirmations and denials he told me *I lied* and I struck him in the face one blow which I might if I wished have repeated but I was heartily sorry that he should forget the gentleman and become *rowdy* enough to give another man the lie and irritate me to become *rowdy* enough to resort to fisticuffs to repel the charge."[10]

Neither man apologized, and the incident was never again discussed between them. To his credit, Wright did not completely dismiss his former friend. He remembered that Dr. Baker had helped him find food and messmates when he joined the expedition outside San Antonio. The doctor had shared his tent with the botanist and had loaned him money when his stipend from Gray ran out. When Wright came down with malaria, the physician had attended him and administered quinine to aid his recovery. While Wright was wracked with fever, Dr. Baker had brought him botanical specimens, one of which proved to be a new species.

Remembering these kindnesses, Wright ends his letter to Gray by saying, "Dr. B. brought to me while I was sick the first specimen of a new sp. [species] of *Leucophyllum*. If it should prove to be new let it be named *Bakeri*."[11] The hard-nosed Connecticut Yankee had room in his heart for the complexities of human nature and the grace to give credit where credit was due, regardless of personal prejudice.

After reading this remarkable letter, we decide to search out this botanical gift to a sick man–this "olive branch" one man gave another on the border of Texas so long ago. Would it bear Dr. Baker's name as Wright proposed? Our new-found herbarium navigation skills help us locate the family section, the case, and the bin of red folders containing type specimens. And here it is! The label reads, "Field No. 823, beyond the Pecos, fl. purp. 2 ft. high, Aug. 15, 1849, *Leucophyllum minus*." Wright's "olive branch" to Dr. Baker was cast aside by Asa Gray. *Leucophyllum bakeri* did not come to pass, and the vain doctor missed his chance at scientific immortality.

The plant, however, lives on. Now called Big Bend silver-leaf, it is a common and attractive staple of the desert landscape of far West Texas. Sturdy branches support a compact shrub that reaches a maximum height of three feet. Silvery gray-green foliage contrasts with showy blue blossoms. Its larger botanical cousins (variously called cenizo, purple sage, or silver-leaf) are popular with xeriscaping gardeners. Being the most hardy of its genus, *L. minus* has been crossed with other species to produce drought-resistant hybrids.[12]

After seeing the plants Charles Wright collected and reading his letters, we realize that the man moved in two worlds of vast dimension. He was at home in the frequently scorching and always prickly Trans Pecos, where human striving shrinks to insignificance in the enormity of its deserts, mountains, and canyons. He was equally at home in the scientific revolution of the nineteenth century that cataloged the natural resources of a nation groping toward its "manifest destiny."

Wright returned to the Rio Grande border country in 1851 with the U.S. Boundary Survey. He explored the Pacific Rim from Australia to Japan with the Ringgold Expedition and spent eleven years tramping around Cuba collecting for his mentor, Asa Gray. The specimens Wright collected helped convince Gray that Charles Darwin was right about natural selection. They provided evidence that strengthened Gray's case in a famous debate with his Harvard rival, Louis Agassiz. The outcome made Gray one of the most influential scientists of the nineteenth century.

His travels over, Wright returned to the family farm in Wethersfield, Connecticut, tended his garden, and died where he was born. Charles Wright never married, but a host of plants carry his name and bear witness to his life-long passion. His intellectual remains are scattered throughout the botanical catacombs of the Gray Herbarium at Harvard. But down in Texas, along the border, beside the Rio Grande, wild snapdragons, four o'clocks, and silver-leafs still spread their leaves and raise their heads to the same sun that beat down on a vagabond for science 150 years ago.

WALT DAVIS

Letters from the Ghost Mountains

The stream bed above us is a wonderful, rich place,
half tropical and half boreal, pines and agaves . . .
where rare hummingbirds come and feed.

L. A. FUERTES,
in a letter to his family

THE RIO GRANDE almost dies of thirst in the desert below El Paso. Water gathered in the San Juan Mountains of Colorado and the Sangre de Cristos of New Mexico is siphoned off downstream to irrigate farms and supply water to cities and towns. Sometimes the Great River dries up completely.

Relief comes when the Rio Conchos brings a life-saving transfusion out of the mountains of northern Mexico and injects it into the Rio Grande at Presidio. After that, the Rio Grande is a real river again, rolling on through some of the more spectacular landscapes in Texas. To the north, it is flanked by the Bofecillos Mountains and the Solitario Uplift. It slices through the Mesa de Anguila to create Santa Elena Canyon, then angles across the sun-baked Chihuahuan Desert to Mariscal Canyon. After another stretch of desert, it passes between the six-hundred-foot walls of Hot Springs Canyon where, on the morning of May 29, 1901, a young man faced a problem.

Louis Agassiz Fuertes in Pine Canyon, Chisos Mountains,
Big Bend National Park

Louis Agassiz Fuertes had climbed four hundred feet up a cliff on the Texas side, only to find his way blocked by a boulder. Handholds and footholds, useful on the way up, were invisible looking down, and the muddy waters of the Rio Grande swirled below. Unwilling to retreat and unable to advance, he did what any graduate of Cornell University and enthusiastic member of its glee club would have done—he sang. For an hour he carried on a duet with his echo bouncing back from the cliff on the Mexican side.[1]

He was still enjoying himself when two men appeared at the top of the cliff and called down to him. Coils of rope sailed out, straightened, and fell back against the sheer rock within reach of the stranded singer. With the rope's help, he climbed past the offending boulder and up to the canyon rim where, reaching into a fold of his shirt, he pulled out the limp body of a beautiful black hawk.

Fuertes had just collected the first scientific specimen of a zone-tailed hawk (*Buteo albonotatus*) from Texas. Fuertes was the official artist on a U.S. Biological Survey expedition to the Big Bend.

He had been hunting the hawk for three days. When he finally brought the bird down, it fell over the edge of Hot Springs Canyon, and Fuertes was not about to leave his prize unclaimed, regardless of the risk.

Scientists at the time demanded definitive proof from anyone claiming to have seen a bird where it had never been seen before. Without cameras capable of recording reliable images, the only acceptable evidence was the body of the bird. It was shot, skinned, filled with cotton or some other inert material, and sewn back together. A label attached to its leg recorded the date, location, collector's name, and other pertinent information. The resulting scientific specimen was commonly called a "study skin."

But the protocol had a weakness. Colors fade over time, and valuable clues to the bird's identity are lost. The colors of some parts, such as eyes and the skin around them, beaks, legs, and even some feathers, can change in a matter of minutes. That is where the artist came in. He could record these nuances before they disappeared, and that is exactly what Fuertes did with his hawk. In a letter to his parents back in Ithaca, New York, Fuertes said, "I painted him fresh that afternoon & am mighty glad of it, for all his lovely plum bloom has gone, in the skin, & he is still splendid, but nearly dead black instead of like a rich ripe black plum."[2]

The expedition camped on the banks of Tornillo Creek, close to its confluence with the Rio Grande and a stone's throw from the famous Big Bend Hot Springs. Vernon O. Bailey, chief field naturalist for the Biological Survey, was in charge. He was a small man, thirty-seven years old, wiry and tough as nails. With full beard, piercing eyes, and a cartridge belt around his waist, he looked more like a border bandit than one of the foremost mammalogists in North America. Harry C. Oberholser was a thirty-one-year-old ornithologist—tall and professorial with angular features, long nose, and deep-set eyes. At twenty-seven, Fuertes was the youngest in age but midway between his companions in size and proportion. Photographs of him capture the wide-eyed good humor of a young man enjoying life.

Bailey was busily collecting mammals while the two bird men waited for the main event—a ride into the heart of the Chisos Mountains, shimmering in the distance. As the first scientific party to enter this well-watered island surrounded by a sea of desert, they were convinced that birds never before seen in the United States awaited them there. Along the river they saw only familiar species. But in the high country, there could be Mexican forms—subtropical varieties that reached the northernmost extension of their ranges in the Chisos—the "Ghost Mountains" of the Big Bend.

Bailey finally finished collecting, and the party packed up and headed for the high country. Travel by horseback was slow, and by late afternoon, the temperature was approaching one hundred degrees Fahrenheit. Clear desert air made distant objects seem deceptively close. Their destination, Pine Canyon, proved farther away and higher up than they realized. The sun set long before they found water and a campsite.

❀

Today, Isabel and I are looking for that same campsite as our pickup lurches and bounces up the unpaved road to Pine Canyon. In the book box on the seat behind us, clipped into a loose-leaf binder, are photocopies of letters Fuertes wrote to his family in Ithaca more than a century ago. They preserve the joyful enthusiasm of a young man at the beginning of a distinguished career. When words failed, Fuertes enclosed pencil sketches of his surroundings. Two drawings of Pine Canyon are so detailed we believe we can use them to locate the expedition's 1901 Chisos Mountains campsite.

We have a back-country permit to overnight in the highest campsite in Pine Canyon–close, we think, to where Fuertes camped. We arrive to find a gravel tent pad, bear-proof trash cans, and not much else–no water and no latrine. The wind picks up and soon sets the guy-ropes of our tent humming and the rain-fly flapping madly. We anchor the corners with heavy rocks before it all takes off for Mexico.

Dinner of cold ham and pasta salad, garnished with a quartered tomato, is washed down with cold beer. After dinner we settle into camp chairs to enjoy the quiet desert twilight, but our reverie is short-lived. A black SUV appears out of a plume of dust in the distance. It grows larger, and we realize it is on the road to Pine Canyon. We planned a solitary night in this one-party-only site in the Chisos foothills to sample the mountain magic Fuertes described in his letters. When cigar-smoking Burt and his wild-haired, grown son William park beside our truck, we learn that the Park Service double-booked "our" campsite. The new neighbors are nice enough, but we are sorely disappointed at the loss of our much anticipated night alone in the wilderness.

Fuertes described his own journey up Pine Canyon in a letter written the first week of June, 1901, addressed from "6,000' up in the Chisos Mountains, 100 miles from the R. R. [railroad]."

> We left our Tornillo camp on the 31st of May, at 9:30 A.M. & made for "town," or Ernst's Store, an adobe affair where they sell beans & shoe-soles, & a few other things. Ernst had gone to Boquillas to buy a pair of confiscated horses, but he'd left the place open, so we ate lunch, shod the horses, got our stuff, left a note & dug out. The store is ½ way to the mts., so we tho't we'd get here about 5 P.M. But we didn't, & had a long hard ride & walk up the road, alias creek bed, finally had to cache ½ our load, as the mules were nearly done for, & found H2O by moonlight in a great impressive valley. Next A.M., B. [Bailey], O. [Oberholser] & I came out afoot & lit the up trail for timber, & found the place we are now camped in.

Fuertes, a recent college graduate, wrote regularly to his parents and favorite sister back home. However, he was disappointed that his accompanying pencil sketches and quick watercolor paintings did not do the Chisos justice:

> I'm sorry I can't paint in ten minutes all the surroundings of our splendid place here, & at night, when the big southern moon comes cooly up from behind her great mountain & floods the cañon [sic] & valley with soft light, & the owls & whippoorwills & other night lovers come out & give it all a new and unsolved life, it makes me long to have some power to get your senses, at least, down here to help me hold it. Bailey laughs at me for refusing to get under a tree at night instead of lugging my bed out into

the open mountain meadow–but I wouldn't miss the cool breeze on my head & the wonderful throbbing bigness of these glorious nights for anything he could name.

He went on to describe a spectacular thunderstorm that lashed their camp:

The other night we (the Chisos) and the Boquillas had a competitive thunder storm & it was the most awful and superb thing I ever saw. It hailed as usual, and the stones were so big & came down so terrifically hard that our poor horses couldn't stand it, & tore around on their ropes till all but Baylor, (one mule) broke loose and tore frantically down the valley. I started out to get them to bring under a tree, but I hadn't gone a yard before a great "hail-ball," as Surles [camp cook] calls them hit me on the shoulder blade & stung for ten minutes–& as I could hardly see thru' the storm as far as the horses, I decided to give it up. I found one stone as big as this–[pencil sketch of golf ball-sized, pumpkin-shaped, hail stone] & it would be no joke to get pelted in the head with "such an one." Next A.M. the ground was all covered with twigs and small branches that the storm had cut off. It took place just at sun down & lasted about an hour in all–then it stopped, cleared, & after we had watched it doing the Boquillas & the intervening valley for a time, it had a relapse as a cold rainstorm for about another hour, & then it all cleared off–the ground drained dry, & by 10 P.M. we were all in bed.

Isabel and I should have seen trouble coming, but the arrival of Burt and William has distracted us. Faint lightning and distant thunder announce an approaching storm, and we have a ringside seat. The four of us stand mesmerized by the gathering clouds and watch the drama unfold around us until Isabel says, in a hushed voice, "Look at William's hair." It is standing straight out from his head. Electrons are getting organized. Lightning is eminent. We rush for our vehicles to wait it out. The air is full of moisture, but none falls. The danger passes, and a double rainbow arcs across an eastern sky inflamed by the setting sun. Later, a peach-colored glow lingers in the west until night finally falls, and we retire to our tents and sleeping bags.

We are on the trail for the high country by 9 A.M., sketches in hand, alert for the alignment of spires and ridges that will tell us where Fuertes camped. His sketch of the view down-canyon looks out over the top of a dome-shaped mountain to the Sierra del Carmen range across the Rio Grande in Mexico. Looking back as we climb, the top of Nugent Mountain begins to line up with the Carmens just as Fuertes's drawing indicated. We are close and begin to look up-canyon for an unusual spire of rock to the left and a ridge to the right.

Finally, the much anticipated rock and ridge materialize, precisely as Fuertes recorded them. This is where the 1901 Biological Survey expedition camped. We are standing in the mountain meadow where Fuertes spread his sleeping bag under the stars. Ahead is the canyon that the big southern moon filled with soft light to the sounds of owls and whippoorwills.

We leave the meadow behind and enter a mixed forest. Juniper and piñon give way to oak, maple, madrone, and ponderosa pine. The trail grows steeper as high clouds burn off, and the sun breaks through. Perspiration flows freely as we approach the end of the trail at the foot of a cliff. The sound of splashing water attracts us to a tiny waterfall. Individual drops descend through sunlight and shadow, giving the whole scene a delightful sparkle. I strip to the waist and take a stand-up shower, gasping in the cold water. After assurance there is no one within ten miles of us, Isabel does the same, just as three young men round the bend. It is hard to pull a dry T-shirt over wet skin, but Isabel manages it in record time.

After setting up camp, Fuertes, Bailey, and Oberholser went to work immediately collecting specimens of the animals they found in this zoological wonderland:

> The stream-bed above us is a wonderful, rich place, half-tropical
> & half boreal, pines & agaves—the big thick Mexican century
> plant with flower stalks 15 ft. high & 6 inches through, where rare
> hummingbirds come and feed. Maples & a lot of things I don't
> know. In this woods we found the 1st day 5 birds new to Texas
> & one new to U.S. & in the next 2 days we found 2 or 3 more
> new ones. A big jay [Mexican jay], soft blue all over & white
> below, a magnificent big pigeon [band-tailed pigeon], California
> Woodpeckers [acorn woodpeckers] & a fine big hummer [blue-
> throated hummingbird] are common in the gulch, & many other
> things keep us pretty busy keeping tab on them. 2 kinds of deer
> [mule deer and white-tailed deer] (if not 3) [Carmen Mountain
> whitetail][3] & probably bears & panthers are in the surrounding
> cañons as we have probably scared them out of this one.

The artist in young Fuertes responded deeply to the exotic landscape of this desert mountain range. The letters he sent home from his mountain campsite contain some of the most lyrical descriptions of the Chisos high country ever written:

> I wish I could describe, so you could see it, this magnificent
> place. The deep lovely colors of the rocks, covered in places with
> a light green moss, but for the most part some tone of light
> gray, deep brown or rich cinnabar red, towering up out of high
> banks of broken slide rock, the rich green of the forested parts,
> the lovely yellow stretch of grass-grown bottom reaching down

between the enclosing ridges to the mouth of the valley, which is blocked by a blue mountain, and beyond the broad lazy valley 15 or 20 miles the filmy outline of the Mexican Boquillas (Carmen ranges) mountains–the color of the palest blue morning glory.

That is the gentler side to look at, but we are just at the entrance to a great Sunday-quiet gulch with immense cathedral rocks which hit the clear blue sky up at 45° from our camp, and which hang over you as you go up nearer–and if a gun should be fired, the echoes roll back & across, up and down and around & end in a long thunder-roll that seems to come from nowhere & everywhere.

Things did not always go smoothly, however. The horses and mules provided essential transportation and could haul enough supplies to keep the men in the field indefinitely, so long as a "store" could be found within a day's ride from camp. But the animals also made life difficult, as on the night of the big hail storm, when they spooked and ran. On one occasion, disaster flirted with the expedition:

Now Baylor is a big strong mule that hates everyone in camp but Surles, & he only stands him because he has to. Well, he took the saddle all right, & Bailey got on all right, & started off, with Surles on a rope around Baylor's nose to snub him if he got gay . . . First off all was well . . . when all at once old Baylor's eyes sparkled black, his ears lay back, he got a good grip on the bit with his grinders and lit out like the Black Diamond Express, with little Bailey on his back like a boy.

He tore loose from Surles in a second, and went straight for a little gulch about 50 yards ahead, jumped it, landed on the other side with hunched feet & began to buck, as only a big strong mule can buck. Bailey gripped his saddle horn, cut loose all other holds, and devoted himself to hanging on for dear life . . . He succeeded for about 30 yards of liver-tearing wrenching, pitching, bucking, when I saw the old mule give a great leap forward, and throw the little man head first over his shoulders, high in the air, to go down like a log over the crest of a little rise that lay between me & him. He gave a little yell as he left his saddle, & I could hear, at my distance, the thud as he hit the ground.

In about no time . . . I was over there . . . little Bailey, on his face, having hit on the back of his head, rolled thro' a summersault & rolled over from the force of his terrific pitch. He was insensible when we found him, and bleeding from somewhere on his head or neck, or ear, we couldn't tell . . . But when I called him he came to enough to say "It's all right boys," in a dull way, slowly, & we carried him back to camp & put him on his bed . . . Well, to relieve you as we were relieved, he is all right but for a headache & a lame hip & shoulder.

Isabel and I have now seen the "Sunday-quiet gulch with immense cathedral rocks" Fuertes sketched for his family back home. We have been to the Chisos high country where, in a single day, he and his companions found five birds new to Texas. Overgrazing threatened the area for a while, but it recovered after it became a national park. The Mexican jay, band-tailed pigeon, acorn woodpecker, and blue-throated hummingbird still live there. The century plant and madrone still grow in the rocky soil.

But the sky has changed, and with it the clarity of the atmosphere. On nights when the wind is out of the south, the stars are not the bright points of light Fuertes described. Industrial pollution from Mexico now stains the desert sky. As we load our pickup for the trip back down, we can barely make out the faint outline of the Sierra del Carmens twenty miles away. Pollution now draws a smoky veil across mountains once the color of the "palest blue morning glory." Leaving the grassy slopes of the

Chisos behind, we descend into the Chihuahuan Desert where strawberry cactus and ocotillo are in full bloom after recent rains. The "gravel" road is rough with rocks the size of apples and oranges—sometimes grapefruit and melons. We negotiate washed-out areas slowly and carefully, but it is not enough. Less than a quarter mile from pavement, an ominous growling from the driver's-side front tire brings us to a halt. We have a flat—the modern equivalent of a recalcitrant mule.

The jack is under the back seat. We unload all the gear from the cab and pile it in the dust beside the road. The spare underneath the truck bed is lowered by a crank and chain mechanism. I insert the crank and turn the handle. Nothing. I try again. Still nothing. I crawl under to investigate.

The mechanism is hidden from view between the spare and the undercarriage, and I reach in to explore by touch. A cotter pin has sheared off. I retrieve a nail from my toolbox and a pair of pliers. It should be a simple matter to insert the nail and bend the end so that it will stay in place. But this must be done upside down and out of sight. To line things up, Isabel and I must communicate precisely about the rotation of the crank: "Turn it a quarter-inch counterclockwise . . . stop, stop . . . too far . . . back it up an eighth."

Suddenly I hear voices. Isabel is talking to someone. From under the truck, I can see mountain bike tires and three pairs of cycling shoes. A man crawls under and scoots over beside me. His name is Mark. I explain the problem and my proposed solution. He takes over, and I crawl out to rest my back and neck. Mark gives his friend Dan instructions for rotating the crank, then inserts the nail, bends it over, and the job is done. The spare drops on cue and a routine tire change proceeds without further complication.

By now Isabel is explaining to Jenny, the third cyclist, that we are retracing the steps of Louis Agassiz Fuertes through the Big Bend, using his letters as a guide. Dan overhears and replies, "So, you have copies of his letters, too? My favorite passage is the one about the 'throbbing bigness of the night sky.'" E. Dan Klepper is a freelance writer from Marathon who has just finished an article for *Texas Parks and Wildlife Magazine* about Fuertes and the Biological Survey expedition of 1901. We enjoy the irony of a chance meeting of Fuertes fans in such a remote place, made possible by letters written a century ago from "6,000' up . . . and 100 miles from the railroad."

☙

Vernon Bailey fully recovered from the injuries inflicted by Baylor the mule and led the expedition through the Davis Mountains and the Guadalupes before summer's end. He returned to the state twice more, spending a total of 425 days on six different occasions studying its plants and animals.[4] In 1905, he published the *Biological Survey of Texas*—the first and still the most comprehensive report ever written about the plants and animals of the state. It incorporated the work of twelve field agents, who spent over two thousand days, exploring more than two hundred sites scattered across all ten of its ecological regions.[5]

Bailey went on to publish biological surveys of New Mexico, Oregon, and North Dakota.[6] His work was part of a nationwide plan to inventory the birds and mammals of the United States and map their distribution. In the first fifteen years of this effort, the list of known species and subspecies of mammals almost quadrupled. C. Hart Merriam, Bailey's boss at the Biological Survey, alone described 660 new mammals. Detailed maps of their distribution revealed patterns of variation linked to Darwin's theory of evolution.[7]

Oberholser did not complete his account of the birds of Texas in time to be included in Bailey's report. It needed more work. By the time he died in 1963, at the age of ninety-three, Oberholser's manuscript had grown to 11,754 typed pages including 961 pages of introduction.[8] After his death, editors managed to trim his tome to publishable size while maintaining the essence of sixty years of field work, research, and writing. In Oberholser's *Bird Life of Texas,* the paintings and drawings done by Fuertes at the dawn of the twentieth century finally found a home.

Fuertes traveled widely after his visit to Texas. He explored North America from Alaska and California to Florida and the Bahamas. The American Museum of Natural History invited him to go on expeditions to the Yucatan and Colombia. In 1926, he was the official artist for Chicago's Field Museum trek into the highlands of Ethiopia and down the Blue Nile to Khartoum. Just three months after returning from this last trip, Fuertes was killed when the car he was driving was struck by a train in Unadilla, New York, not far from his home in Ithaca.[9] He was fifty-three years old.

Frank Chapman, noted ornithologist and personal friend, remembered Fuertes as something more than a cheerful comrade and skillful artist. "He was an experienced woodsman, a good packer, a capital cook, a master hand with tools, who could mend anything, and in adversity and sickness no mother could have been more tender."[10]

Louis Agassiz Fuertes's paintings introduced a generation of Americans to the beauty of birds, much as Roger Tory Peterson and David Allen Sibley have done for subsequent generations. The letters Fuertes wrote from the "Ghost Mountains" of the Big Bend now reside in the library of his alma mater, Cornell University. They capture the excitement and hardship of life in the field for a turn-of-the-century bird artist at the beginning of an all-too-brief career.

Today, however, we realize there is more at stake here than just a memory. The place itself, the creatures that inhabit it, the air and water that give it life, are fragile, finite things. They are changing even now. The land is safe inside a park, but what about the sky?

WALT DAVIS

Wild and Scenic River

In one cañon the walls are carved into the most remarkable
perpendicular pillars, resembling columns of the Egyptian type,
each of which is over one hundred feet in height.
ROBERT T. HILL,
"Running the Cañons of the Rio Grande, Part 1"

S AFELY BACK ON PAVEMENT after our foray into the Chisos
Mountains, Isabel and I face a fifty-mile drive to the put-in
point for our float trip through the Lower Canyons of the
Rio Grande. We turn north, leave Panther Junction behind,
and cross the desert flats between the Rosillos Mountains
to the west and the Sierra del Carmens on the eastern horizon. Shortly
after climbing through Persimmon Gap on U.S. Highway 385, we turn
right onto Ranch Road 2627, pass the old Stillwell Store, and begin
a roller-coaster ride through the scraggly hills of Black Gap Wildlife
Management Area. The road crosses the Rio Grande into Mexico at La
Linda, the starting point for our six-day trip down an official U.S. "Wild
and Scenic River."

❧

The scenic canyons of the Rio Grande were even wilder in 1899, when
Robert T. Hill floated through. He traveled 350 river miles from Presidio
to Langtry to study the geology of the region and make the first accurate map of the river's course. Hill later recalled, "There were but few

Adobe ruin in Hot Springs Canyon on the Rio Grande

inhabitants in the Big Bend country . . . Neither were there automobiles nor many wagon roads. Watering places were few and hard to find . . . the country was, at that time, a dangerous one to travel in, owing to its proximity to a brigand-infested portion of Mexico. It was . . . called the Bloody Bend. The only white men (two in number) encountered on the trip on the Texas side . . . were murdered by bandits within the next twelve months."[1]

At the time of his adventure, Robert T. Hill was forty-two years old. A photograph taken at the end of his voyage shows a short, stocky man in a battered hat, canvas jacket, and muddy high-top boots. He sports a handlebar mustache and beard with a touch of gray on its grizzled tip. Narrow eyes hide in shadows under a furrowed brow. The picture was one of his favorite portraits, and he often added the caption "Eat 'em alive!"[2] The man who came to be called the "Father of Texas Geology" could have easily been mistaken for a river ruffian.

When news of Hill's plan to run the Rio Grande reached Del Rio, local land agent Henry Ware wrote to him: "Buy no outfit, boats or anything until I see you. I can furnish you the only living guide who has ever made the trip from El Paso to Laredo by boat on the Rio Grande."[3] The guide was James MacMahon, a beaver trapper who made his living on the river and was considered by many to be the ugliest man in Texas. His own brother claimed that "when Jim was born his mother had to be tied to the bed before she would let him suckle."[4]

At MacMahon's suggestion, Hill bought lumber for his boats in San Antonio, loaded it onto a Southern Pacific train, and transported the raw materials 150 miles to Del Rio. There MacMahon constructed three boats, each one thirteen feet long and three feet wide, with cleats along the bottom to protect against rocks. Hill shipped the finished boats another two hundred miles by rail to Marfa, where he transferred them to hay wagons for the seventy-five-mile haul to Presidio on the Rio Grande.[5]

In Marfa, Hill made a difficult but wise decision. He knew there would be few chances to buy supplies once the expedition left Presidio and no chance at all for the last one hundred miles. A month's provisions for six men had to fit into three boats, so Hill decided to leave tents and other camp "luxuries" behind. Only photographic and surveying equipment, guns, ammunition, and supplies were allowed—no personal baggage other than what could be rolled into bedding.[6]

The expedition included Hill, Ware, and MacMahon plus Hill's adventuresome nephew Prentis, a cook named Serafino, and an extra boatman, Shorty Franklin.[7] At high noon on October 5, 1899, three boats pushed off into the muddy waters of the Rio Grande on a journey through the heart of what some have called the *despoblado*—the empty place. MacMahon was "cautious as a cat." He watched the water for a safe channel through rocks and gravel bars, scanned the bank for beaver slides, and kept an eye out for a border bandit named Alvarado. He had murdered several men along the river, some in their sleep. Locals called him "Old White Lip" because of his distinctive mustache—white on one side, black on the other.[8]

Hill kept his camera ready, made notes in his journal, and started a letter to his wife that he amended from time to time, until he found a place to mail it.[9] On the morning of the second day, they arrived at the remains of old Fort Leaton and a cluster of six adobe houses that made up the town of Polvo ("dust" in Spanish), the last habitation they would see for 150 miles. They took time to chat with the friendly storekeeper, who showed them bloodstains on the floor and wall where he said his predecessor had been robbed and murdered by the mustachioed Alvarado (within a year, Hill learned later, the storekeeper met the same fate). From that point on, the geologist kept his pistol by his side and began to suspect that Ware and MacMahon secretly hoped to meet up with "Old White Lip" and put an end to his violent career.[10]

A few miles downstream, the boats entered the first of many canyons—this one appropriately named Murderer's Canyon. Below its mouth lay a series of rapids where five of the men struggled with the boats while the sixth, cocked rifle in hand, stood guard. Safely through, they floated on past a ranch where a man, standing on the riverbank with a baby in his arms, watched them glide by. Only after they were well downstream did they realize that the man was Alvarado. They had missed the telltale mustache. Hill said later, "I breathed easier on finding this out, but the men swore audibly and long at their misfortune in not recognizing the supposed monster."[11]

One hundred river miles from Presidio (only fifty as the crow flies) a new threat confronted Hill and his crew. The river ran on a collision course toward an imposing cliff, then, at the last minute, funneled into a narrow canyon. Abruptly the Rio Grande turned a corner. The bright light of the desert gave way to perpetual twilight, as the water flowed swiftly and silently between sheer rock walls towering one thousand feet overhead. Hill describes what came next: "We had gone only a few miles when a halt was suddenly forced upon us. Directly ahead was a place where one side of the great cliffs had caved away, and the debris spread across the narrow passage of the river. This obstacle was composed of great blocks of stone and talus rising two hundred feet high, which, while obstructing the channel, did not dam the waters, but gave them way through the interstices of the rocks. The boulders were mostly quadrangular masses of limestone fifty feet or more in height, dumped in a heterogeneous pile, like a load of bricks from a tip-cart, directly across the stream. At this place, which we appropriately named 'Camp Misery,' trouble began. Although the obstruction was hardly a quarter of a mile in length, it took us three days to get our boats across it."[12]

The Rio Grande exits the canyon suddenly, makes a hard right turn to the south, and is immediately assailed by the glaring heat of the Chihuahuan Desert. Looking back, the men could see the great escarpment from which the canyon emerged. The Rio Grande had cut through an immense fault-block mountain seventeen hundred feet high and sixty miles long. It looked as if a huge knife had sliced into a stony layer cake to make way for the river. The spectacular landmark had no name and appeared on none of the maps Hill had consulted.[13] We now call the canyon Santa Elena, and the spilled brick cart of boulders at "Camp Misery" is known as the "rock slide" by river guides and tourists.[14]

Days stretched into weeks as the expedition navigated the canyons that punctuate the sweeping big bend of the Rio Grande. Leaving Mariscal Canyon, Hill realized that the river had changed course. It no longer trended southeast; instead, it flowed northeast toward Abilene, Chicago, and Lake Michigan rather than toward Brownsville and the Gulf of Mexico. The Rio Grande makes the necessary course correction in a scramble of mountains, deserts, and canyons that remain one of the most remote regions of Texas. Modern-day river runners call this stretch of wild river the Lower Canyons.

The guide for our own trip through the Lower Canyons is not a beaver trapper but a seasoned employee of the commercial guide service Far Flung Adventures. Our party of six is the same size as Hill's, but we are all female, with one exception. Three are paying customers: a nurse from Houston named Irene, Isabel, and me. The lead boatman and guide is Tammi Besmehn, a powerful, compact woman with the shoulders of a gymnast and a beaming smile that even a crooked tooth can't spoil. Friends call her Taz (for Tasmanian Devil) because of her incredible energy and drive. Taz's sister Terri is a slender blonde with long hair done up in a French braid. She rows the gear boat. Third sister Jean, an olive-skinned brunette, is assistant cook and general helper.

We replace the low-tech wood plank rowboats of a century ago with high-tech inflatable rubber rafts stiffened by metal frames. We follow a map. Hill made one. We eat gourmet meals with fresh vegetables and hot-out-of-the-Dutch-oven desserts that are a far cry from the grease-laden grub Hill and party endured.

Our drive to the river begins in light fog with a slow drizzle; but the sky clears, and by the time we reach the put-in point at La Linda, there is not a cloud in sight. The Rio Grande, swollen by recent rain, flows gray between muddy banks lined with dense stands of giant cane. Beyond the green wall of rank vegetation, the tawny gray hills of the Chihuahuan Desert stretch away to the horizon. The gravel bar where we load the rafts is coated with viscous mud–slippery as a field of greased bowling balls. A sprained ankle or broken bone is just one careless step away.

Rigging and loading the rafts takes two hours. After Taz's boat flipped on a wild river in Nigeria, she vowed to pack so tightly that nothing would ever fall out again. Watching her lash equipment onto a raft is like watching a spider wrap its prey. She glances up to cast an experienced eye at the river. "Too thick to drink, too thin to plow," she says, quoting a familiar description of this and several other Texas rivers. As we shove off a pair of zone-tailed hawks soar overhead, and a peregrine falcon engages them in an aerial dogfight.

Taz and her crew serve lunch on the river bank–turkey sandwiches on wheat rolls with lettuce and sprouts. We spend the afternoon on a watery highway through the desert. A strong headwind slows our progress, and we stop for the night where Maravillas Canyon opens into the Rio Grande. An imposing mesa stands guard over the confluence–its impregnable summit isolated from the surrounding desert by sheer limestone cliffs. If the river at its base had been the Rhine, there would be a castle here.

Remembering the recent rain, Taz supervises construction of a shelter over the "kitchen" using a tarp, oars, and driftwood. We look like survivors of a shipwreck thrown upon a beach. When Taz sets up the propane stove to cook supper, it will not light. The prospect of seven days without a hot meal dampens spirits, but Terri diagnoses the problem and fixes it. Supper is grilled chicken with fresh broccoli and stove-top stuffing, capped off with fresh-baked brownies. Threatening clouds and wind come to nothing more than a few sprinkles during the night. But, morning arrives with an ominous sign. An entire tree, uprooted by a flash flood upstream, floats by as we eat breakfast.

When Robert T. Hill and his expedition camped at Maravillas Creek, the river was running low, not high. He did not see uprooted trees floating by. He described the view up the dry creek bed: "This is a horrible desert arroyo, leading northward for one hundred miles or more to Marathon. It has a channel sufficient for the Hudson, but is utterly void of water. Now and then, in the intervals of years, great floods pour down its stony bottom, giving the boulders and other desert debris a further push toward the Rio Grande and the sea . . . The mouth of Maravillas Creek marks the end of the great northerly stretch of the Rio Grande, and from there on the algebraic sum of the direction of the river's course is almost due east to the mouth of the Pecos."[15]

The hard-nosed leader of the expedition struggled to adequately describe the landscape through which they passed: "These cliffs are cut into many lobes and buttes. Occasionally one of these stands out and apart from the main cliff-line in lonely grandeur." He described Castle Butte as a masterpiece of nature's architecture: "[It] rises fully fifteen hundred feet above the river. Its circular, flat top, the square-cut escarpment cornice, and the gracefully sloping pediment are beautiful illustrations of the wonderful symmetrical sculpture seen along the river."[16]

The full moon bathed the landscape in a different light that mesmerized the practical-minded geologist: "Long before its face could be seen, its light would tip the pinnacles and upper strata of the cliffs, still further gilding the natural yellows of the rocks. Slowly this brilliant light sank into the magma of darkness which filled the cañon [*sic*], gently settling from stratum to stratum as the black shadows fled before it, until finally it reached the silent but rapid waters of the river, which became a belt of silver. Language cannot describe the beauty of such nights, and I could never sleep until the glorious light had ferreted out the shadows from every crevice and driven darkness from the cañon."[17]

In spite of spectacular scenery and geological surprises around every corner, Hill and his men grew weary. They had been on the river nearly a month, with provisions running low and tempers growing short. Just then the expedition encountered a wilderness Eden where, according to Hill:

In the depths of a beautifully terraced cañon, we came upon another copious hot spring running out of the bluff upon a low bench, where it made a large, clear pool of water. We reached this place one Sunday noon. The sight of this natural bath of warm water was tempting to tired and dirty men, and here we made our first and only stop for recreation. After lunch, most of the party proceeded to the warm pool, and, stripping, we literally soaked for hours in its delightful waters, stopping occasionally to soap and scrub our linen. While here the party indulged in guessing the height of the inclosing cliffs. The air was so clear in this country that one always underestimated the magnitude of the relief. None of our estimates exceeded five hundred feet. Seeing a good place for the first time in all our course to scale the cañon walls, I climbed them and measured the exact height, which was sixteen hundred and fifty feet.[18]

Our first full day on the river is the hardest of the trip for Isabel. Once the sun comes out, the temperature begins to climb, and the glare off the water takes its toll. The only shade is from her hat. She downs as many aspirin as the warning label allows and drinks water constantly, but it isn't enough. The headache worsens. We stop mid-afternoon, set up camp, and pitch a tent in the thin shade of an acacia tree where Isabel takes a fitful nap. She has no appetite at supper and soon loses what little she was able to eat. Totally exhausted, she falls asleep on top of her bedroll, covered only by a sheet. This would not be a life-threatening problem at home, but here on the river our medical options are limited.

Day three finds Isabel weak but recovered—headache gone. By two o'clock we arrive at the head of Hot Springs Rapids, where Taz beaches our rafts to scout ahead on foot. The river presents an appalling spectacle. Huge boulders pile up pillows of roiling water upstream, carve deep holes downstream, and throw up "rooster tails" of spray and foam.

Taz studies the currents and eddies for a long time, plotting a safe course through the chaos. She talks her sisters through the route she has devised. Jean and I board the first raft, and Taz takes us on a wild ride. Once the current takes hold, there is no turning back. At times the raft rises high on the water only to plunge forward and down until it is almost hidden from view. Spray soaks everyone, but the gear is secure and nothing goes overboard. With an exultant shout Taz turns the raft toward the Mexican shore, and I jump out to tie our bowline to a half-buried snag.

Now it is Terri's turn. She is younger, slimmer, and not as strong as her more experienced sister, who by now has scrambled back overland to join her. Terri takes oars in hand, and Taz shoves off. Isabel and Irene have the ride of their lives, with grins and shouts to match. Terri is having a rough time though, her strength no match for the power of the rushing water. In the middle of the run, sisters precariously trade places. Once both rafts are safely ashore, Taz confides that even though she has been through these rapids before, the high water changes them completely. Past experience counts for nothing. It is a new river with new problems to solve.

Taz decides to set up camp and spend a lazy afternoon recuperating from the strain and excitement of the day. The rapids take their name from hot springs that bubble to the surface in and beside the river. This is the spot where Robert T. Hill declared a holiday for his crew—where they soaked for hours and washed their clothes. Isabel and I find a shaded pebble-lined pool filled with delightfully warm, crystal clear water. It is just right for two people, and we soak a while, dry off, then soak some more. Clouds gather late in the day. After supper, a thunderstorm brings rain, hail, and tent-flapping wind. The show is over by bedtime, and cooler air in the wake of the storm brings a good night's sleep.

Morning light slants into the canyon, enticing us to explore beyond our campsite where we make an unsettling discovery. Pieces of tin roofing laid across the smoke-stained corner of a collapsed rock house create a human lair. Inside, a jug of water, a neatly folded shirt, and portable radio suggest that the occupant is still nearby.

This must be a regular crossing point from Mexico into Texas on the pedestrian highway from poverty to the land of plenty. We wonder how this lone traveler can cross the desert on foot with so little gear. We have two large rafts loaded with food and equipment for a week-long trip down the river. If he is watching, he may be wondering why we have so much, when so little is necessary.

After lunch, Taz decides we need to give up the idea of a full day layover at Hot Springs and move on. Our pace so far will require seven days to reach the take-out point. Ahead lay several more stretches of rough water and the infamous Madison Falls. Any unexpected delays could prove costly, so we load up and push off. It is hot on the river, and we are all glad, late in the day, to find a shady spot for camp.

Under a make-shift awning, the sisters prepare steak, potatoes, and coleslaw, followed by hot pineapple upside-down cake. Cooling shadows fall over camp, and Isabel and I walk up a beautiful little side canyon of sculpted limestone where water stands in *tinajas*—natural basins carved out of solid rock. Earless lizards streak away as we approach. A tiny cicada sings loud enough for an insect ten times its size, and bats begin to flit about in a darkening sky.

Breakfast of blueberry pancakes and bacon fortifies our team for today's big challenge—Upper and Lower Madison Falls. We hear them before we see them and pull out to scout ahead. These rapids are even bigger than Hot Springs, and one spot, near an immense block of lime-stone, is especially dangerous. Downstream from another boulder, a standing wave keeps floating objects turning end over end. Years ago we lost a friend to such a wave on the Guadalupe.

We listen carefully as Taz reviews emergency procedures: "If you go overboard, don't try to swim or fight the current. There is so much air in turbulent water that normal swimming strokes won't do any good. Trust the life jacket. It will keep you afloat. Face downstream and be prepared to fend off rocks with your feet and the strength of your legs."

Before we push off, Taz has visualized the entire run. She knows the angle the raft must enter the rapids in order to exit in position for the next and subsequent maneuvers. She has decided whether to pass to the right or left of the most dangerous boulders, and where to pull out at the end. As we approach the shimmering "V" that marks the beginning of the rapid, Taz says, "When I give the signal, fall forward onto the front of the raft. That will keep us from flipping when we hit the wall of water on the far side of a hole." With that, we are committed, and the wildest ride of all begins.

We glide, and lurch, and turn. On cue, we fall on the bow as a wave breaks over us. At times, the raft seems to rush forward, nose down; then it rises and all but stops, before the current pulls us on again. Now Taz pulls hard for shore and, too soon, it is all over. We are still shouting with exhilaration, as the adrenalin rush slowly subsides. Taz brings the second raft safely through, and we go on to negotiate Lower Madison without incident.

After the excitement of the morning, it is good to slow down and enjoy the countryside. We glide along at the speed of drifting clouds, watching the water change color from chocolate brown in the sun to sky blue in the shadows. Black phoebes dart back and forth across the river from one patch of cane to another. Cliff swallows swoop low to skim a drink off the calmer stretches. An occasional horse, mule, or burro grazes on grass-covered terraces called *vegas*. We stop at a riverside hot spring where Isabel shampoos her hair, careful not to let the soap contaminate the spring or river. It is a delicious luxury.

✽

After their brief vacation at Hot Springs, Hill's expedition continued downriver as the geologist struggled to describe the landforms rising on all sides: "Queer eccentric pinnacles . . . spires, fingers, needles, natural bridges . . . every conceivable form of peaked and curved rocks."[19] As they crossed the 102nd meridian, Hill recorded the " . . . most beautiful and picturesque effects . . . The walls are no longer of orange color, but are of chalky limestone of purest white, which weathers into great curves rather than vertical ledges. In one cañon, for instance, the walls are carved into the most remarkable perpendicular pillars, resembling columns of the Egyptian type, each of which is over one hundred feet in height."[20]

But beauty was not enough to sustain the weary men. According to Hill, "We no longer appreciated the noble surroundings. We longed only to escape from the walls, upon which we now began to look as a prison. Ten hours of hard rowing each day . . . constant wetting . . . baking due to a merciless sunshine . . . [and] the ever-present apprehension of danger, had put us all in a condition of quarrelsome, nervous tension. . . ."[21]

They knew that escape from their canyon prison was eminent when they sighted an immense eagle nest on a cliff on the Mexican side. It had been a landmark for as long as anyone could remember. Hill thought it might be the largest bird's nest in America. It signaled that the village of Langtry was near. The men beached their boats and hired a packhorse to haul their gear from the river to the railroad.[22]

So ended the first recorded descent of the canyons of the Rio Grande. Robert T. Hill and his five companions had navigated and mapped 355 miles of the most remote, dangerous, and spectacularly beautiful geography in Texas. Hill's article in *The Century Magazine*, illustrated by Thomas Moran, introduced U.S. readers to one of their nation's premier wild rivers.[23]

News of the epic journey encouraged the U. S. Biological Survey to send a team of naturalists into the Big Bend region the following year—Vernon Bailey's team that included a young bird artist by the name of Fuertes.

Our last days on the river become a lazy blur of sunny days on a liquid boulevard; campsites on shore in the cool of the evening, and hearty meals morning, noon, and night. Steep-walled canyons are now behind us, and we are surrounded by desert that comes close to flirt with the river. Our trip is nearing the end when we come upon an idyllic campsite on the Mexican side. A level, grass-covered *vega* rises behind a sandy beach, all bounded by a cliff holding back the desert. We set up camp and the crew starts supper.

Without warning, the calm is broken by an explosion of sound from a nearby patch of cane. Something large is thrashing about inside. Suddenly, two gleaming-white Charolais bulls emerge in a cloud of dust and debris. Heads down and muscles bulging, they are locked in a blind dispute over our once-peaceful *vega*. We take a quick look around, hoping there is enough room for two testy bulls and six shaken travelers. The bulls, oblivious to us, settle their argument and wander off to graze in peace. We trust that coexistence is possible if we keep a respectful distance.

After supper we meet another citizen of this place—a large and beautifully patterned copperhead snake. We take a long look and make photographs. Our visitor then insists on crawling toward our tents rather than back to the safety of the rocks. We stamp our feet and try to turn him with sticks, but he will not be deterred. So we zip up our tent doors and watch where we put our hands and feet until bedtime. The night passes without incident, and morning brings a cool fog and the chance to explore beyond our beachhead.

We climb to the top of the plateau bordering the river for a bird's-eye view of our final campsite. We look down into an exotic rock garden nearby, where limestone has eroded into free-standing columns that tower above the riverside trees and shrubs. This must be the place Hill described as having "columns of the Egyptian type." On the rim, over-looking this picturesque spot, we find deep mortar holes where Native Americans processed desert foodstuff, grinding and pulverizing it with stone pestles. They certainly knew how to pick a kitchen with a view.

A few miles from the take-out point near Dryden, we pass beneath a cliff encrusted with the gourd-shaped mud nests of cliff swallows. Birds fill the air, and blue-black faces with white foreheads peer out from nest openings. A fluttering disturbance in the water beneath the cliff turns out to be a young swallow fallen from the safety of its home and strug-gling to stay afloat. I suggest that, tragic as it may seem, it is best to let nature take its course. There is probably a catfish lurking nearby that needs a meal. Jean will not hear of it. She has encountered a creature in need and will do whatever it takes to rescue and rehabilitate the poor unfortunate. She scoops it up, and we move on. Now, at every stop, we scurry about catching grasshoppers, crickets, and other insects we think the little swallow will eat.

A Far Flung Adventures van waits for us at the take-out point. We flip, drain, and wash the rafts before deflating them. We lash oars and metal frames to the top of the vehicle, roll up the rafts, and stow them inside. Before leaving, we take a last long look at the river that has been our lifeline through the desert.

Tears flow as we transfer gear from the Far Flung van to our pickup. The "All Woman (but one) Lower Canyons Expedition" has come to an end. We want to hold our little community together. We long to sus-tain the childlike sense of wonder and excitement life on the river has rekindled. We dread the erosion of memory that will preserve the shell but not the living substance of our experience. But none of that is pos-sible. The currents of our lives sweep us on, around the bend, and out of sight.

Weeks later we receive a postcard from Jean with a picture of the swallow. She had nursed it all the way back to her home in Montana, catching enough insects along the way to keep it alive. Sadly, the next letter reports that the little foundling has taken a sudden turn for the worse. In the end, Jean's devotion is not enough. The fledgling swallow of the Lower Canyons is buried near Yellowstone National Park, far from the cliff beside the Rio Grande where it was born.

Border Botaniʒt

· ·

If you lived here you had to know the plants.
If you didn't know, you didn't survive.
BENITO TREVIÑO,
in discussion with the authors

A FTER LEAVING ITS LOWER CANYONS, the relentless Rio Grande glides past Langtry and the eagle nest already old in 1899 when Robert T. Hill saw it high on a cliff on the Mexican side.[1] Older yet is Parida Cave overlooking the Rio Grande downstream from its junction with the Pecos. Centuries ago, Indians painted pictographs on the ceiling and left deep layers of ash on the floor from countless campfires. Louis Agassiz Fuertes stopped here briefly in 1901 and made sketches.[2] He described a spring-fed pool fringed with maidenhair ferns that remains to this day, but the view downstream from the cave's mouth has changed dramatically. The river is wide and still. A dam near Del Rio has made a lake of the Rio Grande—International Amistad Reservoir.

The river that escapes the lake encounters an environment different from all that has gone before—an environment that will continue to change as the Rio Grande approaches the Gulf of Mexico. It now enters the sun-drenched South Texas Plains. This is brush country. Plants without spines are rare. Sometimes even the thorns have thorns. These scruffy survivors have earned names like prickly ash, catclaw, horse crippler, and crucifixion thorn.[3] Sparse foliage conserves moisture but makes poor shade.

Indigo snake, Santa Ana National Wildlife Refuge

To remove the brush and make the land productive, owners use root plows, roller choppers, shredders, and root rakes to sever roots below the surface or rip them from the ground. Sometimes they string a ship's anchor chain between two bulldozers and pull it across a field or pasture. A three-hundred-foot long, twelve-thousand-pound chain wreaks havoc with every growing thing in its path.[4] In South Texas, brush control takes on the lusty intensity of a blood sport.

It was not always so. The land was once quite different and attracted an unusual visitor in 1828. Jean Louis Berlandier came from Geneva, Switzerland, home to some of the best watchmakers and bankers in Europe. It had been a sophisticated center of learning since John Calvin founded the Academy there in 1559.[5] The city embraced both banks of the Rhone River where it flows out of Lake Geneva, a sky-blue crescent of clear water over a thousand feet deep. Beyond the town, farms and vineyards filled the Rhone Valley, bounded on one side by the Jura Mountains and on the other by the Bernese Alps. What could entice an urbane man like Berlandier to leave such a place behind–to trade its fertile valleys and mountain meadows for the arid scrub of the muddy Rio Grande–to exchange gooseberry and edelweiss for wolfberry and tasajillo?

The answer lay in Geneva's Academy. Its resident botanist, Auguste DeCandolle, ignited intellectual fires in ambitious young men and sent them around the world as scientific missionaries. DeCandolle saw potential in Berlandier, cultivated his talents, and prepared his mind for the opportunity of a lifetime. Another of DeCandolle's students had become Minister of Foreign Affairs for the new Republic of Mexico. He needed a botanist to accompany an expedition being sent out to survey the U.S./Mexico boundary. DeCandolle recommended his star pupil for the position.

On the October day in 1826, when Berlandier boarded ship for Mexico, he had no way of knowing that he would not return.[6] Determined to live up to the high expectations of his professor, Berlandier went to work as soon as he reached Panuco on the Mexican coast two months later. He continued to collect specimens as he traveled through Huasteca, Toluca, and Cuernavaca. Arriving in Mexico City, and eager to move on to the Rio Grande, the young botanist found the wheels of bureaucracy turning slowly.

More than a year passed before the expedition headed north in November, 1827. The survey party was led by General Mier y Terán who arranged for a wagon to carry indispensable books, scientific instruments, and collecting supplies. A small military escort provided security. By the time Berlandier reached the banks of the Rio Grande on February 2, 1828, he had been on the road for thirteen weeks.

Laredo was an impoverished and isolated military outpost, but for the young botanist, it was a botanical treasure trove. He collected there for seventeen days in February before the expedition moved on to San Antonio. As they penetrated deeper into what would become Texas, weather and sickness began to take a toll on the men. Rains fell incessantly, damaging the priceless collection of dried plants. Clouds of mosquitoes pestered both men and animals. First Berlandier, then General Terán, and eventually several more of his men came down with the debilitating fever and delirium of malaria.

The travel-worn botanist who returned to Laredo in August, after six months on the road, was a changed man. Despite difficulties unimaginable by his colleagues in Geneva, Berlandier managed to make important botanical discoveries that led to the description of many plants new to science. Along the way, he fell in love with the border country.

From Laredo, the expedition crossed the Rio Grande and proceeded down the right bank through a series of towns established by José de Escandón in the mid-1700s. One of these towns was called Guerrero. Dr. Rubén Flores Gutierrez, a former resident, recalls it as a place where "art and architecture seem to have harmoniously merged." He remembers the parish church, the public market, and many other buildings that were "expertly built and embellished with beautifully carved decorative details." According to Dr. Gutierrez, "the expertise of the masons of

Guerrero, especially their knowledge of constructing arches, was known throughout the region, and these craftsmen were hired to execute work in other towns."[7]

In 1953, the good people of Guerrero were forced to abandon the place where art and architecture lived in harmony and move to a new town twenty miles away. The United States and Mexico had agreed to build a dam across the Rio Grande. Falcon Reservoir not only flooded a unique riparian habitat, it also drowned a living piece of history. Guerrero Viejo (old Guerrero) was frozen in time by the rising water of the lake.

The sun breaks through morning clouds as we drive across Falcon Dam on our way to see what is left of the town Berlandier visited one hundred and eighty years ago. A stately raft of white pelicans floats on the still water of the reservoir as we cross into Mexico. Beyond the lake and the river, mesquite dominates the brush land on both sides of Highway 2, the busy two-lane artery of commerce between Matamoros and Laredo.

Things change dramatically once we leave the pavement and begin following small blue signs with arrows pointing toward *"Antigua Ciudad Guerrero."* Dangerously deep ruts warn that the hard-packed dirt can become a quagmire in the rain. The burned-out shell of a car sits ominously in the middle of the road, engine and hood missing, windshield a mosaic of scorched shards draped across the dashboard. We stop at a locked gate just as a pickup pulls in behind. A man gets out, unlocks the gate, and motions us through. Forty minutes, and eight-plus miles, after leaving the highway, we finally arrive at the windmill standing guard over the entrance to the old village.

A decade of drought has shrunk the reservoir, letting Old Guerrero rise from its watery grave. The pattern of streets is still etched in the dried mud of the lake bed. Grass has returned. Prickly pear and tasajillo grow in piles of rubble that once were houses. The graceful arches of the public market remain—proudly upright. White plaster with blue trim still covers the hand-hewn sandstone in better-preserved ruins.

We drive into the center of town, park the truck, and step out into a timeless scene. A herd of multicolored goats engulfs us, bells tinkling, kids and nannies bleating. All are on the move, pausing only briefly to nibble grass or balance on hind legs to snatch a leaf overhead. The goatherd emerges from the brush. "*Buenas dias,*" he says, and follows his charges across the open plaza in front of Guerrero's ruined parish church, Nuestra Señora del Refugio. Portions of its crumbling bell tower date back to 1755, according to a sign at its base.

An octagonal bandstand dominates the center of the plaza with stairs leading to a concrete platform open to the sky. The place is well-remembered by a woman who reminisced with a local reporter about her old hometown. The waters of Falcon Reservoir flooded the town plaza, she recalled, but not the upper portion of the bandstand. More than once, it served her family as an island campsite. With their boat tied alongside, they built a fire and cooked a meal in the stilled heart of old Guerrero. She found it strange to take a boat into the flooded church, but was outraged one day to see a man casting his lure where the altar once stood.[8]

A late model white pickup rounds the corner and brings us back to the twenty-first century. Two young girls stand in the back, elbows on the cab, air rifles at the ready. The well-spoken man behind the wheel explains in English that they are hunting birds. The family is from Laredo and has bought land nearby. They are restoring one of the old buildings on high ground that escaped the rising lake. Despite these distractions, we can still visualize Guerrero as Berlandier saw it. The town would have been a noisy, prosperous place with homes, businesses, and civic structures built of stone to last long after their builders passed from the scene.

But the goats that greeted us when we arrived remind us that the landscape had changed dramatically long before the botanist arrived. After listening to old-timers telling about the early days of settlement,

Berlandier said, "The first colonists of the towns on the banks of the Rio Bravo all declared, with one accord, that when they arrived . . . forests were rare, and that before the introduction of their herds, only grassy prairies were to be seen."[9]

In 1757, before Escandón's colony was ten years old, eighty thousand cattle, horses, and mules, plus three hundred thousand sheep had been turned loose on the native prairies flanking the Rio Grande.[10] As the herds grew in the decades that followed, colonists noticed thorny brush invading the grassland. They were forced to move their animals north across the Rio Grande to ever-shrinking stands of native prairie that were also home to growing herds of wild horses and long-horned cattle.[11] Old Guerrero had seen many changes before the Rio Grande rose up to send its people to higher ground and fill its church with catfish.

We are headed back to the truck, when I call Isabel over to see a sad sight. The keystone in an arch above a window is about to give way. When it goes, the leaning wall will crumble, and another piece of the old Spanish Colonial town will slip away. "What is that?" Isabel asks, aiming her binoculars at the shadowy crack above the arch. Something is inside. Eyes closed, it remains motionless, as if carved from the stone on which it stands. A screech owl. Mottled gray plumage blends with the weathered rock around it. Striking pale gray eyebrows echo shapes left by a mason's chisel in sandstone over its head. The little owl has found refuge in the midst of decay.

Another of the Rio Grande Valley's residents has found refuge farther downstream. His name is Benito Treviño, and he traces his family back to Spanish colonial times when the King of Spain granted his great-great grandfather use of land along the Rio Grande in what was then called Nuevo Santander (now Starr County, Texas). We are on our way to meet this man who bridges two cultures and two ways of knowing.

Benito Treviño is the sixth of fifteen children. His parents lived through the Great Depression that hit the Rio Grande Valley especially hard. They gleaned food and medicine from the plants around them, relying on the collected wisdom of previous generations to see them through. Botanical knowledge was not a matter of grades, degrees, or prestige; it was a matter of survival.

By the time Benito came of age, he had the luxury of doing something impractical. He enrolled in the University of Texas and graduated with a degree in botany and a minor in chemistry. Unable to earn a living in botany, Treviño took a job as a chemical analyst for Atlantic Richfield Company (ARCO) in Houston, where he met and married another chemist named Toni Reese. Together they developed a plan to leave the corporate world behind and strike out on their own. It would be risky and would require serious money to jump-start their project. Both took good-paying jobs in Alaska, lived on little, and saved the rest. After two years, they returned to the Rio Grande Valley and bought a piece of history.

The original Spanish land grant had, by this time, passed into other hands. As the family grew, the land was divided among heirs and then divided again. As parcels became smaller, heirs found it harder to make a living on shrinking farms and ranches. By the time Treviño left home, it was all gone. Then a small tract located on the edge of the original grant came on the market. It was only 170 acres, but they were especially valuable acres to a trained botanist from a family of traditional herbalists and gleaners. It had never been root plowed. The living soil with all its accumulated microorganisms was still intact. Native species had been spared from the relentless brush wars of the 1950s. It was a botanical refuge waiting for the right custodians to come along and put it to good use.

The Treviños have built a home there, started a nursery for native plants, and put in RV sites for tourists. Now they are constructing a large facility for educational programs, native plant workshops, and special events. They intend to reclaim and preserve the botanical folk wisdom of previous generations, protect remaining species, and encourage their use in urban landscapes. The couple's work is widely known and respected throughout the Rio Grande Valley.

There is nothing unusual about the fifteen-minute drive from Rio Grande City to the Treviño's place. Modest homes on small acreages appear more often than large fenced ranches or neglected tracts of mesquite brush. A pair of gigantic century plants with twenty-foot-tall dried bloom stalks flanks the entrance to the property. An iron gate stands open, hinged to sturdy posts made of concrete and polished river rock. Almost hidden in the brush to the left, yellow letters on a red sign spell out "Rancho Lomitas."

We are late and drive through quickly. Parking in the shade of a two-story frame and brick house, I turn off the motor, and we listen as a cactus wren calls far off in the brush. Up close, a curve-billed thrasher scolds us with sharp, liquid double-whistles. I knock on each of three doors. No answer. I circle the house, knocking louder, to no avail. We check our notes to confirm date and time and settle down to wait for our host.

Bird feeders, watering places, and butterfly-friendly plantings are signs that this is the right place. Peacocks and chickens cackle and cluck nervously from big wire cages out back. A haughty pair of llamas glare over the top rail of their plank and goat-wire pen, as their half-grown youngster tries to decide whether to be frightened or bored. Close by, a rusty but serviceable John Deere 4010 diesel tractor stands idle.

The crunch of tires on gravel announces the arrival of Benito Treviño in a Ford F250, 4x4 pickup. The driver is a small man dressed in faded black jeans and T-shirt, round-toed, well-worn work boots, and a black leather belt with Mexican coin conchos. There is less gray in the dark hair and moustache than you would expect in a man of sixty. His voice is a distinctive blend of precision and musicality. He is so careful to enunciate all parts of every word that we feel obliged to match his careful speaking with careful listening.

After introductions, Treviño drops to one knee, picks up a stick, and draws a wavy line in the dirt to represent the Rio Grande. He wants us to understand the idea behind *porciones,* the oddly-shaped parcels of land common in the Rio Grande Valley. He adds two narrow rectangles to his drawing, their short ends touching the wavy line. By keeping river frontage narrow, Treviño explains, the Spanish king maximized the number of revenue-producing ranches he could pack into an arid landscape. At fifteen miles long by two miles wide, each tract provided ample land and sufficient water to sustain flocks of sheep and herds of cattle and goats.

Treviño draws a small box on the line separating the two rectangles. "This is Rancho Lomitas," he explains. "And this part," he says, touching the right side of the box, "is across from the front gate." He turns to point his stick toward a piece of history. "That is part of my family's original *porcion,* granted by the King of Spain in the mid-1700s."

"Let's go inside where we can talk," he says, ushering us through the house to a screened-in patio looking out onto a rock garden. Treviño directs us to a round glass table opposite arched windows through which we can see butterflies visiting a blooming bougainvillea. "What is it that you want to know?" he asks. I open the book we have brought with us, *A Field Guide to South Texas Shrubs.*[12] Its pages bristle with orange post-it notes marking the various plants having some connection to Jean Louis Berlandier. The first marked entry is *anaqua,* also called sugarberry (*Ehretia anacua*). M. Terán and J. Berlandier are credited with its discovery, probably during the Mexican boundary survey sometime between the spring of 1827 and the fall of 1830. A photograph shows a cluster of orange and yellow berries against a backdrop of dark green leaves.

"What can you tell us about this plant?" Isabel asks.

"This was a great tree," he says, as if remembering a favorite uncle. "Almost all year it had flowers, green fruit, and ripening fruit. They have a sweet but turpentine-ish, volatile taste. They are very nutritious because they have a lot of sugars that give quick energy. We put a whole bunch of them in our mouths and worked our way through, then spit out the seeds. This was a very dependable food source."

"Where do they grow?" I want to know.

"You often see old ranches that have been abandoned for years," he answers. "The house is falling down, the corrals are dilapidated, but near the house you see an *anaqua* tree. They were planted because they provided food throughout the year and also real dense shade. When the *vaqueros* would come in from their cattle drives, they could always tie their horses underneath the *anaqua* tree or, when they were working at the house and they needed a break from the heat, they could sit under the *anaqua* tree."

He pauses, then smiles as he decides how to deliver the next bit of information.

"There are katydids that feed on the *anaqua*. They're feeding on one end, extracting all the sugar, and they're spitting out water on the other end. So you get under an *anaqua* tree and you are so much cooler because you get this mist continually coming down. At the time I don't think people realize what's happening. They just know it's cool under an *anaqua*."

As we go from plant to plant through the book, Treviño explains how some could be put to good use, while others created problems. Spaniards used *canatilla* (*Ephedra antisyphilitica*) to treat syphilis, but Treviño's family made a tea from the green stems that reduced hunger pangs. His grandmother boiled the leaves of Berlandier's croton (*Croton humilis*) to make a tea that cured *enpacho,* a painful intestinal condition that afflicted nursing babies. Mimosa-like *guajillo,* on the other hand, was the cause of a serious illness in goats. An animal that ate too much of it became sensitive to light and hid from the sun. It was said to have the "wobbles" if it lost control of its legs and would die if it continued to eat *guajillo.*

Treviño's enthusiasm overflows when we open the page to Texas ebony or *ebano* (*Chloroleucon ebano*). "This was a lifesaver," he says, "this and mesquite. I don't think we would have been able to survive without it." He taps his finger on the photograph in the book showing two pale-green seed pods the size of obese English peas. "These are called *naguacatas*," Treviño says. "You take the *naguacata* in your hand like this," he explains, gripping opposite ends of an imaginary bean. "You twist in opposite directions and they split. The seeds inside have a white seed coat, and inside that white seed coat is the actual seed which is light green in color. You pop the seed in your mouth, put it sideways between your front teeth, split the seed coat, turn it around and press to pop the seed out, then spit out the seed coat. Within two seconds you've already cut it, split it in half, removed the seed, and spit out the skin."

Treviño goes on to recite recipes for boiled and roasted *naguacata*, describing with epicurean precision the different flavors each preparation elicits. His highest praise goes to a concoction derived from roasted seed coats ground into coarse powder and added to boiling water. "To me, it's like premium coffee, because, when I drink regular coffee, I get an aftertaste. The few times I've had the privilege of drinking expensive premium coffee, I enjoy the flavor and there is no aftertaste. The coffee you make from *naguacata* has no aftertaste. I like my coffee with a lot of milk and a little sugar. With *naguacata* I don't put anything in it, and I still get that taste—nice and smooth and a little sweet."

Long before Berlandier brought these plants to the attention of the learned men of science back in Geneva, indigenous people had named them, cataloged their uses and dangers, and incorporated the information into encyclopedic oral traditions that were cultural treasures. Benito Treviño is passionate about preserving those traditions. "I must know a very small amount of what they knew then," he admits. "It was common knowledge. If you lived here, you had to know the plants. If you didn't know, you didn't survive. I feel guilty that if I don't do something to record it, I'm contributing to the disappearance of that information—information that other generations would not benefit from."

As we walk back outside, preparing to leave, Treviño stops beside an ebony tree he grew from seed to tell a story. "One year we had this one girl. She was studying pharmacy, and she came on a tour. Later on she called me and said she wanted to come back by herself and just walk with me, and I would tell her about the plants. She was working on her master's degree. She wanted to know what work I thought needed to be done with native plants dealing with medicine. I gave her a list to take back to the university to determine the chemical composition. I think we need to catalog just what each of these important plants contains. Then maybe somebody else can take it another step."

Treviño is trying to build a bridge between two ways of knowing: between scientific knowledge and folk wisdom. He believes that what indigenous people have learned about a place they have inhabited for generations, can enrich what specialists have learned through the scientific method. There is hopeful urgency in Treviño's voice as he concludes his story and we say goodbye.

Hope and urgency were also at play when DeCandolle dispatched Berlandier to catalog the plants of the Rio Grande Valley for science. The bridge-building opportunity that Treviño recognizes today was available in that earlier time as well. Berlandier might have taken that "next step" himself. With his early training in pharmacy, Berlandier was in a position to collect more than dried plant specimens. He could have recorded their medicinal uses. He might have learned from the locals which plants were edible and which were poisonous and recorded that information for science. The opportunity to do more disappeared, however, when Berlandier learned that DeCandolle was deeply disappointed in what his student had been able to accomplish.

In a letter to a colleague, DeCandolle complains that Berlandier "sent some dried plants in small number, badly chosen, and badly prepared; he neglected completely the sending of animals and seeds, and the communication of notes on the country. At the end of some time he neglected even to write, so that for a long interval we did not know whether he was living or dead. We then found that we had spent some sixteen thousand francs for some dried plants that were not worth a quarter of that amount."[13]

With his scientific reputation destroyed, Jean Louis Berlandier decided not to return to Europe. He started a new life in Matamoros near the mouth of the Rio Grande. He married a Mexican woman, established a pharmaceutical business, and became a well-respected physician. After Berlandier's untimely death by drowning in 1851, Lt. D. N. Couch purchased his extensive collection of plant and animal specimens, books, and publications. From those who knew him, Couch learned that Berlandier "was universally beloved for his kind, amiable manners, and [his] regard for the sick poor of that city; being always ready to give advice and medicine without pay."[14]

The good fortune of the *Matamoreños* seems to have been due to a misunderstanding between student and professor. Evidence in the archives of the U.S. National Museum indicates that the young botanist did a creditable job of collecting, in spite of the hazards of wilderness travel. Berlandier's handwritten list of specimens sent to Geneva includes "188 packets of dried plants totaling some 55,077 specimens; 198 packets of plant seeds; 935 insects; 72 birds; 55 jars and bottles of material in alcohol; and more than 700 specimens of land and fresh-water mollusks."[15]

DeCandolle may have had unrealistic expectations—some shipments may not have arrived in a timely manner. In any event, Berlandier did not defend himself against unjust criticism. It would be many years before the record was set straight by DeCandolle's successor in Geneva, Dr. John Briquet. "The collections of Berlandier have furnished . . . materials for the description of a great number of new species; it is by no means rash to affirm that the importance of the herborizations of this naturalist has gradually increased in the course of the last eighty years, and that the outlay of the little coterie of botanists at Geneva was not made in vain."[16]

Fortunately, people like Berlandier, the Treviños, the young pharmacy student, and others are working to document the plant life of the Rio Grande Valley. The place has changed radically since the time of the first Spanish colonial pioneers two-and-a-half centuries ago. Grazing pressure from vast herds of livestock allowed native brush to invade the original grassland on the South Texas Plains. Ingenuity and mechanical muscle enabled farmers to clear the brush and make way for intensive agriculture. An attractive climate has encouraged urbanization that now threatens to engulf what little original habitat remains.

As our long journey down the Rio Grande comes to an end, Isabel and I take a short walk on a favorite trail in Santa Ana National Wildlife Refuge. Green jays hop nimbly from limb to limb then fly away. A kiskadee flycatcher whistles its name nearby, and chachalacas gabble in the brush just out of sight. "Do you see what's at your feet?" Isabel asks in a hushed voice. I was looking for birds and did not notice the glistening black creature lying motionless beside the trail—a six-foot-long indigo snake. Its head is broad, its eyes unblinking. I remember the tenacity of one that bit me many years ago and refused to let go. Four rows of small but sharp, backward-curling teeth extinguished any hope of quick escape. When it finally released me, tiny beads of red appeared on the back of my hand. I have no desire to disturb the one at my feet today, and it glides noiselessly into the shadows.

The indigo snake is now on the endangered species list in Texas, along with the ocelot, jaguarundi, and northern aplomado falcon. The Texas tortoise is threatened.[17] As native prairie and brush become increasingly rare, many of the attendant animals reach the verge of extinction, and their significance, belatedly, comes into focus. The natural wonders of the Lower Rio Grande Valley have begun to attract economically significant numbers of visitors to the region.

Birds, butterflies, sea turtles, and even snakes are gaining ground in the financial calculations that ultimately determine how much room will be allotted to the indigenous species of a place. Hopefully, the tenacity of the original inhabitants of South Texas will enable them to hold on long enough to populate the world we bequeath them.

WALT DAVIS

CHAPTER 7

The Great Feather Fight
· ·

A bird in the hand is a certainty, but a bird in the bush may sing.
BRET HARTE,
source unknown

TREES WERE ONCE SO SCARCE on the coastal plain between Brownsville and Corpus Christi that any significant grove was given a name. Late in April of 1900, three travelers stopped for the night at San Ignacia, a cluster of venerable live oaks in the middle of a sandy plain otherwise devoid of plant and animal life. When one of the men shot a rattlesnake, dozens of startled scissor-tailed flycatchers exploded from the trees. The other man lassoed dead branches and pulled them down to build a fire. The woman remembered the place and the night they spent there for many years to come: "The stars came out so temptingly that we carried our sleeping bags out under them on the open prairie . . . the dream of years was to be realized at last! As if from a raft on the ocean the entire circle of your horizon is star-filled sky! As night closes in around you, you seem to be alone with the stars. Mortal no longer, you become a point in the universe. All human cares, all the littleness of human life drop from you, and the great universe lies close around you."[1]

The woman's name was Florence Merriam Bailey, and she was on her honeymoon. Her husband, Vernon Bailey, was a field agent for the U.S. Biological Survey. She was thirty-six years old, dark-eyed with soft features and thick hair piled artfully on top of her head. At thirty-five, Vernon was pale-eyed, thin, and wiry with a bushy mustache. The other

Texas tortoise and great egret, Laguna Atascosa National Wildlife Refuge

man was a crusty old Texan Bailey had hired as camp cook and guide. They traveled in a wagon drawn by mules. Fifteen years later, Florence Bailey published the story of that trip to Texas with her new husband at the dawn of a new century. She called it "Meeting Spring Half Way."

It was the most recent in a long list of articles she had written for scientific journals and popular magazines. Her first book–*Birds Through an Opera Glass*, came out in 1890, her latest–*A-Birding on a Bronco*, in 1896. Before meeting Vernon, she had given up the idea of marriage and devoted herself to nature writing and bird conservation. Now, she could share her life's work with a kindred spirit who loved nature and nature's creatures as much as she did.

The couple had traveled by train from Washington, D.C. through Texarkana, Austin, and San Antonio. In Corpus Christi, they transferred to a wagon for the 360 mile trip to Brownsville and back. They left winter behind and found what they were looking for on the coastal prairie of Texas. Florence wrote: "It was a pleasant surprise to meet the spring flocks [of dickcissels] on their way north. We began meeting them on our first day out. Long rows, rows sometimes reaching hundreds, were lined up on the fences like Swallows on telegraph wires. Their flat heads and hanging tails marked them when too far away to see their chestnut backs or yellow chest patches. Their familiar song with its mouthed furry burr suggested the wheat fields of Illinois, for which some of them may have been bound."[2]

They traveled slowly, stopping now and then to identify a flower, collect a specimen, or take a photograph. She carried books of poetry from which they read to one another. "After Wordsworth," she wrote, "we were well attuned to the quiet prairie sunset . . . the round pink ball going down on the level horizon. . . ."[3] They brought along a star chart to study during the day in preparation for nights under the clear Texas sky. With morning, came the flowers: "On the dry prairie we drove through bands of color, miles of low pink phlox and pink primroses, yellow Coreopsis, Senecio, or Oenothera, orange brown Thelesperma, scarlet painted-cup and white daisies. During the day we noted the Blue Grosbeak, Red-winged Blackbird, and Maryland Yellow-throat. In an oak mott that we crossed, there was an interesting old stage station, a Mexican pole house with thatched roof, its pole walls chinked with mud, a brush corral adding to the foreign picture."[4]

Near this spot, the Baileys met "three fellow travelers, an old Mexican with a pointed hat, a boy with a three-story water jug in his hand, and a solemn little burro with a peccary skin spread on his back."[5] Vernon bought the skin for his collection of Texas fauna. At night, he set out traps for small mammals. An acquisitive wood rat stole one of Bailey's traps and installed it prominently atop the pile of sticks the animal called home. For Florence, however, birds were the main attraction: "The green level stretching away to the horizon was dotted with ponds, some bordered with tules, some merely flood water ponds with submerged tufts of marsh grass, but all covered with water fowl, some of which were resting and feeding on their way from Argentina to Alaska. Among those seen were the Solitary, the Western, and Buff-breasted Sandpipers, Dowitchers, Black-necked Stilts, Killdeer, Greater and Lesser Yellowlegs, feeding in flocks together, besides quakerish Willets, and comfortable looking Shovelers. How interesting to meet the travelers half way!"[6]

⚜

Isabel adds willets and yellowlegs to our growing list of birds seen as we drive north from Brownsville toward Laguna Atascosa National Wildlife Refuge. A green and level landscape stretches to the horizon. We have come to see if the place Florence Bailey wrote about a century ago is still intact. The sky is full of birds as we enter the refuge. Overhead, laughing gulls joke and jostle one another, and Forster's terns pass on their way to appointments elsewhere. Green jays hop about in the brush crowding the front door of the visitor's center. Inside, we find Jody Mays, the wildlife biologist who has agreed to take us on a tour of Laguna Atascosa.

She is a hazel-eyed blonde in her twenties with a crisp gray short-sleeved shirt tucked into dark green pants. She wears lace-up hiking boots and a watch with wide leather band. We climb into her U.S. Fish and Wildlife Service extended cab pickup and head down an oyster-shell road flanked by tall brush. It has rained recently. Mays is worried that roads on the far side of the refuge may be too muddy to travel. Gray clouds hint at more rain to come.

A cottontail rabbit darts across the road and dives into the brush. Two more nibble grass in the ditch on the other side. "That's a good sign," Mays says. "Cottontails are a favorite food of our ocelots, and we love our prey base." Jody Mays looks after the endangered species on the refuge. "We've got ocelot, jaguarundi, aplomado falcon, piping plover, Kemp's ridley sea turtle. And then there's the state-listed ones: horned lizard, indigo snake, reddish egret, and the Texas tortoise." This last animal, *Gopherus berlandieri,* is named for the Swiss botanist who discovered so many new species of plants along the Rio Grande.

Not far from a sign that says "Ocelot Crossing," what looks like a TV antenna rises above the brush. "That's for the ocelot project," Jody explains. "This is good habitat for them. They could be right there, and you couldn't see them. They stay back in the brush." This beautiful spotted cat looks like a pint-sized jaguar. Old-time Texans called it the "tiger cat."

We surprise a family of chachalacas in the middle of the road. Mother and five young run for their lives in front of the truck, unable to find an opening in the wall of brush on either side. "Pick a spot, pick a spot," Jody urges. "Get over to one side, goofy." Leaning my way she adds, "See how her tail feathers are all different lengths? She's molting."

We finally exit the brush and catch the broad glint of water ahead. "This is Laguna Atascosa," our guide announces. "It means 'muddy lagoon' in Spanish." We learn that the lagoon narrows to become Cayo Atascosa then empties into the Laguna Madre near a place called Green Island. Refuge managers control the flow of water through the system to insure optimum conditions for wildfowl and shorebirds. Too much or too little water means life or death here.

"Now this is natural coastal prairie habitat," Mays says, stopping the truck and pointing to a wide sweep of grassland lying just inches above the level of the marsh. Vastly different habitats (marsh, prairie, and brush) exist side by side with only a few inches change in elevation separating them. Too much water would drown the brush and take out the ocelots. Flood the prairie—lose the aplomado falcon and the Texas tortoise. Dry up the marsh—say goodbye to the wildfowl and shorebirds. Strike the perfect balance, and you have one of the most dynamic ecosystems in Texas and one of its most dramatic coastal landscapes.

"What's that in the road up there?" Isabel asks.

"That's a tortoise," Mays answers, hitting the brakes.

"That's our guy!" I shout, slamming the door behind me, as I hit the ground running.

"Try not to handle him too much," Mays cautions, "or he will drop his water, he'll pee. He'll lose stored water, and that will stress him."

The Texas gopher tortoise is an oddly constructed creature. With hind legs appropriate for a tiny elephant and fore legs befitting a sea turtle, it looks like a miniature Galapagos tortoise. Scutes on its back seem carved in high relief. Protruding from the bottom of its shell, and extending forward under its neck and head is something resembling the business end of a crowbar. Males use the device to flip adversaries on their backs when jousting for the favors of females.

The tortoise at our feet has withdrawn into its shell. We wait. Finally it extends its head, rises, and sprints for cover. For a turtle, it is remarkably fast, but I manage to shoot half-a-dozen pictures before it disappears into the grass. What a stroke of luck, to see and photograph one of the refuge's rare endangered species! But, back in the truck, I discover that my camera battery is dead. There are no pictures—only indelible mental images. Mays says we've come about half way as she turns the truck around and we start back to headquarters to retrieve spare batteries.

Florence and Vernon Bailey reached the halfway point of their trip on May 1, in Brownsville, on the banks of the Rio Grande. They had come 180 miles in six days. Florence noticed a blend of cultures there. Fair-skinned girls in shirtwaist dresses rode bicycles past *señoritas* with blue or black *rebozas* on their heads. Locals pointed out the little frame house where Porfirio Díaz purportedly planned the Mexican Revolution. "The plaza and market place were characteristic," Florence wrote, "and the picturesque old cathedral . . . had bullet holes left from war times."[7]

Cotton, corn, and sugarcane grew in irrigated fields. Trees laden with oranges, lemons, bananas, and guavas gave the place a tropical flavor. Florence remembered that "with all this foreign setting it was a surprise to find an enthusiastic botanist, a woman connected with the Presbyterian mission, actually teaching botany to the Spanish Señoritas. Would that some one could have taught them the birds!"[8]

On the return trip to Corpus Christi, Florence was amazed at how much had changed in just a matter of days: "Not only had the great waves of migration passed north, but in places the prairie carpet had changed completely during the interval. An entire set of social plants had gone out of bloom and been replaced by others. In one section we were nearly a day with a newly laid carpet of yellow tar weed that gave a softly tinted picture, the yellow green floor having a wall of dull green mesquite and a roof of soft blue sky. Between Petranilla [Petronila] Creek and Corpus Christi where, on April 24, the ground had been pink with evening primroses, on May 11 it was covered with white mint as far as the eye could see in all directions. The change was so complete that it was positively startling."[9]

Florence was soon to hear something even more startling and far more disturbing. She and Vernon spent two weeks camped out near Corpus Christi, collecting and preparing specimens for the Biological Survey. Some "poor settlers," as Florence called them, dropped by to see what the Baileys were up to. One man was surprised at the small number of animals they were skinning. He claimed that in 1889, he shot 816 birds in just five days and 1,023 more in a six- to seven-day period. The man listed least and black terns, black skimmer, great blue heron, long-billed curlew, willet, and avocet among the birds he shot. He could sell black terns for five cents apiece, least terns for twenty cents, and great blue herons for forty. "We gradually discovered that we were in the heart of a plume hunting district," Florence Bailey wrote.[10] Before they left Corpus Christi, the Baileys visited an island where one thousand pelicans once nested. They were all gone. "We saw only six pelicans in the neighborhood, and those flying over, a pitiful band contrasted with the hordes which had been driven from their homes."[11]

In his book, *Feather Fashions and Bird Preservation*, Robin Doughty reports that in 1900, the year the Baileys came to Texas, "approximately 83,000 people, mostly women, were employed in the United States in making and decorating hats."[12] Most of those hats bore plumes supplied by middlemen who bought from individuals. For example, hunters from Long Island supplied seventy thousand birds to New York dealers in the mid-1880s. After exhausting local sources, middlemen went farther afield to secure plumes. One dealer acquired 11,018 birds during a three-month trip through South Carolina and reported handling thirty thousand birds per year.[13]

Florence Bailey was incensed that dealers had arrived in Texas. No wonder. She had been active in bird conservation for fifteen years. The prestigious American Ornithologist's Union (AOU) named her its first female associate member in 1885, and she immediately joined its influential Bird Protection Committee. Less than two months after George Bird Grinnell started the Audubon Society in 1886, Florence convinced classmates to organize a chapter on the Smith College campus.[14] Since then she had written articles, given talks, led field trips, and published four books advocating respect and appreciation for nature's creatures.

But the effort to protect birds flew in the face of deeply rooted fashion trends. European royalty and women of the upper class had worn plumes in their hats from the time of Marie Antoinette. During the Victorian era, the rising wealth of the middle class greatly expanded the millinery market. By the 1880s, magazines like *Godey's Lady's Book, Delineator,* and *Harper's Bazar* carried pictures of fashionable feathered hats into the parlors of women across America.[15]

As the fad spread, designers found ways to make each season's offerings different and more exciting. Why have a plume or two when you could have a whole wing? Why not have the head of an owl, a whole bird sitting on a nest, several hummingbirds perched on flowers? One fashionable lady in Paris wore a dress edged with swallow's wings, while another in London had her gown hemmed with the heads of finches.[16] But, as the twentieth century dawned, the tide of public opinion began to turn. According to conservation historian Robin Doughty, "The cavalier manner in which birds were sacrificed on the altar of vanity began to arouse feelings of disgust and outrage, not admiration."[17]

What outraged Florence Bailey was an article in *The Auk,* a scientific journal published by the AOU. It reported four hundred thousand hummingbirds sold in one week to milliners in London.[18] Dealers traveled to the ends of the earth to supply the trade. During one four-month period in 1885, a London auction house sold "404,464 West Indian and Brazilian bird-skins, and 356,389 East Indian, besides thousands of Impeyan pheasants and birds-of-paradise."[19] The idealistic young graduate of Smith College determined to do all she could to stop what an article in *Science* magazine in 1886 called "a war of extinction."

It is no surprise that Florence Bailey immediately blew the whistle on the Texas operation. Her exposé appeared in the *Report of the Committee on the Protection of North American Birds for the Year 1900:* "The plume hunters themselves, as we found them, are mainly poor settlers in a country where it is hard to make a living, and they shoot the birds merely to add a little to the meagre [sic] support they can give their families. Moreover, they generally sell through middlemen who reap the real profits of the trade. It would be both cruel and useless to prosecute this class of hunters. The middlemen and the rich millinery firms are the ones who should be made to pay the penalty for their disregard of the laws."[20]

It took another twenty years for plummeting bird populations to stabilize and then begin climbing back from the brink of extinction. The Audubon Society played an important role in that eventual comeback. Five years after Florence Bailey sounded the alarm, Captain M. B. Davis of Waco took up the cause and helped organize more than one hundred chapters throughout the state. As one of only eight field agents employed by the National Association of Audubon Societies, Davis joined forces with the Texas Farmers Congress to launch an effective state-wide educational campaign aimed at ". . . those folk who were in the day-to-day position of protecting and managing the state's wildlife." He successfully advocated strict enforcement of game laws when lobbyists for market hunters tried to weaken them.[21] When Davis died in 1912, the outcome of the struggle to protect Texas birds was uncertain. He had not been alone, however, and new forces soon came into play.

In 1921, the Texas legislature voted to lease Big Bird Island, Little Bird Island, and Green Island to the Audubon Society for fifty years, at no charge. Located in the Laguna Madre between Brownsville and Corpus Christi, these were three of the most important nesting sites for herons, pelicans, and other coastal birds in all of Texas. One island contained the only breeding colony of reddish egrets left in the nation. As its first warden, the Society hired R. D. Camp who immediately rented a houseboat in Port Isabel and towed it to Green Island. There he took up residence and stayed through the nesting season to protect the birds from trespassers.[22] Texas and the nation had turned a corner. A new ethic regarding wildlife had been born.

The somber gray of the morning sky has given way to bright blue as we retrieve spare batteries and head back toward Laguna Atascosa. Isabel adds more birds to our list: great egret, snowy egret, tricolored heron, green heron, great blue heron. Mays points out an immature little blue heron, mottled duck, and short-billed dowitchers. Florence and Vernon Bailey would be thrilled. A reddish egret goes into its signature fishing dance. Wings akimbo, it staggers one way, leans precariously, then darts off in another direction. Although it remains threatened, at least its nesting place is protected, giving it a fighting chance to survive.

"Phalaropes," Isabel announces from the back seat. In a shallow pond beside the road, eighteen small shorebirds spin in place like a troop of folk dancers. From time to time birds stab the water, snapping up insect larvae and other aquatic morsels stirred up by their whirling. Isabel adds Wilson's phalarope to our daily list.

Mays drives on, pointing out an alligator path and a spot where feral hogs have stirred the mud and uprooted plants. A mother pied-billed grebe leads her zebra-striped brood out of harm's way as we rumble past. At a culvert where Cayo Atascosa flows under the road, we come upon a pack of aquatic predators. Spotted and alligator gar lie in wait for anything edible that might be swept through the pipe. Like thick-bodied, scaly submarines, they sink and rise, appear and disappear. One monster is three feet long.

Conversation inevitably turns to the endangered predator that commands so much of Jody Mays's time—*Felis pardalis*—the ocelot. To better understand the life history and habitat requirements of this rare cat, she has joined a team of researchers to study the animal in the wild. Mays and her colleagues trap ocelots in cages baited with live chickens. She quickly explains that the chickens are protected in cat-proof compartments. The same birds are used over and over. Rookie chickens are terrified by the experience, but soon learn they will not be hurt. After a night in a cage next to a confused and disappointed ocelot, veterans are usually found the next morning pecking corn from a dish and clucking contentedly.

The captured cat, on the other hand, is ready for a fight. Mays approaches its cage with a syringe attached to the end of a pole. A quick jab from a safe distance delivers a precise dose of anesthetic. Ten to fifteen minutes later, the sedated animal is removed from the cage, placed in a tote bag, and weighed with a spring scale. Next, Mays takes a series of measurements, draws a sample of blood from the ocelot's foreleg, and gives it a rabies shot. She inserts a PIT tag under the skin between its shoulder blades. This is the same kind of Passive Integrated Transponder used to keep track of domestic dogs and cats. Around the ocelot's neck goes a collar holding a miniature battery pack, radio transmitter, and six-inch-long wire antenna. Finally, she snaps a photo of the animal to add to the growing album of ocelot portraits back in her office.

Geneticists, analyzing blood samples taken by Jody Mays and her colleagues, have concluded that there are only two viable breeding populations of ocelots left in Texas. One, on private property in Willacy County, contains ten to twelve individuals. The other, centered on the Laguna Atascosa refuge, contains twenty-five to forty. Although only ten miles separate the two groups, they do not co-mingle. As a result, inbreeding is a serious problem in spite of the fact that genetically healthy populations live across the border in Mexico.

According to Mays, ocelots eat rabbits, rodents, opossums, and a surprising number of feral hog piglets. Collared peccaries are also common on the refuge, but their young do not show up in the ocelot diet. Mays says peccaries stay close to their young when feeding and keep them in the middle of the herd when moving from place to place. By contrast, feral hogs often let piglets wander from the herd or straggle behind, leaving them vulnerable to hungry cats.

"This is good ocelot habitat," Mays says, pulling to the side of the road. "See all the fiddlewood in here, see all the red berries? That's granjeño with the orange berries."

Three rabbits nibble grass at the edge of the road, a sight we've seen throughout the refuge. "That's a good indication of our prey base," Mays observes.

"Could I go in there?" I ask, nodding toward a solid wall of fiddle-wood. "I want to see what it's like inside."

"Sure, just be careful. Everything in there's got thorns."

I leave the machined precision of the truck, step over the roadside grass, and immediately enter another world. The broad vista of marsh, lagoon, and prairie narrows to a cramped and shadowy space. Unable to stand, I crawl ahead carefully on hands and knees under a snarl of tangled branches. Yellow-green light filters down through layers of thin foliage. Thorny twigs and tiny yellow leaves litter the ground like prickly confetti.

So this is where the ocelot lives. I imagine the place at night when the "tiger cat" is on the prowl, *the faint sound of its footsteps lost in the nocturnal chorus of frogs and insects. Coyotes bark and yammer in the distance. A striped feral piglet does not recognize a cat in the pattern of spots, circles, and bars that camouflage its fur. The cat's tail, almost as long as its body, twitches expectantly. Large, unblinking eyes, short alert ears, and a blunt but discerning nose pick up signals missed by other creatures. A pounce, a panicked squeal, then silence . . . until the night-time chorus swells again.*

"There are four big things going on with ocelots," the biologist explains, as I climb back into the truck. "Habitat loss, habitat fragmentation, road mortality, and genetic erosion." Tiger cats, we learn, once lived in brushy places from the Big Thicket to the Hill Country and down into South Texas. Most of that habitat has been cleared, and what remains has been broken into isolated tracts. Cats that risk a trip to another patch of brush are often hit by cars and trucks. Now the Border Wall, designed to stop illegal immigrants from crossing the Rio Grande, may permanently isolate Texas ocelots from healthy populations of their Mexican relatives. As the population shrinks, inbreeding threatens the few remaining ocelots. "All four problems are increasing," Mays cautions. "They are not in good shape. They're still declining."

As our tour of Laguna Atascosa ends, Isabel adds up the morning's list of sightings: one endangered tortoise, one curious coyote, a dozen or so rabbits, a white-tailed deer, and thirty-six species of birds, including the threatened reddish egret. The list would have been much smaller if plume hunters and dealers had completed their campaign of extermination a century ago.

That campaign was rooted in a fatal misconception. Most Americans believed that the natural resources of North America were inexhaustible. They read about earth-shaking herds of bison roaming limitless prairies. They saw sky-darkening flocks of passenger pigeons rise from immense forests. Rivers, lakes, and coastal marshes teemed with countless living things. In the face of such fecundity, it seemed reasonable to take as many bison, pigeons, herons, or hummingbirds as you might need or want. There would always be more to take their place.

It took passionate advocates like Florence and Vernon Bailey to correct that misconception. Along with Captain Davis, the Audubon Society, the AOU Bird Protection Committee, and others, they challenged their generation to reject the greed and vanity that threatened whole species with extinction. They called for tolerance and appreciation instead, and the nation responded. A stately great egret, its immaculate white plumes mirrored in the water of Laguna Atascosa, is a living monument to their accomplishment. What will the absence of the ocelot memorialize?

WALT DAVAS

Bird Lady of the Texas Coast

. . . in Wildness is the preservation of the world.
HENRY DAVID THOREAU,
"Walking"

CCOMPANIED BY THUNDER, lightning, and pouring rain, Isabel and I ride the cresting wave of a March cold front rolling south toward the Texas Coast. Eighteen-wheelers and big-rig RVs hurtle past on the narrow blacktop. Their tires kick up sheets of water that slash across our windshield, stopping wipers mid-stroke and knocking the side mirror cockeyed. For anxious seconds I am unable to see what is ahead or behind, aware only that several tons of steel are rushing by just inches from my ear. Meanwhile, out in the Gulf of Mexico, tens of thousands of exhausted birds battle headwinds that drain the last reserves of energy from weary bodies. Spring migration is underway.

The rain has stopped by the time we arrive at Goose Island State Park where we face a dilemma. If we set up camp on the bay front, wind will buffet us day and night. If we camp in the live oaks, mosquitoes will make life miserable. According to the ranger, they made their ear-buzzing, cheek-slapping spring debut just yesterday. We choose the mosquitoes. They will be the airborne banquet for flocks of swallows, flycatchers, warblers, and other hungry birds about to make landfall after crossing the Gulf. Camped under the moss-draped oaks, amid the greenbriar, poison ivy, and coral bean, we will be in the thick of the action. Tomorrow we hope to track down some of those tenacious spring migrants and learn

Common yellowthroat in a live oak thicket, Rockport

more about the woman who brought them to national attention–the Bird Lady of the Texas Coast, Connie Hagar.

☙

Americans met this remarkable woman in the September 10, 1956 issue of *Life* magazine. Famed photographer Alfred Eisenstaedt flew down from New York to shoot some pictures and was startled by his first sight of Mrs. Hagar. She was not the rugged outdoors type he expected. She was small and frail. Her freshly-waved hair behaved itself beneath a barely visible net, and her lilac sweater matched her starched dress. Delicate white slippers completed the outfit. The photographer suggested she tousle her hair, remove the makeup, and pick a more "suitable" dress (she had no shorts or pants of any kind).

The photo that made it into the magazine bore a caption calling her ". . . probably the world's champion bird watcher."[1] She was seventy years old. Missing from the story was any hint of the obstacles this dainty woman overcame in rising to a prominent position in the birding community. There was no mention of the extraordinary chain of events that brought her to the Texas Coast.

According to friend and biographer Karen McCracken, Martha Conger (Connie) Hagar was plagued with health problems from infancy. When she was one month old, her parents, Robert and Mattie Neblett, had her baptized because they feared the small and sickly child would soon die. Neither her doctor nor her family realized that the milk forced upon her for her health's sake was the problem, not the solution. Food allergies were unknown in Corsicana, Texas in 1886.[2]

The small but energetic girl loved animals and the outdoors. She took long spring and summer strolls around the family's shady yard, holding her father's hand as he pointed out birds and called them by name. Younger sister Robert (pronounced Ro-bert) shared her love of nature.

Connie and Bert became true pals and enjoyed one another's company, despite a healthy dose of sibling rivalry.

Their mother wanted them to grow up to be ladies, have good manners, and dress well–to dance, sing, and recite poetry. Their father wanted them to develop their minds and think for themselves.[3] Connie learned both lessons well. But the life she would fashion by combining her mother's social grace and her father's intellectual rigor would not be what any of them expected.

As Connie Hagar reached adulthood, the pillars of a traditional Victorian lifestyle began to fall away. She married a globe-trotting Navy man and found herself home alone most of the time. Her grandmother died at the age of eighty-five, and within months, her father succumbed to a kidney infection and pneumonia. When Connie's marriage failed four years later, friends whispered that the best years of her life were behind her.[4] She was thirty-five years old.

Connie returned to the family home in Corsicana, arriving by train at five o'clock in the morning with one large suitcase, a painted bunting in a tasseled bird cage, and a white pit bull named Mark Antony. As she trudged past an all-night café, a middle-aged man stepped forward and offered to carry her suitcase. He would prove to be the key to Connie's new life.

Morning comes slowly to our campsite down in the oaks as the sun struggles to break through a moisture-laden sky. Cardinals begin to sing, and Carolina wrens chime in with their syncopated "*chirpity, chirpity, chirpity, chirp.*" A male tufted titmouse whistles just outside our trailer window. We begin to count the notes–three notes and a pause, two notes, then five. It becomes a game. How many notes in the next stanza? As few as one, as many as eleven.

In the background, we detect another sound. Ignoring the soloists, we begin to hear a faint chorus of very different notes—high-pitched buzzes and twitterings, lisping whispers, and trills. The warblers have arrived! We are unable to identify species by sound alone and wish for a warbler expert to sort them out for us. Yesterday's southward rush of cold, wet weather collided with the northward push of warbler migration and forced the birds to stop and refuel before flying on. With conditions just right for a birder's dream day, we sign up for a morning walk with park host Polly Freese.

Dream days were ahead for Connie Hagar too, back in 1921. The man who carried her bag on the morning of her painful homecoming was Jack Hagar, a successful real estate broker and oilman. Bostonian by birth, he had recently moved to Corsicana from Oklahoma. Five years later, on April 2, 1926, Connie and Jack married as the first waves of spring migration began to spread across Texas.

Shortly after Connie's forty-seventh birthday, she and sister Bert packed their bags, bid their husbands goodbye, and headed south for a month-long vacation in Rockport. Their doctors had prescribed sunshine and salt air for the arthritis that afflicted them both.[5] The nature-loving sisters saw the prescription less as a treatment and more as a chance to learn about coastal wildlife.

There were only three "tourist courts" in Rockport at the time, and the Neblett sisters picked the one off the beaten track—Rockport Cottages. Eight small, frame cabins faced Aransas Bay with their backs to ancient live oaks leaning away from the constant onshore breeze. Beyond an oyster-shell semicircular driveway, a blanket of colorful gaillardia (Indian blanket or firewheel) spread across the sand between cottage number seven and the beach. Their room had a double bed, dresser, and two chairs. One bare light bulb hung from the ceiling. A curtain hanging from a broomstick nailed across one corner of the room made a closet. The kitchen was outfitted with a two-burner stove, ice box, sink, table, and chairs. There was no hot water, but the place was clean and remarkably cool.[6]

The profusion of life along the beaches, in the marshes, and out on the coastal prairie moved Connie deeply. She wanted to sort out the tangle of creatures that flew, and ran, and crawled there. She longed to learn their names, observe their behavior, and record their comings and goings. Upon returning to Corsicana, she approached her husband with an unexpected proposition: "I would like to live in Rockport. I want to study birds. Is there any reason why we should not move there?"[7]

A telegram from the real estate agent helping them locate a place to live settled the issue. The Rockport Cottages were up for sale. Would the Hagars be interested? Here was a project Jack could embrace while Connie was off birding. Maintaining, improving, and promoting the cottages would be a worthy challenge.[8]

✿

Isabel and I have a challenge of our own—putting names and faces to the chorus of migrating warblers singing in the brush around our oak grove campsite. The bird walk with Polly Freese is scheduled to start in ten minutes. We wolf down cold cereal with bananas, drain our coffee cups, and slather on mosquito repellent and sun screen. Grabbing binoculars and field guide, we head out the door. Rounding a bend in the park road, we notice a gaggle of people ahead looking skyward. They have all the field marks of birders, and Polly welcomes us into the group.

She is from New Hampshire and introduces us to a couple from the Midwest, a man from Chicago, and another couple from somewhere back East. One man carries an umbrella and sports a bushy snow-white beard worthy of a Maine lobsterman. He turns out to be a nature photographer, who, with his wife, has birded all over the world. Another distinguished-looking man, a doctor I believe, occasionally lags behind, pulls a digital recorder from his pocket, and whispers into it the names of the birds we identify.

Chipping sparrow, catbird, brown thrasher—we see nothing unusual at first. Then the first warbler appears high in a live oak overhanging the trail. Polly tries to point it out. A tiny silhouette against the bright sky; it flits from limb to limb, darts under a leaf to snatch a bug, perches for a split second facing one way, then, in the blink of an eye, reverses position and is off again.

My neck aches and my binoculars have grown heavy before I can confirm the field marks—blue-gray head and back, tiny white arcs above and below the eye, yellow throat, and a breast that shades from black through dark orange to bright yellow. Two white wing bars and white tail corners complete the picture of a bird whose body is no bigger than a strawberry. The doctor steps aside and whispers into his recorder, "northern parula." We walk on.

There's more commotion up ahead.

"He is perched on the fence beyond the trees," Polly says, stooping slightly to point through an opening in the nearby foliage to a larger bird with a long tail.

"Oh," gasps the woman from the Midwest, "just look at the pink along his side. That's a lifer for me."

For some of us, a scissortailed flycatcher is a common sight, but the excitement of the others reminds us how exotic the bird seemed when we first saw it. A zebra-striped black-and-white warbler hitches up a tree trunk. In the bushes not far away, a raccoon-faced, canary-colored yellowthroat peers out at the intruders. The doctor whispers more names into his little machine—"black-throated green warbler, blue-winged warbler, ovenbird, downy woodpecker, orchard oriole, white ibis, roseate spoonbill. . . ."

As the walk ends, we compare notes and tally up the morning's sightings. In three hours we have seen forty-seven species including ten different warblers—an average of one new bird every four minutes. Yesterday's cold front delivered the goods. We have experienced a classic "fall out" of migrants—an unusual concentration of birds colliding with a spring cold front and rain. It is a birder's equivalent to a bowler's perfect game or golfer's hole-in-one. We have long dreamed of such a day and have timed our trip to the coast to put us in the right place at the right time, but the weather is beyond our control. It is a gift.

A gift of another kind came to one of America's leading ornithologists in the summer of 1937. Sitting at his desk in the Washington, D. C., office of the U.S. Bureau of Biological Survey, Harry C. Oberholser shook his head in disbelief. He was reading the latest copy of *Gulf Coast Migrant*, a privately published bulletin listing birds seen along the Texas coast. That spring, a "Mrs. Jack Hagar" reported a warbling vireo nesting outside her bedroom window in Rockport. Impossible! Oberholser knew that the nearest nesting record of that species was four hundred miles farther north. Not long after, the same woman claimed to have seen a sooty shearwater—a bird never before recorded in Texas.[9]

Dr. Oberholser wrote to Mrs. Hagar, and counseled her to keep more detailed records of time and location for her observations. He also requested copies of her bird lists, and they arrived with more surprises. If this woman from Texas was right, he would have to revise portions of his life work, a project he had pursued for thirty-six years. It was time to go to Texas and find out if Mrs. Hagar knew what she was talking about.

Oberholser's credentials were impressive. At sixty-seven, he had already spent forty-three years studying American birds. He first came to Texas in 1900, and over the next three years spent a total of 397 days in the state. By the time he retired in 1941, Dr. Oberholser had published nearly nine hundred technical papers, belonged to forty scientific and conservation organizations, and had amassed a three-million-word manuscript entitled *The Bird Life of Texas.*[10]

Biographer Karen McCracken paints a vivid picture of the morning the scientist met the "bird lady from Texas." It was August 23, 1937: "She returned early from the bayfront, bathed, combed her hair, laid out the dress she would wear [lilac voile], and pulled on a loose robe. Jack left for the post office. The no vacancy sign was out, and she felt secure from interruption. Barefooted she propped against a pillow at the foot of her bed, her back to the door, and began listing species seen that morning. The doorbell tinkled. She was tempted to ignore it, but she could not be rude to Jack's guests. At the door she confronted a tall man whose face was vaguely familiar. 'Are you Mrs. Jack Hagar?' the man inquired in an unmistakably Eastern city voice. 'I am Harry Oberholser.'"[11]

Without giving his hostess a chance to collect her wits or change her clothes, Dr. Oberholser–formal, polite, unsmiling–got down to the business of assessing her birding capabilities. After an initial round of questions, Connie excused herself, dressed, and returned to the court of inquiry. "This sooty shearwater, how near land was it? What was the weather? Did the bird land or take off while you were watching it?" They went to the marine laboratory, site of the discovery, and interviewed two observers who also had seen the bird.[12]

After lunch, the inquisitor and his witness took a field trip. Oberholser interrupted polite conversation to demand identifications. "What is that? . . . name the bird . . . identify." Cooly confident, Connie responded, "Yellow legs, mostly greater . . . white-faced glossy ibis among spoonbills . . . black-and-white warbler on the tree, empidonax flycatcher above . . . you mean the willet or those dowitchers?"[13] She added information about nesting behavior, feeding habits, arrival and departure dates for migrants. Realizing that this kind of detailed information could only come from considerable first-hand experience, Oberholser asked,

"You say you observe every day, Mrs. Hagar?"

"Yes, morning and afternoon if not all day."

"You don't mean every day, Mrs. Hagar. How often, exactly?"

She was not exaggerating. Connie Hagar had by now lived on the Texas Coast for thirty months–roughly nine hundred days. She had already spent more than twice as much time as Oberholser observing Texas birds in the wild. He visited occasionally, dividing his time between different parts of the state and different seasons. She focused primarily on the Rockport vicinity and saw firsthand the seasonal variation of the local population. Dr. Oberholser had to admit that the once-mysterious Mrs. Hagar did indeed know what she was talking about.

Since Rockport is just across Copano Bay from our campsite on Goose Island, Isabel and I decide to drive over to see what remains of Connie and Jack's world. Passing through Fulton and Rockport, we turn onto Church Street and begin looking for Rockport Cottages–the magnet that drew the best of the birding world to this part of Texas between 1935 and 1967.

We arrive to find a stoutly-constructed observation platform and a sign identifying the Connie Hagar Cottage Sanctuary. The semicircular drive remains, but the cottages themselves are gone. An artificial pond, its tattered black liner exposed around the edges, has lost its water and is filled with silt and cattails. Sad and disappointed, we wander down a path that leads into a ragged grove of live oaks and enter an untamed place where the understory is choked with shrubs and vines. Fallen limbs litter the ground. Life and death are side by side here. Growth and decay share the same shadowy space.

"What was that?" I ask, straining to hear a bird calling from the brush. "*Witchity-witchity-witchity-witch.*" The sound is closer now, its notes more clear. "It's a yellowthroat," Isabel answers. Flitting about in a tangle of limbs and leaves is a small yellow creature with a black mask–a tiny bandit stealing caterpillars. "*Witchity-witchity-witchity-witch.*" Another calls from farther away. The grove is full of them. The cottages may be gone, but the warblers keep coming back.

❁

The bird lady of Texas eventually added more than twenty new species to the list of birds known to occur in the state. Thirty-five years of daily observation and faithful recording netted a total of five hundred species for Rockport, Aransas Bay, and the surrounding prairies and marshes—nearly three-fourths of all species reported between Canada and Mexico.

Connie Hagar lived into her eighty-seventh year—unusual in a family whose members seldom saw seventy. Asked to what she attributed her longevity, Connie replied, "It must be the birds. I live for the birds, and they just won't let me go."[14] But hypertension and arteriosclerosis began to take their toll. Minute hemorrhages in the eye and brain stole her sight.[15] Friends surrounded her. Acquaintances sent cards and letters of support. Disorientation, hallucinations, and episodes of paralysis marred the last thirty months of Connie's life and stood in grim contrast to her first thirty months in Rockport—her birding honeymoon on the Texas coast.

Connie Hagar died on November 24, 1973. Now that the birds had finally let her go, who would greet the warblers that filled the oak mottes in the spring? Who would care that warbling vireos built their nests in Rockport? Who would look at the drab legions of shorebirds and call them by name as if they were friends?

Connie herself had already supplied the answer. Scores of ornithologists, hundreds of amateur birders, and thousands who read her articles in newspapers and magazines would continue to greet, and care, and call the birds by name. She had struck a spark or fanned a flame in many of the guests of Rockport Cottages, and they would keep her passion alive.

I remember from Connie's biography something about the morning flight of black skimmers. She loved to take visitors to Fulton Beach at daybreak to watch hundreds of birds fly in unison out over the water toward the rising sun, disappear for a while then return en masse. It is late in the afternoon. If they honored the start of the day, they might also honor its end. We drive to the beach to check it out.

Behind a post and cable fence we find a sandy lawn littered with crushed oyster shell. Skimmers by the hundreds stand motionless on tiny feet, beaks to the wind. Have we missed the action? Have they already returned from their mass flight? Isabel retrieves Connie's biography from the book box on the back seat and reads the passage again. I have remembered only part of the story. The skimmers fly out to meet the sun in the winter. We are late by a couple of months.

In the fading light, the eastern horizon dissolves as sky and water merge into a luminous ultramarine haze. A disturbance passes through the assembled skimmers. A few rise into the air, then more. Some circle and return. Then they all leave, flying toward the Gulf, away from the sun. Binoculars gather just enough light to make out bird-like shapes as they recede into the distance. Soon their slim torsos dissolve, leaving only a beating web of disembodied wings flying into the night. I lower my binoculars and look at Isabel. No words can express the melancholy beauty of the moment.

The surreal evening flight of the black skimmers is not a mystery to Ray Little. He has lived in Rockport more than thirty years and knows its birds well. We have invited this local legend to our trailer to tell us what that was like. He drove the car for the Bird Lady on many excursions in the late sixties and early seventies. We mention last night's evening flight of skimmers, and Little explains, "They will feed at night because a different set of crustaceans is active at night. It's not just skimmers. Roseate spoonbills, a lot of birds will work that shallow water at night. You get a bright moonlit night, and they will work all night by that moon."

Ray Little sits opposite me at the kitchen table. Isabel perches on the edge of the bed behind him. His silver hair, cropped short, frames a deeply tanned face. Behind thick-lensed glasses, his left eye seems tired, but the right is lively and alert. A white T-shirt peeks out beneath the collar of a short-sleeved plaid shirt. It soon becomes clear that Ray Little was interested in birds long before he met Connie Hagar. I ask how his passion began.

"My dad was abusive," Little answers, matter-of-factly. "Now they call them alcoholic. When he became abusive, I would go sleep on the creek. We lived in a little place just outside of Dallas."

A glance at Isabel tells me she's as surprised as I am about this unexpected answer. What does it have to do with birding?

"There were several coveys of quail along the creek that I got to know pretty well," Little continues, as if to answer my question. "This gentleman would work his bird dogs in a nearby field, and I got acquainted with his dogs. Then I got acquainted with him. I would tell him where there was a covey here, and over across the creek, and up by those trees."

While speaking, he points one way, then waves his hand across a remembered creek toward trees still standing in his mind's eye: "One night he saw me running across the field. My dad was chasing me through town, and I ran into the creek. This man came down to get me, and he says, 'What is your problem?' When I told him he said, 'Well no, you're not going to sleep on the creek. I got a place up here for you.' So I went up there and slept in his storeroom, and he brought a cot out there. Within a week he had a buzzer fixed up so that anytime I wanted to go in there I could push that buzzer, and most of the time his wife would bring me out something to eat. He would get me up the next morning so I could go to school." Little's weathered hands, now resting quietly on the table before him, testify that these things happened a long time ago.

The man who befriended him was vice president of the local bank—a quail hunter and bird watcher. Gathering three or four friends into his car, the man would drive to the creek, pick up Little, and pay him to guide his party to the best birding locations. Earning two dollars a head, the boy pocketed from eight to ten dollars for an afternoon's work.

To keep his father from finding and spending the money, Little hid it. He took a Prince Albert tobacco tin, stuffed the money inside, and buried it under a brick in their driveway or patio. He wrote the "combination" for the hiding place on a beam under the house. "Down six bricks this way and over three bricks . . . I saved enough money to help pay my way through college."

After graduation and a stint on Okinawa during World War II, Little realized he could not support a family on bird-watching wages. But the lure of the birds led to an ingenious plan. He discovered that a medical equipment salesman was most productive between the daylight hours of nine and two-thirty. That left early mornings, afternoons, and evenings free—the hours birds were most active. Until he retired in 1970, Ray Little led a double life—salesman by day, birdman the rest of the time.

"Things aren't the same now," he says, "not like it was thirty years ago. Frandolig Island, where herons and egrets nested by the thousands in Connie's time, is now a fancy real estate development. I remember when you had to go out there by boat. It had mesquite trees and brush and understory all over the thing . . . You could be over here on the mainland, and you could see a solid wall of color out there. You see what man has done."

"But we've seen plenty of birds," Isabel responds.

Little explains that clearing out the brush beneath the trees removes vital food for migrating birds. Insects thrive in brushy habitat and provide food for migrating birds flying on empty after crossing the Gulf of Mexico.

"There was one place where I used to take elderhostels and different school groups to see the birds. Then they came in with bulldozers and cleaned it up . . . They called it brush. I call it understory. We still have that going on in Rockport today. It's sickening. They have more birds up around Houston and High Island and in that area than we have down here. Right now the birds are going up the coast."

"So you can tell that there are fewer birds today than thirty years ago?" I ask.

"I can see that every day," he insists.

As Ray Little drives away, Isabel and I realize that a piece of history goes with him. He is a living connection to a time and place fading fast. We had asked him to take us on a vicarious bird walk with Connie Hagar. Instead, he had revealed the source of his own life-sustaining connection to wild places and their inhabitants.

"In wildness is the preservation of the world." Henry David Thoreau said it in the nineteenth century. Ray Little and Connie Hagar confirmed it in the twentieth. They found ways to live in harmony with creatures who, like a tough little boy and a frail little girl, deserved to be sheltered and sustained.

Isabel and I leave Goose Island State Park and drive past carefully-pruned groves of live oaks devoid of sheltering underbrush. No longer quaintly picturesque, the bare trunks pose a question. How much "wildness" will our generation leave to nourish the next?

WALT DAVIS

Ivory-bills on Buffalo Bayou

Its meanderings and beautiful curvatures seem to have been directed
by a taste far too exquisite for human attainment.
J. C. CLOPPER,
"Journal of J. C. Clopper, 1828"

ROM ROCKPORT AND COPANO BAY we drive inland to Victoria, pick up U.S. 59, and turn northeast toward Houston. Our route takes us through the heart of the Gulf Prairies and Marshes ecological region and across the lower reaches of the Colorado and Brazos rivers. Nearing the outskirts of the city, we are drawn into a torrent of traffic coursing through a landscape dominated by concrete and glass. We have been lured into one of the nation's largest metropolitan areas by something John James Audubon saw here in 1837. The capital of the Republic of Texas was less than a year old when the artist visited and recorded his impression of Buffalo Bayou. It was a deep, sluggish stream winding through dark woods where Audubon found ivory-billed woodpeckers "in abundance."[1]

Of all the places to find the holy grail of the birding world, Houston seems one of the most unlikely. Back in the early seventies, the stretch of Buffalo Bayou that had become the Houston Ship Channel was so polluted Houstonians were afraid that a spark might touch off a firestorm rivaling the San Francisco disaster of 1906. Docks and warehouses crowded its banks, effluent poisoned the water, and trees of any kind were scarce. Ivory-billed woodpeckers on Buffalo Bayou? We will need

Great egret on Buffalo Bayou, Houston

hard evidence to convince us that *Campephilus principalis* once lived in a place that is now one of the busiest seaports in the United States.

In Audubon's day, Houston and its fledgling port were primitive out-posts on the edge of civilization. Getting there was not easy, but the artist arranged through contacts in Washington to "borrow" a fifty-five ton revenue cutter, the *Campbell*, and her twenty-one man crew. The ship's captain, Napoléon Coste, was an old friend with whom Audubon had explored the east coast of Florida. Audubon's son John Woodhouse Audubon and their friend Edward Harris completed the party that set out from New Orleans on April 1, 1837, bound for Texas.[2]

The *Campbell* arrived in Galveston Bay twenty days later "having had a fine run from Atchafalaya Bay." Four days after that, Audubon reported that a "heavy gale blew all night, and this morning the thermometer in the cabin is sixty-three degrees. Thousands of birds, arrested by the storm in their migration northward, are seen hovering around our vessels and hiding in the grass, and some are struggling in the water, completely exhausted."[3] When the storm abated, the three naturalists waded into the shallow bay to collect shorebirds and herons.

On May 2, while stalking roseate spoonbills on a sandbar, they encountered something unexpected. "The back fins of a large fish resembling those of a shark appeared meandering above the surface of the shallow waters. We called to John, and he, wishing to kill the monster, which moved but slowly, rammed home a couple of bullets, and lodged them in the body of the fish."[4] Soon a boatload of sailors joined the chase, beating the wounded fish with oars and cutting off its tail.

A crowd gathered round as the sailors dragged the creature to shore with a gaff-hook through the eye. Only then did they realize that their prize was not a shark. "It proved to be a sawfish, measuring rather more than twelve feet in length. . . . From her body we recovered ten small sawfish, all of them alive and wriggling about as soon as they were thrown on the sand. The young were about thirty inches in length, and minute sharp teeth were already formed."[5]

Clearly, the study of living things was a death-dealing discipline in the nineteenth century. Audubon knew if he reported a bird (or a sawfish) in an unusual location, the sighting would be disregarded without the body as proof. Before photography was widely available, artists had to immobilize their subjects long enough to sketch or paint them. For Audubon, this meant shooting the bird and arranging the limp form on a web of wires to simulate a lifelike pose. New technologies have radically changed the way scientists and artists work with their subjects today, and death is no longer the tool of choice.

Almost a week after the battle with the sawfish, Audubon's expedition left Galveston harbor and headed inland. His journal vividly records the hazards of travel in nineteenth-century Texas:

Monday, May 8.–Today we hoisted anchor, bound for Houston; after grounding a few times, we reached Red Fish Bar, distant twelve miles, where we found several American schooners and one brig. It blew hard all night, and we were uncomfortable.

Tuesday, May 9.–We left Red Fish Bar with the schooner *Crusader* and the gig, and with a fair wind proceeded rapidly . . . We passed several plantations and the general appearance of the country was more pleasing than otherwise. About noon we entered Buffalo Bayou, at the mouth of the San Jacinto River, and opposite the famous battle-ground of the same name. Proceeding smoothly up the bayou, we saw abundance of game . . . This bayou is usually sluggish, deep, and bordered on both sides with a strip of woods not exceeding a mile in depth . . . It was here today that I found the Ivory-Billed Woodpecker in abundance, and secured several specimens. . . .

Wednesday, May 10.–It rained again today, but we pushed on in the gig toward Houston. The rain had, however, so swollen the water of the bayou and increased the current that we were eight hours rowing twelve miles.

Monday, May 15.–We landed at Houston, the capital of Texas, drenched to the skin, and were kindly received on board the steamer *Yellow Stone* [by] Captain West, who gave us his state-room to change our clothes in, and furnished us refreshments and dinner.[6]

The *Yellow Stone* was just six years old when Audubon and his party went on board. In that short time, she had already pioneered navigation of the upper Missouri River for John Jacob Astor's American Fur Company. She had carried legendary artists George Catlin and Karl Bodmer into the wilderness, chief Black Hawk back to civilization, and smallpox vaccine to the Indians of Kansas. In 1836, she ferried Sam Houston and his rag-tag army across the Brazos on their way to San Jacinto. Before the year was out, she conveyed Stephen F. Austin's body to its final resting place at Peach Point Plantation beside the Brazos. Two weeks after playing host to Audubon, the *Yellow Stone* disappeared from history. Some say she struck a snag and sank in the Brazos or in Buffalo Bayou. Others believe her name was changed and she ended her days on some other river. Whatever happened was unrecorded, as was the disappearance of the last ivory-bill a generation later.[7]

Today, Isabel and I have a date with Buffalo Bayou and its passionate apostle Don Greene. Environmentalists, historians, and outdoor adventurers of our acquaintance all agree that if we want to see Buffalo Bayou as it was in Audubon's day, Greene's our man. He worked for many years with the river guide service Far Flung Adventures out of Terlingua on the Rio Grande. Through his own company, White Water Experience, he has led canoe trips down many Texas rivers. More recently, he has focused his activities on the waterways of Houston, especially Buffalo Bayou. He completed a rigorous workshop in applied fluvial geomorphology (river science for engineers) and has served on the boards of several conservation organizations in Houston.

Greene agreed to show us the bayou, and we are to meet him at a designated take-out point near the Shepherd Drive bridge. He arrives in a well-traveled Chevrolet suburban, its original shiny blue skin now chalky with age. Paddles, life jackets, and coolers are piled to the roof in back. The twenty-foot Old Town canoe lashed to the luggage rack wears its scuffs and patches proudly, like an old gray whale that has seen a lot of the world and has the scars to prove it.

Our guide, tall and big-boned, opens the door and slides out from behind the wheel, landing solidly on a pair of Birkenstock sandals. He wears a red-checked shirt, open at the collar, over faded blue shorts. Unruly hair and beard frame a deeply tanned face with dramatic arching eyebrows. He greets us warmly in a booming voice and suggests we leave our truck here and ride with him to the put-in point.

Heading west on Memorial Drive, Greene begins our indoctrination with a brief history of Memorial Park and its champions, including people like Terry Hershey and her friends Army and Sarah Emmott. In fact, the canoe we will use on the bayou has "Sarah Emmott" hand-lettered on the bow. It's soon clear that Don Greene is on a mission to keep Buffalo Bayou from being swallowed by the city that surrounds it. Our conversation is awash in fluvial geomorphology, micro-habitats, sedimentation, and erosion control.

Greene parks his suburban at the bridge over Buffalo Bayou, near the intersection of Post Oak and Woodway. We ferry gear down the grassy bank to the launch site and immediately enter another world. It is shady and cool beneath the bridge. Two men sit on plastic buckets playing cards at a make-shift table. They live here. I recall a brief passage in Audubon's journal. "We . . . passed two little girls encamped on the bank of the bayou under the cover of a few [clapboards], cooking a scanty meal."[8] Greene greets two other men returning from a morning float on the upper reaches of the bayou. The older man gently lifts a sleek, handcrafted wooden canoe from the water, deftly negotiating the mud and concrete rubble at water's edge. The stream continues to lure an odd assortment of people to its banks.

Gear and passengers safely aboard, Greene shoves off and settles into the stern seat for his third trip of the week down Buffalo Bayou. We glide out to mid-stream and head east with the sun at our backs and traffic noise rapidly receding. The water is the color of iced-coffee with milk. Blue sky and green foliage, however, create reflections that keep the color lively and ever-changing. A veneer of mouse-gray sediment coats the bank, and occasional slabs of mossy sandstone protrude from the mud. Sycamore, pecan, water oak, and black willow create a Gothic green arch overhead.

There is no doubt that this is an urban stream. Glass and steel buildings rise above the riparian forest. Plastic bags, Styrofoam cups, and aluminum cans share the shore with raccoon tracks and beaver-peeled logs. A storm drain empties into the bayou through four huge openings, each big enough to belch out a taxicab. We are tempted to paddle in but decide to continue downstream, leaving unexplored the mysteries of the Houston underground.

Herons escort the *Sarah Emmott* and her passengers. Greene points the canoe toward a gleaming white great egret standing in the shallows up ahead. We lay our dripping paddles across the gunnels and drift close enough to see the green skin between the egret's eye and the yellow-orange bayonet of its bill. Flying downstream, it lights on a pile of driftwood. When we catch up, it flies again, and again, until it finally rises high above our heads and returns to its preferred hunting grounds. A prehistoric apparition stands motionless in the shadows—a great blue heron. A little green heron calls from the bank, and a little blue sails around a bend and out of sight.

"Hear that?" Greene asks.

"Hear what?" I answer.

"Exactly," he says, having successfully sprung his trap. "When was the last time you heard traffic noise?"

It is there if you listen, a barely audible hiss on the edge of consciousness. But the sound of leaves jostling in the wind and the songs of cardinals and Carolina wrens dominate. Here, nature holds the city at bay. Ahead, a white sand beach lines the left bank. Beyond that, a red clay bluff forces the bayou into a right turn beside towering sycamores. We land, pull out a cooler with drinks, a dry-box with snacks, and let our senses inventory a time-forgotten place. This is Don Greene's sacrarium—a place where he and others like him reconnect with something profound, something worth investing a lifetime to preserve, protect, and share. In the heart of Houston, we have come face-to-face with the Buffalo Bayou that ivory-billed woodpeckers once called home.

Refreshed in body and spirit, we shove off again, drifting lazily in and out of shadows, alternately warmed by the sun and cooled by its absence. Suddenly the three of us see something that instantly changes the tenor of the day. A log on the bank seems to sprout legs and sprint for the water. I fumble for the camera and fire off a shot. Isabel shouts, "Alligator!"

The creature's corrugated back is as wide as a truck tire caked with dried mud. Its tail swings heavily side to side, as the gator sprints toward the water and slides in. "He hangs out here a lot," Greene tells us. "Once, when I was closer than this, I estimated that he was a lot longer than a canoe paddle. That would put him at more than six feet."

Our guide keeps up a steady commentary on stream-side vegetation, erosion abatement, and the politics of flood control in Houston. After three-and-a-half hours of paddling, traffic noise intrudes again, and the smell of exhaust fumes signals our approach to the Shepherd Drive bridge—our take-out point.

But Greene has one more surprise in store, and we continue downstream. The forest thins, and the bayou's current slows. Greene says that back in the early fifties, Harris County crews cut down the trees in the flood-plain to rush water downstream away from expensive properties crowding the bayou. "There were huge native magnolias all along here," our guide explains. Audubon mentioned them, and so did Frederick Law Olmsted, when he passed through Houston in 1854. In his *Journey Through Texas*, Olmstead recalled that "in the bayou bottoms near by, we noticed many magnolias, now in full glory of bloom, perfuming delicately the whole atmosphere. We sketched one which stood one hundred and ten feet high, in perfect symmetry of development, superbly dark and lustrous in foliage, and studded from top to lowest branch with hundreds of great delicious white flowers."[9]

No magnolias perfume the air today. As we float into the shade of another bridge, Don Greene asks if we can smell anything. Somewhere between traffic fumes and the musty aroma of the bayou, I pick out another odor. It is musky and familiar.

"Bats?" I speculate.

"Mexican freetails," Greene confirms. "You can see the guano scattered on the concrete apron, and if you listen, you can hear them."

We stop paddling, stop talking, and strain to filter out the muffled groaning of traffic overhead. What is left is not so much a sound as an irritating disturbance of the ear—a signal from another world. "This is Houston's version of Austin's bat colony under the Congress Avenue bridge," Greene explains. "If it were not for this bridge, and others like it, the Mexican freetails would still be in their limestone caves on the Edwards Plateau." The city that takes away also gives back—a magnolia forest in exchange for a bat-festooned bridge. What is the net worth of such a trade?

In 1828, J. C. Clopper, a Cincinnati land speculator and sometime rancher, described Buffalo Bayou as "the most remarkable stream I have ever seen . . . the water being of navigable depth close up to each bank giving to this most enchanting little stream the appearance of an artificial canal in the design and course of which Nature has lent her masterly hand . . . most of its course is bound in by timber and flowering shrubbery which overhang its grassy banks and dip and reflect their variegated hues in its unruffled waters. . . ."[10]

In Clopper's day, the stream was 150 yards across and twenty feet deep where it joined the San Jacinto. Upstream it narrowed until it was just forty yards wide at the mouth of White Oak Bayou, where the city of Houston would be born in 1836. Three years later, French newspaper editor Frédéric Gaillardet described Buffalo Bayou as being "so hemmed in between its two banks that the trees growing close to the water tear into the hulls of the plucky crafts and sweep their decks of anything which has been rashly left lying on them. A steamboat never arrives at Houston without having left along the way a few portions of its stern rail, or who knows? Perhaps even a passenger!"[11]

In spite of its upstream constriction, Buffalo Bayou and the San Jacinto River were wide enough to provide an outlet to the sea for Texas's inland riches. Plantation owners hauled bales of cotton from fertile fields in the Brazos River bottoms and on the coastal prairie to Allen's Landing at Houston. From there, steamboats took the white gold down to Galveston where ocean-going vessels waited to carry the cargo to ports in the United States, Mexico, and England. The same route took lumber harvested from primeval forests of longleaf pine along Buffalo Bayou to the Mexican boomtown of Tampico. Sawmills had begun slicing up ivory-bill habitat a decade before Audubon arrived and collected his specimens.[12]

Had the artist come in January rather than May, 1837, he would have found only one house and twelve residents in the little town beside the bayou. Five months later, fifteen hundred people had moved in, and one hundred houses lined its muddy streets.[13] The meteoric rise of Houston unleashed social and economic forces that sent seismic waves of change through the landscape. More than two million residents now live in the six hundred-square-mile metropolis that has become the fourth largest city in the United States. The Port of Houston consistently ranks second or third busiest in the nation. In 2006, more than seven thousand ships carried 81.6 billion dollars worth of petroleum, iron, steel, cereals, and other goods to and from ports all over the world.[14]

None of that would have been possible had lower Buffalo Bayou not been dredged and widened. The village born of the bayou consumed its progenitor in order to fulfill its potential and become a great city. Who can fault a transformation that put food on the table for generations of Texans? Who would take back changes that generated wealth to reinvest in a growing community—educating its citizens and enriching the cultural life of a major metropolitan center. Looking back, it seems inevitable and irreversible, and yet . . .

As we haul the *Sarah Emmott* out of Buffalo Bayou beneath the Shepherd Drive bridge, Isabel asks Don Greene how the stream we just floated escaped the chain saws, bulldozers, and dredges of progress. "You'd have to go back forty years or more to answer that question," he says. "You need to talk to Terry Hershey. She was there and can tell you how it happened."

The morning rush hour wanes as we exit Interstate 10 on our way to Terry Hershey's home in the exclusive Sherwood Forest neighborhood, between Memorial Park and the Houston Country Club. We have traded yesterday's insect repellant and sunscreen for lipstick and cologne, Tevas and shorts for wing tips and slacks. We pass a security booth and wind our way down Friar Tuck through an emerald tunnel of pine and water oak. At the Hershey house, we park our mud-spattered pickup beside a Mercedes station wagon. One bumper sticker admonishes tailgaters to "Protect Texas Rivers." Another says "No Wetlands/No Wildlife."

Mrs. Hershey's home rises like a minor Mayan temple emerging from the jungle, as if archeologists have just begun to clear away the brush and vines. A massive stone chimney injects a serene note of right-angled order into the leafy chaos. The front door stands ajar with a handwritten note on the jam. "Doorbell does not work, please knock on door." Twice I knock. Twice no answer. Finally, a gangly, un-clipped Airedale, the consummate canine doorman, comes out to greet us, followed by Mrs. Hershey.

Her hair, silvered at the temples, is pulled back and clipped into a casual knot in back. A maroon blouse, belted at the waist, hangs loosely over her autumn-colored skirt. Necklace, bracelets, and rings of silver, turquoise, amber, and red coral bring a hint of Santa Fe chic to hot and humid Houston. She ushers us through a room with fifteen-foot-tall windows looking out into the woods. We pick up mugs of coffee in the kitchen and follow our hostess outside to a table and chairs beside a rock-rimmed pool bathed in filtered green light.

We soon learn that Terry Hershey has a degree in philosophy, opened the first art gallery in Fort Worth, and is passionate about preserving her environment. Her late husband Jake, a member of the Hershey chocolate family, founded American Commercial Barges and was a member of the Permanent International Navigation Congress. Mrs. Hershey has been involved with waterways for a long time.

Isabel switches on the tape recorder and picks up a chorus of bird song, as I ask the first question: "How is it that this island of wildness has survived in a rough-and-tumble town like Houston?"

She describes the shock of finding a nine-acre tract of beautiful woods cut down along upper Buffalo Bayou—the first step in a flood control project. Learning that a portion of the stream closer to her own home was next on the list, she called her county commissioner to confirm what she suspected.

She remembers him saying, "Aw Mrs. Hershey, them big government fellas have come in here and are pushing us around."

"What government fellas?"

"The Corps of Engineers."

"If it's the Corps," she asked, "why does it say Harris County Flood Control District all over those trucks?"

"I'm too busy to talk to you," he said.

"He hung up on me. He made me mad, and I've stayed mad for forty years. You don't like your elected officials hanging up on you when you ask a perfectly valid question. So I dug into it to see what was going on, and who was doing what."[15]

Although Terry Hershey has a mellow contralto voice and hearty laugh, she speaks these last words in a whisper as the old anger resurfaces. To make a stand, she joined an informal group of concerned neighbors that became the Buffalo Bayou Preservation Association. Its second president was George Mitchell, developer of the Woodlands, an upscale planned community north of Houston. Uniting with wealthy and influential property owners were several local garden clubs, the Outdoor Nature Club, and the Junior Bar Association. Together they confronted city, county, and federal agencies bent on taming the last of Houston's original bayous.

"Was there ever a moment when you felt the tide turn in your favor?" I ask, as a pileated woodpecker calls from the nearby forest and gray squirrels play tag through the trees overhead. Mrs. Hershey says, without hesitation: "Yes there was. George Bush, the father, not the son, was our senator at the time, and we had convinced him that what was billed as flood control was nothing more than flood transference–moving the water downstream faster–transferring the problem rather than solving it. Funding for channelizing Buffalo Bayou was coming up before the Senate Appropriations Committee, and I was invited to the hearing.

George asked that the project not be funded, and the chairman, looking George straight in the eye, said, 'Do we understand that you are asking us not to spend money in your district?' George gulped and said, 'There must be a better way to manage storm water than to concrete a river.'"

The Buffalo Bayou Preservation Association, according to Mrs. Hershey, went on to educate community leaders and government officials in the art and science of sustainable flood control. She introduced the incoming Harris County Flood Control District director, Art Storey, to fluvial geomorphology expert Dave Rosgen. Storey sent several of his staff to take Rosgen's course in river mechanics and flood control. "Harris County Flood Control has changed one hundred percent," Mrs. Hershey says. "They have a re-foresting project, and they're re-vegetating the banks as much as they can."

We thank this remarkable woman for the gift of a wild bayou, and tell her about the last item on our agenda. So far we have only seen Buffalo Bayou upstream from Allen's Landing. Audubon experienced the downstream stretch that has since been widened to accommodate ocean-going ships. Houston-based urban historian Janet K. Wagner believes, however, that engineers bypassed a loop of the original bayou when they dredged the Houston Ship Channel.[16] She has given us directions to the spot, and we are on our way to look at what remains of the picturesque stream Audubon traveled and described.

From Sherwood Forest, we take Memorial Drive, through downtown Houston, past Allen's Landing (where Audubon dined aboard the *Yellow Stone*), and out to Brady Island, where Bray's Bayou empties into the channel. Sure enough, we locate a bridge across a shallow backwater–Buffalo Bayou. The stream J. C. Clopper described as having "meanderings and beautiful curvatures [that] seem to have been directed by a taste far too exquisite for human attainment"[17] is now a parking lot for barges.

Downstream from the bridge, the *Buffalo 251* is tied up to the left bank; its slab-sided sister is tied beside it. Beyond, three tugboats wait for assignment. Upstream, a barge lies dormant in dry-dock as a workman sandblasts rust from its hull. The ear-splitting hiss of his hose obliterates all other sound. Coils of rope, pipes, re-bar, and rotting timbers litter the muddy banks. The air reeks of sour mud, diesel, and hot asphalt.

I reach for my camera to record the scene. To frame the desolation before me, I include an abandoned sailboat to anchor the lower right corner of the image. Something sits on the shorter of its two masts. It's not a seagull. I zoom in for a closer look. It's an osprey! Here in the graveyard of Buffalo Bayou sits a top predator of the bird world—the symbol, in my mind, of wild unfettered places.

Maybe rumors of the bayou's death are premature. Maybe there's life in the old stream yet. Thanks to George H. W. Bush, George Mitchell, Terry Hershey, Don Greene, and others, its upper reaches are free-flowing and vital. The Bayou Preservation Association has shown that beauty and practicality can live together, and that there is room for wildness, even in a bustling, prosperous city.

Isabel and I have found the hard evidence we sought. Ivory-billed woodpeckers did once live in a shadowy forest beside a magnolia-scented bayou in tidewater Texas. They and the magnolias are gone now. But fragments of their world remain, thanks to people with a deeply rooted conviction that the fourth largest city in the United States need not completely devour the bayou that made their city possible. An osprey, an alligator, and an escort of herons testify that such conviction can bear surprising fruit.

WALT DAVIS

CHAPTER 10

Searching for Longleaf Pine

The longleaf pine . . . forms miles of dense forest . . . the cleanest, most uniform, and symmetrical body of pine to be found on the continent.

VERNON BAILEY,

North American Fauna No. 25, Biological Survey of Texas 1889–1905

S TATE HIGHWAY 87 HUGS the northern rim of the Gulf of Mexico from Galveston to the Louisiana border. Along the way it passes through some of the best birding spots in Texas–High Island, McFaddin Marsh National Wildlife Refuge, and Sea Rim State Park. At Sabine Pass the road turns inland and skirts the western shore of Sabine Lake through Port Arthur to Orange on the banks of the Sabine River. Before logging changed the landscape, this was where the Gulf Prairies and Marshes ended, and the Pineywoods began.[1]

Nineteenth-century steamboats left Orange loaded with staple foods and merchandise and churned upriver to remote plantations and farms in East Texas and Louisiana. They came back loaded with bales of cotton, stacks of hides, and bushels of corn, beans, and potatoes.[2] For a hundred years, the Sabine also carried longleaf pine and cypress logs to lumber mills along its banks.

Upstream from where shipyards and giant sawmills once stood, Interstate 10 now arches over the Sabine on its way to Louisiana. Beyond that, the old steamboat landing and Civil War fort at Niblett's Bluff have been replaced by a state park. An hour or so by boat farther upriver, in

Don McCaughey and his homemade log-pulling barge

a straight stretch near a bluff, a small barge is tied to the bank. A well-muscled young man in bathing suit, baseball cap, and tennis shoes tends a yellow hose that leads from a compressed air tank into the water. Bubbles rise periodically from somewhere below.

The barge is a simple plywood platform twelve feet wide and fourteen long, atop two pontoons three feet in diameter. A welded pipe frame stands like a metal sawhorse over a square hole in the middle of the deck. A cable runs from a hand-cranked winch, through a pulley attached to the pipe frame, through the hole in the deck, and into the water.

The young man stirs as an older man, fully clothed, emerges from a cloud of rising bubbles and breaks the surface. White hair plastered to his head, he pulls off diving goggles and spits out his air-hose mouthpiece. The young man cranks the winch while the other, still dripping, stands by. The barge sinks a bit as the cable draws tight around something heavy down below. Gears clatter and bubbles roil the surface as the cable reels in, ever so slowly. Both men whoop and holler at the first sign of their prize rising from the murky water. It is a "sinker" longleaf pine.

A century or more ago, when lumbermen floated fresh-cut logs down the Sabine to giant sawmills at Orange, many sank along the way. In the oxygen-poor environment of silt and mud at the river's bottom, they lay for decades without rotting. Brought again to the surface and dried out, these "sinkers" are sawed and milled into high-quality, highly desirable lumber. The eighteen-foot log suspended beneath their homemade barge could bring as much as thirteen hundred dollars.

Alive, this tree was a tall and graceful aristocrat in one of the most extensive woodland ecosystems in North America. According to forestry historian Lawrence S. Earley: "Longleaf pine was the dominant tree over about 60 million acres of the Southeast when the Spanish arrived in the early 1500s, and it mixed with other pines and hardwoods on an additional

30 million acres. These great conifer forests sprawled over nearly 150,000 square miles, covering a wide swath of every coastal state from the James River in southeastern Virginia . . . west to southeastern Texas, interrupted only by the vast floodplain of the Mississippi River . . . You could travel for months through it and feel as if you had never left home."[3]

Earley says that individual trees grew to a height of one hundred to one hundred fifty feet with occasional specimens two hundred feet tall. Many were three feet thick at the base—some as much as four or five. Most were bare of branches from ground to crown. Frequent fires kept the forest floor clear of shrubs and saplings. Travelers talked of driving a carriage or galloping a horse through a park-like landscape. Vernon Bailey (chief field naturalist for the U.S. Biological Survey) described the longleaf pine forest of Texas as "the cleanest, most uniform, and symmetrical body of pine to be found on the continent."[4]

When a tree is twenty to thirty years old, it begins producing cones from four to twelve inches long bearing seeds bigger and heavier than those of other pines. Storing more moisture and nutrients than its competitors, a longleaf seed sprouts and grows quickly. Before it is a year old, it may have a tap root eight feet long. Above ground, it puts up a tight cluster of tall green needles that look more like grass than a tree. After several years in this "grass" stage, the young longleaf puts on an impressive growth spurt, gaining as much as five feet in height in a single year.[5] The mature tree grows more slowly, adding only one-sixteenth of an inch of new wood per year. As a result, longleaf pine lumber is notoriously dense and hard. Carpenters drill pilot holes before driving nails into it.

Isabel and I decide to find what remains of the Texas longleaf pine forest. Our trailer is parked in the Whispering Creek R.V. Park in Newton, not far from the Sabine River. Buddy Hollis is coming by to give us some pointers on the natural wonders of Newton County. Hollis was once a duck and goose hunting guide and worked for a time in the chemical industry before becoming a professional nature guide. He grew up here, knows the county well, and has agreed to show us some longleaf pine.

Hollis is a tall, big-boned man with gray beard and glasses. The emblem on his camouflage cap says "Hollis Nature Guide Service, Newton, Texas." A plain white T-shirt is tucked into the top of gray field pants with cargo pockets. He says there may be a few "old timers" in the woods, but no significant stands of virgin timber. Hollis remembers a forester friend who found a big tree in a small tract of longleaf savannah habitat complete with hanging bogs and pitcher plants. The friend extracted a pencil-thin plug of wood from the tree using a "corer" with a hollow drill. Counting the rings in the plug, he concluded that the tree had been growing in that spot since 1776.

But a single grizzled survivor does not a forest make. Where can we go to experience the splendor of the great conifer forest of the south? "Nowhere in Texas," according to Hollis. He does tell us about a place where we can see a recovering stand of longleaf. We climb in the truck and head north on State Highway 87 to check it out. Hollis is a Newton County nature encyclopedia. "Around this next bend is the best place to see the rare Indian pink," he says. Sure enough, hidden in the roadside grass is a small tubular flower, red with yellow interior, flaring into six pointed petals. "By the way," he announces a bit farther on, "we've got a new yucca in the county that's just been discovered two years ago, new to science, *Yucca cernua*, weeping yucca. It's blooming out west of town."

Descending a hill before dropping into the floodplain of a creek, Hollis asks if we want to see some insectivorous plants. We park beside the road, cross a fence (he knows the owner), and find ourselves in a soggy little sphagnum bog. The swollen stems of pitcher plants rise out of the mud. They look like green snakes, mouths agape, trying to swallow something too big for their throats. Some are blooming. Quarter-sized sundews grow close to the ground. Their round leaves bristle with tiny hairs, each tipped with a drop of amber-colored, insect-trapping glue.

Our final destination is a high sandy ridge and a stand of pine that at first seems no different than one hundred others we have seen throughout East Texas. But then we notice the young ones with trunks the size of broomsticks pushing a mop of foot-long needles six to eight feet into the air. They look like giant green bottle-brushes—like something out of Dr. Seuss. These are longleaf pines. All but hidden in the tall grass are the little ones—stiff clusters of bright green needles.

Isabel walks into the woods among the older trees and brings back a pinecone as big as a pineapple. From "grass stage" seedlings to mature seed-bearing trees, here are the prime ingredients of a long-lost ecosystem. Leave these trees alone for a hundred years, and this place might resemble the primeval forest Vernon Bailey described a century ago. Some of these youngsters could still be alive three hundred years from now. We have come face to face with forest aristocracy.

Seeing our delight, Hollis suggests we pay a visit to an unusual botanical garden in Orange—a place called Shangri La. It closed its doors fifty years ago but is about to reopen. He thinks we will be interested in what the staff is doing with longleaf pine.

When we arrive, Orange is decidedly gray. It has rained in the night and might start again any minute. We park in a remote lot and board a shuttle bus bound for Shangri La. This is not the mythical place James Hilton wrote about in *Lost Horizon* and Frank Capra made into a movie. We are headed for a different kind of dream, one that died decades ago in a snowstorm, but is coming back to life. The dreamer was Lutcher Stark, heir to a family fortune made in the lumber industry. He was well-educated, well-read, and widely traveled. Impressed with spectacular gardens he visited in various parts of the world, he decided to create a horticultural showplace in his home town.

With money to match his idea, Stark set to work transforming swampland along Adams Bayou, a tributary of the Sabine, into a garden paradise. He built ponds, installed statuary and fountains, planted acres of azaleas, and moved full-grown trees to new locations. In 1946 he opened his dreamscape to the public, and thousands came to see what he had done.

Twelve years later, a freak winter storm blanketed Stark's tropical paradise with snow followed by several days of freezing temperatures. Shangri La was ruined. Stark gave up all hope of recreating it and closed it to the public. As nature reclaimed the gardens, sneaking in to see the eerie ruins became a rite of passage for the young people of Orange.

Today, from the window of our shuttle, we see banners saying, "Welcome Back Shangri La." Yesterday's headline in the local paper read, "Paradise Park opens Tuesday." We step from the bus and join the stream of people walking toward the front gate. Looking skyward we hope rain will not spoil the celebration. The gathering crowd includes city leaders, Chamber of Commerce boosters in bright orange jackets, families with children, and a cadre of firemen in dress blues with white caps. TV cameras roll as the executive director of the Stark Foundation welcomes the guests, and the mayor lauds the civic benefits of the renovated gardens.

A representative of the Green Building Council compliments the environmentally and socially responsible way Shangri La was designed and built. She awards it her organization's platinum award–the first project in Texas so honored, and only the fiftieth in the world. The sun comes out and a stately flock of white ibis flies over as dignitaries cut a flower-bedecked vine, and the doors to Shangri La open once again.

Clever combinations of rustic pine logs and glass walls create a cluster of transparent, climate controlled boxes in the woods. A theater, exhibit building, gift shop, classroom, and café fit seamlessly into the landscape. We walk paths and boardwalks of recycled materials to enjoy azalea gardens, pools, fountains, and outdoor sculpture. A bird blind at the edge of a pond provides an intimate glimpse of life in a nesting colony of herons and egrets.

But where are the longleaf pines Buddy Hollis told us about? Shangri La's director, Michael Hoke, tells us the story. "Hurricane Rita hit us really hard," he says. "We lost fifty-two thousand trees. We know how many because we had to remove them. Most were loblolly pine." These faster-growing trees, Hoke explains, replaced the original longleaf forest that was clear cut in 1895. "We have replanted seventeen thousand longleaf seedlings," he continues. "It's only 150 acres, but it's a start."

Our visit to Shangri La ends with a motorized barge trip up Adams Bayou to an outpost in the swamp that will be an outdoor classroom. A boardwalk meanders from the riverside dock through cypress and palmetto to a dry knoll with an unusual building at its crest. Peeled logs combine with screen wire, steel, and glass to inject a note of modernity into this wilderness setting. "Here," Michael Hoke says proudly, "children will come into close contact with nature and learn to be kind to their world."

❀

Behind the long-awaited reopening of Shangri La—behind its award for environmental and social sensitivity and its goal of living in harmony with nature—lies an irony. None of it would have been possible without the Stark family fortune inherited from one of Texas's most successful lumber barons, William Henry Stark, Lutcher Stark's father.

When the elder Stark married Miriam Lutcher, he gained not only a wife but also a business partner. W. H. Stark's father-in-law, Henry Jacob Lutcher, had joined forces with G. Bedell Moore to create Lutcher and Moore Lumber Company in 1877.[6] The two men staked their financial futures on a risky plan. They decided to build one very large sawmill and equip it with the best steam-powered machinery money could buy. Producing more lumber faster, they reasoned, they could sell cheaper and undercut the competition. The idea worked. The mill they erected at Orange had four times the capacity of any competing mill and could sell at a third the cost.[7]

But the plan required peak production year round. The beast they created had an insatiable appetite for trees. As the need for lumber, railroad ties, bridge timbers, and shingles grew, Lutcher and Moore modernized their operation. They borrowed money to buy bigger, more powerful saws, replaced ox and mule teams with steam skidders and tram lines for hauling logs out of the woods. They hired more men. Lumber was shipped to East Coast and Mexican ports aboard their own fleet of lumber schooners.[8] It was a race to keep ahead of the saws and the bank. Company accountant F. H. Farwell recalled, "Mr. Lutcher traveled in a cycle. He ran the operations, sold the lumber, borrowed the money with which to buy more timber land from which to cut more lumber. He was always broke."[9]

Lutcher bought out Moore's interest in the company in 1901, and when Lutcher died in 1912, son-in-law William H. Stark gained control of a lumbering empire.[10] Through it all the nation's need for lumber and the mill's appetite for trees continued to grow. At the peak of production in 1929, a new mill at Wiergate produced two hundred thousand board feet of lumber per ten-hour day.[11] It would take one hundred trees per hour to supply that much raw wood—one thousand trees per ten-hour day.[12]

The same story was repeated with variations from Virginia and North Carolina to Louisiana and Texas. The longleaf pine forest of the South had been traded for the homes, churches, businesses, warehouses, railroads, bridges, docks, and ships of a booming nation. In Texas, what Vernon Bailey considered to be, "the cleanest, most uniform, and symmetrical body of pine to be found on the continent," disappeared. Lutcher and Moore lumber helped build the infrastructure for a modern, economically vibrant state.

It also created a family fortune managed by W. H. Stark's son H. J. Lutcher Stark and his wife Nelda. In 1961 they created the Stark Foundation in order to put the family inheritance to good use in Southeast Texas.[13] This is the foundation that resurrected Lutcher Stark's dream of Shangri La. It was a lumber baron's fortune that funded one of the most ambitious and innovative environmental education projects in Texas.

One innovation in particular grabs our attention. Project designers and architects used lumber cut from "sinker" cypress and longleaf pine for many of the walls, railings, and moldings in various buildings. Wood from these resurrected logs is as good, and in many ways better than, fresh-cut lumber. Michael Hoke tells us that the man who found some of these ghosts from lumbering's past, Don McCaughey, lives just across the river in Vinton, Louisiana. We decide to pay him a visit.

❧

Vinton is a prosperous little town north of Interstate 10 in what used to be prime rice-growing country. Majestic, moss-draped live oaks give the simple frame houses a sense of grandeur. "Crawdads" have decorated many of the lawns with jaunty little towers of dark mud. The McCaughey place sits on a corner lot with grass-lined drainage ditches along one side and the front. There are canoes in the yard and a pirogue in the shed behind the carport.

A small, square-faced man with white hair and beard answers the door. He is dressed for a cool day in wet woods—fleece-lined canvas vest, gray shooting shirt, jeans, and rubber boots with lace-up leather uppers. His wife, Lorraine, is a petite, gray-haired woman, Cajun by birth. He is a Cajun in Scotch/Irish wrapping.

Two canoes hang from the ceiling of the McCaughey living room. One is a beautifully restored 1923 guide model, the other a 1922 HW. A set of drums stands silent in one corner. Amplifier and microphone, flanked by speakers, take center stage in front of the fireplace. This is the practice studio for McCaughey's band. He plays bass, guitar, harmonica, and accordion.

After hearing Don explain his connection to Michael Hoke and Shangri La, I ask how he got started raising "sinkers" out of the Sabine.

"I always wanted to build a dugout canoe," he says. "It takes a big log to build a dugout, at least thirty-six inches. I started looking and found some logs and decided to cut one of them up. A friend of mine had a sawmill on the river. He built it by hand—a Rube Goldberg thing. It was amazing to watch it work. I brought one of my logs down to him, and while he was cutting it the thing came apart on him. The wheels weren't balanced properly and just threw iron all over the woods. My son was out of a job, so I said, 'Why don't we buy us a little sawmill, one of those portable deals, and start pulling some logs and cutting them ourselves?' So that's what we did."

"What about the dugout?" I ask.

"The only log I found that was big enough, I had in partnership with somebody else, and we needed the money, so we just sold the wood. I never did make the dugout."

"How much can you get for a good-sized log?" Isabel asks.

"Oh, we were getting less than most people. They were getting eight dollars a board foot, so it's not unusual to make four thousand dollars off of one log. We've been selling ours for two-fifty. We've gone up to four dollars for cypress and pine. It's like treasure hunting. That's why we do it."

Lumber companies stopped floating logs down the Sabine around 1930.[14] The sinkers that log-pullers like McCaughey dredge up are 75–125 years old. McCaughey tells us that when the Toledo Bend dam was built on the Sabine, the river began to deposit sand downstream and covered up most of the old sinkers.

"They are going to be there forever," he says, "and, every once in a while, one will come up. I was in a bayou the other day, been there a hundred times, and all of a sudden, I saw the end of a log sticking up. It was a sinker pine that had just popped up for some reason or other. I've got it on the sawmill now. Would you like to see it? It's out at our place on the river."

McCaughey owns some land near Niblett's Bluff on the Sabine. He offers to drive us out there, cook hamburgers for lunch, and show us around. It is a rare opportunity to see an old-growth longleaf pine, even if it is just a log.

Light rain falls as McCaughey drives past the "Private Property" sign marking the entrance to his riverside camp. "This whole area was covered with downed trees after Hurricane Rita," he says. "We couldn't even get through on a four-wheeler—had to walk in. I never thought it would look this good again." He points to an orange contraption on wheels surrounded by logs and slabs of lumber. "That's my portable sawmill over there. We'll come back and look at it when this rain lets up."

The McCaughey camp house is low-slung with a wide porch on two sides, the longer side facing the river. Rain drums on the tin roof as our host unlocks the door, ushers us in, and starts a pot of coffee. He lights a fire in the fireplace, as we take a quick look around. The plywood floor of the dining area is marked off in squares, and McCaughey has painted a different kind of fish in each. Tromp l'oeil water lilies decorate the floor of the living area. The faux rug in front of the fireplace has a decorative oak leaf border.

Even more remarkable is McCaughey's creative use of wood. Outside edges of door moldings are the irregular outside edges of the trees from which they were cut. The lacy bottoms of ceiling moldings are the work of insects on the outer layer of sinker cypress logs. Doors, wainscot, paneling, ceilings, escutcheons, furniture—all are loving tributes to cypress and longleaf pine.

From a wooden chicken coop made into a coffee table/book case, McCaughey pulls out a photo album. A cup of coffee in one hand, he opens the album and points to a picture.

"That's my barge. It has thirty-six inch pontoons."

"Like the ones people make house boats from?" I ask.

"No. Somebody gave me an old heater-treater from an oil field, a big round pipe they use to treat the oil with. It was twenty-eight feet long. I cut it in two, welded pipe caps on the ends, and made pontoons out of it."

The frame, he explains, is made from cast-off channel iron and junk pipe. He paid a Wyoming rancher fifty dollars for a discarded but serviceable winch.

"Where is the motor?" Isabel asks.

"It doesn't have one. We just put the bow of my skiff between the pontoons and push it like a barge."

Another photo shows McCaughey, fully clothed, wearing goggles, neck deep in the muddy water between the pontoons of his barge.

"How far can you see in that water?" Isabel asks.

"You can't see," he answers, "I just crawl around on the bottom. I don't wear flippers. I have an air tank on the boat with a forty-foot hose and a mouthpiece. Belt weights keep me down."

"I couldn't do that," Isabel says. "I'm claustrophobic."

"The type of job I had, I couldn't be claustrophobic," McCaughey answers. "I inspected refineries—had to go down flair stacks and vessels, everything. They'd drop us down pipes that were fifteen stories tall. We would have to go down in a little chair."

McCaughey looks for logs with his feet. When he finds one, he digs it out of the mud, sometimes with the help of compressed air blowing through a hose. He then attaches a line from the winch to the freed end of the log and reels it in. If all goes well, the log pops free in a cloud of bubbles and silt and rises to the surface. Secured to the barge, it neither floats nor sinks, but lies inertly just beneath the surface. McCaughey then cranks the outboard on his skiff and pushes his barge and his prize back to Niblett's Bluff.

While we have been looking at photographs, the rain has stopped. It is time to see what McCaughey has found. We walk to a little cove sheltering a weathered boathouse and step into his flat-bottomed aluminum skiff. The motor putters along quietly as we nose out into the Sabine and turn downstream. Just past the cabin he reverses course, points the bow into the current, and slowly approaches the bank. At first I can't make out the logs he says are tied up here. Then I see them. They lie low in the water–long, dark forms–like a pod of dead whales. "That's a longleaf pine," he says, pointing to one. "See that round hole? That's where they pegged on a crossbeam to make a raft."

The river is quiet today–no other boats, no fishermen on the banks. When this longleaf pine sank to the bottom of the Sabine, the river was full of logs on their way to the mill. Many floated free. Others, like the one McCaughey found, were assembled into rafts with wooden pegs through crossbeams holding the logs together. Some rafts had shacks on board where men could sleep and cook and keep the valuable cargo moving downstream. When spring rains, like the one today, caused the river to rise and turned the Sabine into a commercial highway, steamboats had to wait their turn for a place in line among the logs.

McCaughey turns his skiff upstream to show me his barge with its handcrafted pontoons, scrap metal frame, and cast-off winch. Back on shore we walk through wet grass under still-dripping trees to his portable sawmill. He has a story for every log, but it is the one on the machine that interests me–the sinker longleaf McCaughey found after it came to the surface recently.

The bark is gone, and the outer layer of wood is ash gray. It is full of shallow holes and little depressions where insect larvae and other aquatic organisms have burrowed in. The log's exterior looks old, but where Mc-Caughey cut off the end and exposed the interior, it looks as new as the day it was felled. It is the color of fresh-cut pine with annual rings so symmetrical they could have been laid out with a compass. McCaughey pats it lovingly, as a groom would pat a thoroughbred or a rancher his prize bull. It is the booty from a practical man's treasure hunt in the murky water of the Sabine.

Driving back from Vinton to Orange in a river of traffic on Interstate 10, Isabel and I talk about the contrast between McCaughey's operation and the giant Lutcher and Moore lumber mill. We try to imagine the old-growth longleaf forest with its tall, stately trees and open, park-like understory. It was a well balanced ecosystem adapted over millennia to the soil, rainfall, climate, and recurring fires of the humid South. Ivory-billed woodpeckers flew among its trees. Black bears roamed beneath them.

Life, however, was hard for the people who survived in this forest before the Civil War. Cholera, malaria, yellow fever, and other maladies threatened health. Bad roads and unpredictable rivers made it difficult to get produce and products to markets or supplies to remote farms. Economic stagnation resulted.

The lumber industry changed all that. It provided badly needed jobs and stimulated the growth of railroads that connected Southeast Texas with the rest of the country. Timber barons like Lutcher, Moore, and Stark made life better for thousands of people. Lumber from their mills built family fortunes that later generations shared philanthropically with their neighbors. But the price for economic prosperity in longleaf country was high. It was paid by every state along the Gulf Coast and Eastern Seaboard from Texas to Virginia. Lawrence Early, in his book *Looking for Longleaf,* puts it in context: "By 1996 only 2.95 million acres of longleaf remained out of the original 92 million acres . . . Almost all of the old-growth forest is gone . . . By any measure, longleaf's decline of nearly 98 percent is among the most severe of any ecosystem on earth. It dwarfs the Amazon rain forest's losses of somewhere between 13 and 25 percent. It is comparable to or exceeds the decline of the North American tallgrass prairie, the coastal forests of southeastern Brazil, and the dry forests of the Pacific Coast of Central America. It surpasses the losses of the old-growth Douglas fir forests of the Pacific Northwest."[15]

We have found signs of hope, however. Buddy Hollis showed us a thriving young stand of longleaf pine. He described efforts by timber companies, private landowners, and the Nature Conservancy to grow more. Relic stands of these forest aristocrats are preserved in the Big Thicket National Preserve. Michael Hoke told of planting seventeen thousand longleaf pines in Shangri La where a new generation is learning how to "live in harmony with the earth." But a hard truth is inescapable. What was, will never be again. What remains is but a souvenir of what was lost.

WALT DAVIS

CHAPTER II

Exploring Bear River

*When the bear got scarce we didn't quit hunting. We'd hear of
one over here, one over there, go hunt it and kill it. They're all gone.
It was the greatest sport on earth!*
CARTER HART,
quoted in Campbell and Lynn Loughmiller, Big Thicket Legacy

ON DECEMBER 17, 1718, two bound men awaited their
fate aboard a boat anchored in the Mississippi River
not far from New Orleans. On the opposite side of the
vessel, other men held ropes that led under the hull
to the prisoners. Pushed overboard, the accused men
were pulled under the boat, across the keel, and up the far side. Bénard
de la Harpe dutifully recorded the event in his journal: "The 17th, I had
keel-hauled from on board the vessel of M. Bellanger two mutineers of
my troop."[1]

The French government had ordered La Harpe to establish a trading
post on the Red River near present-day Texarkana. He knew the journey
ahead would be long and dangerous. Only strict discipline would keep
his men in line. The two mutineers probably survived their punishment,
but from that moment on, Bénard de la Harpe was the undisputed, iron-
willed leader of this expedition into the wilderness.

Through the rest of December, La Harpe's crew struggled to paddle
their pirogues and row their two *bateaux*, loaded with six tons of merchandise and supplies, up the Mississippi–against the current. They passed
isolated French plantations and numerous Native American settlements.

Jason and Jacob Scurlock on the Sulphur River

On January 10, 1719, the expedition reached the mouth of the Red River. Persistent rain dampened spirits, and chronic food shortages added anxiety to the fatigue of travel.

Hunters of the Avoyelles nation took pity on the Frenchmen. La Harpe recorded their generosity: "They killed for me ten deer and a bear, a number of bustards, some duck, some hares and several squirrels; they caught also many fish for me; I made a present to them of two muskets."[2] In the years that followed, war and disease decimated this once proud and generous people. By 1805 only two or three women remained.[3] Similar tragedy befell every group La Harpe met on his journey upriver.

Crewmen fought against the relentless current for every foot of progress. Rain increased the flow. They encountered rapids. At times the men shipped oars, threw a tow line to shore, and pulled the heavy boats by brute strength closer and closer to Texas. Their immediate goal was an island in the middle of the Red River—a place called Natchitoches named for the Caddoan Indians who lived nearby. Fort Saint John the Baptist, built there just four years earlier, was the westernmost outpost of French Louisiana.

Unfortunately, the closer La Harpe's flotilla got to the fort, the harder it was to proceed. Believing the island to be near, a Frenchman fired his musket and was answered by a shot from Natchitoches. Shortly thereafter the expedition ground to a halt. Leaving the vessels, La Harpe walked the short distance to the fort and secured help to clear a path through log jams that clogged the river.

It took a local chief and thirty of his men four days to cut away the timber. When the exhausted crew tied up at Natchitoches on February 25, they had been fighting their way upstream for two months and eight days. The shake-down cruise was over. The real adventure was about to begin.

Isabel and I, inspired by La Harpe's vivid portrayal of his journey, decide to retrace a portion of his route by canoe. He crossed into Texas by way of the Sulphur River near the northeast corner of the state. However, our journey begins 450 miles to the west. We have come to the opening of an art exhibit at the Panhandle-Plains Museum, where we meet a woman from Texarkana. When we mention our proposed trip to her part of the state, Linda Scurlock, with a twinkle in her eye, says we must meet her husband.

Linda and Bill Scurlock are the editor and publisher, respectively, of *Muzzleloader* magazine. They live and work in Nash, Texas, on the outskirts of Texarkana and just happen to own a piece of the north bank of the Sulphur River close to the Arkansas line—precisely where we want to put in for our float trip. It turns out that Bill has wanted to canoe the Sulphur for years. We decide to join forces.

Forty-eight days later Isabel and I stand beside two olive drab Kubota ATVs (all terrain vehicles) in a muddy track walled in by yellow ragweed growing head-high. River bottom greenery glistens with morning dew, and the musty odor of rotten wood mixes with the smell of gasoline and crushed vegetation. We review the ATV starting procedure Bill Scurlock taught us yesterday. Isabel mashes the starter button, kicks it into low gear, and roars off. Bunjee straps secure dry-bags, tent, and army surplus ammo boxes to the rack behind the driver's seat, next to plastic milk crates cradling stove, cooking pots, and utensils.

Our careful packing passes its first test as I nose the machine into a hub-deep puddle of mud and churn through to dry ground on the other side. A tree across the trail presents another challenge. Isabel inches forward until front tires touch the obstacle, then throttles up to push the front end up and over. After the briefest pause, she hits the gas again pulling herself, her cargo, and the back tires over to the other side. Driving an ATV focuses the mind wonderfully. The noise obliterates distracting sounds like singing birds and rustling leaves. Hairpin turns, mud holes, and downed trees keep the eyes focused on the road ahead. When we arrive at the river bank and switch off the engines, the silence is deafening. Our tunnel vision broadens to survey the wide-flowing river and surrounding forest.

There is no time to sightsee, however, as our leader has organized the expedition with military precision. Within minutes, the second squad (Scurlock's teenaged sons Jason and Jacob) arrives at the staging area where Isabel meets them and hands over her ATV to transport their gear. She then uses our pickup to escort the third unit (her brother-in-law Randy Mallory) from a nearby country church to the staging area. The final contingent (Scurlock and his father-in-law Earnest Cook), having left a vehicle at the take-out point in Arkansas, arrives at the put-in last. We load the boats and push off at 10:30 A.M. sharp, entrusting our little band to the indolent but inexorable current of the Sulphur River.

Bénard de la Harpe entrusted his own flotilla of pirogues and *bateaux* to the unrelenting current of the Red River on March 6, 1719. He had rested his men for nine days at Fort St. John the Baptist, but it was time to push on. A Natchitoches chief agreed to serve as guide and brought along twelve of his men. Eight days later La Harpe made this entry in his journal: "The 14th, we sailed along the high shore a league; then we found some timbers so thick that it seemed incredible to be able to go through them. There was on the branches of these trees an infinite number of snakes, upon which it was necessary for us to fire some musket shots from fear that they might fall into our boats. This route was very painful and fatigued our men extremely. We entered afterwards into a channel full of alligators where the currents were frightful. We passed through it by the tow line and by pulling ourselves from branch to branch; we stopped then on a prairie. The route for the day was north two leagues."[4]

For the next two weeks, the expedition struggled up the Red River traveling two to seven leagues a day (roughly five and one-half to twenty miles). Soaking rain and bitter cold slowed their progress. When no dry campsite could be found, they slept in the boats. Natchitoches hunters managed to kill a buffalo, some deer, and turkeys. On one occasion, La Harpe planted a cross near the river and ordered the French coat of arms carved on a tree. Then more rain and cold weather.

On April 1, after twenty-six days of grueling toil, the expedition pitched camp 324 miles north of Natchitoches where another river joins the Red. The guides called the stream Bear River, but today it is known as the Sulphur. La Harpe's final destination was a large village of the Nassonites, one of many subgroups of the Caddo. The village lay 154 miles farther up the Red River, but the guides knew a shortcut. Paddling up Bear River and marching overland to the same destination would save one hundred miles. It was time to make a decision.

La Harpe sent all of his men, both *bateaux,* and most of his pirogues the long way around. Six tons of valuable merchandise required deep water to keep it afloat and military protection to keep it safe. La Harpe took the Bear River shortcut accompanied by three Natchitoches guides. They forced their way through numerous log jams and spent the night camped on an island in the middle of the stream.

On the second day, the river lived up to its name. La Harpe's journal entry reads: "The 3rd [of April], the three savages I had with me killed two bears; this stream is full of them. We continued to advance toward the west-northwest to some very great high grounds which we sailed along, leaving them on our left. [He had just crossed into what would become Texas]. At two o'clock in the afternoon we arrived at the portage that goes to the Nassonites . . ."[5]

The next day, leaving their canoes behind, the party set out overland, and one of the guides hurried ahead to inform the Nassonites that they were coming. At ten o'clock the next morning seven tribal notables arrived with horses to carry them the rest of the way. La Harpe described crossing "some great prairies and very fine country" before entering a forest. At three o'clock in the afternoon, he arrived at the home of the seventy-year-old leader of the tribe.[6] La Harpe describes the welcome he received: "This chief with those of the Caddodaquious, Nadsoos, and Natchitoches [all subtribes of the Caddo Confederacy] was awaiting me at this dwelling, outside of which, under an *antichon,* they had prepared a feast, consisting of bread and boiled corn, prepared in different ways, and some bear meat and buffalo meat and fish. We maintained a profound silence during the repast; it is even the custom of the savages to ask not one question to their new guests until they may be refreshed or that they should speak themselves."[7] Following the meal, La Harpe told the distinguished gathering of tribal leaders that the King of France pledged to support them in their struggles against neighboring enemy tribes. What began as a wilderness journey now became a high-level diplomatic mission.

The mission of the Scurlock, Cook, and Davis expedition is more modest, but still daunting. The river is quiet today, but moving water can be treacherous. Evidence of the river's power surrounds us—oaks, elms, box elders, and sycamores are broken and contorted by floods. Downed trees thrust gnarled roots from the mud and water. Pencil-straight but lifeless pines lie scattered about like pick-up-sticks dropped from a child's hand. The riverside forest is not a pretty sight—it is a war zone in which the river gods have the upper hand.

We have timed our trip well, however. Early March has brought clear skies, cool temperatures, and gentle breezes that nudge us along. Bill Scurlock paddles a replica Louisiana pirogue—a wooden, flat-bottomed boat that navigates obstacles and shallows with ease. Earnest Cook powers his own well-traveled, square-ended canoe. Randy Mallory serves as bowman. Jason and Jacob Scurlock lurch downstream in a leaky, borrowed canoe with a broken thwart. Isabel and I struggle along in our seventeen-foot Lowe's Ouachita. It has served us well on the Brazos, Guadalupe, and Trinity Rivers, but is designed for lake travel with a keel more hindrance than help on this river. Changing course is difficult and slows us down. We soon take up a permanent position at the rear of the fleet.

Shouts up ahead shatter our river-induced reverie. A long dark form on the bank rises up on wide-spread legs and lumbers into the water. Alligator eyes and reptilian snout soon pop to the surface and glide slowly to mid-river. We decide to stop for lunch. As we snack on sandwiches, Beanie Weenies, and sardines, the gator lingers, cruising back and forth, eyeing the intruders. Back on the water, we round a bend and encounter a second alligator larger than the first. These living relics from the ancient past give the river a more menacing, less benign character.

At three o'clock we begin looking for a place to pitch camp. Several candidates are too muddy, and others have impossibly steep banks. One is covered with poison ivy, and another has no level spots for pitching tents or building a proper campfire. Two hours and several miles pass before we spot a weathered sign that says, appropriately, "campsite." Cook knows this place well. A road comes in to the bluff bank overlooking the river where a large fuel tank stands sentinel. Game managers periodically pump water out of the river to flood wildfowl habitat nearby. They haul the pump in and out as needed and store fuel in the tank.

The place has an industrial look about it. I suggest to Isabel that we pitch our tent on the riverbank out of sight of the intruding signs of civilization. But fresh sign from a beast with a prior claim abruptly changes my mind. Hand-sized tracks tipped with stubby claw marks announce the presence of yet another alligator, approximately my size, that takes occasional strolls through our would-be campsite. Instead, we pitch our tent high on a slope covered with purple vetch so thick we have to tramp it down to clear a spot for our ground cloth.

I heat Texas Goulash over a roaring backpacking stove as we sip the one-beer-each carefully packed for just this moment. Randy votes his thirst quencher "the best beer ever." We have paddled nearly sixteen miles today–a personal best for everyone including the veteran Earnest Cook. Shortly after sunset a full moon rises, and as evening turns to night, coyotes howl in the distance. A barred owl hoots, *"who cooks for you, who cooks for you all"* somewhere deep in the woods.

Around the campfire after supper, Bill Scurlock tells a story about a hike he once took across the Cumberland Plateau. It was a reenactment of an eighteenth-century journey. David Wright, one of Scurlock's friends, had invited twenty men on a week-long, cross-country hike, hunting and gathering as they went. Fifteen showed up with flintlocks, lead shot, and black powder. Scurlock came dressed in knee breeches, leather leggings, plain shirt, leather jacket, a flat-brimmed felt hat, and moccasins.

Wright explained the rules of engagement. His friends would assume the roles of backwoods hunters who had run out of food. They would carry no provisions but live off the land. Accordingly, fifteen men subsisted for seven days on one-half to three-quarters of a squirrel a day plus one or two handfuls of blueberries, fox grapes, or muscadines. A crow and one copperhead added variety to the menu.

Scurlock does not remember feeling hungry, but he does recall vividly what a little food did for their depleted bodies. Once, after climbing out of a steep gorge, the men fell to the ground exhausted. They finally roused enough to eat some grapes gathered earlier in the day–barely enough to give each man a slim handful. Those few grapes delivered a jolting load of sugar to fifteen torpid bodies. In minutes the men were bustling about with suddenly renewed energy.

Scurlock lost twelve pounds that week. At the conclusion of his walk across the Cumberland Plateau, he joined his fellow travelers in a restaurant to celebrate their survival. After a dozen bites of rich food, however, they could eat no more. The sudden bounty overwhelmed digestive systems calibrated to process small amounts of food at infrequent intervals. Bowels that had little cause for action during the past week came back to life slowly. Scurlock's experience brings home the harsh reality of La Harpe's constant struggle to find enough food to keep his crew fit enough to fight the brute strength of the river.

When Scurlock finishes his story, I leave to check on Isabel. After supper, her arms began to ache, and she went back to our tent to take some pain relievers and rest. Pulling back the tent flap, I am startled by what I see. Isabel lies on top of her sleeping bag, shivering uncontrollably, tears in her eyes. Six hours of hard paddling has taken a terrible toll. The pain in her arms is excruciating. I begin rubbing, first one and then the other. An hour passes. Finally, the pain subsides enough that she can sleep, but she is restless through the night. I drift off thinking of six-ton *bateaux*, tow lines, and fatigued men straining against the current.

Morning finds mist rising from the river. While the rest of the camp sleeps, the forest is quiet, and the river rolls silently by. Sunlight sets the mist in motion. Miniature hurricanes spin across the water. Little tornadoes of vapor twist briefly, then leap into the air and disappear. By the time camp begins to stir, the show is over, and the Sulphur River regains its composure. Isabel wakes tired but much improved. Day two begins with steaming cups of camp coffee and homemade breakfast bars. We load the boats and coax sore muscles into paddling again as we point our bows downstream toward the Red River.

We thread through flood debris caught in the ruins of a bridge proudly bearing the date of its construction–1930. Later, Cook points to a grove of pines on a bluff where an old trading post once stood. Years ago he explored the site with a team of archeologists. Called a factory, it was one of a series of government-sponsored outposts intended to control trade with local Indians and win them away from Spanish influence. John Fowler built the Sulphur Fork Factory in 1818, one hundred years after La Harpe passed this way. By 1822 it was gone.

Far ahead we catch the gleam of white sand marking the east bank of the Red River. Soon the Sulphur gives up its water to the Red that will, in turn, pass it on to the mighty Mississippi. Our journey ends here. We load our canoes onto Scurlock's flat-bed trailer, pile into his pickup, and drive back to our starting point to retrieve cars and ATVs. We have come to appreciate the edgy beauty of the Sulphur River. But even though we have traveled the same stream Bénard de la Harpe did, we did not experience the Bear River of his day.

❦

Sixteen days after La Harpe arrived at the Nassonite village on the Red River, the rest of his expedition hove into view. Crewmen were exhausted, but La Harpe joined them in singing the *Te Deum*, a hymn of joy and thanksgiving for the safe arrival of men and merchandise. In the days that followed he took time to describe in his journal the forests and prairies near the village. Reading his account is like pulling aside a curtain and looking back at Northeast Texas in its primeval state—a place accessible today only through the imagination: "The common trees are red and white cypresses, cedars, pines, sweet gum, white woods, willows, ashes, oaks, walnuts, pecans, whose nuts are very good, mulberries, persimmons, which produce a fruit similar to the medlar, but much better, plums whose fruits are very good and an infinite abundance of grape vines, whose grapes are very delicate; my men made six casks of good strong wine there. Game is abundant . . . especially in winter; buffalo are killed at twenty leagues [forty-eight miles] from the establishment; bear, deer, hare, and rabbit are not far away, nor are the turkey, the snipe, and other fowls."[8]

As soon as La Harpe could leave the Nassonite Trading Post in the hands of his subordinates, he set out westward on an overland trek, hoping to open trade with the Spanish and Native Americans in New Mexico. He secured twenty-two horses to carry men and supplies out of the forests, through the foothills of the Ouachita Mountains, and onto the Great Plains. There he saw herds of buffalo and a curious animal he called a unicorn (probably a pronghorn), before turning back toward the Red River.[9] He and his men narrowly escaped a band of Comanches, got off course in the mountains, ran out of food, lost some of their horses, and ate the rest. On October 13, the bedraggled explorers reappeared at the post of the Nassonites ". . . extremely fatigued from a route so painful."[10]

After two weeks of recovery, La Harpe bade farewell to his men and his many Caddo friends and boarded a pirogue bound for Natchitoches and New Orleans. The wilderness gave him up grudgingly however. Just four days into the return voyage, a debilitating fever struck La Harpe down. He lay for days in the bottom of a boat, protected from the cold and rain by a buffalo robe. When low water halted progress on the river, La Harpe's men set out overland to find food and help. They left their suffering leader in an abandoned hut with two aides to care for him. The three subsisted on haw berries and wild purslane after their corn ran out.

Assistance arrived in the form of a Natchitoches chief, three of his men, and fifty Adayes recruited along the way. They found La Harpe so close to death that they dared not move him. Later, the Frenchman described their ministrations: "Recognizing the peril I was in [they] sent in diligence to search for three of the medicine men, whom they call sorcerers . . . They arrived at two o'clock after midnight and commenced by chanting . . . I being extraordinarily swelled, they laid me on the ground naked, stretched upon a buffalo robe, where these medicine men sucked all the most afflicted parts of my body; I found myself a little relieved by it."[11]

Having given him the best medical care available, these eighteenth-century EMTs carried La Harpe on a litter to the nearest navigable water, then transported him by pirogue to Natchitoches. A steady diet of wholesome food soon revived the intrepid explorer, who continued to New Orleans.

Bénard de la Harpe accomplished his mission in the face of capricious rivers, merciless weather, and ruthless enemies. Success required physical strength, emotional drive, and the kindness of countless strangers. He penetrated deep into an alien world and lived to give an account of his adventure. It had been an epic journey. His journal remains a priceless record of a time long ago—when the woods were full of "savage" princes—and "unicorns" roamed the plains.

Bear River has changed in the ensuing years, and its namesake has fallen on hard times. In the eighteenth century bear meat was considered a delicacy, and everyone extolled bear grease as a flavorful cooking oil and clean-burning fuel for lamps. La Harpe reported meeting a trader from Nachitoches bound for New Orleans with corn, bear oil, and tobacco.[12] A century later, John Fowler, factor of the Sulphur Fork Trading Post, loaded three hundred bear skins and the skins of forty cubs onto a keelboat bound for the same city.[13]

The remainder of the nineteenth century was hard on the animals. Forests were cleared, swamps drained, and war declared on any creature accused of livestock depredation. By the beginning of the twentieth century, one of the most common and widespread large mammals in Texas had retreated into the inaccessible mountains of the Big Bend or the impenetrable Big Thicket. Oddly enough, the discovery of oil in 1901 dealt a death blow to the few bears remaining in East Texas.

Oil made many avid bear hunters rich overnight. Freed from the necessity to work for wages, they turned to full-time hunting, and made short work of their quarry. According to Carter Hart, one of Texas's last bear hunters, "Most of the good bear hunting was over around 1910. The last one I killed was in 1911, I believe, although I was with Ben Hooks on a deer hunt in 1918 when we happened to strike a bear and he killed it and that was his last . . . When the bear got scarce we didn't quit hunting. We'd hear of one over here, one over there, go hunt it and kill it. They're all gone. It was the greatest sport on earth!"[14]

The animal that gave Bear River its name no longer lives on the Sulphur. But that may be changing. Bill Scurlock says that a black bear appeared in downtown Texarkana not long ago, and Earnest Cook read about one that walked through nearby Spring Hill, Arkansas, the same year. They theorize that young males, known to wander a bit after leaving their mothers, are coming down from the foothills of the Ouachita Mountains where the species is thriving. Bears may soon return to Bear River.

The epic journey of Bénard de la Harpe means more to us now than a distant footnote in history. We have traveled the river he traveled, seen its beauty, and sensed its dangers. Bill Scurlock has demonstrated the gritty reality of living off the land as La Harpe and his men were forced to do. Scurlock and Earnest Cook have shown us what modern day woodsmen are like. Attuned to nature, they are thankful for its gifts and tolerant of its tolls and tariffs.

The Sulphur River is no longer a blue line on a map. It is a living thing—both ancient and brand new—a force equally capable of creation and destruction. Along its banks, across the centuries, people have come and gone like the vapor that dances briefly above its muddy waters, then leaps, and vanishes in the sun.

WALT DAVIS

Red River Trading Post

· ·

Thousands of deer were met with daily . . . it was no uncommon
sight to see from one to two hundred in a single herd.
RANDOLPH B. MARCY,
The Prairie Traveler: A Handbook for Overland Expeditions

B ÉNARD DE LA HARPE never returned to the trading post
he built on the banks of the Red River. For almost sixty
years, it continued to operate in the wilderness. A few
soldiers, never more than fifteen, protected a handful of
settlers and traders. Alex Grappe revitalized the project in
1737 when he built and fortified a smaller post and trading house nearby.[1]
Twenty-five years later, decisions made on the other side of the Atlantic
sealed the fate of La Harpe's enterprise.

When France ceded Louisiana to Spain in 1763, the Nassonite post
was closed and its soldiers withdrawn. Grappe and his family held on
for two more years before finally moving away. By 1778, the site was
completely abandoned.[2] Red River floods spread sand and silt over the
once-prosperous Nassonite post. As the water receded, a green shroud
of vegetation grew over the place where people had exchanged goods,
blended families, lived, and died. What was buried there would not be
seen again for almost three hundred years.

As time passed, floods continued to erase human history and rearrange the landscape. Most of nature's earth-shaping work is done in
slow motion, too gradual to notice—erosion measured in millimeters per
year, uplift in fractions of an inch. But water can rise several feet an hour

Deer hide, rifle, and horse trading network in a Caddo village

during a flood. What was the main channel one day can be an isolated oxbow lake the next. To witness a flood is to see geologic force at work on a human time scale.

Strong thunderstorms and tornadoes pounded much of Texas for several weeks in the spring of 1990. Bowie County and the Texarkana area were especially hard hit. On Sunday, May 6, the Red River overflowed its banks and water again covered the site of the old French trading posts.[3] The National Guard came in to shore up levees and rescue stranded livestock. People were evacuated in airboats. One state official called the calamity " . . . some of the most destructive . . . weather ever to hit the state of Texas in modern times."[4]

CBS Evening News sent Connie Chung to report on the disaster. "I want to talk to somebody that's been in there," she said to the people gathered at the water's edge where a rescue boat had just landed. "He can tell you all about it," someone said, pointing to a cowboy in a mud-spattered hat wading ashore with a saddle slung over his shoulder and a Winchester under his arm. "What do you think about the Red River?" she asked. "Fuck the Red River," he snapped and walked right on by.[5] To those who knew him, the answer was no surprise. The cowboy's name was Meredith Edwards. He and his wife Ethel still live in the Red River "bottoms," and we are on our way to get the rest of his story and to find out what he knows about some unusual artifacts that have turned up near his house.

The road to the Meredith's place runs across level flood plain. Willow, sycamore, box elder, and pecan grow along the shore of Roseborough Lake, an oxbox left behind long ago when the Red River changed its course. A small herd of well-fed longhorns grazes in a green pasture to one side of the road; corn grows in a big field on the other; and in the distance, an old drag line sits idle beside an open sand pit. We park in the shade of giant pecan trees that tower over the Edwards's house, and a blue healer barks to announce our arrival.

Ethel Edwards greets us at the gate. She is a stout, gray-haired woman with an open, friendly face. There is a corn bread, black-eyed peas, and fresh sliced tomatoes aura about her. Meredith is a surprise. The brash cowboy, now sixty-four, walks with a cane. His left arm is withered from a childhood bout with polio. He is a small man with the face of a leprechaun but the demeanor and vocabulary of a drill sergeant. Dark eyes, set back under unruly eyebrows, serve notice that this is not a man to trifle with.

Our conversation begins uneasily, but Edwards soon warms to his story, and to us. As a young man, he was a wizard with a rope and a serious contender on the rodeo circuit. Later, he turned to farming and ranching. The angry man Connie Chung met wading ashore in 1990 had just lost 306 head of cattle to the rampaging Red River. He had himself come close to drowning.

Old resentment rises as he recalls the drama. "The Army Corps of Engineers said they were trying to check out places where cattle were not being cared for so they could drop feed to them. But what they actually did was working against us. We had [the cows] on high ground where they could get feed and be cared for, and [the helicopters] were flying down over them stirring up the water. Wind from the [rotors] caused a current that would just suck them under."

But it was a horse that nearly cost Edwards his life. "You know, a horse will swim in current real good until he sees something coming by, like stumps and stuff like that. If a horse has any wildness in him whatsoever, he is going to go crazy. They get to cuttin' up, and the only thing you can do is get away from them. This horse, he went crazy, and I mean I got away from him, and when I did I went to the bottom. I don't swim very good."

Desperate to kick off his water-filled boots, Edwards accidentally spurred himself in the leg. Reaching safety he called to the horse but watched helplessly as the animal drowned before his eyes. "I got my lariat rope and tied him off because I didn't want to lose my saddle." That was the saddle Edwards carried on his shoulder when he told Connie Chung what he thought of the Red River.

He didn't know it at the time, but the river had one more deadly surprise. The witch's brew of flood water swirling around Edwards's lacerated leg contained staphylococcus bacteria. When a friend rushed him to the hospital two weeks later, Edwards was delirious and his leg had swollen to twice its normal size. "When I got there," he recalls, "they cut my britches leg off. They started with a knife, and it was so tight it just ripped out by itself. The doctor said I was going to lose that leg. I said I'd rather be dead than have my leg cut off." Doctors managed to save both his leg and his life.

Meredith Edwards had survived four previous floods. When he saw this one coming, he sent his daughter, a high school senior, to town to buy supplies. "Stuff that you could just open and eat," he said. When the water got close, he sent wife and daughter to town telling them, "I don't want to have to look after anybody but myself." Ethel Edwards remembers the Parks and Wildlife air boat pulling up to their house. "I stepped out of the back door and into the boat. Had to take my daughter's prom dress with me. It was just half-finished, and I didn't know when I'd be coming back." Soon, the house was ankle deep in water. Edwards lifted furniture onto oil cans filled with sand and kept their new carpet high and dry on buckets.

Rising water also delivered food to the door. "The Red River is a living mass of fish," he recalls. "The dog could catch her fill every night. She caught a lot of catfish and buffalo. Some of the buffalo were thirty to thirty-five pounds." The water also brought less welcome visitors. "That barn over yonder never did get under water, and I've forgotten how many snakes I killed over there." What her husband forgot, Mrs. Edwards remembers clearly. "They kept a running tally, but finally lost count after a thousand. Everybody who worked here at that time carried a gun because you go to move a piece of machinery, or move anything, you'd run into a snake. They were everywhere." Any patch of dry ground became a stationary ark where deer, coyotes, raccoons, and armadillos found refuge. Even the moles evacuated their waterlogged tunnels.

Meredith Edwards lived for eighteen days in the grasp of the flood and watched the Red River rearrange a familiar landscape. He concludes the account of his ordeal with a story about some rearranging of his own. "In 1960, I took a John Deere tractor and a half-yard fresno, and all during Christmas vacation I hauled dirt up here. When I thought I was through, Daddy said, 'Keep on going.' I raised this thing six feet–six feet higher than the surrounding country." Later, Edwards built his house on that mound. "I was kinda proud of raising it and hauling all that dirt, he recalls. "Daddy said, 'Son, I won't ever see it–but you'll see water in that house.' He was right."

Talk of the flood recedes as our conversation turns to the unusual artifacts we have heard about. Edwards tells of picking up arrowheads in plowed fields and finding cannonballs in local sand pits. We tell him what we know of La Harpe and the Nassonite trading post. He says that, as a child, his father saw poles from some old building sticking out of the ground; but, according to Ethel, the origin of the poles is disputed by historians. Both remember archeologists digging in the area but are not sure what they found. Edwards turns to his wife and says abruptly, "Ethel, get your car keys. Let's take 'em in our car. I don't want them driving on that road in their car."

Minutes later we are parked on the shoulder of a dirt road less than a mile from the house. We passed this spot on the way in–field to one side, pasture and oxbow lake to the other. Edwards points to a tarp-covered stack of hay bales in the field and says, "That is where they dug." It is an unassuming place. Row upon row of stunted corn stretch into the distance. Far away, a faint line of trees marks the present channel of the Red River.

Could this be the place La Harpe described nearly three hundred years ago? His journal contains this description: "The terrain of the

Nassonites is a little elevated, the soil is sandy, but at half a quarter of a league from the river, the country is fine, the earth black, and the prairies most beautiful and most fertile. Near the place that I have chosen for my establishment, there is an expanse (lake) two leagues long covered with ducks, swans, and bustards. Although the land there may be sandy, it does not fail to be very fertile for cultivation."[6]

Mrs. Edwards drives and her husband narrates the rest of our tour of local attractions. Just beneath the surface of another corn field, according to our host, lies the wreck of an old river boat. A monstrous hackberry tree marks the boundary of the old family farm. Mysterious mounds in a pecan orchard are attributed to the Caddo. The Red River slides serenely under the bridge where we turn around and head back to the house. Blue sky and white clouds are mirrored in the sun-struck water midstream, but in the shadows the water runs deep red. Today, Edwards seems to be at peace with his old nemesis, but he has shown us the dark side of this river and teased us with some of its mysteries.

☸

Today a large brown envelope shows up in our mailbox. It has come from one of Isabel's colleagues in the library at West Texas A&M University. Inside is a copy of a paper originally published in the *Bulletin of the Texas Archeology Society* entitled "Bénard de la Harpe and the Nassonite Post." It includes a map showing Roseborough Lake and a road we recognize. Could this be proof that the corn field near Meredith and Ethel Edwards's home is the site of the long-lost Nassonite trading post?

I am encouraged to find that one of the paper's authors, R. King Harris, is a man I met many years ago. While working on a project for the Dallas Museum of Natural History, I visited Harris at his home near White Rock Lake. The imposing man who met me at the door had close-cropped gray hair, the face of a benign bulldog, and a passion for archeology. He had transformed the family dining room into a working laboratory. The table was set with books, lab reports, journals, maps, and meticulous drawings of chipped stone artifacts. Boxes of worked flint and pottery sherds were stacked against the wall.

Harris, though an amateur, pursued his passion with the rigor of a professional and made significant discoveries in Texas archeology. His good friend and frequent collaborator Wilson Crook called Harris, "the extant national authority on Historic period trade beads and the preservation and identification of gun parts, knives, glass and ceramic artifacts . . ."[7]

We could not have asked for a better man to help answer the question that has troubled us since our visit with Meredith and Ethel Edwards. We are surprised to learn that no less than nine amateur archeologists worked on that very question, off and on, for fifteen years. They collected artifacts, dug test pits, and searched out historic documents pertaining to La Harpe's Nassonite Post. Working as a team, they combined their research and published their findings.

Sometime before World War II, M. P. Miroir, one of the team members, discovered the skeleton of a thirty-year-old woman in a shallow grave. Nine pots, some intricately decorated, had been buried with her. More than a thousand trade beads lay near her head. All but one were typical of beads available at the time La Harpe built the Nassonite post.[8]

The final inventory of Native American artifacts collected over many years included pendants, pipes, pottery figurines, arrow points, and beads. Pottery is more easily dated than most of the other artifacts, and, according to the research team, "all of the decorated pottery examples recovered fall within the Historic time frame."[9]

Even more interesting are the "European Trade Goods"—axes, bottles, mirrors, ceramics, and horse trappings. Some items are utilitarian such as scissors, kettle fragments, and part of the blade of a carpenter's draw knife. Others are less so—a briefcase lock and two pieces of a sleigh bell. Cocks, frizzens, butt plates, and trigger guards appear to have come from "French trade guns."[10]

Some of the best evidence for the age of the Roseborough Lake site came from some of the smallest artifacts–glass trade beads–2,958 of them. They are to historical archeologists what phone records and security cameras are to detectives. Knowing when the beads were made helps date the sites in which they occur. Harris and his colleagues sorted the Roseborough Lake beads into seventy-five types, twenty-six of which date back to the early 1700s.[11]

But there was more. An unusually large number of beads, unearthed in one small area, dated nearer the middle of the century than the beginning. This led Harris and his team to speculate that "... this may be the site of Alex Grappe's little fort and trading house built shortly after he settled the site in 1737."[12] Thirteen years later, Kathleen Gilmore examined additional artifacts and studied historical documents describing the posts and their locations. She came to the same conclusion.[13]

There is little doubt that the corn field Meredith and Ethel Edwards showed us near Roseborough Lake was the site of a busy trading post almost three hundred years ago. The evidence, however, points to Grappe, not La Harpe as the builder.

What the documents did not disclose was a close connection between the French trading posts and something unusual going on at the same time one hundred miles farther west. While Harris and his colleagues were still excavating at Roseborough Lake, they began to dig another site near Lake Fork Creek east of Lake Tawakoni. They soon realized that similar artifacts were turning up in both locations. Decorated pottery as well as gunflints and brass sideplates from flintlocks were strikingly similar. Fragments of two French case knives found at the new Gilbert site bore the same maker's marks as two found at Roseborough Lake.[14]

As digging continued, however, significant differences emerged. The new site was not a trading post or even a village. Hundreds of deer bones and hide scrapers suggested that it was a temporary hunting camp probably run by the Kichai, an opportunistic group related to the Caddo.[15] It was the eighteenth-century, deep-woods version of a twenty-first-century factory ship on the high seas. Hunters brought their kills to a central location, skinned them, and packed them onto horses for transport to the trading post. From there, Texas deer hides were shipped to France where craftsmen transformed them into fashionable clothing and accessories.

A key player in this trade network turned out to be the Comanche and other southern plains groups who had surplus horses while most woodland Indians had few. Simply put, French traders had guns and wanted hides. Kichais had hides but needed horses to transport them to market. Comanches had plenty of horses but needed guns. Out of this supply and demand dynamic grew a hide-gun-horse trade network linking the Texas plains and forests to France through trading posts on the Red River. Long before buffalo hunters, ranchers, lumberjacks, or wildcatters tapped into the natural resources of Texas, French traders worked with indigenous entrepreneurs to provide deer and buffalo hides to a European market.

In the years that followed two of the key players in that market met very different fates. Sadly, war and disease took a terrible toll on the Native Americans involved. La Harpe reported that twenty-five hundred people lived in the immediate vicinity of his trading post ten years prior to his arrival. Only four hundred remained by the time he opened for business. The Kadohadacho had been there longest. De Soto saw them in 1541. They had disappeared as a distinct tribe by 1805.[16] The Kichai, who operated the deer processing camp in the woods, were confined to a reservation near the Brazos River in 1855 and were driven out of Texas three years later. About fifty Kichai were reported living with the Wichita in Oklahoma in 1912.[17]

And what of the white-tailed deer—the heart of the hide-gun-horse trade network?

Early on, western explorer Randolph B. Marcy sounded a warning. Passing through southern Texas in 1846, he reported that "thousands of deer were met with daily, and, astonishing as it may appear, it was no uncommon spectacle to see from one to two hundred in a single herd; the prairies seemed literally alive with them; but in 1855 [the year the Kichai went to the reservation] it was seldom that a herd of ten was seen in the same localities . . . I was puzzled to know what had become of them."[18]

The decline accelerated as firearms became increasingly plentiful and more accurate. Local markets for deerskins and venison grew with the population. Distant markets opened up with the advent of railroads and refrigeration.[19] In his book *Texas Natural History: A Century of Change*, noted mammalogist David Schmidly says, "Native deer were virtually eliminated in Texas by the end of the nineteenth century because of indiscriminate slaughter by commercial meat and hide hunters."[20] It took fifty years to reverse the slide toward extinction. Game laws and conservation education slowed the decline. Restocking gradually increased the population. By 1950 deer once again thrived in suitable habitat throughout East Texas.[21]

Three hundred years ago, when deer were plentiful and bears still roamed the woods of northeast Texas, the Red River flowed past thatched houses amid thriving fields of corn, beans, and melons. The French flag flew over wilderness trading posts where Kichai hunters unloaded deer hides from Comanche horses. Today, corn still grows beside the river and ducks still swim in oxbow lakes like the one Bénard de la Harpe described long ago.

Without the hard work and determination of amateur archeologists like R. King Harris, much of what we know about that earlier time would still lie underground. Without the conviction and perseverance of farmers, sportsmen, conservationists, and policy makers, the deer that once roamed the floodplain forest might have disappeared forever.

Meredith and Ethel Edwards are only the most recent in a long line of sturdy folk who have lived within the embrace of the Red River. It has sustained them. It has all but washed them away. After eighteen days in the swirling belly of a flood, Meredith Edwards cursed the river. But he came back. He and Ethel live there still, in a house on a six-foot pile of dirt scraped together when Meredith was a boy; and his father, remembering the past, saw into the future.

WALT DAVIS

A Singular Object from Texas

Hearing more of this singular metal, to which they attributed singular virtues in curing diseases, I resolved to obtain permission to see it if I could and proposed to them to go with me.

ANTHONY GLASS,

Journal of an Indian Trader: Anthony Glass and The Texas Trading Frontier

UPSTREAM FROM MEREDITH EDWARDS'S FARM, the Red River twists and turns through a series of horseshoe bends north of Clarksville, Paris, and Bonham before reaching Denison Dam and massive Lake Texoma. To travel farther upriver is to leave the forests of East Texas behind and enter a region of prairies and crosstimbers. Nomadic bands of Comanche and Kiowa hunted bison here. More sedentary people related to the Caddo planted fields of corn, beans, and melons in the floodplain of the river.[1]

Around 1757, a mixed group of Taovaya and Wichita people established a large village near present-day Spanish Fort, fifty miles east of Wichita Falls and ten miles north of Nocona. An unusual palisade fence, probably inspired by French traders, protected an exceptionally large and diverse population thriving under the enlightened leadership of a Taovaya chief named Awahakei. Historian Dan Flores calls it "the most important Euroamerican trade base on the Southern Plains."[2] It was also the place where an American trader in 1808 first heard of a "singular object" that would spark an international incident and lead to a startling scientific discovery.

The "singular object" before leaving Texas

John Sibley, an Indian agent stationed in Natchitoches, Louisiana, received word that chief Awahakei was interested in trading with Americans. Sibley authorized Anthony Glass to make the trip deep into what was technically New Spain, and required him to keep a written record of his travels. Glass arrived in the village on August 11, 1808, and soon befriended a Spaniard known as Tatesuck. Captured as a child and raised by the Indians, Tatesuck elected to stay with his adopted people rather than return to his home when given a chance. Glass described him as, "the most distinguished man in the nation as a warrior and the first Leader of war parties . . . a Brave, Subtle and intrepid man."[3] Tatesuck told Glass of a singular object "some days journey distant to the southward on the waters of River Brassos [Brazos]." The object was venerated for its ability to cure diseases. More significant to Glass, it was described as being a metal, like iron, that did not rust. The trader thought it might be "Platina [platinum] or something of great value, no white man at this time had seen it."[4]

Glass persuaded Tatesuck to take him to see this wonder. They left the village on October 3, traveled southwest, and two weeks later Glass recorded in his journal:

We approached the place where the metal was; the Indians observing considerable ceremony as they approached. We found it resting on its heaviest end and leaning towards one side and under it were some Pipes and Trinkets which had been placed there by some Indians who had been healed by visiting it. The mass was but very little bedded in the place where we found it. There is no reason to think it had ever been moved by man. It had the colour of Iron, but no rust upon it. The Indians had contrived with Chisels they had made of old files to cut off some small pieces which they had hammered out to their fancy . . . it was obedient to the magnet—. Very malable [sic] would take a brilliant polish and give fire with a flint. I had some scales cut off and left it.[5]

Glass went on to capture a large herd of Texas mustangs, and the following March he and his men started the long trip home. Arriving in Natchitoches the first week of May 1809, the trader delivered to Indian agent Sibley the journal in which he had recorded the nature of the land he explored and the people who inhabited it. On May 10, Sibley sent an urgent letter to U.S. Secretary of War William Eustis reporting that Glass:

> Saw in Large Masses of many thousands of pounds weight a Singular Kind of Mineral . . . If it is not Platina, I do not know what it is; I have Some of it in my possession & have Sent a piece of it to Philadelphia to be tried. Capt. Glass says an hundred Thousand pounds of it Could be Obtained should it prove Valuable.[6]

Before June ended some of Glass's men, led by George Schamp and Ezra McCall, formed an expedition to retrieve the mineralogical wonder and secured Sibley's official blessing and financial support. Their plan was to return to the Taovaya-Wichita village, negotiate the purchase of the sacred stone, load it onto a wagon, transport it to the Red River, float it by canoe four hundred miles downstream to Natchitoches, sell it, and reap a rich reward for their Herculean effort. Other veterans of the Glass expedition had a simpler plan—head straight for the metal, steal it from the Indians, and sell it to the highest bidder. Rumors of these illegal incursions into foreign territory reached San Antonio by early fall, and a Spanish expedition set out to thwart both American plans.[7]

Veteran plainsman John Davis led the unofficial expedition and reached the metal first. However, without a wagon for transport, his men were unable to ferret it away. Instead, they rolled it a short distance, buried it, and camouflaged the site, planning to return with the necessary equipment. A few days later, the official expedition, having bought the metal, arrived on the scene and found it missing. A suspicious clump of grass led them to the hiding place. They dug it up and went to work with tools brought for the purpose to build a "truck wagon" on site. Using saplings for levers, they loaded the metal onto the wagon. Six horses strained to set the prize in motion.[8]

The men wanted to escape Spanish territory before their treasure was confiscated, so they turned north for the Red River instead of east for Natchitoches. Along the way, equally entrepreneurial Indians stole the expedition's horses, leaving the men afoot with an immovable payload. Schamp and a man named Piper walked four hundred miles back to Natchitoches, secured horses, and returned for their prize.[9] Meanwhile the fifty-two-man Spanish cavalry patrol was on its way north to intercept them. After traveling through places we now call Waco and Fort Worth without encountering any Anglo-Americans, the Spaniards returned to San Antonio empty-handed.[10]

By late October, the official expedition and the metal reached the banks of the Red River. The men felled a large walnut tree and hollowed it out to make a freight canoe substantial enough to carry their booty downriver to Natchitoches. Details of the seven-month journey that followed went unrecorded. Somehow they found a way around the notorious log jams of the Red River, avoided capsizing and losing their cargo, and escaped notice by the various parties hoping to intercept them and relieve them of their prize.

On June 4, 1810, one year after their departure, the expedition returned to Natchitoches creating a sensation that lasted another twelve months. Speculators offered small fortunes for their find. But expedition members held out, convinced that they would all be wealthy men once their metal was properly assayed.[11]

We know where the singular object from Texas ended its journey out of the wilderness—Natchitoches, Louisiana. We know where the river portion of that journey began—somewhere near Spanish Fort, Texas. What we do not know, and probably never will, is where the sacred stone was when Anthony Glass first saw it and where Schamp and McCall loaded it onto their wagon. Glass said it was near the Brazos River, and historian Dan Flores believes it was close to present-day Albany, Texas. Wanting to make tangible contact with this two hundred-year-old saga, Isabel and I visit the site of the Taovaya-Wichita village, the one scene of action that can be located with some assurance. But even a certainty turns out to be more elusive than we expect.

☙

We drive into Nocona on a cold and drizzly February day to meet Robert Fenoglio. He may be able to tell us how to find the famous village where the story of the singular object began. Walking into his Ranch House Café and Filling Station, we are confronted by a sign warning, "This is not Burger King, you don't get it your way, you get it my way, or you don't get the damn thing at all." Nailed to the wall behind the griddle, next to a rack of knives, is what looks like a leather pouch cradling two golf balls. The not-so-subtle reminder of how bulls become steers has us just a little apprehensive about how Fenoglio will react to our questions.

Sporting a grease-stained cowboy hat and red apron, he proves to be friendly and forthcoming, allows us to record our conversation, and even poses for a photograph. We leave with directions to the village site, a list of people to contact, and information about a private collection of artifacts gleaned from the farm fields that replaced the once-famous Indian metropolis. Heeding Fenoglio's warning not to wander off onto the muddy ranch roads in this kind of weather, we stick to pavement and head north on FM 103 to the steady beat of windshield wipers.

Signs to the Spanish Fort cemetery hint that we are getting close. We round a bend and there it is—a lonesome collection of neglected farmhouses, scattered house trailers, and a boarded-up store. The sign on the storefront reads, "Hutsons's Hunters Supplies: Spanish Fort Coon Hunters Association." A placard on the front door advertises, "Red Adair Co., Oilwell Fires—Blowouts." Another warns, "This Property Protected by a 12 Gauge Shotgun." We are beginning to get the idea that folks in this part of Texas are a little wary of strangers. Across the road from the store sprawls an open grassy area with picnic shelter and flagpole.

Our first clue that we are close to the Taovaya-Wichita village is a decidedly out-of-place 1936 Art Déco monument of pink Texas granite. Sculptor Raoul Sosset's bronze bas-relief of a stylized Indian with bow and war club stands guard over an inscription: "The Town of Spanish Fort occupies the site of an ancient Taovayas village, scene of the first severe defeat of Spanish troops by Indians in 1759 . . . Permanent white settlement began in this vicinity after 1850." In another place the reader is encouraged to "let the grandeur of the pioneer be discerned in the safety he has secured, in the good he has accomplished, in the civilization he has established."

We hear a more sober account of the town from retired teacher and goat farmer Adrian Hill, who lives in Spanish Fort with his wife, Cliffie. They say nearby rich bottomland along the Red River once supported ten large farm families. Five hundred people called Spanish Fort home. With the advent of mechanized row farming, three families could do the work of ten, and the rural population declined. After the road to Nocona was paved, folks found it more convenient to live in town and drive out to the farm. Only forty-six people live in Spanish Fort today.

Hill remembers something of his childhood that we find fascinating. As a boy he frequently walked the fields where the "old Indian village" once stood. He picked up beads "by the handful" and sold them to Joe Benton—one of the names Fenoglio had mentioned back in Nocona. Benton began collecting arrowheads when he was a boy and later bought artifacts from locals. According to Fenoglio, he amassed a large collection that professional archeologists have described as one of the best in the state. We realize that we are talking to one of Benton's paid collectors.

Later we drive out to the fields along Village Creek where Hill says he found hundreds of beads. Cattle graze in close-cropped pastures. It is beautiful rolling country with no hint of the battles fought here in front of the famous stockaded village. Maybe we will find more tangible evidence in Joe Benton's collection.

We return to Nocona and drive out 11th Street to where the town ends, and ranch land begins. Brick gateposts topped with Spanish tile flank a cattle guard marking the entrance to the Benton-Whiteside Ranch. Beyond the gate, a gravel road curves up a hill, past a stately grove of post oaks, to a sprawling ranch house. Clarice Whiteside greets us in a tailored red and black outfit that makes us regret our jeans and muddy boots. Clarice is Joe Benton's daughter. She inherited the ranch after her father died, and with it, his museum full of artifacts.

We follow Mrs. Whiteside to a separate brick building where a stuffed longhorn stands guard just inside the front door. Beyond is a room lined floor to ceiling with glass-front bookcases. Display cabinets fill the rest of the space, leaving only narrow pathways for visitors. Peering through glass frosted with dust, we finally find what we have been looking for–tangible evidence of the metropolis on the Red River, the Taovaya-Wichita village.

Benton organized his artifacts by type, with pottery in some cases, projectile points in others. Dozens of metal arrowheads provide sure evidence of contact with non-native traders. We wonder if any of the metal came from the object Schamp and McCall plucked from the prairie. Bits and pieces of swords and knives are surprisingly common, as are trigger guards and hammers from flint-lock rifles. There are copper kettles, scores of clay pipes, and trade beads by the hundreds–somewhere among them the beads Adrian Hill picked up as a boy.

Some artifacts suggest a close tie to the French trading posts established downstream by Grappe and La Harpe. Fired clay horse figurines, wooden-handled metal hide scrapers, and butt plates from French flint-lock rifles are similar to those found in the Roseborough Lake site near Meredith Edwards's farm.[12]

But the object that once triggered an international incident is not in Joe Benton's collection. The sacred metal that Tatesuck showed to Anthony Glass went downriver in a dugout canoe two hundred years ago. What happened to the "singular object" from Texas after it reached Natchitoches?

※

Schamp, McCall, and their partners decided to ship it to New York where it could be assayed, its value determined, and their fortunes secured.[13] The healing stone of the Taovaya, Wichita, and Comanche—the priceless metal of the Anglo-Americans and their government—embarked on a journey that would bring heartbreaking disappointment to some and breathtaking discovery to others.

Months passed before Sibley received the bad news and passed it on to Schamp and McCall. The assayer in New York declared that the metal was iron, not platinum, and virtually worthless. Imagined fortunes disappeared in the space of a breath. The men who risked life and limb for a year to bring the thing out of Texas never accepted the verdict and died believing they had been duped.

But the arrival of the metallic object from Texas coincided with the arrival of an outlandish idea circulating in scholarly circles on the East Coast and in Europe. For some time, scientists had been puzzled by similar objects whose origins they could not explain. A few suggested that these curiosities did not originate on earth but in outer space. When they entered earth's atmosphere, they created the streaks of light called meteors. If they survived the fiery plunge, they were called meteorites.

Professor Benjamin Silliman of Yale University came to this conclusion after examining fragments from a spectacular meteor shower that hit Connecticut in 1807, the year before Glass saw the sacred stone in Texas. Silliman was excited to learn of a newly discovered mass of metal whose properties he recognized and whose weight far exceeded anything known to science. But, he was not the only one to realize what had been found. Noted mineralogist George Gibbs bought the Red River meteorite just before it was to be shipped to Europe and sold as a New World curiosity.

Professor Silliman examined "Red River," the object's new name, and set out to learn all he could about its discovery. He corresponded with Sibley in Natchitoches, who told him of the journal Glass kept during his time in Texas. Silliman asked for a copy, and Sibley obliged. The original has since been lost, and only the facsimile remains to keep the story alive.

Having already fallen from the sky, survived a canoe trip down a wilderness river, and traveled to New York via New Orleans, Red River's journey was not yet over. In 1820, Gibbs loaned what was, at the time, the largest meteorite ever found in North America to the Lyceum of Natural History in New York. When Gibbs died, his widow gave it to the Cabinet of Mineralogy at Yale; and in 1877, it was transferred to the Peabody Museum of Natural History where it resides today.

The singular object from Texas had seen a lot of the grit, determination, greed, and devotion of the human race. Geographer William Darby met several of the men who brought the meteorite out of the wilderness and gave it to the civilized world. Reflecting on their rejection of the assay results that robbed them of an imagined fortune, Darby said, "The persons engaged were in general too ignorant to understand the decisive results of such tests, and unwilling to abandon a pleasing delusion; and the Cabinet of science stands indebted to their infatuation for its possession."[14]

✤

Isabel and I decide that it is high time for a Texas delegation to go back East, pay its respects to Red River, and confirm that our meteorite is being well cared for. We fly to New Haven, Connecticut, and check into a hotel across the street from the university. We have arranged an appointment with Barbara Narendra in the Meteorite and Planetary Science Department of the Peabody Museum. She is intimately acquainted with the Peabody's meteorite collection and is an old friend of Red River.

The museum is housed in an impressive Gothic Revival building complete with decorative roof pinnacles and a pointed arch over the entrance. Narendra greets us just inside. "Follow me," she says, indicating that it is a bit of a hike to Red River's temporary home in the astronomy building. It seems that while they are preparing a new meteorite exhibit, Red River has to stay elsewhere.

We enter a plain brick and glass building and ride the elevator to the second floor. The doors slide open to a dimly-lit lounge with cinder block walls, institutional gray tables, and orange vinyl chairs. There, in front of a window on a makeshift table with pipe legs, resides the holy grail of Sibley, Schamp, and McCall–the sacred object Glass found on the Texas plains.

A dark rust-colored patina hides its shiny metallic surface. Pock-marked from its fiery ride through Earth's atmosphere, it is also scarred from the gouges of worshipers taking away flakes of metal for arrow points and amulets. One end has been amputated, cut into small pieces, and shared with universities around the world. Chunks of it now reside in Vienna, Calcutta, Moscow, Fort Worth, and the Vatican.[15] An inscription is carved into the cut end of it.

IN MEMORY OF

George Gibbs

A LOVER OF

SCIENCE

AND HIS

COUNTRY

PRESENTED TO

Yale College

By

LAURA W. GIBBS, 1835

———

Meteoric Iron of Texas

WEIGHT 1635 LBS.

Clearly the singular object from Texas has suffered well-intentioned indignities, but it has survived and has an honored place in a venerable museum that appreciates its importance.

Before we leave, Narendra escorts us to the science library to read some of Professor Silliman's earliest scientific descriptions of the meteorite. There we make a chilling discovery. Included among the scientific papers is a clipping from the New York Daily Tribune, August 11, 1877. According to the unnamed reporter: "One of the meteorites under Prof. Dana's care has a history that points a moral for New-Yorkers. It had been deposited with the Lyceum of Natural History in New-York, by Mr. George Gibbs, but by some inexplicable neglect was allowed to lie for years uncared for in City Hall Park. One day, when a Fall election made it necessary to find work for unemployed voters, some Irishmen were ordered to bury this great black stone out of sight. They had dug a hole for the purpose, and the meteorite was about to disappear forever from human view when Mrs. Gibbs interposed, rescued it and sent it to Yale College, where it has ever since borne the name of the donor, being known as the Gibbs meteorite."[16]

In spite of greed and risk and negligence, the meteorite, Red River, survives. Out of ignorance and delusion came a scientific breakthrough. From the wilds of Texas came a singular object, and it arrived from outer space.

WALT DAVIS

Death in the Redbeds

The summer temperatures approximate those of hell. Almost all the animals bite or sting. Water is scarce and usually unpleasant . . . but the people of the region are among the finest, and the fossil reptiles to be found there are the world's best.

ALFRED SHERWOOD ROMER,

"Fossil Collecting in the Texas Redbeds"

O N A HOT AUGUST DAY, months after our trip to New Haven and our winter visit to Spanish Fort, Isabel and I return to the Red River Valley to continue our journey along the edge of Texas. U.S. Highway 82 takes us through Nocona, Ringgold, and Henrietta, where we pick up U.S. 287 to Wichita Falls. According to *A Historical Atlas of Texas*, we have just passed from a region of the state where rainfall is "usually adequate" into one where it is "critical."[1] Before us stretches the southern Great Plains—the epic outdoor stage upon which so much of the history of the American West unfolded. We are on the trail of an obscure player in that drama who made a startling scientific discovery. In 1876, Jacob Boll unearthed a fossil skull that opened the door to a time long past, when this part of Texas was a steaming tropical swamp.[2]

A few miles west of Electra, we turn north on FM 1763, a two-lane blacktop that parallels the Pease River. There was no road at all when Jacob Boll came this way in the waning days of the cattle drives. You still see a few pet longhorns from time to time, but the open range has been replaced by a checkerboard of dry-land farms where cotton, peanuts, and

Eryops *in a Permian swamp*

grain sorghum grow in soil the color of pulverized clay pots. Up ahead, two half-grown coyote pups gambol across the road followed by their haggard mama. The weatherman predicts a high today between 106 degrees and 110 degrees. Dust devils spin like dervishes in the shimmering heat.

⁂

The U.S. Cavalry was still fighting Comanche, Kiowa, and Cheyenne warriors on the Texas plains in the decade following the Civil War. It was an unlikely time and a dangerous place to find a university-trained Swiss naturalist hunting for rocks, bugs, and fossils. Jacob Boll regularly sent large collections of such things to his friend and mentor Louis Agassiz, founder of the Museum of Comparative Zoology at Harvard College in Cambridge, Massachusetts.

In 1870, Boll shipped a spectacular collection of Texas insects to the museum—fifteen thousand specimens representing sixteen hundred species. He picked up most of the moths and butterflies as chrysalises or raised them from caterpillars, feeding them until they metamorphosed into adults.[3] He did significant field research for the U.S. Entomological Commission, and when the Texas governor and the legislature considered establishing a state geological survey, Jacob Boll was their choice to head it up.[4]

He was a small man with full beard and grayish-blue eyes, who often wore a feathered Swiss *alpenhut* and long yellow linen duster. Biographer Samuel Geiser pictures him returning from a long walk in the country: "Over his shoulder hangs a naturalist's tin collecting box. In one hand is gathered an insect net and a looped stick for collecting snakes and lizards, while in the other hand he carries a turtle by the leg."[5] Boll was a curiosity to his Dallas neighbors. But had he been a military man, he would have been awarded a Medal of Honor for the important work he did under dangerous circumstances.

In 1877 Boll met a man who sent him on his most hazardous field trip to date. Edward Drinker Cope came to Dallas on a recruiting trip. Locked in fierce competition with fellow paleontologist Othniel C. Marsh to describe new species of prehistoric animals, Cope needed a collector to explore northwestern Texas. He was willing to pay three hundred dollars a month plus expenses. In addition he would provide a span of mules, double harness, and wagon.[6]

Boll took the job and gave his new employer some bones he had collected along Onion Creek, near present-day Archer City. In a letter to his wife, Cope reported meeting a "German" naturalist in Dallas who had given him some "very fine objects." "In fact," he wrote, "I learned of wonderful things from him, which I will use in the future."[7]

Before the year was out, Cope published the description of a new species of prehistoric amphibian in the *Proceedings of the American Philosophical Society*. He named the animal *Eryops megacephala*, noting that "this interesting fossil was found in the Triassic [*sic*] formation of Texas by my friend Jacob Boll."[8] Their partnership netted a total of thirty-two new species of reptiles and amphibians from what would come to be known as the Permian redbeds of Texas.

All too soon their collaboration came to a tragic end. According to scientific historian Samuel Geiser: "Death came to the explorer in the dugout hut of a collecting camp on the Pease River near its confluence with the Red River on September 29, 1880. Here, surrounded by the fossils he had collected, and attended only by his teamster—a mere boy terrified by the sufferings of the naturalist—Boll succumbed to peritonitis after an illness of ten days."[9]

Boll had ventured far beyond the reach of medical help when appendicitis struck him down. The teamster buried his employer in a temporary grave and drove the wagon back to Henrietta and civilization—a five-day trip. Henry Boll returned with a coffin, unearthed his brother's body, and brought it back to Dallas for proper burial in Greenwood Cemetery.[10]

Isabel and I are trying to retrace that fatal journey and locate some of the ancient red rock outcrops that lured Boll to his untimely death. The prairie landscape he traversed has long since disappeared. Cattle and plows have seen to that. Today, the most conspicuous landmark in the area is the Crown Quality grain elevator in Vernon. In this flat country it can be seen for miles in every direction.

We wait for an east-bound coal train to clear the Burlington Northern tracks, then drive north on U.S. 283 and cross the silt-laden Pease River flowing red between gray-green walls of feathery salt cedar. On the far side of the bridge we find what Boll was looking for—an outcrop of what he called the "Texas redbeds."

Three layers are exposed: six feet of crumbly brick-red clay on the bottom, a one-foot-thick bed of gravel in between, and four or five feet of lighter red sand on top. Only one thing is missing—fossils. There is nothing here to interest a man paid to collect prehistoric animal remains. We turn the truck south toward Onion Creek where Boll made some of his first, and most important, discoveries. Finding the remains of long-dead animals was just the beginning of a story that unfolds like a cold case murder mystery—a really cold case—almost three hundred million years cold.

It is late afternoon when Isabel and I arrive in Archer City. The setting sun casts deceiving shadows across the Archer County courthouse lawn—shadows that look cool but aren't. We check ourselves into the Spur Hotel. The manager has already left for the day, so we haul our bags up two flights of stairs to room nine on the third floor. A note says we will be the only guests tonight and asks that we lock the front door when we go to bed. After cold beer in the empty hotel lobby, we walk over to the Onion Creek Grill for supper.

John Wayne is already in the house, looking down from a handful of movie posters on the wall. The radio is tuned to KARL in Wichita (locals never use the town's full name), and George Strait is singing. I pass up #22 on the menu—the Onion Creek Burger—"Double Meat and Cheese, Lettuce, Tomato, Grilled Onions, Jalapenos, $5.00." Isabel orders a chicken strip basket, and I opt for a barbecue plate.

According to the menu cover, "Onion Creek . . . traverses gently rolling terrain, surfaced by clay and sandy loam that support scrub brush, mesquite, cacti, and grasses. The area has been used for rangeland." That's like saying the Alamo is an abandoned church. Scratch the surface anywhere in Archer County, and it will bleed history. Dig and you will find stories that challenge the imagination. We know. We have the book: *Trails Through Archer* by Jack Loftin.

The author has agreed to meet us at seven sharp tomorrow morning and take us to the place where Boll found the skull that made scientific history. Better than that, Loftin will take us to even more prolific sites where a new generation of fossil detectives has pieced together an incredible story. It took place before the age of dinosaurs; before the Rocky Mountains rose up in the west, or the land split apart to make way for the Atlantic Ocean.

Jack Loftin is a solidly built man with a kind but serious face. He has the alert eyes and ample ears of a man equipped to see and hear things others might miss and strong hands for hanging on tight. Dressed in jeans, cowboy boots, and a black-and-white checkered shirt, he wears a sweat-stained cap from "ABC Transmission and Motor Company." Eyeglasses rest in a vinyl case in his shirt pocket, and a gray plastic digital watch fits tightly around his thick left wrist.

He pulls a battered, thirty-two-ounce, plastic drink bottle from the front seat of his car and asks, "Do you have plenty of water? I thought this was full but it isn't." Loftin introduces his friend Steven Young, an amateur archeologist, who is going along today to learn a little paleontology. Steven and Isabel squeeze onto the back bench of our extended-cab pickup. I drive, and Loftin keeps up a steady commentary from the passenger's seat.

Riding around with Jack Loftin is like moving the cursor around an interactive computer map. Click on any spot and up pops a message telling the history of the place. For instance, Loftin notices a blackened spot beside the road and tells me to pull over.

"I thought this was gone," he says, as if locating a lost friend. "Until this drought the grass was so high you couldn't see it."

We gather around a pile of clinkers, slag, and fire-scorched brick.

"This was the McCracken and Baggett Bit Shop. For years they did all kinds of metal work for people around here. During the oil boom they sharpened drilling bits—the kind you had to heat in a forge and beat into shape with a sledge hammer."

Loftin stoops to pick up something.

"See these bricks? These are fire brick from the forge. I'm going to take one to put in the museum."

Jack Loftin is on a mission to remember. It pains him to see this fragment of history disappear under the grass and sink back into the earth. The brick will keep the story of the blacksmiths alive, at least for a while. The "rememberer" will add it to the collection of the Archer County Museum, of which he is chief curator.

We stop again at the place where Bell Road climbs out of the valley of Onion Creek. Loftin points to the west and asks,

"Can you see that ridge in the distance?"

I strain to pick out any break in the monotony of the rangeland sprawling in all directions.

"You're not looking where I'm pointing," he says impatiently. "Look right where my finger is."

He is standing behind me now, his arm arching over my head, his finger right in front of my eyes. Beyond that finger I can just make out a blip on the horizon—a sliver of gray above the red and green of dirt and mesquite.

"Yes, I see it now."

"That's the Citadel. That's how I know this is the place where Boll found *Eryops*."

Loftin believes that Jacob Boll found his fossil bonanza by following the wagon tracks of an earlier expedition looking for copper ore. M. K. Kellogg and his party spent the night of July 29, 1872, camped on Onion Creek. The next morning, riding up a hill, Kellog saw in the distance "a fine fortress-like work commanding extended views—a prominent landmark for many miles."[11] According to Loftin we are now standing on the only hill along that creek providing a view of the "prominent landmark" now known as the Citadel. If Kellogg passed this way, then so did Jacob Boll.

"Where on Onion Creek did Boll find the *Eryops* skull?" I ask.

"About a mile-and-a-half from here, around that bend you can see in the distance, on the north side of the valley."

We are near the spot where Jacob Boll made his life-changing find. Take away the mesquite, and we are looking at the same landscape he did. We have come as close as possible to the beginning and the end of Jacob Boll's brief but successful fossil-hunting career.

Interest in the prehistoric animals of the Texas redbeds, however, did not end in that dugout camp on the Pease River. Cope hired other collectors who found other bones in many more locations. Rather than solving an age-old mystery, Boll merely brought it to light. Were this a murder case, Boll would be credited with finding the first victim, but as the body count climbed past thirty, other fossil detectives wanted to know what killed so many, how they were related in life, and what their world was like so long ago.

In 1923, a young man from Harvard followed Boll's trail into the Texas redbeds. His name was Alfred Sherwood Romer, and he would spend almost fifty years combing through the evidence, finding more bones, and assembling them into beautifully articulated skeletons. Romer wanted to know what it was like for the animals that pioneered life on dry land—early reptiles and amphibians.

Important clues often turned up in "redbed" deposits found in several places around the world. But, according to Romer: "Nowhere are they better exposed or richer in fossils than in northern Texas. In these beds are numerous amphibians, not far removed from the first backboned animals which ventured out of water onto land. Here, too, are found the oldest well-preserved reptiles just beginning the evolutionary story of that group . . ."[12]

Toward the end of his career, Romer told Jack Loftin that his best find was the Geraldine bone bed where, in 1939, "we found . . . over an area 30 or 40 feet square . . . within a foot or so of the surface, a whole mass of reptilian and amphibian bones, mostly in the form of articulated skeletons of *Eryops* . . . and *Edaphosaurus* . . . It was a spectacular find. But some years later when I went back there, I found to my astonishment that no trace of our dig could be found."[13]

"Now this is where Geraldine was," Loftin says as we roll to a stop where two dirt roads cross in a mesquite thicket. "This was one of those land speculation schemes that went bust when they found out there wasn't enough water. The Geraldine bone bed is named for it."

Loftin has relocated the lost dig site northwest of Archer City, checked the location with a GPS unit, and driven a stake in the ground to make it easy to find it again. He is taking us to see Romer's "best find." From the intersection of Geraldine and River Roads just north of the Little Wichita River, we drive on to a place where a pipeline crosses the road. Loftin gets out, opens a gate, and motions me through.

Years ago bulldozers pushed the brush aside to make way for the pipeline. The scrape has since scabbed over with buffalo grass. What looks like a long brown lawn walled in by brush runs straight from our bumper to the horizon. Loftin cautions against running over the innocent-looking mesquite saplings sprouting up between the tire tracks ahead. If a thorn punctures a tire we will be changing a flat in all this heat. After ten minutes of careful maneuvering through a mine-field of thorns, Loftin calls a halt: "We'll walk from here."

Romer has vividly described our destination: "The summer temperatures approximate those of Hell. Almost all the animals and plants bite or sting. Water is scarce and usually unpleasant either before or after taking, or both. But the people of the region are among the finest, and the fossil reptiles to be found there are the world's best."[14]

Right away we are confronted with the sharp truth of his description. Prickly pear and pencil cactus grow in profusion. The latter cactus sports inch-long thorns like miniature knitting needles complete with the hook on the end. Extract one from an arm or leg, and that little hook will pull the skin with it before tearing loose with a stinging snap. Harder to see and even more diabolical are the aptly-named horse-cripplers, a squatty species of barrel cactus that bulges from the ground with rosettes of thorns stout enough to penetrate a hoof, a boot, even a tire.

"Looks like good rattlesnake habitat," Isabel warns. The place has diamondback written all over it—hot, dry, lots of flat rocks. Scattered piles of sticks, prickly pear pads, and mesquite beans are sure signs of a rattlesnake delicacy—woodrat. All eyes scour the ground as we pick our way through the brush.

"Here it is," Loftin shouts, pointing to an orange pipe planted in the ground. "We had a little trouble finding it but checked it out with a GPS. This is the Geraldine bonebed. If you watch real close we might find you a piece."

We fan out, heads down, trying to detect bone in red dirt at our feet.

"OK, here's you a little piece. Here, let the lady pick it up."

Isabel stoops to pluck a dark, maroon-colored rock from the ground.

"That's a rib . . . that's right down where the rib ties on."

I spot a similar piece nearby and hand it to Loftin.

"This is the spine of an *Edaphosaur*. See that little tit? That's where the crossbar tied on. That's how you tell the difference between an *Edaphosaur* and a *Dimetrodon* spine."

Both animals had "sails" on their backs–vertical webs of skin held up by bony spines as much as three feet long. The *Edaphosaur* is sometimes called the ship-lizard because the crossbars on its spines suggest spars on the mast of a ship.

"Right in front of you, Ma'am," Loftin says. "I see a piece."

"Is it a tooth?" Isabel asks.

"It is. That's a good find. That's a tooth of a *Dimetrodon,* one of those big ones."

Steven has been sorting through a pile of bone and calls us over to take a look. "What happened here?" he asks.

"I'll tell you why they're here. Sander told those kids to leave those fossils. They took some, but he told them to leave some so we could find this place next time."

The "Sander" Loftin mentions is a paleontologist from Zurich (P. Martin Sander) who has been studying the Geraldine site. The "kids" are Sander's student assistants.

"Now what's this?" I ask. "This is a different color."

"The stuff is taking on iron, see?" Loftin rolls the fragment over with his thumb. "That's another piece right above the backbone . . . one of those lizards." He mentally sorts through the possibilities. "I'm not sure." He hesitates, then looks up and concludes, "It's probably *Eryops*."

Here at last is the beast that started it all–*Eryops megacephala*–the "interesting fossil" E. D. Cope's friend, Jacob Boll, found in Texas. Alfred Sherwood Romer's best find, the Geraldine bone bed, is still giving up clues about the tragic event that killed and then preserved dozens of animals an unimaginably long time ago.

Something scurries under a rock. Loftin glances my way, smiles; and, looking toward Isabel, whispers, "Let's show her." I'm not sure what he saw, but as Isabel approaches, he bends down, grabs the far edge of a big flat rock and heaves it over. A scaly tail is coiled beneath, and the head on the other end is three fingers wide. Then it runs. "Red-headed mountain boomer!" Loftin shouts, as a large male collared lizard sprints away, clattering over the bones of its ancestors.

✺

The Geraldine bone bed has puzzled paleontologists since the day it was discovered. At least forty-four skeletons have been removed from a relatively small area. Imagine a crime scene with that many bodies piled up in a space roughly twenty by thirty-five feet. But these victims are decidedly un-human. One (*Eryops*) looked like a two hundred-pound frog with teeth and tail, except that it lumbered along spraddle-legged instead of hopping. Another (*Dimetrodon*) was a lizard-shaped but alligator-sized carnivore with a spectacular leathery sail on its back.[15]

As fossil evidence accumulated, the mystery deepened. Many of the animals (lungfish and freshwater sharks) lived in water, some (*Archeria* and *Eryops*) were amphibious, still others (*Dimetrodon* and *Edaphosaurus*) lived on land. Scavengers did not scatter the bones as they often do, and many of the skeletons lay parallel to one another. Bits of charcoal were found among fragments of plant leaves, stems, and seeds.[16]

P. Martin Sander, the paleontologist whose assistants left the bone pile at Geraldine, has a theory about what happened. The story begins almost three hundred million years ago in a steamy tropical swamp. Tree-sized ferns and towering horsetail clubs dominated the landscape instead of today's mesquite and prickly pear. One day a forest fire swept through the area, as they still do today in the Okeefenokee Swamp and the Everglades. Animals choked to death in the poisonous smoke or succumbed to the scorching heat. Bodies of some victims floated down a stream into a pond where they stacked up like driftwood, parallel to the shoreline. Within months, a flood buried all evidence of the disaster in a protective layer of sediment.[17]

{ 201 }

As the eons passed, sediment turned to rock and bones fossilized. During this time the Geraldine site rode on the back of the North American tectonic plate as the forces of continental drift pushed it slowly northwest from a point five hundred miles south of the equator where the story began.[18]

As we climb back into the truck, minds reeling from the immensity of time and geography we have just encountered, Jack Loftin suggests we take a look at some of the evidence for this epic story in the Archer County Museum. The temperature has been inching up all morning, and the sun is directly overhead by the time we arrive at the brown sandstone building that once served as the Archer County Jail. A red tile roof caps the third story with windows secured by bars. Keys jingle and the door rattles as Loftin ushers us from the heat and glare of a Texas summer into the barely cooler shade of the museum.

As our eyes adjust to the dark interior, we can see that every square inch of wall space is covered with photographs, charts, posters, and labels. Artifacts fill exhibit cases packed together so tightly that we move single file through the rooms. Chunks of local history rest in piles on the floor, and all is covered with a thin layer of red dust. The march of time has stopped to take a breath here. The air is still. Beads of sweat gather on Loftin's forehead.

He pauses at an open shelf where empty eyes stare back from a flattened skull shorter but wider than that of an alligator. It is a replica of an *Eryops* skull that Loftin made after years of collecting bits and pieces like the ones we found earlier this morning. With perspiration dripping from the end of his nose, our guide moves on to a dusty glass case in which *Edaphosaur* bones laid end-to-end give a rough impression of the living animal. The room is stuffed with fossils found over the years and brought here for safekeeping. Jack Loftin stands proudly in this stifling memorial to the deep past. It is the product of a lifelong passion to save the evidence so the story can be passed on.

❀

Results of a similar passion are displayed in another museum fifteen hundred miles away, and we have come here to see the remains of the animals that Romer dug from the earth—the clues Sander used to reconstruct an ancient tragedy. Cambridge, Massachusetts, is as cool and shady as Archer City was hot and dry. The Museum of Comparative Zoology, on the Harvard University campus, fills three floors of a brick building the color of the Texas redbeds. Block letters over the arched entrance spell out "Agassiz Hall" in honor of the museum's founder and Jacob Boll's old mentor, Louis Agassiz. Inside we discover a relic of another time—a cabinet of curiosities gathered from around the world. Skeletons of whales and porpoises hang from the ceiling. Glass cases trimmed in dark wood enshrine exotic animals—giraffe, gorilla, rhinoceros, and okapi.

We pass a three-foot-long, fish-like creature suspended in a covered aquarium filled with yellowish liquid. According to the label, the *Coelacanth* was thought to have become extinct sixty-five million years ago, until fishermen pulled one up off the coast of South Africa in 1939. Around the corner from the nightmarish skeleton of *Zeugladon,* a fossil whale with teeth worthy of *T. rex,* is the quiet alcove we have been looking for. Here, in the "Texas Room," Alfred Sherwood Romer deposited the finest specimens gleaned from over forty spring and summer field trips to Texas between 1926 and 1973.[19]

Ribs drape in gentle curves from a *Dimetrodon's* reassembled backbone, and the spines that supported its dramatic sail are in their proper place again after almost three hundred million years. A flat-headed, spraddle-legged *Eryops,* has been cobbled together from thousands of fragments of broken bone. The reconstructed skeletons are graceful and serene—a far cry from the reeking tangle of bloated bodies Sander described.

Today, Charles Schaff manages the museum's vertebrate paleontology collections. He takes us behind the scenes to see where much of this remarkable work was done. A sepia-toned portrait of Alexander Drinker Cope hangs over the door to the collection room as if to bless those who enter. Snapshots of field trips fill a bulletin board. The dirty, sweat-soaked men look more like death march survivors than scientists. In one photo, Dr. Romer sits wearily on the running board of a car. He could be a bit player on the set of *Grapes of Wrath.*

Gray metal cabinets stacked two-high are arranged in rows in this scientific morgue. Schaff opens the door to a case marked "Geraldine Site" and pulls out one of twelve drawers. It is lined with shallow boxes, each filled with fossils bearing tiny numbers inscribed in white ink. Another drawer contains hundreds of *Edaphosaur* sail bones, none more than three inches long, most an inch or less. To reconstruct the skeletons we saw on exhibit, Romer and his assistants reassembled thousands of fragments like these. And we are looking at only one site from one period of geologic time.

Near the collection room, Dr. Romer's office remains unchanged since his death in 1973. It is a scientific time capsule. Floor-to-ceiling bookshelves are crammed with reprint boxes, journals, and scientific texts. Portraits of distinguished paleontologists hang on one wall. Among them is a face we recognize—Jacob Boll. Romer paid tribute to the man whose scientific passion cost him his life but also introduced the fossil riches of Texas to the scientific world. Beside the portrait is a small black shadowbox enclosing a thumb-sized rock. Peering through the glass we can just make out an inscription, "First Fossil Bone from Redbeds, Collected by Jacob Boll, 1871."

The story of the Geraldine bone bed is only one of many recorded in the redbeds of north-central Texas. Every time it rains, evidence for other episodes washes from the ground and tumbles down Onion Creek, the Little Wichita, and the Pease. Ancient history bleeds into the Red River and flows irrevocably toward oblivion in the Gulf of Mexico. Without the intercession of men like Loftin, Sander, Romer, and Boll, all that evidence of long-ago Texas would be lost. What a debt of gratitude we owe them. Remembering is the least we can do.

WALT DAVI

Panhandle Petrified Zoo

Oh day and night, but this is wondrous strange.
And therefore, as a stranger give it welcome.
WILLIAM SHAKESPEARE,
Hamlet

ISABEL AND I DRIVE WEST out of Wichita Falls on U.S. 287 headed for Childress, on the other side of what many of our friends claim is the most boring part of Texas. Andy Adams didn't think so in 1882 when he helped push a herd of longhorns across the Red River at Doan's Crossing, north of present-day Vernon.[1] Neither did the young Comanche braves who climbed the Medicine Mounds between Chillicothe and Quanah on vision quests that gave them names and set the course of their lives. Cynthia Ann Parker never forgot the campsite on the Pease River south of the Mounds. She had been happy there in 1860, before Capt. Sul Ross and Charlie Goodnight stole her back from the Comanches, killed her husband, and broke her heart. Boring is not a word that fits the place.

At Childress we turn north on U.S. 83 and strike out across the Rolling Plains. Before fences parsed the prairie, this was open range, home of big spreads with colorful brands–Shoe Nail, Diamond Tail, Rocking Chair, RO, T bar T, and Laurel Leaf. In 1892 one of the Laurel Leaf hands started a place of his own and called it Cabin Creek Ranch.[2] One of his granddaughters is a friend of ours. She has invited us to spend a few days at her weekend house on the family ranch overlooking the Canadian

Margaret and C. Stuart Johnston at the Coffee Ranch dugout

River near the Oklahoma border. We trade U.S. 83 for State Highway 33, then County Road 21, exchange blacktop for caliche, and finally a dirt track. The raking sunlight of late afternoon reveals undulations in what had seemed to be a flat landscape. I stop at a cattle guard and Isabel unhooks the single strand of barbed wire that serves as a gate. Ahead we can barely make out a tiny shape on the horizon. Eleanor Glazener's house sits alone on the prairie at the end of a road that rises and falls over a series of treeless hills. From the gathering shadows beyond a glint of silver escapes the Canadian River, all but hidden in a distant grove of cottonwoods.

Stars wink on in the afterglow of sunset, as we linger over a dinner of barbecued brisket, beans, and potato salad and listen to Eleanor's tales of growing up on the family ranch. With dishes stacked and table cleared, she pulls out her grandmother's diary to illustrate the pluck and determination required of women living on the plains.

Isabel responds with the saga of Margaret Johnston. During the Great Depression, she was the only woman in the United States to supervise Works Progress Administration (WPA) crews. As many as twenty-five men labored under her tough-minded direction on a project to extract fossils from the Dust Bowl. Today visitors can see a spectacular collection of bones from one of those digs in the Panhandle-Plains Historical Museum (PPHM). Tomorrow West Texas A&M University paleontologist Dr. Gerald Schultz will take us to one of those dig sites—a place as famous for prehistoric mammals as the Geraldine site is for reptiles and amphibians. He may also shed some light on the troubling story of Margaret and C. Stuart Johnston whose passion for fossils blazed briefly on the Texas plains.

Morning brings a clear sky, light breeze, and brisk air that makes a long-sleeved flannel shirt feel good—a perfect day to be outdoors. After a driving tour of the sprawling family ranch, we start for town. An hour later we roll to a stop in front of the Roberts County Museum in Miami and park beside Schultz who has just arrived, still dressed for class. A plaid long-sleeved shirt complements khaki Dockers, leather belt, and casual walking shoes. No hat protects his smooth, tanned crown surrounded by a fringe of gray. His powder-blue backpack, the kind students fill with books, is loaded instead with zip-lock bags, geologist's hammer, chisel, and other paleontological paraphernalia.

Eleanor Glazener, with obligations elsewhere, leaves us after lunch. Schultz climbs into our van, and we drive north toward a place near in distance but far away in geologic time. "When was the Coffee Ranch site discovered?" I ask, as we head out of town.

"Back in 1929 or so," Schultz answers, "two geologists were doing a survey for the Rio Bravo Oil Company. They discovered about two dozen fossil sites, mostly in Hemphill County. This one was deemed the most productive."

He explains that the Coffee Ranch location dates back to the Miocene and Pliocene periods, six to six and one-half million years ago. That places it just before the Pleistocene—the Ice Age. Dinosaurs were long gone by then. Humans were not yet on the scene.

The morning's promise of a perfect day unfolds as we follow Red Deer Creek toward the Canadian River. Stream-side cottonwoods are turning from lime green to yellow. Their days of golden glory will come soon, but the first blue norther of winter will strip it all away. The road reaches the top of a hill, and long vistas open to the north and east. Pulling onto the grassy shoulder, I turn off the engine, set the brake, and turn to look at Isabel. She loves the plains and the unobstructed view of the sky. A scene like this can bring tears to her eyes. Today, she smiles instead.

"When we get over the fence it will take me a bit to get my bearings," Schultz says, scanning the hill for remembered landmarks. After a three hundred-yard ramble we come to a ledge of chalky rock. The skeleton of a tree silhouetted against the sky anchors one end, and a thicket of shoulder-high aromatic sumac protects the downslope approach. We wade through the brush, watching for snakes.

"This is it," Schultz announces, pointing to a brushy depression to the left of the ledge. "This is the dugout right here. Have you seen the picture? It was a stone building with a little doorway in front, built right into the bank where they kept tools and equipment. The quarry is over there." A few more cautious steps and Schultz points to a layer of rock–soft as an after-dinner mint–white, with a touch of green. "We are starting to get some of the ash right here. It came from Idaho."

According to our guide, airborne debris from volcanoes erupting hundreds of miles away fell to earth here, killing animals gathered around a waterhole and burying their bodies. Survivors of the catastrophe left tracks in ash that blanketed the plains. Isabel asks if we might find fossils today. Schultz answers in a voice absent of encouragement, "You might. I've picked up a few pieces of turtle and a rabbit bone and a little toe bone of a carnivore one day."

Undeterred, Isabel continues her search, while Schultz fills me in on various scientific reports written about Coffee Ranch and its fossils. I am amazed to learn that one paleontologist sifted samples of green clay through wire mesh sieves and found the bones of tiny mice, shrews, and a prehistoric mole.

Isabel returns to announce, "I found some little pieces of bone. It may be historic though."

"No, that's fossil bone," Schultz confirms, and all eyes are now glued to the ground.

Isabel finds something else and brings it over. "That's a horse tooth. Now that's a good one. I might be able to do something with that," Schultz says, as he slides Isabel's prize into his pocket.

Schultz reels off a mind-boggling list of exotic animals found here, including four different kinds of camels, a small antelope, a ground sloth, and a rhinoceros–twenty-five to thirty species in all. But it is Isabel's horse tooth that seems to interest him today. From time to time he pulls it out, looks at it, and returns it to his pocket. We find the imprint of raindrops in one bed of ash and camel tracks in another.

When we catch up with Isabel again, Schultz pulls her find from his pocket. "I think you may have added the tooth of a different horse in here. It looks very much like *Neohipparion leptode*, which is rare. You may have done me a great favor in finding this."

According to Schultz several species of horses lived in the same place at the same time. I am surprised, but he points out that it is not unusual to see several species of antelope together on the Serengeti plains of Africa. The difference is that the horses in North America did not survive.

"Why?" I inquire. "Things were going so well for horses here, and when the Spanish brought them back, they thrived again in the same place. What happened to wipe them out?"

"Oh, I think it probably had something to do with climate change and seasonality, changes in the vegetation, changes in the length of the growing season," he says. "That's still debated."

Isabel has found something else. "It's a lower jaw fragment of a horse," Schultz says. "Right lower jaw fragment, was there any more?"

We all begin searching, and I am the lucky one this time. Protruding from a ledge of soft white rock is something more animal-like than mineral. It is the rest of the jaw with five teeth still in place. Schultz glances toward the sun, estimates that we have a couple of hours before dark, and decides to collect the specimen.

He pulls a battered wooden-handled screwdriver and geologist's hammer from his pack and starts to work. The rock is soft, but the bone is fragile and riddled with cracks. The jaw comes out in pieces that Schultz will have to reassemble in the lab. He settles into a wordless rhythm—tapping, brushing away debris, prying, bagging the pieces. Thirty minutes pass. Eight sandhill cranes flap lazily overhead, bugling as they go. Blades of grass barely stir in the slightest of breezes. Autumn seems to hold its breath.

I picture this scene six million years ago. *A large river meanders through expansive plains where scattered ponds shine with reflected sky. Herds of grazing animals move slowly across the landscape. What seems like a pack of stiff-legged dogs far away proves to be a herd of miniature pug-nosed horses as it draws nearer. A distant giraffe turns out to be a towering, long-necked camel. Llama-like animals graze near an oddly shaped boulder that moves— a giant land tortoise. A grotesque dog with huge bone-crushing jaws skulks away from a lion with teeth like ivory butcher knives. Animals abound in bewildering variety and staggering numbers.*

The afternoon sun casts faint shadows—its dimly glowing disk barely penetrating an ash-laden atmosphere. At day's end, the western sky seems to catch fire. During the night miasmic clouds of volcanic ash blow in from violent eruptions eight hundred miles to the northwest. Toward morning it rains. Dawn breaks over a gray landscape. Raindrops have left tiny craters here and there, and wind has rippled sediment in the bottom of a shallow pond. A crane-like bird impresses its three-toed calling card in the damp crust near the still body of a small horse.

A thin slice of the past, no more than a few days in duration, has been preserved here. Now, a twenty-first century paleontologist is trying to save a piece of that past before erosion washes it away. After an hour of patient chipping, Schultz bags the last fragment of bone, shoulders his pack, and turns toward the van. During supper at the KNT Cafe in Miami, Schultz explains how the fossils we have just seen fit into the larger picture of Panhandle paleontology. On a page in Isabel's journal, he sketches out various periods and epochs along with appropriate fossil sites and dates.

Driving back to the ranch house, Isabel and I talk about the men and women who spent untold hours in field and laboratory collecting the information Schultz so casually sketched out after supper. Geologists, paleontologists, and vulcanologists compiled mountains of data. Some spent entire professional careers making that little chart Schultz drew as accurate as possible. Tomorrow we hope to explore one such career and piece together the story of an extraordinary couple who turned depression-era economic policy into a scientific bonanza.

Some people say the Panhandle-Plains Historical Museum in Canyon is the Smithsonian of the plains. Others call it the Panhandle's attic. In 1934, a year after it opened to the public, the museum welcomed the arrival of C. Stuart Johnston, the new professor of paleontology and anthropology at West Texas State Teacher's College. In addition to his teaching duties, Johnston had been promised access to the resources and collections of the museum.[3] Within five years Johnston and his wife, Margaret, had become Panhandle legends. Isabel and I want to know how this remarkable couple managed to accomplish so much in their short time together. The museum archive is the place to start.

Betty Bustos, matriarch of the archival collection, greets us warmly at the door. We feel like family invited into her kitchen for a feast of information. Bustos thumbs quickly through an antique wooden card catalog then pulls a stack of folders from an olive-green file cabinet with faded, typewritten labels.

We divide the spoils. Isabel looks for articles written by Johnston, while I comb the files for photographs. In no time I come across the picture Schultz mentioned yesterday—the one of C. Stuart and Margaret Johnston in front of the dugout at Coffee Ranch. He leans against the rock wall that stabilizes the front of the structure. Margaret sits on the corner of a stone slab table. Four college students lounge on a broad bench scraped from bedrock in front of the dugout. Shovels and picks lean against the wall. Indiana Jones would look right at home in this scene.

In another photograph, two white horses stand in what looks like a bomb crater. Piles of dirt lie on both sides of a ditch in which a refrigerator-sized block of stone sits at an awkward angle. Ropes run from the block to collars around the horses necks, and reins lead to the upraised hand of the driver in bib overalls. Down in the ditch, another man in his undershirt heaves aside a shovelful of dirt. They are removing a slab of six-million-year-old rhinoceros, camel, and horse bones from the Coffee Ranch bone quarry. That slab is now on public display in the paleontology hall at the museum.

Other photographs capture the charisma of the Johnstons. In one, Margaret stands at the edge of an excavation with a shovel at her feet and workmen laboring behind her. She wears a checkered flannel shirt, jodhpurs tucked into tall lace-up boots, and a leather aviator's helmet with flaps covering her ears. She looks straight at the camera—a serious, commanding presence.

In another, C. Stuart Johnston poses stiffly for a publicity photo. His partially open dark leather jacket reveals his trademark white shirt and tie. Black hair is parted on the left. Dark eyebrows angle sharply over piercing eyes, and a pencil-thin moustache perches above unsmiling lips. A half-smoked cigar smolders in his left hand. There is a hint of the outlaw in his demeanor.

Isabel has accumulated a pile of documents that reveal the prolific scientist behind Johnston's rakish exterior. She hands me the 1936–37 annual report to the Panhandle-Plains Historical Society. In that year alone, Johnston's one-man Department of Archeology and Paleontology enrolled approximately one hundred students in courses ranging from anthropology and archeology to geology and paleontology. He also acknowledged his wife's work saying, " . . . under the supervision of Mrs. Margaret Johnston, twenty-five men are engaged in collecting material in Donley and Randall Counties." C. Stuart, gifted teacher and dedicated fossil hunter, also found time to author six scientific papers that year.

Isabel hands me one entitled, "Tracks from the Pliocene of West Texas." Could they be from the site we visited yesterday? Captions under some of the illustrations list Coffee Ranch as the location. The photographs show well-defined impressions as sharp as if made yesterday, but a thousand times older than the pyramids of Egypt.

"Do you think these tracks could be downstairs in the museum's fossil collection?" Isabel asks.

"Let's find out," I suggest, closing the folder and taking off the white gloves Betty Bustos provides to protect her treasures.

A short elevator ride takes us from the third-floor archive to the basement collection storage area. Assistant Curator of Archeology Rolla Shaller meets us, unlocks a door, and ushers us into the pitch-black inner sanctum of Panhandle prehistory. At the flip of a switch, banks of fluorescent lights flicker on, revealing a long room filled with row upon row of gray metal storage cabinets. Archeology Curator Jeff Indeck joins us. He suggests we start with the open shelves at the far end of the room where larger specimens are stored.

We look through *manos* and *metates*, bison skulls, and mastodon bones before noticing a familiar three-toed track in a block of white ash. It is the one pictured in Johnston's 1937 paper—the one made by a bird similar to a crane. Bubble wrap separates it from another slab bearing the imprint of the bone-crushing dog, *Osteoborus*. I remember, as a Cub Scout, making plaster casts of animal tracks. These fossil footprints are as sharp as any I made from the freshest dog tracks around.

Shaller directs us to cabinets marked "Coffee Ranch," opens the door, and pulls out a drawer filled with bones and teeth. In another, chunks of a massive rhinoceros jaw have been reassembled and rest beside molars the size of walnuts and incisors as big as bananas. The handful of horse teeth we found yesterday would be lost among the hundreds piled into a third drawer. Then we notice a bit of human history mixed in with the fossils.

Fragments of bone lie in an old Roi-Tan cigar box. Did the cigar in Johnston's hand in his publicity photo come from this box? Who emptied the Almond Joy and Hollywood Butternut candy boxes now filled with fossils? Who spent $15.95 at Warren's Department Store for the size 7½ AAA shoes, then donated their box to science? During the Depression, adaptive reuse often made up for cash shortfalls. In other drawers, secondhand boxes have been replaced with standardized containers, zip-lock bags, and computer-generated labels. I compliment Indeck and Shaller on the improvement, but regret losing contact with that earlier time.

We are not the first to be intrigued by the Johnstons, however. A few years ago, Archeologist Christopher Lintz decided to play detective. Combing through letters, papers, photos, and the like, he pieced together the human story behind this enigmatic couple.[4] C. Stuart Johnston, it seems, was a university-trained paleontologist. He taught school briefly before signing on as a structural geologist with Tulsa-based Carter Oil Company in the late twenties. Soon he had a boots-on-the-ground familiarity with plains geology and its fossil-producing potential. As the Great Depression deepened and demand for oil dropped, Johnston was laid off.

Luckily, Classen High School in Oklahoma City needed a science teacher, and Johnston accepted the position, agreeing to take four college-level courses leading to a teaching certificate. The decision profoundly affected both his personal and professional life. At Classen High he found the attractive blonde who would become his wife, and at the University of Oklahoma he found his professional passion.

Moving far beyond the required courses, Johnston decided to go for a Ph.D. and, in 1931, he began work on an unprecedented double degree program in paleontology and anthropology. It was an audacious undertaking that would have dire consequences. That same year, Miss Margaret Counts turned nineteen, graduated from Classen High, and married the man who had been her teacher. She quickly became a contributing partner to his rapidly rising career.

Another contributor to Johnston's career was the president of the United States. When Franklin D. Roosevelt established the Federal Emergency Relief Administration (FERA) in 1933, he did more than provide quick cash for jobless Americans. Johnston's professor at the University of Oklahoma saw FERA as a way to fund archeological digs. Tax revenue spent on science was a good investment, he argued, as well as a boon to the local economy. The professor got his grant, and his star pupil got the assignment.

Margaret helped her husband fix up an old dugout on the Stamper

Ranch, where the couple lived while he supervised the FERA-funded excavation nearby. He made the most of his opportunity, and his success did not go unnoticed. Before he could complete his degree, C. Stuart Johnston was offered a teaching position at West Texas State Teachers College (WT). He and Margaret immediately closed the Stamper site, left their honeymoon dugout, and moved to Canyon.

Johnston parlayed his FERA funding experience into a phenomenally successful field research program funded by the Works Progress Administration (WPA) and Civilian Conservation Corps (CCC). He published twenty scientific articles in just five years while writing two dozen popular essays in the *Fort Worth Star-Telegram* and installing a number of exhibits in the museum. The man was driven to learn, teach, dig, and explain. But prodigious effort came at a cost. Work toward his Ph.D. languished, and his health began to falter.

In 1937, the year his first son was born, WT administrators pressured him to complete his doctoral program. Already overextended, he audited a summer class at Berkeley, completed a correspondence course from the University of Chicago, and, the following summer, traveled to Harvard for additional course work. The deadline for completion was fast approaching in 1938 when a serious stomach disorder required medical treatment. A year later, C. Stuart Johnston faced the collapse of his ambitious degree plan and the implosion of his career.

❧

It is nearly noon, and the parking lot at the Ranch House Cafe is already full. Minivans and SUVs are wedged between Dodge Ram 4x4s and Chevrolet Silverados. An intimidating blue heeler stands guard, Marine-like, on the flat bed of a mud-splattered Ford F150. Friday lunch at the Ranch House Cafe is Canyon's version of town and gown. Our friends from the university and the museum already have ordered by the time Isabel and I find two seats at the end of a long table reserved for the "curmudgeons."

Over the clatter of dishes and competing conversations, Rolla Shaller tells us how C. Stuart Johnston's brief career came to an end. In the summer of 1939, C. Stuart left Margaret in charge of the WPA field crews and drove to the University of Oklahoma for one last attempt to complete his degree. He needed to publish a paper on the results of a WPA excavation known as Antelope Creek 22.

Field notes and specimens from the dig had been deposited in the Panhandle-Plains Museum and would provide the basis for his paper. He made a serious mistake, however, by failing to ask the godfather of Panhandle prehistory for permission to use the material. Floyd Studer, passionate protector of Panhandle fossils and artifacts, blocked publication of Johnston's unauthorized report, and put his degree at risk. Johnston's trip to Oklahoma was a last desperate attempt to salvage his career.

While there, according to Rolla Shaller, a curious thing happened. "He was in the cafeteria eating when someone came in. Johnston got up and climbed in the car with this student; just took the clothes on his back, and they drove to Boston without telling Margaret. You hear so many stories . . . Maybe he was going to do some research or check on some fossils."

Dr. Schultz joins in. "He had some kind of attack. I think he probably drank a lot. He might have had stomach problems. They found him in a fifty-cent-a-night Boston flop house. He was comatose. They took him to the hospital, and he died. When they called to tell Margaret, she didn't even know he was up there and said, 'No, he's over in Oklahoma.' Funeral was here at First Methodist Church. He was buried out at Dreamland Cemetery."

The waitress interrupts to refill tea and water glasses; then Isabel asks, "What about Margaret? What happened to her?"

"We tried to find Margaret back in the seventies," Shaller remembers. "All the leads went cold."

Schultz clarifies, "She's dead now. We did find the death record." Then, looking to Rolla, he recalls, "Remember, she married that guy from

Paris, after the war, in 1946, and they moved to North Carolina. Funny, that's where C. Stuart was from."

"And the boys?" Isabel asks.

"We know their names," Shaller answers. "Robert Stuart and John Sidney–they were born in 1937 and 1938." He is quiet for a moment. "Wonder if she ever told them about their father?"

"Someone gave the little one a toy shovel," Schultz adds. "He used to like to dig in the dirt."

Shaller remembers one last thing before we leave: "A few years ago I went out to Dreamland and asked if Johnston was buried there. They said yes, but, when I found the grave, there was only a temporary metal plate marker like the funeral home puts on a new grave."

"Yeah," Schultz interjects, "and it was so beat up by mowers you could hardly read the name."

Shaller continues, "We decided our curmudgeons bunch should take up a collection and put a headstone out there. But you know about this," he says, looking me in the eye. "I think you donated money for that headstone."

He is right. When we lived in Canyon and I worked at the museum, Isabel and I did donate to the cause, but more out of courtesy than informed appreciation. The last two days have opened our eyes to the scope and significance of his work and the key role Margaret Johnston played in his success. Together they documented the phenomenal diversity of past animal life on the plains. Their work, and that of the scientists who followed them, lives on in scholarly papers and scientific specimens that combine to open a window on a world "wondrous strange."

Beyond the Latin names and scientific jargon lies a story mythological in its sweep and its challenge to the imagination. In this epic, animals rivaling those of a medieval bestiary roam across vast plains under a reddening sky, while ash falls like otherworldly snow.

What is a story like that worth? For the Johnstons, it was worth all they had to give.

WALT DAVIS

CHAPTER 16

From Buried City to Chill Hill

. . . .

As their remains are meagre and their history unwritten, an air of
the mysterious and the unknown will always cling about this place,
"The Buried City of the Panhandle."
T. L. EYERLY,
"The Buried City of the Panhandle"

SABEL AND I TURN OUR ATTENTION from prehistoric animals
buried in volcanic ash and the tragedy of a promising career cut
short, to a place called the "Buried City" in the northeastern
corner of the Texas Panhandle. We drive north on U.S. Highway
83 through rolling hills and along tree-lined tributaries of the
Canadian River en route to Ochiltree County. Members of the Texas
Archeological Society (TAS) are gathering at Lake Fryer on Wolf Creek
for their forty-sixth annual field school. Four hundred and fifty men,
women, and children will spend the next week exploring the place where
Texas archeology was born. We are joining them "in the trenches" to look
for clues to a centuries-old mystery.

Wolf Creek is a picturesque stream of clear water shaded by trees
that seem out of place on the plains. Anglo buffalo hunters camped along
its course in the 1870s and brought back stories of unusual stone ruins
marking what they believed was a buried city.[1] Serious study of the site
began thirty years later and continues today. Anthropologist David T.
Hughes of Wichita State University led large-scale excavations from
1985 to 1990.[2] The ruins have given up some of their secrets, but many
remain.

Excavations on Chill Hill, Courson Ranch

Experts now believe the structures were built between six hundred and eight hundred years ago by people quite different from the nomadic bison hunters who later roamed the plains. Residents of the Buried City shared traits with the pueblo people farther west and with the woodland farmers to the east. They used stone slabs to build permanent homes and grew corn, squash, and beans in stream-side fields. But they also hunted bison and deer and gathered wild fruit, seeds, and edible flowers.[3] For three hundred years, they prospered on the plains.

Long before Coronado crossed the Llano Estacado, however, the Buried City lay in ruins. Some researchers say the Apaches drove the people out. Others blame drought or population growth that exceeded the carrying capacity of the land. Still others suggest that the people who abandoned the Buried City moved east, modified their lifestyle to accommodate changes in their environment, and are known as the Wichita and related tribes of southwestern Oklahoma.[4]

We may never know exactly what happened on Wolf Creek six hundred years ago, but archeologists still look for evidence to complete the story. Today there is a sense of urgency about their work. Oil and gas production in the northeastern Panhandle destroys potential sites every year. Bulldozers scrape out drilling platforms, mud pits, and new roads. Workmen carry off artifacts and turn potential clues into worthless curios. The problem is not new. During the oil boom of the twenties, one archeologist worried about the "indiscriminate digging on the part of visitors from the oil fields . . . [that threatened to remove] every vestige of primitive occupation."[5] Oil and gas production is vitally important to a nation on the move, but there are hidden costs, and this is one.

Fortunately there is good news as well. Professional and amateur archeologists have been accumulating evidence along Wolf Creek since 1907. In that year the principal of a preparatory school in Canadian, Texas, took twelve of his students on a field trip. Digging into piles of rubble at the Buried City, T. L. Eyerly and his young excavators discovered several burials and concluded that the site was a graveyard.[6]

Eyerly's excavation and subsequent report are now considered the first organized dig, and the first scientific documentation, of an archeological site in Texas.[7] One of the students on that trip was fifteen-year-old Floyd Studer. His portrait in the 1907 school newspaper shows a serious young man in suit and bow tie. His hair, parted in the middle, curls just above prominent ears. Thin lips lie flat and expressionless above an ample chin. With tenacity already evident at fifteen, Floyd Studer championed the archeological significance of the Texas Panhandle and brought it national attention.[8]

In 1920 he accompanied one of the leading archeologists in the United States, Warren King Moorehead, on an expedition that identified more than one hundred sites in the Canadian River valley. Moorehead spent three weeks excavating the Buried City and exploring the Wolf Creek valley. He concluded that ". . . this small and picturesque plain may be justly considered one of the strategic centers in American archeology."[9]

At the time, the Panhandle oil boom was in full swing, and it gave Studer an idea for protecting places like the Buried City. If oil men could obtain leases from landowners to drill wells, why couldn't he secure leases to dig for artifacts? That way, he could control who dug where and protect the growing number of sites he had discovered. Studer talked the newly-established Panhandle-Plains Historical Society into sponsoring his effort. Signs soon began appearing on ranch gates reading:

EXCLUSIVE PRIVILEGE to
INVESTIGATE this LOCATION
and other Archeological and
Paleontological Sites on this ranch
HAS BEEN LEGALLY GRANTED
Trespassers will be prosecuted under the law
Panhandle-Plains Historical Society
–sign posted by Floyd Studer[10]

Throughout his long life, Studer continued to spend weekends and holi-days searching for new sites. Looking back on forty-five years of work he said, "Every means of transportation made available in those years was used—shanks' mare [on foot], horseback, buckboard, motorcycle, Model T, later models—until finally the airplane solved a lot of the problems." By 1955 Studer had "located, mapped, and fully recorded over two hundred Indian sites."[11]

Unfortunately, his idea of fully recording a site was crude by today's standards. He looked for walls, doorways, fireplaces—the major features of a structure. Burials were significant, but animal bones, charred plant material, and other "insignificant" debris were tossed aside. He probed many sites, but never produced a complete report on any of them.[12] But Studer was no worse than many of the professionals. Standards were dif-ferent in those days. Things they considered trivial are deemed valuable today.

Studer's protective attitude grew as the years passed, until he came to believe that the archeological sites of the Texas Panhandle were his personal "turf." No one collected without his permission. No one dug unless he sanctioned their project. He gave Warren Moorehead a map of the sites he had discovered, but left off the more sensitive locations. When archeologists tried to use the map later, they discovered that many of the sites were intentionally mis-located. Studer promised to produce an accurate and complete map before he died, but he never did.[13]

※

Isabel and I turn off of U.S. 83 onto County Road U where a sign points east to Wolf Creek County Park. We are on our way to the TAS Field School campground. For the next week, amateur and professional arche-ologists will work side by side to learn more about the people who lived along Wolf Creek and the Canadian River. This is our chance to work in the trenches of a real excavation—to see what it takes to piece together the story of people long dead.

Wolf Creek still flows freely in the shade of ancient cottonwoods that have since been joined by drought-tolerant Chinese elms. A Mississippi kite soars overhead, turning in slow circles, trimming its wings, and adjusting its tail to the currents that keep it aloft. We turn where a sign points to the TAS camp. Early birds in pop-up campers, travel trailers, and RVs have already taken the sites with water and electricity. All the shady level spots are covered with tents.

We finally locate an empty patch of ground between two sets of portable toilets across the road from the cook trailer and a couple of refrigerated trucks. Noise from the generators is a problem. But our lakeside location provides cool breezes, and we watch the setting sun bathe thunderheads along the eastern horizon with pastel shades of peach and gold.

Night comes, but not sleep. Dogs bark incessantly in the public campground across the lake. Loud voices and raucous laughter drift across the water. One man yells to a child, "If I have to put this leg on and come get you, I'm gonna beat you within an inch of your life." Generators on the refrigerated trucks kick on periodically, drowning out one noise with another. After a few hours of fitful sleep, a new sound intrudes. The camp boss is driving around, lights on, horn blaring, speakers broadcasting *You Are My Sunshine* at peak volume.

This is the TAS version of an alarm clock. It is 5 A.M., and breakfast will be served in thirty minutes. The workday starts at seven and ends at one, to take advantage of the cool morning air and avoid the afternoon heat. We dress quickly, grab our trays, and walk across the road to the cook trailer. Thirty people are already in line. Four women in matching straw hats and blue blouses begin ladling out food—scrambled eggs, bacon, fried potatoes, biscuits, and gravy.

The sky is brighter by the time we finish breakfast, pick up our day packs, and join the throng of people walking up a grassy hill toward a blue-and-white striped tent big enough for a small circus. A woman, who has been through this before, says the crew chiefs and lab directors will be holding up signs bearing their names. Sure enough, I spot a tall man in jeans, T-shirt, and baseball cap holding up a placard that says "Art Tawater." I introduce myself and meet my team. Isabel locates the lab crew she has been assigned to.

The first rays of sunlight touch the treetops down in the campground as Tawater briefs the crew on its assignment. He is a soft-spoken man with sad eyes and a long face. He reminds me of Gary Cooper, but with a mustache, and the voice of Tommy Lee Jones. I am disappointed to learn that we will not be digging at the Buried City. Instead we will open up a new site thirty miles away in Roberts County at a place called Chill Hill on the historic LIPS ranch.

Briefing complete, we load our gear and join a caravan of pickups, SUVs, and cars headed for the excavation. Leaving Wolf Creek, we cross rolling ranchland, top out among irrigated wheat fields, and turn south on State Highway 70. Ten miles later, the High Plains seem to break apart and tumble toward the Canadian in a jumble of arroyos, buttes, and rock-strewn hills, carrying us with it. We pass a concrete-block building with overhead doors open at both ends to let in the breeze. This is the Chill Hill lab where Isabel will be working. The road stops here, but we drive on and park in the grass beyond. Shouldering my pack and carrying shovel and water jug, I trudge upslope toward clusters of awnings marking the dig site.

Art Tawater gathers his team and outlines our mission: "We will be digging two, two meter squares, and we will go down ten centimeters at a time. A magnetometer survey indicates there may be a hearth thirty centimeters or so beneath the surface. Use your line levels often to make sure you don't go too deep too fast. If you find anything, stop and let me take a look. Don't remove it unless I say so."

I understand most of his instructions, but decide to stay close to Robin and Ann Martin, a retired couple from Austin who seem to be old hands at this. Later, Robin interrupts my digging to show me the yellow string tied to a stake that we use to measure depth. He stretches the string tight, slides the line level over the spot where I am working, moves the string up and down until the bubble registers level, and measures the distance from string to dirt.

"Fifteen centimeters," he announces. "We are going to twenty, so you can take off another five, but no more."

The dirt is as hard as concrete and makes a scratching noise as I pull my trowel across it. Tawater orders us out of the square and hoses it down. Moisture transforms hard-packed dirt into pliable soil, and digging speeds up noticeably. My small pile of dust quickly grows into a couple of gallons of mounded earth. Test excavations done earlier turned up one thousand artifacts per ten-centimeter layer including stone tools, chert flakes, animal bone, and pottery sherds.[14] I can't wait to get down to the good stuff.

As I dig, however, I can't help thinking about something Rolla Shaller and Gerald Schultz told us about another site nearby. Floyd Studer and C. Stuart Johnston were involved, and things did not turn out well. What happened underscores the vulnerability of sites like Chill Hill and the importance of the work we are doing today to collect and preserve artifacts before they are lost.

In 1920 Floyd Studer took Warren King Moorehead to the ruins of a multi-room house on a bluff overlooking Antelope Creek. After inspecting the house, Moorehead declared that it was the work of people whose culture was a unique blend of plains and pueblo traits. He called it the Canadian Valley or Texas Panhandle Culture.[15] In 1938 and 1939 archeologists led Works Progress Administration (WPA) crews in an extensive excavation of the ruins.[16]

This was the site that C. Stuart Johnston intended to write about in order to complete the requirements for his PhD. Ever protective of his "turf," Floyd Studer objected, complaining that Johnston had failed to ask permission before proceeding. After Johnston died, Studer relented, and allowed the controversial paper to be published.[17] Antelope Creek 22 became one of the most important archeological sites in the state.

Then, in 1994, a company installing a natural gas pipeline decided to locate a pumping station on a bluff overlooking Antelope Creek. When the bulldozer operator began clearing a place for a pad, he noticed stone ruins and decided to investigate . . . with his machine. When he finished, walls that had stood for over six centuries were demolished, and orderly layers of artifact-bearing soil had been shoved into chaotic piles. A priceless cultural resource had been senselessly destroyed.[18]

The same thing nearly happened to the site we are working on today. Landowners Harold Courson and his son Kirk planned to drill an oil well on top of Chill Hill. But first they asked their staff archeologist, Scott Brosowske, to do some test excavations. When he discovered thousands of pottery sherds, projectile points, shell beads, and bone tools, the Coursons directed the drillers to move the well to a new location.[19] Harold and Kirk Courson are passionate about preserving the archeological sites scattered throughout the ranches they own and operate.

Isabel and I are curious about how they balance the conflicting demands of oil and gas production and historic preservation. After completing our morning shift at Chill Hill, we drive over to Kirk Courson's weekend home to talk about that. He lives on Wolf Creek just a stone's throw from the Buried City. The modest frame house with well-kept lawn sits back among trees and bushes that take the curse off the prairie wind. The air-conditioned interior is a delightful change from the glare and heat of the afternoon. Courson is a slimmer, younger version of his father, bald on top, hair close-trimmed on the sides. He wears a blue, short-sleeved, two-pocket shirt, and jeans. Courson motions for us to sit down at the dining table.

"What would you like to know?" he begins. Isabel asks what sparked his interest in archeology and learns that it began when he and his father bought the ranch where his house now stands. Mr. Handly, the previous owner, had kept the place going for fifty years, but when he died, several people expressed interest in buying and developing it.

"We decided collectively that whatever it cost, we would acquire the ranch ... Besides, it's a beautiful place, and we had always wanted to own a piece of land on Wolf Creek." Kirk's father was on the Texas Historical Commission at the time and had developed a deep interest in historic preservation. That's when the idea first came up to create a conservation easement and insure the long-term protection of Buried City.

"Bob Malouf was the State Archeologist back then," Kirk says, "and he approached me with the idea. We ended up using, as a pattern, a document that the state of Kansas had created. It was the first archeological conservation easement in Texas."

He explains that an easement is a deed restriction on a specified piece of property. The owner agrees not to damage any known, or unknown, archeological features within the confines of the easement. The owner is free, however, to continue historic farm and ranch practices that do not harm the site. The Texas Historical Commission serves as "watchdog" to see that the agreement is honored by present and subsequent owners, in perpetuity.

"How much land are we talking about?" Isabel wants to know.

"About sixty acres. There are eight to ten ruins within that easement."

Courson describes a second easement of about thirty acres with a half-dozen ruins and hints that there may be a third. The Coursons' archeologist, Scott Brosowske, believes Chill Hill could turn out to be an important site. TAS was invited to excavate in order to test Brosowske's hypothesis.

"Is it a smart move to put a deed restriction on valuable land?" I ask. "Do these easements make economic sense from your point of view?"

Kirk Courson leans forward, forearms on the table, and says with conviction, "From my perspective as a historic preservationist, there's absolutely no reason in the world not to grant a conservation easement, unless you intend to perform an activity on a piece of property that would destroy the site."

He acknowledges that private property rights are important to Texas landowners who should be free to use their land as they see fit. But it disturbs him to see hundreds of prospective archeological sites destroyed needlessly each year. Education is the key, he believes. Besides, there are significant tax advantages for the owner who sets up an easement. We are encouraged to hear these ideas from the president of a successful oil and gas exploration and production company—a man with a degree in finance who oversees ranching operations on more than one hundred thousand acres of valuable land.

Courson looks at his watch. "I have a job to do at five o'clock. I'm cooking hamburgers for the crew chiefs."

"Is that part of your job description?"

"No, it's just something I pride myself in. I like to cook beef."

The next day Isabel and I return to the lab and the excavation with a new appreciation for the significance or our work. I drop to my knees, pull out my trowel, and resume digging. I sweep my scrapings into a dust pan then empty it into an orange five-gallon bucket. The dirt will be washed through a wire screen to make sure I haven't missed anything. The tedious effort becomes routine as the trowel slices through soft dirt with a satisfying earthy crunch. Lean forward, set the trowel, lean back and pull, over and over again. Each pull exposes another layer of dirt exactly like the last but deeper. Now I notice a slight difference. Something protrudes from the last layer exposed. I touch it with my finger. It is hard. I wipe it, and a shape appears . . . triangular . . . man-made. Columbus had yet to discover the New World when a human hand last touched this artifact.

"Art, I think I have a point here."

All digging stops as Art Tawater drops to one knee to look at the thin, translucent piece of chert at the tip of my trowel.

"Yes you do. It's a Washita point. It's diagnostic of the Plains Village Culture that we believe occupied this site. That's a good find."

It is less than an inch long and wafer thin. The tip is broken, but the base is intact. Robin brings in the measuring tape to record the exact location of the point in the square. Someone makes an official photograph, and my "good find" goes into a zip-lock bag destined for the lab. Word spreads to the adjacent squares. I have a few minutes of archeological fame as "the one who found the point." Then a woman a few squares away finds a broken pot with intact rim, and I am just another digger on Chill Hill.

The next morning, fellow excavator Kay Woodward takes me to the washing station to show me how it's done. She is an energetic pixie of a woman in her seventies. She stops at a bright-blue metal water trough on legs where six washers are at work. There are two such stations. Every ounce of dirt removed from every square passes through here to insure that not even the smallest artifact is lost.

Six wood-framed wire mesh screens sit on top of each trough, and six hoses with pistol grip nozzles provide water to wash dirt through the screens. Wind whips the spray in all directions, and silt sluices out the other end to create an expanding delta of glistening mud. Kay shows me a bucket marked Tawater 1, the square I have been digging. I dump five gallons of dirt onto the screen and begin spraying. Soil melts away leaving behind small white rocks, grass roots, and two or three tiny grubs . . . but no artifacts. Another bucket of dirt yields the same disappointing result. As the buckets multiply, my arms begin to ache. I strain a wrist and worry about my back.

I am relieved an hour later when ranch owner Harold Courson

arrives to check on our progress, giving me a break. Starched blue dress shirt and Stetson set him apart from the muddy screeners. Khaki slacks held up by suspenders are tucked into high-top black boots. A tiny red American Legion poppy sticks out of his breast pocket. I ask where the water comes from that we so generously spray onto our screens.

"From a well," he answers. "When we dig a site on the ranch and need water to wash the dirt, I dig a well."

The average water well, I learn, runs about ten thousand dollars. Pipe, fittings, hoses, and screens add to the cost. The troughs are left over from the first TAS Field School in 1985–86. Courson had them sandblasted and repainted for this year's excavations.

"You get so many more artifacts with water screening," he explains, then turns and points to one of the screeners. "I saw a shell bead over there—an olivela shell. You wouldn't have found that dry screening."

He explains that shaking dry dirt through a screen scratches some artifacts and grinds softer items, like bone and shell, to dust.

After Courson leaves, I return to work thinking about the enormous effort going into the excavation of Chill Hill. Scores of diggers and screeners move tons of dirt and thousands of gallons of water every day. Crew chiefs, site supervisors, and lab workers make sure we dig carefully, keep accurate records, and take good care of the artifacts. Years from now, people will have no idea how much work it took to verify the simple statement, "Plains Village people of the Canadian River valley made beads from Pacific Coast olivela shells."

When I return to the excavation, things are not going well. The more we dig, the less we find, until Art Tawater declares that our "unit" has "gone sterile." He instructs the crew to tidy up the old square and move to a new location. Sterile squares are to be expected when opening a new site. It's a bit like playing battleship. With each miss, the chances for a hit increase. Our site supervisor comes by with a word of encouragement. The productive layer is at least thirty centimeters down, and most of the other squares are beginning to find things at that level.

Three days later, the field school comes to an end, and archeologist Scott Brosowske summarizes the findings: "We found two structures at Chill Hill. One was a large, dark, charcoal-stained feature full of trash and debris. Most likely the inside of a house. The other was a two-meter-wide group of units that went right through a house. We could see the east wall and the west wall, but weren't able to get it clearly defined by the end of field school."

"Do you think Chill Hill is going to be as important as Buried City?" I ask.

"Yeah, in a lot of ways it will."

Brosowske explains that back in the thirties and forties, when the Buried City and similar sites were excavated, workers missed a lot of clues. They took fewer samples and screened less. Before the advent of the radiocarbon dating technique, they could not say with confidence how old things were.

"We have a lot of questions about those sites," Brosowske concludes. "Chill Hill will fill in a lot of gaps."

Our time in the archeological "trenches" has come to a close. TAS will return next year hoping to find more houses and artifacts. With luck, they may come up with new evidence about who the Plains Village people were, why they left their homes, and where they went so long ago. Evidence already gathered must now be analyzed and interpreted—a process that will take years. While that is going on, hundreds of potential new sites and the evidence they contain will be destroyed.

In Texas, the race to extract priceless information from archeological sites before they are lost began when a teacher and twelve students dug into the Buried City and published their findings. The effort to protect such sites in perpetuity originated in the same place when Harold and Kirk Courson established the first archeological conservation easement in the state.

Future archeologists will benefit from their stewardship. Improved techniques will solve puzzles that seem unsolvable today. One day, a citizen of Oklahoma, not yet born, may learn that her ancestor tended fields of corn in "the bend of a creek with an abundant supply of crystal waters." The story will grow as long as clues keep turning up.

As we roll up our tent and pack away the gear for the trip back home, we realize that this is the last campsite on our tour around the border of Texas. It has been an amazing journey full of twists and turns, interesting people, and natural wonders. A half-century ago, when Frank X. Tolbert returned from a similar trip, he wrote to the readers of the *Dallas Morning News:* "We can report that all the Texas borderlands are intact."[20] As our own tour comes to an end, we must deliver a different report: the Texas borderlands are changing. The rate of change is accelerating. And the agent of change increasingly comes in human form.

Epilogue

Our journey around Texas has come to an end. Our companions have included archeologists, artists, bird banders and watchers, botanists, cowboys, ecologists, explorers, geologists and paleontologists, log-pullers, map-makers, river-runners, writers, and zoologists.

Some served as modern-day guides. They escorted us onto the plains, across deserts and mountains, down wild rivers, up the coast, into the dark recesses of an urban wilderness, and through the shadows of the Pineywoods. Those who came before us left poignant firsthand accounts of an earlier Texas teeming with plant and animal life. Through their diaries, journals, and official reports, we have seen how much Texas has changed in the last three centuries.

Some of that change has been tragic. Whole nations of Native Americans vanished, decimated by war and disease. Seemingly limitless herds of bison were hunted to the brink of extinction. A primeval forest of longleaf pines was chopped down, cut up, and carted away.

But there were success stories as well. Florence Bailey, the Audubon Society, and many others prevented plume hunters from robbing the Gulf Coast of its elegant herons and egrets. Concerned sportsmen and effective legislation halted the wholesale slaughter of white-tailed deer at the hands of commercial hunters. Citizen activists Terry Hershey, George Mitchell, and their allies kept the verdant upper reaches of Buffalo Bayou from becoming a concrete ditch.

Our four thousand mile long, three century deep journey around the state has taught us two important lessons. First—people are more likely to preserve and protect things they know about and value. Kirk Courson, the Panhandle oil man, put it simply, when he said that education was the key to preserving archeological sites. That insight applies to a wide range of cultural and environmental resources. Lutcher Moore, the East Texas lumberman, once considered saving some stands of longleaf pine for the future, but he knew his competitors would not relent. Reluctantly, he gave up the idea and cut till the last tree fell. Had he known then, what we know now, he might have decided differently.

But knowledge of the natural world comes at a price—that is the second lesson learned from our journey. Hardworking men and women took risks and invested their lives in the search for information that enlightens. A botanist walked nearly seven hundred miles collecting plants. A fossil hunter died on the prairie looking for fossils. An ornithologist spent sixty years studying Texas birds. What they and others learned has changed the way we look at the natural world. We know names and histories of our plant and animal companions. We understand how our actions affect them—how our decisions impact land, water, and air.

The extraordinary men and women who explored the Texas borderlands left a priceless legacy. They helped write the natural history of the state. The stories they pieced together highlight the value of our cultural and natural resources, inform our public discourse, and enrich our lives.

On a more personal level, Isabel and I agree that bird artist Louis Agassiz Fuertes best captured the spirit of our trip when he described a night spent high in the Chisos Mountains of Big Bend:

> When the big southern moon comes cooly up from behind her great mountain & floods the cañon & valley with soft light, & the owls & whippoorwills & other night lovers come out & give it all a new and unsolved life, it makes me long to have some power to get your senses . . . down here to help me hold it. . . . I wouldn't miss the cool breeze on my head & the wonderful throbbing bigness of these glorious nights for anything [you] could name.

We have learned, as Fuertes did, that life is an unsolved mystery, and regret, as he did, that we cannot capture moonlight or convey the throbbing bigness of the Texas sky. Such things are gifts, not possessions. We encountered many on our trip around the state . . . left them where we found them . . . and wouldn't trade the memory of them for anything you could name.

Notes

···························

Chapter 1

1. James W. Abert, *Gúadal P'a: The Journal of Lieutenant J. W. Abert from Bent's Fort to St. Louis in 1845* (Canyon, Tex.: Panhandle-Plains Historical Society, 1941), 51–52.

2. Ibid., 52.

3. Frederick W. Rathjen, *The Texas Panhandle Frontier* (Austin: University of Texas Press, 1973), 113.

4. Ibid.

5. Abert, *Gúadal P'a,* 54.

6. William H. Goetzmann, *Exploration and Empire: The Explorer and the Scientist in the Winning of the American West* (Austin: Texas State Historical Association, 1993), 251.

7. Rathjen, *The Texas Panhandle Frontier,* 112–113.

8. LeRoy R. Hafen, *Broken Hand: The Life of Thomas Fitzpatrick: Mountain Man, Guide and Indian Agent* (Denver: Old West Publishing Co., 1973), 219.

9. Ibid., 318–19.

10. Ibid., 1.

11. Goetzman, *Exploration and Empire,* 251.

12. Rathjen, *The Texas Panhandle Frontier,* 121.

13. Ibid., 121–122.

14. Gerald Schultz, (Professor of Geology, West Texas A&M University), in discussion with the authors, October 17, 2006.

15. Jeffrey A. Schneider, "Environmental Investigations: The Great Underground Sponge: Ogallala," Department of Chemistry, State University of New York, http://www.oswego.edu/~schneidr.CH300/envvinv/EnvInv12.html (accessed June 2, 2008).

16. Abert, *Gúadal P'a,* 53–54.

17. Ibid., 54–55.

18. Ibid., 58.

Chapter 2

1. George G. Shumard, *The Geology of Western Texas* (Austin: State Printing Office, 1886), 95.

2. Ibid.

3. Frederick R. Gehlbach, *Mountain Islands and Desert Seas: A Natural History of the U.S.—Mexican Borderlands* (College Station: Texas A&M University Press, 1981), 107–108.

4. W. Frank Blair, *Vertebrates of the United States* (New York: McGraw-Hill Book Company, 1957), 491, 522, and 527.

5. Gehlbach, *Mountain Islands Desert Seas,* 106–108.

6. Ibid.

7. Ibid., 98.

8. Frederick and Nancy Gehlbach, in discussion with the authors, December 6, 2007.

9. Douglas H. Chadwick, "Crown of the Continent," *National Geographic,* September 2007, 69.

Chapter 3

1. Samuel W. Geiser, *Naturalists of the Frontier* (Dallas: Southern Methodist University, 1948), 191.

2. Ibid., 192.

3. Clinton P. Hartman, "Charles Wright: Botanizer of the Boundary, Part I," *Password* 37, no. 2 (1992): 60–63.

4. Charles Wright, "Field notes of Charles Wright for 1849 and 1851–52" (typewritten transcription with commentary by Ivan M. Johnston, Library of the Gray Herbarium, Harvard University, February 1940), 33–34.

5. Samuel W. Geiser, "Charles Wright's 1849 Botanical Collecting-trip from San Antonio to El Paso; with Type-localities for New Species," reprinted from *Field & Laboratory* 4, no. 1 (1935): 32.

6. Samuel Gibbs French, Senate Executive Document, *A Report in Relation to the Route over which the Government Train moved from San Antonio to El Paso del Norte, Made in Pursuance to Order . . . dated May 30, 1849,* 31st Cong., 1st sess., 1850, vol. 14, no. 64, p. 48.

7. Geiser, "Charles Wright's 1849 Botanical Collecting-trip," 30–32.

8. Charles Wright to Asa Gray, December 1849, Wright-Gray correspondence, Library of the Gray Herbarium, Harvard University.

9. Ibid.

10. Ibid.

11. Ibid.

12. Sally Wasowski with Andy Wasowski, *Native Texas Plants: Landscaping Region by Region* (Houston: Gulf Publishing Company, 1991), 249.

Chapter 4

1. Louis Agassiz Fuertes to his family, 29 May 1901, Louis Agassiz Fuertes Papers, #2662. Division of Rare and Manuscript Collections, Cornell University Library.

2. Quotations, unless otherwise noted, are exact transcriptions (including ampersands, abbreviations, etc.) from letters that Fuertes wrote to his family between 29 May and 9 June, 1901. Louis Agassiz Fuertes Papers, #2662. Division of Rare and Manuscript Collections, Cornell University Library.

3. David J. Schmidley, *Texas Natural History: A Century of Change* (Lubbock: Texas Tech University Press, 2002), 270–271.

4. Ibid., 25.

5. Ibid., 8.

6. Ibid., 25.

7. Ibid., 7.

8. Harry C. Oberholser, *The Bird Life of Texas* (Austin: University of Texas Press, 1974), xix.

9. Robert McCracken Peck, *A Celebration of Birds: The Life and Art of Louis Agassiz Fuertes* (New York: Walker and Company, 1982), 162–164.

10. Ibid., 161.

Chapter 5

1. Robert T. Hill, "Running the Cañons of the Rio Grande, Part 1," *The Dallas Morning News*, August 5, 1934.

2. Nancy Alexander, *Father of Texas Geology: Robert T. Hill* (Dallas: Southern Methodist University Press, 1976), 116.

3. Ibid., 123.

4. Ibid.

5. Robert T. Hill, "Running the Cañons of the Rio Grande," *The Century Magazine,* January, 1901, 373.

6. Alexander, *Father of Texas Geology,* 124.

7. Ibid., 116, 123–124.

8. Hill, "Running the Cañons," *The Century Magazine,* 375.

9. Alexander, *Father of Texas Geology,* 125.

10. Hill, "Running the Cañons," *The Century Magazine,* 376.

11. Ibid., 377.

12. Ibid., 379.

13. Ibid., 381.

14. Ross A. Maxwell, *The Big Bend of the Rio Grande: A Guide to the Rocks, Geologic History, and Settlers of the Area of Big Bend National Park, Guidebook 7* (Austin: Bureau of Economic Geology, University of Texas, 1968), 89–90.

15. Hill, "Running the Cañons," *The Century Magazine,* 384.

16. Ibid.

17. Ibid., 383.

18. Ibid., 384.

19. Ibid., 385.

20. Ibid., 386.

21. Ibid., 387.

22. Hill, "Running the Cañons, Part 5," *Dallas Morning News,* September 16, 1934.

23. Hill, "Running the Cañons," *The Century Magazine,* 372.

Chapter 6

1. Hill, "Running the Cañons," *The Century Magazine,* 387.

2. Louis Agassiz Fuertes to family, April 29, 1901.

3. James H. Everitt, D. Lynn Drawe, and Robert I. Lonard, *Trees, Shrubs, & Cacti of South Texas* (Lubbock: Texas Tech University Press, 2002) 62, 78, 108, 183.

4. Harold T. Weidemann, "Factors to Consider When Sculpting Brush: Mechanical Treatment Options," http://texnat.tamu.edu/symposia/sculptor/18.htm (accessed September 29, 2007).

5. Geiser, *Naturalists of the Frontier,* 31.

6. Ibid., 30–54.

7. Ruben Flores Gutierrez, "Guerrero Viejo: An Architectural Legacy," in *A Shared Experience: The History, Architecture and Historic Designations of the Lower Rio Grande Heritage Corridor*, ed. Mario L. Sanchez (Austin: Los Caminos del Rio Heritage Project and the Texas Historical Commission, 1994), 202.

8. Unidentified newspaper clipping posted in Falcon State Park visitor center.

9. Jean Louis Berlandier, *Journey to Mexico During the Years 1826 to 1834*, trans. S. M. Ohlendorf (Austin: The Texas State Historical Association and University of Texas, Austin, 1980), vol. 6, chap. 4, p.483.

10. V. W. Lehman, *Forgotten Legions: Sheep in the Rio Grande Plain of Texas* (El Paso: Texas Western Press, 1969), 15.

11. Robert S. Weddle, "Nuevo Santander," in *The New Handbook of Texas*, ed. Ron Tyler (Austin: Texas State Historical Association, 1996), 4:1074.

12. Richard B. Taylor, Jimmy Rutledge, and Joe G. Herrera, *A Field Guide to Common South Texas Shrubs* (Austin: Texas Parks and Wildlife Press, 1999).

13. Geiser, *Naturalists of the Frontier*, 48.

14. Ibid., 53.

15. Ibid., 52.

16. Ibid., 48.

17. Texas Parks and Wildlife Department, "Wildlife Fact Sheets," http://tpwd.state.tx.us/huntwild/wild/species/?=endangered (accessed October 4, 2007).

Chapter 7

1. Florence Merriam Bailey, "Meeting Spring Half Way, Part II," *Condor* 18 (1916): 188.

2. Ibid., 183.

3. Ibid., 188.

4. Ibid., 187.

5. Ibid.

6. Ibid.

7. Florence Merriam Bailey, "Meeting Spring Half Way, Part III," *Condor* 18 (1916): 217.

8. Ibid.

9. Ibid., 218.

10. Witmer Stone, "Report of the Committee on the Protection of North American Birds for the Year 1900," *The Auk* 18 (1901): 74–75.

11. Ibid.

12. Robin W. Doughty, *Feather Fashions and Bird Preservation: A Study in Nature Protection* (Berkeley: University of California Press, 1975), 23.

13. "The Destruction of Birds for Millinery Purposes," *Science* 7, no. 160 (Feb. 26, 1886): 196.

14. Harriet Kofalk, *No Woman Tenderfoot* (College Station: Texas A&M University Press, 1989): 32–35.

15. Doughty, *Feather Fashions*, 14–15.

16. Ibid., 16.

17. Ibid., 15.

18. Kofalk, *No Woman Tenderfoot*, 44.

19. "The Destruction of Birds," 197.

20. Stone, "Report of the Committee . . . ," 75–76.

21. Robin W. Doughty, *Wildlife and Man in Texas* (College Station: Texas A&M University Press, 1983), 167–170.

22. Ibid., 172.

Chapter 8

1. Karen Harden McCracken, *Connie Hagar: The Life History of a Texas Birdwatcher* (College Station: Texas A&M University Press, 1986), 224.

2. Ibid., 4.

3. Ibid., 4.

4. Ibid., 19.

5. Ibid., 38.

6. Ibid., 39.

7. Ibid., 46.

8. Ibid.

9. Ibid., 63–64.

10. David J. Schmidly, *Texas Natural History: A Century of Change* (Lubbock: Texas Tech University Press, 2002), 34.

11. McCracken, *Connie Hagar*, 67–68.

12. Ibid., 68.

13. Ibid.

14. Ibid., 271.

15. Ibid., 281.

Chapter 9

1. Geiser, *Naturalists of the Frontier,* 91.

2. Ibid., 82.

3. Ibid., 87.

4. Ibid., 90.

5. Ibid.

6. Ibid., 90–91.

7. Donald Jackson, *Voyages of the Steamboat Yellow Stone* (New York: Ticknor & Fields, 1985), 4, 47, 79, 111, 130, 142.

8. Geiser, *Naturalists of the Frontier,* 91.

9. Frederick L. Olmstead, *A Journey Through Texas* (Austin: University of Texas Press, 1978), 362.

10. Joseph Chambers Clopper, "Journal of J. C. Clopper, 1828," *The Quarterly of the Texas State Historical Association* 13 (1909–10): 52.

11. Frédérick Gaillardet, *Sketches of Early Texas and Louisiana,* trans. James L. Shepherd, III (Austin: University of Texas Press, 1966), 53.

12. Janet K. Wagner (Houston-based land use historian), in discussion with the authors, April 3, 2006.

13. David G. McComb, "Houston, Texas," in *The New Handbook of Texas,* ed. Ron Tyler (Austin: Texas State Historical Association, 1996), 3:721–723.

14. Port of Houston Authority, "Trade Development Division: Trade Statistics," http://portofhouston.com/busdev/tradedevelopment/tradestatistics.html.

15. Terry Hershey (Houston-based environmental activist), in discussion with the authors, April 4, 2006.

16. Wagner, discussion.

17. Clopper, "Journal of J. C. Clopper, 1828," 52.

Chapter 10

1. James Van Kley, "The Pineywoods," in *Illustrated Flora of East Texas,* ed. George M. Diggs, Jr. et al. (Fort Worth: Botanical Research Institute of Texas, 2006), 1:77.

2. Keith Guthrie, *Texas Forgotten Ports* (Austin: Eakin Press, 1995), 3:135.

3. Lawrence S. Earley, *Looking for Longleaf: The Fall and Rise of an American Forest* (Chapel Hill: The University of North Carolina Press, 2004), 1.

4. Vernon Bailey, *Biological Survey of Texas*, North American Fauna 25, (Washington: U.S. Department of Agriculture, Division of Biological Survey, 1905), 18.

5. Earley, *Looking for Longleaf*, 23–25.

6. Rickey Thibodeaux, "The Story of Timber in Southeast Texas," *Industrial Times*, supplement to *Beaumont Enterprise*, August, 2001.

7. Donald R. Walker, "Harvesting the Forest: Henry Jacob Lutcher, G. Bedell Moore, and the Advent of Commercial Lumbering in Texas," *Journal of the West* 35, no. 3 (1996): 13.

8. Thibodeaux, "Story of Timber."

9. Hamilton Pratt Easton, "The History of the Texas Lumbering Industry" (Ph.D. dissertation, University of Texas, 1947), 122–128.

10. Walker, "Harvesting the Forest," 16.

11. Robert S. Maxwell and Robert D. Baker, *Sawdust Empire: The Texas Lumber Industry, 1830–1940* (College Station: Texas A&M University Press, 1983), 195.

12. Easton, "History of the Texas Lumbering Industry," 349.

13. Thibodeaux, "Story of Timber."

14. Howard C. Williams, ed., *Gateway to Texas: The History of Orange and Orange County* (Orange, Tex.: The Heritage House Museum of Orange, 1988), 117.

15. Earley, *Looking for Longleaf*, 2.

Chapter 11

1. Ralph A. Smith, trans., "Account of the Journey of Bénard de la Harpe: Discovery Made by Him of Several Nations Situated in the West," *Southwestern Historical Quarterly* 62, no. 1 (1958): 76.

2. Ibid., 81.

3. Ibid.

4. Ralph A. Smith, trans., "Account of the Journey of Bénard de la Harpe: Discovery Made by Him of Several Nations Situated in the West," *Southwestern Historical Quarterly* 62, no. 2 (1958): 247.

5. Ibid., 250.

6. Ibid.

7. Ibid., 250–251.

8. Ibid., 255.

9. Ralph A. Smith, trans., "Account of the Journey of Bénard de la Harpe: Discovery Made by Him of Several Nations Situated in the West," *Southwestern Historical Quarterly* 62, no. 4 (1959): 533.

10. Ibid., 535.

11. Ibid., 538.

12. Ralph A. Smith, trans., "Account of the Journey of Bénard de la Harpe," *Southwestern Historical Quarterly* 62, no. 1, 82.

13. Russell M. Magnaghi, "Sulphur Fork Factory, 1817–1822," *Arkansas Historical Quarterly* 37, no. 2 (1978): 177.

14. Campbell and Lynn Loughmiller, *Big Thicket Legacy* (Austin: University of Texas Press, 1977), 108.

Chapter 12

1. M. P. Miroir, R. King Harris, and others, "Bénard de la Harpe and the Nassonite Post," *Bulletin of the Texas Archeological Society* 44, (1973): 162.

2. Ibid.

3. Wes Pendley, "Efforts Persist to Shore up Last Defense Lines," *Texarkana Gazette,* May 11, 1990.

4. Wes Pendley, "Hardest Hit: Hightower Says Bowie County Damage High," *Texarkana Gazette,* May 10, 1990.

5. Meredith and Ethel Edwards (Red River land owners), in discussion with the authors, August 8, 2005.

6. Smith, "Account of the Journey of Bénard de la Harpe," *Southwestern Historical Quarterly* 62, no. 2, 254.

7. Wilson W. Crook, Jr., "Recollections, Anecdotes, and Bibliography of R. K. Harris," in *Texas Archeology: Essays Honoring R. King Harris* (Dallas: SMU Press, 1978), 165–166.

8. Miroir, Harris, and others, "Bénard de la Harpe," 115–118.

9. Ibid., 121.

10. Ibid., 148.

11. Ibid., 132–137.

12. Ibid., 137.

13. Kathleen Gilmore, "French-Indian Interaction at an 18th Century Frontier Post: The Roseborough Lake Site, Bowie County, Texas," *Institute of*

Applied Sciences North Texas State University, Contributions in Archeology, no. 3 (May 1986): 39–40.

14. Miroir, Harris, and others, "Bénard de la Harpe," 126–129.

15. Jay C. Blaine, "The Gilbert Site: An Eighteenth-century French Connection in East Texas," *Texas Beyond History*, Texas Archeology Research Laboratory, University of Texas at Austin. http://texasbeyondhistory.net/gib ert/french.html. (accessed February 26, 2008).

16. Smith, "Account of the Journey of Bénard de la Harpe," *Southwestern Historical Quarterly* 62, no. 1, 86.

17. Ibid., 84, 86; Ralph A. Smith, trans., "Account of the Journey of Bénard de la Harpe: Discovery Made by Him of Several Nations Situated in the West," *Southwestern Historical Quarterly* 62, no. 3 (1959): 375.

18. Randolph B. Marcy, *The Prairie Traveler: A Handbook for Overland Expeditions* (New York: Harper and Brothers Publishers, 1859), 239.

19. Robin W. Doughty, *Wildlife and Man in Texas*, 157.

20. Schmidly, *Texas Natural History*, 442.

21. Doughty, *Wildlife and Man in Texas*, 196.

Chapter 13

1. Dan L. Flores, ed., *Journal of an Indian Trader: Anthony Glass and the Texas Trading Frontier, 1790–1810* (College Station: Texas A&M University Press, 1985), 117. Quotations from letters and journal entries written by A. Glass and J. Sibley are exact transcriptions (including capitalization and ampersands).

2. Ibid., 92.

3. Ibid., 61.

4. Ibid.

5. Ibid., 68–69.

6. Ibid., 85–86.

7. John Sibley to Benjamin Silliman, June 2, 1822, Silliman Family Papers, Yale University Library.

8. Ibid.

9. Ibid.

10. Flores, *Journal of an Indian Trader*, 90.

11. Ibid.

12. Miroir, Harris, and others, "Bénard de la Harpe," 121, 129, 146.

13. John Sibley to Benjamin Silliman, June 2, 1822.

14. Flores, *Journal of an Indian Trader*, 91.

15. Monica M. Grady, *Catalogue of Meteorites: with special reference to those represented in the collection of the Natural History Museum, London*, 5th ed. (Cambridge: Cambridge University Press, 2000), 423.

16. "Rare Minerals," *New York Daily Tribune*, August 11, 1877.

Chapter 14

1. William C. Pool, *A Historical Atlas of Texas* (Austin: The Encino Press, 1975), 10.

2. Geiser, *Naturalists of the Frontier*, 24.

3. Ibid., 21.

4. Ibid., 24.

5. Samuel Wood Geiser, "Prof. Jacob Boll Won Fame as Naturalist While Making Home in Dallas From 1869–1880," *Dallas Morning News*, October 21, 1928.

6. Samuel Wood Geiser papers circa 1915–1975, SMU 1991.0001, DeGolyer Library, Southern Methodist University.

7. Geiser, *Naturalists of the Frontier*, 25.

8. Edward Drinker Cope, "Descriptions of Extinct Vertebrata from the Permian and Triassic Formations of the United States," *Proceedings of the American Philosophical Society* 17, no. 100 (Jun.-Dec., 1877): 191.

9. Geiser, *Naturalists of the Frontier*, 29.

10. Geiser, "Prof. Jacob Boll Won Fame."

11. Jack Loftin, *Trails Through Archer* (Austin: Eakin Publications, Inc., 1979), 149.

12. Alfred Sherwood Romer, "Fossil Collecting in the Texas Redbeds," *Harvard Alumni Bulletin* 42, no. 30 (May 24, 1940): 1045.

13. Loftin, *Trails Through Archer*, 159.

14. Romer, "Fossil Collecting in the Texas Redbeds," 1045.

15. Alfred Sherwood Romer, *Vertebrate Paleontology* (Chicago: The University of Chicago Press, 1945), 137, 277.

16. P. Martin Sander, "Taphonomy of the Lower Permian Geraldine Bonebed in Archer County, Texas," *Paleogeography, Paleoclimatology, Paleoecology* 61 (1987): 221.

17. Ibid., 233–235.

18. Ibid., 224.

19. Loftin, *Trails Through Archer*, 157.

Chapter 15

1. Andy Adams, *The Log of A Cowboy: A Narrative of the Old Trail Days* (Lincoln: University of Nebraska Press, 1903), 120.

2. River Valley Pioneer Museum, "Ranching in Hemphill County: Cabin Creek Ranch," http://www.rivervalleymuseum.org/ranching_history.htm (accessed June 1, 2008).

3. Christopher Lintz, "The Stamper Site, Part 1," *Oklahoma Archeology: Journal of the Oklahoma Anthropological Society* 51, no. 2 (2003): 20.

4. Ibid., 19–22.

Chapter 16

1. T. L. Eyerly, "The Buried City of the Panhandle," *The Archeological Bulletin* 3, January-March, 1912, p. 1–2.

2. Steve Black, ed., "Buried City: Credits & Sources," Texas Beyond History, Texas Archeological Research Laboratory, University of Texas at Austin, www://texasbeyondhistory.net/villagers/buriedcity/credits.html (accessed May 1, 2008).

3. David Hughes, "Buried City: Village Life Along Wolf Creek," Texas Beyond History, Texas Archeological Research Laboratory, University of Texas at Austin, http://www.texasbeyondhistory.net/villagers/buriedcity/index.html (accessed May 15, 2008).

4. David Hughes, "Buried City: Who Lived at Buried City," http://www.texasbeyondhistory.net/villagers/buriedcity/who.html (accessed May 15, 2008).

5. Warren King Moorehead, *Archeology of the Arkansas River Valley* (New Haven: Yale University Press, 1931), 96.

6. Eyerly, "The Buried City of the Panhandle," 1.

7. David Hughes, "Research History: Early Days," http://www.texasbeyondhistory.net/villagers/research/early.html (accessed October 14, 2006).

8. Ibid.

9. Moorehead, *Archeology of the Arkansas River Valley*, 106.

10. David Hughes, "Panhandle Pueblo Culture," http://www.texasbeyondhistory.net/villagers/research/culture.html (accessed October 14, 2006).

11. Ibid.

12. Ibid.

13. Ibid.

14. Scott Brosowske, "2008 TAS Field School," Texas Archeological Society, http://www.txarch.org/Activities/fschool/fs2008/archeology02.html (accessed June 25, 2008).

15. Hughes, "Research History: Early Days."

16. Hughes, "Panhandle Pueblo Culture."

17. Christopher Lintz, "The Stamper Site, Part 1," 21–22.

18. Hughes, "Research History: Early Days" (Antelope Creek 22 photo caption).

19. Harold Courson (landowner), in discussion with the authors, June 15, 2008.

20. Frank X. Tolbert, "Summing Up 5,000 Wonderful Miles," *The Dallas Morning News,* July 8, 1955.

Bibliography

Abert, James W. *Gúadal P'a: The Journal of Lieutenant J. W. Abert from Bent's Fort to St. Louis in 1845,* with introduction and notes by H. Bailey Carroll. Canyon, Tex.: Panhandle-Plains Historical Society, 1941.

Adams, Andy. *The Log of a Cowboy: A Narrative of the Old Trail Days.* Lincoln: University of Nebraska Press, 1903.

Alexander, Nancy. *Father of Texas Geology: Robert T. Hill.* Dallas: Southern Methodist University Press, 1976.

Bailey, Florence Merriam. "Meeting Spring Half Way, Part II." *Condor* 18 (1916): 183–190.

———. "Meeting Spring Half Way, Part III." *Condor* 18 (1916): 214–219.

Bailey, Vernon. *Biological Survey of Texas, 1889–1905.* North American Fauna No. 25. Washington, D.C.: United States Department of Agriculture, Division of Biological Survey, 1905.

Berlandier, Jean Louis. *Journey to Mexico: During the Years 1826–1834.* Translated by Sheila M. Olendorf, Josette M. Bigelow, and Mary M. Standifer. 2 vols. Austin: Texas State Historical Association, in cooperation with the Center for Studies in Texas History. University of Texas, 1980.

Blair, W. Frank, Albert P. Blair, Pierce Brodkorb, Fred R. Cagle, and George A. Moore. *Vertebrates of the United States.* 2nd ed. New York: McGraw-Hill, 1957.

Chadwick, Douglas H. "Crown of the Continent." *National Geographic* (September 2007): 60–79.

Clopper, Joseph C. "Journal of J. C. Clopper, 1828." *The Quarterly of the Texas State Historical Association* 13 (1909–10): 44–81.

Cope, Edward Drinker. "Descriptions of Extinct Vertebrata from the Permian and Triassic Formations of the United States." *Proceedings of the American Philosophical Society* 17, no. 100 (1877): 182–193.

Crook, Wilson W. Jr. "Recollections, Anecdotes, and Bibliography of R. K. Harris." In *Texas Archeology: Essays Honoring R. King Harris,* edited by Kurt D. House, 165–171. Dallas: Southern Methodist University Press, 1978.

"Destruction of Birds for Millinery Purposes." *Science* 7, no. 160 (February 26, 1886): 196–197.

Doughty, Robin W. *Feather Fashions and Bird Preservation: A Study in Nature Protection.* Berkeley: University of California Press, 1975.

———. *Wildlife and Man in Texas: Environmental Change and Conservation.* College Station: Texas A&M University Press, 1983.

Earley, Lawrence S. *Looking for Longleaf: The Fall and Rise of an American Forest.* Chapel Hill: University of North Carolina Press, 2004.

Easton, Hamilton Pratt. "The History of the Texas Lumbering Industry." PhD diss., University of Texas, 1947.

Everitt, James H., D. Lynn Drawe, and Robert I. Leonard. *Trees, Shrubs, & Cacti of South Texas.* Lubbock: Texas Tech University Press, 2002.

Eyerly, T. L. "The Buried City of the Panhandle." *The Archeological Bulletin* 3 (January-March, 1912): 1–5. Available as a PDF file at Texas Beyond History, Texas Archeological Research Laboratory, University of Texas at Austin, http://www.texasbeyondhistory.net/villagers/buriedcity/credits.html (accessed May 27, 2008).

French, Samuel Gibbs. "A Report in Relation to the Route over which the Government Train Moved from San Antonio to El Paso del Norte, Made in Pursuance to Order . . . dated May 30, 1849." U. S. Senate, 31st Cong., 1st sess., 1850. vol. 14, no. 64.

Fuertes, Louis Agassiz. Papers #2662. Division of Rare and Manuscript Collections, Cornell University Library, Ithaca.

Gaillardet, Frédéric. *Sketches of Early Texas and Louisiana.* Translated by James L. Shepherd, III, with an introduction and notes. Austin: University of Texas Press, 1966.

Gehlbach, Frederick R. *Mountain Islands and Desert Seas: A Natural History of the U.S.-Mexican Borderlands.* College Station: Texas A&M University Press, 1981.

Geiser, Samuel Wood. "Charles Wright's 1849 Botanical Collecting Trip from San Antonio to El Paso: with Type-localities for New Species." Reprinted from *Field and Laboratory* 4, no. 1, November 1935.

———. *Naturalists of the Frontier.* Dallas: Southern Methodist University Press, 1937.

———. "Prof. Jacob Boll Won Fame as Naturalist While Making Home in Dallas from 1869–1880." *Dallas Morning News,* October 21, 1928.

———. Papers circa 1915–1975. DeGolyer Library, Southern Methodist University, Dallas, Texas, SMU 1991.0001.

Gilmore, Kathleen. *French-Indian Interaction at an 18th Century Frontier Post:*

The Roseborough Lake Site, Bowie County, Texas. Contributions in Archeology. No. 3. Denton, Tex.: Institute of Applied Sciences, North Texas State University, May 1986.

Glass, Anthony. *Journal of an Indian Trader: Anthony Glass and the Texas Trading Frontier, 1790–1810.* Edited by Dan L. Flores. College Station: Texas A&M University Press, 1985.

Goetzmann, William H. *Exploration & Empire: The Explorer & the Scientist in the Winning of the American West.* Austin: Texas State Historical Association, 1993.

Grady, Monica M. *Catalogue of Meteorites: with Special Reference to Those Represented in the Collection of the Natural History Museum, London.* 5th ed. Cambridge: Cambridge University Press, 2000.

Gray, Asa. Papers. Library of the Gray Herbarium. Harvard University.

Guthrie, Keith. *Texas Forgotten Ports.* Vol. 3. Austin: Eakin Press, 1995.

Gutierrez, Rubin Flores. "Guerrero Viejo: An Architectural Legacy." In *A Shared Experience: The History, Architecture and Historic Designations of the Lower Rio Grande Heritage Corridor,* edited by Mario L. Sanchez, 199–223. Austin: Los Caminos del Rio Heritage Project and the Texas Historical Commission, 1994.

Hafen, LeRoy R. *Broken Hand: The Life of Thomas Fitzpatrick: Mountain Man, Guide, and Indian Agent.* Denver: Old West Publishing Co., 1973.

Hartman, Clinton P. "Charles Wright: Botanizer of the Boundary, Part I." *Password* 37, no. 2. (1992): 55–70.

Hill, Robert T. "Running the Cañons of the Rio Grande." *Century Magazine* 61 (1901): 371–387.

———"Running the Cañons of the Rio Grande, Part 1." *Dallas Morning News,* August 5, 1934.

———"Running the Cañons of the Rio Grande, Part 5." *Dallas Morning News,* September 16, 1934.

Jackson, Donald. *Voyages of the Steamboat Yellow Stone.* New York: Ticknor & Fields, 1985.

Kley, James Van. "The Pineywoods." In *Illustrated Flora of East Texas.* Vol. 1. Edited by George M. Diggs Jr., Barney L. Lipscomb, Monique D. Reed, and Robert J. O'Kennon, 76–106. Fort Worth: Botanical Research Institute of Texas, 2006.

Kofalk, Harriet. *No Woman Tenderfoot.* College Station: Texas A&M University Press, 1989.

Lehmann, Valgene W. *Forgotten Legions: Sheep in the Rio Grande Plain of Texas.* El Paso: Texas Western Press, 1969.

Lintz, Christopher. "The Stamper Site, Part 1." *Oklahoma Archeology: Journal of the Oklahoma Anthropological Society* 51, no. 2 (2003): 13–36.

Loftin, Jack. *Trails Through Archer: A Centennial History, 1880–1980.* Austin: Eakin Publications, Inc., 1979.

Loughmiller, Campbell, and Lynn Loughmiller. *Big Thicket Legacy.* Austin: University of Texas Press, 1977.

Magnaghi, Russell M. "Sulphur Fork Factory, 1817–1822." *Arkansas Historical Quarterly* 37, no. 2. (1978): 167–183.

Marcy, Randolph B. *The Prairie Traveler: A Handbook for Overland Expeditions.* New York: Harper and Brothers, 1859.

Maxwell, Robert S., and Robert D. Baker. *Sawdust Empire: The Texas Lumber Industry, 1830–1940.* College Station: Texas A&M University Press, 1983.

Maxwell, Ross A. *The Big Bend of the Rio Grande: A Guide to the Rocks, Geologic History, and Settlers of the Area of Big Bend National Park, Guidebook 7.* Austin: Bureau of Economic Geology, University of Texas, 1968.

McCracken, Karen Harden. *Connie Hagar: The Life History of a Texas Birdwatcher.* College Station: Texas A&M University Press, 1986.

Miroir, M. P., R. King Harris, J. C. Blaine, and J. McVay. "Bernard de la Harpe and the Nassonite Post." *Bulletin of the Texas Archeological Society* 44 (1973): 113–167.

Moorehead, Warren King. *Archeology of the Arkansas River Valley.* New Haven: Yale University Press, 1931.

Oberholser, Harry C. *The Bird Life of Texas.* Edited by Edgar B. Kincaid Jr., Suzanne Winckler, and John L. Rowlett. 2 vols. Austin: University of Texas Press, 1974.

Peck, Robert M. *A Celebration of Birds: The Life and Art of Louis Agassiz Fuertes.* New York: Walker and Company, 1982.

Pendley, Wes. "Efforts Persist to Shore up Last Defense Lines." *Texarkana Gazette,* May 11, 1990.

———. "Hardest Hit: Hightower Says Bowie County Damage High." *Texarkana Gazette,* May 10, 1990.

Pool, William C. *A Historical Atlas of Texas.* Austin: Encino Press, 1975.

Port of Houston Authority. "Trade Development Division: Trade Statistics." Port of Houston Authority, http://portofhouston.com/busdev/tradedevelop ment/tradestatistics.html (accessed April 1, 2008).

"Rare Minerals." *New York Daily Tribune,* August 11, 1877.

Rathjen, Frederick. *The Texas Panhandle Frontier.* Austin: University of Texas Press, 1973.

River Valley Pioneer Museum. "Ranching in Hemphill County: Cabin Creek Ranch." River Valley Pioneer Museum, http://www.rivervalleymuseum .org/ranching_history.htm (accessed June 1, 2008).

Romer, Alfred Sherwood. "Fossil Collecting in the Texas Redbeds." *Harvard Alumni Bulletin* 42, no. 30 (May 24, 1940): 1045–1049.

———. *Vertebrate Paleontology.* 2nd Ed. Chicago: University of Chicago Press, 1945.

Sander, P. Martin. "Taphonomy of the Lower Permian Geraldine Bonebed in Archer County, Texas." *Paleogeography, Paleoclimatology, Paleoecology* 61 (1986): 221–236.

Schmidly, David J. *Texas Natural History: A Century of Change.* Lubbock: Texas Tech University Press, 2002.

Schneider, Jeffrey A. "Environmental Investigations: The Great Underground Sponge: Ogallala." Department of Chemistry, State University of New York, http://www.oswego.edu/~schneidr.CH300/envinv/EnvInv12.html (accessed June 2, 2009).

Schumard, George G. *The Geology of Western Texas.* Austin: State Printing Office, 1886.

Smith, Ralph A., trans. "Account of the Journey of Bénard de la Harpe: Discovery Made by Him of Several Nations Situated in the West." *Southwestern Historical Quarterly* 62, no. 1 (1958): 75–86.

———. "Account of the Journey of Bénard de la Harpe: Discovery Made by Him of Several Nations Situated in the West." *Southwestern Historical Quarterly* 62, no. 2 (1958): 246–259.

———. "Account of the Journey of Bénard de la Harpe: Discovery Made by Him of Several Nations Situated in the West." *Southwestern Historical Quarterly* 62, no. 3 (1959): 371–385.

———. "Account of the Journey of Bénard de la Harpe: Discovery Made by Him of Several Nations Situated in the West." *Southwestern Historical Quarterly* 62, no. 4 (1959): 525–541.

Stone, Witmer. "Report of the Committee on the Protection of North American Birds for the Year 1900." *The Auk* 18 (1901): 68–76.

Taylor, Richard B., Jimmy Rutledge, and Joe G. Herrera. *A Field Guide to Common South Texas Shrubs.* Austin: Texas Parks and Wildlife Press, 1999.

Texas A&M University, Cartographics Laboratory. *Roads of Texas.* Fredericksburg, Tex.: Shearer Publishing, 1995.

Texas Beyond History. Texas Archeology Research Laboratory. University of Texas at Austin, http://www.texasbeyondhistory.net.

Texas Parks and Wildlife Department. "Wildlife Fact Sheets." Texas Parks and Wildlife Department, http://www.tpwd.state.tx.us/huntwild/wild/species/?=endangered (accessed October 4, 2007).

Thibodeaux, Rickey. "The Story of Timber in Southeast Texas." *Industrial Times,* Advertising Supplement of the *Beaumont Enterprise* (August 2001).

Tolbert, Frank X. "Summing Up 5,000 Wonderful Miles." *Dallas Morning News,* July 8, 1955.

———. *Tolbert's Texas.* Garden City, N.Y.: Doubleday, 1983.

Tyler, Ron, ed. *The New Handbook of Texas.* 6 vols. Austin: The Texas State Historical Association, 1996.

Walker, Donald R. "Harvesting the Forest: Henry Jacob Lutcher, G. Bedell Moore, and the Advent of Commercial Lumbering in Texas." *Journal of the West* 35, no. 3 (1966): 10–17.

Wasowski, Sally, with Andy Wasosowski. *Native Texas Plants: Landscaping Region by Region.* Houston: Gulf Publishing Co., 1991.

Weidenmann, Harold T. "Factors to Consider When Sculpting Brush: Mechanical Treatment Options." Texas AgriLife Extension Service, Texas A&M System, http://texnat.tamu.edu/symposia/sculptor/18.htm (accessed July 1, 2008).

Williams, Howard C., ed. *Gateway to Texas: The History of Orange and Orange County.* Orange, Tex.: The Heritage House Museum of Orange, 1988.

Wright, Charles. "Field Notes for Charles Wright for 1849 and 1851–52." Typewritten transcription with commentary by Ivan M. Johnston. Library of the Gray Herbarium. Harvard University.

Index

ISBN-13: 978-1-60344-153-7
ISBN-10: 1-60344-153-0

"A cop!" she gasped

"If you're a cop," she demanded, "where's your badge?"

"I dumped it. And I lost my gun coming after—"

"Get out of here!" she snapped suddenly, aware that hysteria was rising in her. She didn't realize that her voice was also rising. "Cops don't—"

"Shhh! Are you trying to get us both killed? If they even get a whiff of who I am, I'll become shark bait. Listen to me, lady. Listen good. I'm a cop—whether you believe it or not. Go along with me. I'm only going to warn you once, because I can bail out of this real easy by myself. Pull one more stunt against me and I swear I'll jump overboard.

"I don't mind sticking around to do my job, but I'll be damned if I'll keep worrying about getting killed *because* of you instead of *for* you!"

Also available from Mira Books by
HEATHER GRAHAM POZZESSERE

SLOW BURN

Don't miss these upcoming titles by
HEATHER GRAHAM POZZESSERE
Coming soon from Mira Books

KING OF THE CASTLE
STRANGERS IN PARADISE
ANGEL OF MERCY
DARK STRANGER

HEATHER GRAHAM POZZESSERE

A MATTER OF CIRCUMSTANCE

MIRA BOOKS

ISBN 1-55166-005-9

A MATTER OF CIRCUMSTANCE

Copyright © 1987 by Heather Graham Pozzessere.

Printed in U.S.A.

A MATTER OF
CIRCUMSTANCE

wooden docks gave way to the cold reality of the concrete parking lot.

Sean heard a little titter of laughter and gazed sideways, annoyed to realize that he had become an object of fascination for two well-endowed teenagers in string bikinis. He tensed, swearing to himself. If something was going to happen after this long and futile day, it would surely happen now, while the kiddies were in the way.

He lowered his head, feigning a nap, hoping they would go away.

At his side, what looked like a credit-card-sized AM/FM receiver suddenly made a little buzzing sound. Sean picked it up and brought it to his ear.

"Hey, Latin lover!" Anderson teased. Sean looked up; he could see Harvey Anderson in the refreshment stand, chatting while he turned hot dogs on a grill. "You got a fan club going there, you know? I think you should be on grill duty. You're too pretty to blend into the woodwork."

Sean idly moved the radio in front of his mouth. "Anderson, it's not that I'm too pretty—you're just too damned ugly. You'd scare away the devil himself."

Todd Bridges, unseen, but not far away in the parking lot, broke in on the conversation. "Must be those Irish eyes, Sean. Keep 'em lowered, eh?"

"Todd..."

"Hey, who said duty was a chore?" Harvey interrupted. "Will you look at that? I am in love! Thunderstruck and all that junk. Now I really think you should be grilling the hot dogs, Ramiro! Ah, I'd like just a whiff of the air she breathes!"

1

From one of the assorted ketches, catamarans, speedboats and yachts, a Jimmy Buffet tune was rising high on the air, tarnished by only a shade of static. The late afternoon was tempering the heat, and a breeze was flowing in from the water, cooling Sean Ramiro's sun-sizzled arms and chest. To all outward appearances he was as negligent and lackadaisical as the carefree Sunday loafers who laughed, teased, flirted and played around the docks. But when he raised his head for a moment, tilting back the brim of his Panama hat, a careful observer might have noted that he surveyed the scene with startlingly intense green eyes.

All seemed peaceful and pleasant. A lazy afternoon by the water. Girls in bikinis, guys in cutoffs, tourists with white cream on their noses, and old geezers in bright flowered shirts. Kids threw fish tails to the gulls that hovered nearby. Sean arched his shoulders back, grimacing at the feel of the wooden dock piling that grated through the thin material of his cotton shirt. He'd been sitting there a long time now.

Farther down the dock Sunday fisherman were cleaning their catches. A young sailor in tie-dyed cutoffs was hosing down his small Cigarette boat. A group of beer drinkers passed him, heading for the refreshment stand that was located where the rustic-looking

Harvey was always falling in love with anything in a bikini. But Sean idly turned his head, tilting the brim of his hat just a shade. He arched a dark brow and was surprised to discover that his breath had caught in his chest.

This time Harvey was right on the mark.

She was coming in from the end of the dock. She walked slowly and casually, and with the most sensual grace Sean had ever witnessed. She wasn't wearing a bikini, but a one-piece thing cut high on the thighs, and man-oh-man, did those slim sexy thighs go on forever.

If someone were to have asked Sean Ramiro what he first noticed about a woman, he would have given it a little thought, then answered with honesty, "Her eyes." Eyes were the mirror of the soul, as the saying went. And so he looked first at her eyes.

He couldn't see their color, not from his position, not with the way he was forced to squint into the sun. He did see that they were sparkling like the sun, that they were large and exquisite, that they were framed with thick lashes ... that they enchanted.

He didn't know why, but his eyes fell then to take in the whole of her. Her easy, idle movement. Her walk...

He was—even on duty—spellbound by that walk. The never-ending length of her golden tanned legs, the curve of her hips. He liked her waistline, too, smooth and sleek. Just like Harvey, he was instantly in love. Spaghetti straps held the yellow swimsuit in place. The top was straight cut, but she needed no help to display her cleavage. Her still-damp skintight bathing suit couldn't hide the fact that her breasts were firm, round, perfect. Sean realized that he felt a bit like a kid in a candy store, almost overwhelmed by the desire to reach out and touch.

"Will you look at those...eyes," Harvey breathed in awe.

"What is it?" Todd demanded from the parking lot.

"Boy, did you draw the wrong straw!" Harvey told him.

Sean looked back to her face.

It was a perfect oval. High boned. Classical. She could have posed for history's most famous artists, and not one of them could have found a flaw. Her mouth was generous, but elegantly defined. Sean could imagine her laughing; the sound would be as provocative as the curve of those lips. Her nose was long and straight, and her eyes—those wondrous eyes!—were framed by high brows that added to their captivating size and beauty. And her hair...

Her hair matched the coming of the sunset in glorious color. It wasn't blond, neither was it dark. It was a tawny color, like a lion's mane, with deeper highlights of shimmering red to match the streak of the sun against the sky.

"I am in love!" Harvey repeated.

"Oh, watch your hot dogs!" Todd grumbled from the parking lot.

Sean grimaced, jerking involuntarily as the radio suddenly gave out a burst of static. Then Todd's voice came back on the air.

"I just got a buzz from Captain Mallory. Someone pulled in faulty information. Blayne isn't here, and he isn't coming. He's got a reservation on a flight north at six."

For a moment Sean completely forgot the woman, as he closed his eyes in disgust. Damn that Blayne! The senator had received threats against his life, but he had lifted his naive nose to the police, who had bent over backward to protect him. Still, as public servants, it was their job to protect him.

They'd been tipped off today that Blayne, who had mysteriously disappeared, had ordered a catered lunch delivered to the docks this morning for a sailboat registered as the *Flash Point*. Meanwhile, another threat had been phoned in to the police. Of all the lousy details to draw, Sean had drawn this one. He'd had to spend the whole stinking day on the dock, waiting for Peter Blayne to make an appearance and to see that he got off the docks without mishap.

Now it seemed the fool had never been anywhere near the docks to begin with, nor intended to be. The boat had gone out earlier, but without the senator aboard.

Sean opened his eyes again. Not even his disgust at the wasted day could really have any effect on him— not when he was staring at *her*, and she was coming closer. A scuba mask and a pair of flippers dangled from one hand as she moved along, still at that lazy, no-hurry pace. Her face was tilted upward, and the smallest signs of a smile curved her lip, as if she was savoring that soft kiss of sun and breeze against her cheeks.

Just like some ancient goddess, Sean thought, and he could almost see her walking along at that slow confident pace, naked and assured, in some flower-strewn field, while a primitive drumbeat pulsed out the rhythm of her fluid motion and an ancient man bowed down before her.

"Hey!" Harvey's voice, quiet and tense, suddenly jolted Sean from his daydream.

"What?"

"It's back. The *Flash Point*. Way down the dock—she didn't berth where she should have!"

Sean stared down the dock. It was true. The *Flash Point* was in, and two kids—or young men—were securing her lines.

He stood, slowly, carefully, unaware that he grimaced as all the muscles in his six-foot-two frame complained. Absently he rubbed a shoulder and stared down at the ketch. Nice. It had three masts and probably slept a dozen in privacy and comfort.

It was Blayne's boat, and someone had gone out on it. But if Peter Blayne was really catching a six o'clock flight, they couldn't possibly have picked him up and brought him back on the ketch. It was six now.

Someone behind him began an excited conversation, half in Spanish, half in English. Two men cleaning fish were talking about a woman, trying to decide if it was "her" or not. Without thinking, Sean tuned in the words, then tuned them out, more concerned with the arrival of the *Flash Point* than he was with "that rat's old lady."

He supposed he should saunter down and ask a few questions. Pulling his open shirt across his chest to conceal the holster strapped underneath, he stared at his quarry, then started toward it. He rubbed his jaw and the dark stubble there, wondering if he didn't look more than a little like a bum. Good for sitting around on a dock idly, but a little scary, maybe, to the elite teenagers battening down the *Flash Point*.

He didn't realize how quickly he was moving until he suddenly plowed into somebody—and knocked them down. He started to bend down and offer a hand, then he noticed that he wasn't the only person racing toward the *Flash Point*.

From the end of the pier a slim, handsome young Latin with a grim look of purpose and something bunched in his arms was hurrying toward the ketch— or toward the end of the dock. Sean wasn't sure.

What he *was* sure about was the man's identity.

It was Garcia. Definitely. Julio Garcia, old Jorge's son. He had his father's flashing dark eyes and arresting, near-gaunt face.

Sean immediately felt tension riddle him. The police might have been wrong about Blayne's whereabouts, but if so, it seemed a strange coincidence that the people threatening him had received the same faulty information.

"You stupid ox!"

Momentarily startled, Sean stared in the direction of the feminine voice that had spat out the epithet. It was her. The sensually swaying woman with the never-ending legs and great eyes.

Eyes . . .

They were topaz. Not brown. Not green. Not hazel. They were the color of light, shimmering honey, sparkling now like liquid sunlight, like precious gems reflecting the last dying rays of the sun in a burst of rebellious glory.

And he'd just knocked her down flat, without a word of apology. He could reach out and touch her. He could . . .

He offered her a hand. She took it with delicate fingers, watching him warily.

If only Garcia wasn't just yards away . . .

"Hey!" The voice came from down the dock. Garcia was gripping the arm of one of the kids who had been working on the *Flash Point*. "I don't know what you're talking about!"

Even from this distance Sean could hear the kid's angry retort to whatever Garcia had said. Then the kid's voice lowered, and Garcia said something with a frightening vehemence.

Sean didn't know that he had dropped the woman's hand when she was halfway up until she thudded back to the wood with a furious oath. "You are the rudest person I have ever met!"

He barely heard her; he was too tense, watching Garcia.

"Don't you speak English? *Estúpido!*" the woman snapped.

Absently he offered a hand to her again.

"Don't touch me! Just move, please. Honest to God, I don't know what's wrong with people these days!"

Sean ignored her, anxious to reach Garcia. But even as he stepped past her, the kid with Garcia looked up and started yelling. "Hey, Mrs. Blayne! Can you do something with this guy? He insists that the senator is aboard and I keep telling him that he isn't!"

Blayne!

Sean swung around and stared at the beauty he'd just knocked over, then ignored. Mrs. Blayne? His wife? She couldn't be! Blayne was in his mid-forties or early fifties if he was a day; this woman was twenty-five, twenty-eight, tops!

She was impatiently dusting herself off after her fall on the sandy dock, but she smiled at the kid with a rueful shake of her head. "Tell him Peter had to be in Washington tonight. He isn't on the *Flash Point*—he probably isn't even in the state anymore."

The kid started speaking earnestly to Garcia. Sean was momentarily frozen, with two thoughts registering in his mind.

Blayne wasn't here; they had all been wrong, and it was probably for the best. Garcia hadn't identified himself during any of the threatening calls, but who else could be so violently angry with the senator except for some crackpot? And Garcia was definitely a crackpot.

The other thought, which interrupted his professional logic in a way that annoyed him, was about her. She was married to the man. And quite obviously for his money, since the age difference was definitely vast!

It was irritating, and somehow it hurt—for all that any feelings on his part were ridiculous. She was just a dream. The absolute, perfect dream you might see on the page of some magazine, then forget just as soon as the page was turned. Yet he wanted to shake her. To demand where her morals were—and her dignity and pride!—that she would marry an old guy like Blayne just for the sake of material possessions.

But even as he thought that, he smiled a little ruefully. Because the question that was really bothering him was, why him and not me? I'm thirty-three and as healthy as the "ox" you just called me. I'm the one who could show you what life was meant to be, just what you were built for, lady!

He reminded himself that he didn't like blondes. But any man, face-to-face with this particular blonde, would want her.

"Roberto, man, it is her! Julio, the old lady!"

Sean frowned, realizing then that the two fishermen were yelling to Garcia. He was halfway to the man himself, but paused.

The two fishermen jumped into a speedboat.

"Hey, wait—" he called to them. Where the hell was Harvey? Couldn't he tell something was happening? But how would he? Nothing illegal was going on. Two men had jumped into a speedboat, and Julio Garcia was talking to a kid. Nothing to get arrested for, but...

"Get out of the way! Get down!"

The heavily accented command came from Julio Garcia. Sean ducked, then fell flat as a whole barrage of bullets was suddenly spewed haphazardly in his direction. He tasted sand as he fell hard against the wood, reaching for his .38 caliber Smith & Wesson as a second barrage began.

Julio was fast; he kept firing as he raced down the dock. The shots rang out discordantly against the absolute and lazy peace of the afternoon, shocking everyone, causing chaos and so many screams that Sean didn't know where to look.

The woman!

He rolled just in time to see that the thing under Julio's arm had been potato sacking, and that Julio had looped it over her head, thrown her struggling but constrained figure over his shoulder and made a wild leap for the speedboat.

Sean didn't dare shoot; he would hit the woman.

He didn't think; he just reacted. He dove into the water, determined to reach the boat before it could jet out into open water and head for the endless nooks and crannies that the mangrove islands could provide.

2

He wasn't accustomed to making mistakes. A homicide detective simply couldn't make mistakes and expect to live.

But as he dove into the murky water his gun was swept from his hand by a stinging collision with the wood and instantly disappeared into a growth of seaweed. Still submerged, Sean could hear the motor of the speedboat revving up, and he knew he didn't have a spare second left. It seemed necessary at any cost to reach that boat and then come up with a plan of action, minus his gun.

His fingers grasped the edge of the boat while it was already in motion. Water splashed into his face, blinding him, gagging him. He held on, feeling the tremendous force of the pressure against him.

Ass! he accused himself, but too late. To give up now would be to risk the murderous blades of the propeller, so, thinking himself the greatest idiot ever to draw breath, he grated his teeth against the agony of his hold and tried to bring his body as close as possible to the side of the boat.

The motor was suddenly cut, and Sean remembered just in time to ditch his ID card and gun clip.

"*¿Qué pasa? ¿Qué pasa?*"

He heard the furious query, then a colorful spate of oaths in Spanish. Someone reached over the side of the boat to pull his half-drowned body over the edge.

He was dizzy; his head reeled as he lay soaked between two side-to-side seats. He gasped in a breath even as he heard the motor rev into motion again and felt the vibrations with his entire body.

The three men—Garcia and the two fishermen— were fighting away, screaming and gesticulating over the terrible hum of the motor, an occasional word of English slipping into the Spanish tirades.

"What happened? Who the hell is he?"

"I don't know. Why didn't you kill him?"

"We're not murderers!"

"We agreed if we had to—"

Something pounded viciously against his head, and Sean groaned despite himself. Twisting, he saw that the burlap sack containing the girl was stretched out over the seat so that her feet dangled right over his head, only the toes bared.

Of all things he noticed that her toenails were filed and manicured and glazed in a deep wine red. For some reason that irritated him. Maybe he realized he'd half killed himself over some mercenary socialite.

"Why did we take her?" one of the fishermen whined.

"She's twice as good as the old man! Hey, if he wants her back, he'll see that my father is set free!" Garcia proclaimed.

"So who the hell is this guy?" the second fisherman asked.

Sean, blinking furiously, more to clear his head than his eyes, pushed himself up to his elbows. If the stinking motor would just stop! He would need his wits to get out of this one. In the last few minutes the sun had decided to make a sharp fall. The boat was carrying no lights. Everything seemed to be a haze of darkness: the sea joining the sky, the men seated in the motorboat nothing more than macabre silhouettes. There weren't even any stars out. He was grateful that there didn't seem to be any other boats out, either.

He felt, though, that all the men were staring at him. Especially Garcia, who was seated next to the bundled, struggling figure in burlap.

Her toes crashed into his nose when he tried to elbow himself into a better position.

"*Me llamo* Miguel Ramiro," he began, yelling above the motor, but just as he started screeching, the motor was cut.

"*Cállate!*" Garcia snapped. Shut up.

Sean heard the water lapping against the side of the boat, then a woman's shout from nearby, and Garcia's quick answer. They came alongside a much bigger vessel, some kind of motorized, two-masted sailboat. A ladder was dropped down; Garcia motioned the two fishermen up first, then turned to stare down at Sean. Despite the poor light Sean could see the dark, wary glitter in his eyes.

"Who are you?"

"Miguel Ramiro."

"And who is Miguel Ramiro?"

The woman—Mrs. Blayne—could blow the whole thing in a matter of seconds, but he had to come up with something. He damn well couldn't introduce himself as a cop. He inclined his head toward the burlap. "She is mine," he replied in Spanish.

Garcia arched a dark brow, then leveled the gun at Sean. "Then you take her up the ladder—and then explain yourself."

Sean struggled to his feet between the wooden seats. He bent over the burlap, trying to figure out just where to grab her. He obviously made a mistake, because his hand encountered something nicely rounded, and the bundle let out an outraged shriek and began twisting and squirming all over again.

"Stop it!" he snapped in English. A recognizable piece of anatomy swung toward him, and in sudden exasperation he gave it a firm swat. Her outraged cry reached him again, and he tried to murmur convincingly, "It is Miguel. I am with you, my darling."

Garcia's brow arched higher; Sean figured he couldn't press his luck too far and decided it didn't matter in the least right now which part of her anatomy he came in contact with. He reached down, gripped her body and tossed her over his shoulder, wincing as she came in contact with a sore spot, right where he had hit the deck to avoid the gunfire.

"Up the ladder," Garcia said.

Sean nodded and started up. His squirming burden almost sent him catapulting back down.

For Garcia's benefit he swore heatedly in Spanish, then added contritely in English, "My love, please! It is me, Miguel!"

Her reply was inarticulate, but Sean knew what she was saying: who the hell was Miguel?

Maybe he would be better off if she remained wrapped in burlap for a while. He probably wouldn't have to carry this thing off for too long. Harry and Todd had been on the docks. Search boats and helicopters would be out soon.

Yeah, but the coastline was a maze of islands and shoals and shallows and roots.... The mangroves, the islets, the Everglades.... They had sheltered many a criminal throughout the years.

He couldn't think about it that way. He just had to play the whole thing moment by moment.

Starting now.

He crawled over the starboard side of the sailboat to find four people already studying him in the light of a single bulb projecting from the enclosure over the hull. There was a short, graying woman, plump and showing traces of past beauty, and a younger woman, somewhere in her early twenties, with huge almond eyes and a wealth of ink-dark hair. Then the two fishermen. They must have seen him on the dock all day, just as he had seen them. Well, he would just have to make that work to his advantage. They were both in their late twenties or early thirties, jeaned and sneakered, and dark. One wore a mustache; the other was slimmer and as wary as Garcia himself.

Garcia came up the ladder right behind Sean. They all stared at one another for a moment, then the older woman burst into a torrent of questions. What was going on here? Who was this man? Who was struggling in the sack? Where was Peter Blayne? Had they all gone loco?

Then she burst into tears.

Garcia took both her shoulders and held her against his chest. "Mama, Mama! It will be all right! We were wrong, you see. The senator was not on his boat. But his wife was—we've got his wife! And if he wants her back, we must get Papa back first. It's better than the senator."

The woman looked dubiously at the sack that twisted over Sean's shoulder, then pointed a finger in his direction. "Who is he?"

"That," Garcia said, rubbing his chin and looking keenly at Sean, "is something we're still trying to figure out."

Sean sighed deeply and spoke in heavily accented English. "I told you, *amigo*—I am Miguel Ramiro. And I am in love with her."

Garcia started to laugh, and the fishermen laughed with him.

"And she is in love with you, too, *amigo*?" Garcia asked skeptically.

Sean gave them a sheepish look, then gritted his teeth, because the girl in the burlap was screeching something and twisting with greater fury. He smiled grimly and gave her a firm swat once again, which shut her up for several well-needed moments.

"*Sí, sí!*" Sean cried passionately. He irritably muttered a few epithets in Spanish, then added, "But you know these *Americanas!* She's fond of the hot Latin blood in private, but when we are in public I am not good enough to clean her shoes!"

"She's a senator's wife and she's having an affair with you?" Garcia said.

"I told you—"

"I believe it, Julio," the younger woman suddenly interrupted him. Sean paused, gazing her way. She was looking him up and down with an obvious appreciation that was quite gratifying—he needed someone to believe him!

"Maria, I did not ask you."

But Maria put her hand on Julio Garcia's arm and gave him a sexy little smile, her almond eyes wide. "But I tell you, because I am a woman, too, yes?"

"Yes, you are all woman, little one," Julio said pleasantly to her, and she laughed delightedly.

"Latin men make the best lovers, yes, Julio?" She giggled. "I see it all well! She is married to some dull old man, but who can live like that? So she finds Miguel—"

"*Sí!* I was the gardener!" Sean said quickly.

"And he is *muy hombre!*" Maria laughed. "So she calls him in on the side, but pretends, Oh, no! Never!"

The fishermen started to laugh again, too. They were all grinning like the most amiable friends.

Except that Garcia was leveling his gun at Sean's chest.

"Juan!" Garcia said. "Start her up. We leave the motorboat right where it is. We go to the cove where we intended. Mama, Maria, you go below. Now!"

"But—" Maria began.

"Now!" Garcia snapped, and Maria, with one last sultry grin for Sean, obeyed.

Sean and Garcia stared at each other, both ignoring the grunts and oaths that came from the burlap bag.

Sean heard the crank as the anchor was pulled in and felt the motion as the sailboat began to move.

"Amigo," Garcia said softly, "do you know what is going on here?"

Sean shook his head vehemently and lied. "I only know that she is mine. You took her, and I followed."

Garcia shrugged and stared at him a while longer.

"I mean you no harm. I mean no man any harm. All I seek is freedom for my father."

Sean remained mute, thinking that this wasn't the time to explain to an impassioned man that spraying a populated dock with bullets and kidnapping a young woman were not sound means to reach the end he sought.

"I know nothing of your father. I am here for her."

"So stay with her. But if her husband does not produce my father..."

"Then what?"

"Then we shall see. Justice should be equal." He waved the gun.

"Your father is not dead," Sean said.

Garcia shrugged again, then smiled. "But you will be, and the woman, if you cause trouble."

Sean lowered his head. Where the hell was everyone? There didn't seem to be another boat in the water; he hadn't heard a single damned helicopter out searching....

Night had fallen. And the Atlantic was one hell of a big ocean!

"Put her down."

Sean braced himself, then lowered her to the deck.

"Get the hood off her," Garcia continued.

His captors had spoken Spanish to one another, and Sean had spoken Spanish to them, but he was certain that Julio Garcia's English was completely fluent. Once she started to talk he could well be in serious trouble, despite his story.

"The hood!" Garcia snapped.

Sean hunched down and moved to take the burlap from her—a difficult procedure, because she was struggling so wildly. At last it came free, and she stared at him—glared at him—with eyes so wild they might have been those of a lioness, and her hair in such a tangle it could have been a massive tawny mane. She was pale, and those fascinating tawny eyes of hers were as wide as saucers, but she'd lost absolutely none of her fight. She stared at him and recognized him as the long-haired, unshaven, rude Cubano who had knocked her down just before this mess had begun.

"You!" She hauled back and struck him hard on the chin.

His eyes narrowed, and he thought quickly. No self-respecting man in his invented position would accept such behavior.

He hauled off and slapped her back, bringing a startled gasp from her—and further fury. She tore at him, nails raking, fists flying. Grunting as her elbow caught his ribs and her nails his cheek, he managed to wrap his arms around her, bringing them both crashing down on the deck. Scrambling hastily, he straddled her, caught her wrists and pinned them.

That didn't calm her at all. She called him every name he'd ever heard and writhed beneath him.

Garcia, still holding his gun, suddenly caused her to go quiet with his laughter. "Miguel," he told Sean in Spanish. "You have yourself a tigress here. Maybe it is good you are along."

Sean saw that she was struggling to understand the words, but her knowledge of Spanish just wasn't good enough. Then she started to scream again. "What the hell is going on here? I warn you, I will prosecute you to the full degree of the law! You'll go to prison! Let me go this instant! What in God's—"

"Shut up!" Sean hissed at her. "I'm on your side!"

Garcia crouched down beside them. She surely realized that she was in trouble, but if she hadn't before, she must now, because Garcia leveled the gun at her temple.

"Mother of God, but you've got a mouth!" he said in English. "Don't threaten me. Think of your sins. If your husband doesn't get my father out of that prison, you will die." He grinned. "You and your lover will die together."

Her eyes reverted to Sean's again, registering shock. "He's not—"

Sean didn't really have any choice in the matter. His hands were occupied securing hers. He had to shut her up.

He leaned down and kissed her.

Her mouth had been open, and he came in contact with all the liquid warmth of her lips, exerting a certain pressure that he hoped would be a warning.

She struggled anyway.

He held his fingers so tightly around her wrists that she didn't dare cry out. Garcia, chuckling again, rose.

Sean tried to take that opportunity to warn her. He moved his lips just above hers and whispered, "Behave! Shut up and follow my lead. For God's sake, the man has a gun and is upset enough to use the damn thing! I'm—"

"Get off me!" she whispered vehemently in turn. "You . . . kidnapper!"

"I'm not with them! I'm—"

"Get off me!"

"Shut up, then!"

She clamped her lips together, staring at him with utter loathing. He sighed inwardly, wishing that he hadn't bothered to stick with her. The hell with her. Let them shoot her!

Then she was talking again, this time to Garcia. "Look, I still don't get this. If you'll just let me go now we'll forget all about it. I promise. You can't get any money through me. I just don't have any. And as for him—"

"Shush!" Sean interrupted, glaring at her. He wasn't about to be shot and thrown to the sharks for his above-and-beyond-the-call-of-duty attempt to save her.

She was going to try to interrupt him again. He tightened his hold on her, his eyes daring her to denounce him to Garcia. He tried to come up with his best and most abusive Spanish to keep Garcia entertained and drown her words.

She must have put on suntan oil sometime during the day, because one of her hands slipped from his grasp, and she used it to lash out at him. His patience was growing thin. He was even beginning to wish that he had decided to practice law, as his mother had suggested. So far he'd been half drowned, thoroughly abused and was surely bloody and bruised from her flying fists and nails. This couldn't go on much longer.

What had happened to terrified victims?

"Don't touch me! Let me go! Get your filthy paws off me! You son of a bitch! Who the hell—"

He had to do something before they both wound up shot and thrown back into the sea.

She just wasn't going to see reason. Sighing inwardly, Sean twisted her quickly to the side and brought the side of his hand down hard just at the base of her skull. With a little whimper she fell peacefully silent at last.

Mandy hadn't panicked at the sound of gunfire; it had come too suddenly. Nor had she really panicked when the burlap had been thrown over her. That, also, had been too sudden. She hadn't even really panicked when she found herself absurdly cast into battle with the rude, green-eyed, unshaven Latin hulk on deck.

But when she returned to awareness in a narrow bunk below deck she *did* panic, because what brought her to awareness was the terrible feel of rope chafing against her wrists.

She was tied to the headboard of the small bunk, tied so tightly that she couldn't begin to move her arms.

She almost screamed—almost—as a feeling of absolute helplessness overwhelmed her. Not only were her wrists tied, but her ankles, too. Someone had tossed a worn army blanket over her poorly clad figure, but it didn't cover her feet, and adding insult to injury, she could see the cheap, filthy rope that was attached to the same type of panel posts framing the foot of the bunk. Someone knew how to tie knots—good knots.

Oh, hell! Just like a Boy Scout! Did they have Boy Scouts in Cuba?

She closed her eyes and tried to swallow the awful scream that hovered in her throat; she tried to reason, but reasoning seemed to give her little help.

What the hell was going on?

Facts, facts...Peter always warned her to look to the facts. Okay, fact: she had gone out this morning with a few students to study coral markings. Pleasant day, easy day. Peter had seen that a lunch had been catered. They'd done some work; they'd partied and picnicked, and absolutely nothing had been wrong in the least. Mark Griffen had given an excellent dissertation on the shark's incredible survival from prehistory to the present, and Katie Langtree had found some exceptional examples of fossilized coral. Easy, fun, educational, pleasant ...

Her only responsibility—her one big worry for the day!—had been to see that the *Flash Point* was returned in good shape: galley clean, equipment hosed. And even that had seemed like a breeze, because the kids had vowed to do all the work, and they were a dependable group. They also knew they would never use the yacht again if she wasn't returned shipshape.

So ... facts! They'd come in, they'd docked. Mark had started rinsing the deck; Katie and Sue had been at work in the galley; Henry Fisher had been covering the furled sails. Everything in A-B-C order. She had stepped off the *Flash Point*, seen that the kids were hard at work at their tasks, then started lazily down the dock, looking forward to a cold canned soda from the refreshment stand.

Facts....

Next thing she knew, she was out of breath and flat on her back, with a tall dark man standing over her and not paying the least attention to her—even though he had just knocked her down in the rudest fashion. She briefly pictured his face; unshaven; his hair a little long and near ebony in color; his nose as straight as a hawk's; his skin sun-darkened to a glistening bronze. And against all that darkness his eyes had been the brightest, most shocking green. If she lived to be a hundred she would never forget the impact of those kelly green eyes against the bronze of his skin.

Facts!

She had said something to him, something about his rudeness. He had barely paid attention. She'd realized then that he must be Latin—Cuban, Colombian, Nicarauguan. Spanish speaking, as were so many of the area's residents.

English or Spanish speaking, no one had the right to be so rude!

Rude! How the hell could she be worrying about rudeness right now! Fact: she was tied hand and foot to a bunk, and some wacko was running around with a gun. He'd already shot up half the docks; she could only pray he hadn't killed someone.

And she had been the target! Why? Why on earth would anyone kidnap her? She didn't have any money to speak of. She did okay, but paying one's electricity bill on time was tremendously different from coming up with hundreds of thousands of dollars to meet a ransom demand!

No, no... kidnappers demanded ransom from others, not the victim. Peter had money. Not tons of it, but he was certainly one of the affluent. Because of their deep friendship, Peter would surely pay to keep her from being—Don't think of it!

Murdered...

"Oh, God!"

The little breath of a prayer escaped and she fell into sheer panic once again, whimpering and tugging furiously at the ropes. All she managed to do was tighten the knots and chafe her flesh until it was raw.

"Oh, God!" she repeated, panting and lying still. Her wriggling had brought the blanket up to her nose; she was going to sneeze.

Why?

The question came back to haunt her again. There was a lot of money in south Florida. Tons of really rich people lived here. Why not abduct a banker's daughter, or a plastic surgeon's wife? Why her? Peter would pay for her, yes, but Peter just wasn't worth that much!

And who the hell was the green-eyed Cuban? Or Colombian, or whatever he was?

Involuntarily she moistened her lips with the tip of her tongue and squirmed uncomfortably. Panic was zooming in again. The young, intense, dark-haired man had been the one to shoot up the dock and throw the burlap over her. Then everything had been a blur; her strongest memory was of a motor screeching through the night, stopping long enough for her to hear a furious volley of Spanish, then starting up again. And then someone had touched her, and naturally she had tried to escape. The dark-eyed man had first imprisoned her. But once she had been freed from the burlap it had been that same rude, green-eyed man who had imprisoned her a second time. Rude! He was much more than rude! He was brutal. He'd slapped her, subdued her, kissed her—and knocked her out. And the other man had been saying something about Peter being her husband and the scruffy Latin being her lover!

"Oh, God!"

It seemed to be absolutely all she could think of to whisper, but then, the Almighty was surely the only one who could banish her absolute confusion and growing terror.

Once again panic, a sizzling sensation inside of her that grew and swelled and overwhelmed, seemed to be taking charge. She struggled some more and realized sickly that, once again, all she achieved was a greater misery. The knots grew tighter, and the coarse hem of the blanket tickled her nose.

She blew at it, trying to force it beneath her chin. Tears welled in her eyes, and she decided firmly that she wasn't going to cry.

And then she wondered why not. There was a group of crazy Latins outside who were intending to murder her—or worse. She'd already been mauled and bruised, and she didn't understand any of it, and she just very well might wind up shot, so why the hell shouldn't she cry?

For one minute she suddenly lay very, very still, her memory going back... back.

If it had been three years ago she wouldn't have cared in the least. They could have done anything, and she simply wouldn't have cared. She could remember standing over the coffins, Paul's and the baby's, and hurting so badly that she yearned to be dead, too, to be going with them, wherever that might be. She could even remember the thought; take me, God. Take me, too. There is nothing left for me, nothing at all....

She'd cried then. Cried until there were no more tears, cried until she'd been numb, the only thought in her mind that it was so unfair. But of course, no one on earth could explain why life cold be so horribly unfair, and in time, still baffled, she'd had to learn acceptance, because the only alternative was insanity.

Peter had been there for her.

Crushed and nearly broken himself, he had still been there for her. Peter, her parents, her brother. But despite her love for her own family, Peter had been the one who somehow gave her the greatest comfort. Perhaps because his loss had been as keen: his only son, his only grandchild.

Huge burning tears were forming behind her eyes. She blinked furiously, trying to think of Peter. He was so strong, so moral. He'd never wavered under fire; he always did what he thought was right. He always went by principle. She wasn't going to cry, and she wasn't going to break. Somehow, no matter what happened to her, she would rise above these people.

She tensed, aware that someone had come below. Twisting, she could see that she was in the stern of the old sailboat. Another bunk, identical to the one she lay on, was straight across from her, and two small closets at the end of the bunks stood at the stern. There was a slatted wooden door just past her head; her entire space of confinement couldn't have been much more than fifty square feet.

Two people were somewhere beyond that door. At least two people, laughing and talking in Spanish. She strained to make out the words, but they spoke too quickly.

Why the hell hadn't she paid more attention to Spanish in school? Why? Because the teacher had been a horrible nasty woman whom everyone in the entire school had thought was creepy. She'd had the most awful way of pointing her finger and saying, *"¡Repitan, por favor!"* in a sickeningly sweet voice, and no one had paid her the least attention.

Irrelevant! Totally irrelevant right now! She'd been hearing Spanish all her life; surely she could comprehend something of what was being said, she insisted to herself.

She did. At long last she did.

Cerveza.

Someone was asking someone else if he wanted a beer. Great! That bit of genius would surely help her vastly!

But then she stopped worrying about her comprehension or lack thereof. Foootsteps were approaching the door. Her muscles cramped with tension from head to toe, and panic sizzled through her once again.

She was helpless, absolutely helpless. Trussed like a pig on its way to the slaughterhouse. Totally, horribly vulnerable.

The door opened; she thought about closing her eyes, but too late.

One of the men ducked as he stepped through the door. He straightened too soon, cracked his head and swore beneath his breath. He turned to her and she found herself staring into his eyes.

Green eyes. Bright, startlingly...tense as they stared into hers.

He glanced over his shoulder quickly, then moved to kneel down beside her.

"Mrs. Blayne."

He said it in English, and she couldn't detect any hint of an accent.

"Mrs. Blayne, are you all right? Juan was assigned to watch me all night. I couldn't get back to you. Maybe he trusts me now. I'm not sure. This is important, please listen."

He was reaching toward her.

She couldn't help herself; she let out a small scream. Oh, God, what was going on? Who was he? How on earth could he be on her side when he seemed to be just like them?

The young man with the dark eyes suddenly appeared in the doorway, laughing, saying something about *amor.*

"*Amor?*" Mandy shook her head. Lover! "N—"

A hand clamped down over her mouth, stifling her words, stealing her breath. He twisted his head toward the man at the door and laughed, too, and when he spoke next there was an accent in his words.

"Amigo, you got a gag anywhere?"

The dark-eyed man chuckled and responded in Spanish, then turned away. Then the green-eyed stranger leaned his furious face so close to hers that she felt the whisper of his breath and the blaze of his body heat.

"Damn it! The next time I try to say something, you shut up and listen!"

There was no accent at all this time...

He straightened and slowly drew his hand away. Still terrified, and completely baffled, Mandy stared up at him in silence.

"Good," he murmured grimly. "Now—"

"Who the hell—" she began, then froze. He was leaning toward her again, tangling his fingers in the hair at her nape, bringing his mouth to hers....

The dark-eyed man was at the door again, she realized, staring at her. And at him. At the green-eyed stranger.

Who was kissing her again. Pressing his mouth to hers urgently, feverishly, heatedly. Stealing away any words she might have spoken.

3

Cerveza...

He tasted of beer, and though she stiffened and tried to twist away, she was in that horrible position of helplessness, chin caught by his powerful hand, mouth overpowered by his.

But beyond the terror, beyond the fury, beyond that awful helplessness, the kiss wasn't that bad.

Wasn't that bad!

Oh, Lord, she was getting hysterical. This was insane; she was going insane already. So much for inner strength. Not that bad! It was wretched; it was humiliating!

And it could get much, much worse, she reminded herself, and that was her last thought, because suddenly all the little sensations seemed to overwhelm her, and she felt as if she was nothing but burning kinetic energy. She felt the rasp of his bearded cheek and the warm texture of his lips, the moistness that seemed like lava, and the taut muscles of his chest, crushed hard against her breast. She felt the whisper of his breath and thought ridiculously that he smelled rather nice, and that the slight taste of beer wasn't so awful, either, and really, she could live through this, because what other choice did she have?

The man in the doorway chuckled again, saying something and addressing the green-eyed man as Miguel.

At last "Miguel" drew away from her, but those green eyes remained on hers, as bright as gems, sparkling out a warning so potent that it might have been written on the air.

He kept staring at her as he answered the other man. What he said she didn't know, she just kept staring back into those green eyes, wishing with all her heart that she was free, not trussed and tied here so ignominiously. Wishing that she could reach up, wrench out a thatch of that ebony hair and punch him through a wall!

And then she was afraid all over again. Deeply afraid. Because every man on the sailboat could come in at any time and do anything to her, and all she would be able to do in turn was fight until her wrists bled from the cruel chafing of the rope.

She averted her eyes from his at last and suddenly realized that it was day. Ugly old curtains were pulled over the tiny portholes, but light was filtering in nevertheless.

She'd slept here the night through, and of all the ridiculous things, while her life hung in the balance, she was suddenly and desperately the recipient of nature's call. They were still prattling away, so she burst out in interruption, "I have to go to the bathroom."

They both stopped speaking and stared at her.

"*¡Baño!*" she snapped. "I have to...go!"

Then they both stared at each other and started laughing again. Miguel said something; the other man, addressed as Julio, shrugged, then turned away.

She cringed as Miguel pushed aside her hips with his own so he could sit and lean over her. He gave a disgusted oath, granted her another sizzling glance and moved on to his objective: freeing one of her wrists.

She breathed a little more easily, closed her eyes and prayed for strength, and said carefully, "Who are you?"

He glanced back toward the door quickly, then whispered, "For God's sake, trust me! Go along with me!"

Julio was back; she couldn't say anything more. Actually, she could have, because she didn't trust Miguel in the least, but somehow she chose not to.

He kept working on her wrist. She gazed past his broad bare shoulder to Julio. "Señora Blayne," he told her, "we really do not wish to hurt you. If you can behave, you will be well. Miguel says he can handle you—"

She couldn't help but interrupt. "Oh, he does, does he?" she asked, flashing Miguel a glance of pure loathing.

"And for your sake, señora, I hope he speaks the truth."

Her right hand fell free. Miguel clutched it, inhaling with concern at the rope burns there. She tried to snatch it from him, but he held tight, warning her with his eyes once again.

She clenched her teeth against the tears that threatened. He started to free her other hand. When her left wrist was released he moved to her feet. Rubbing her wrists, she turned her head defiantly to stare at Julio.

"Why are you doing this? You're mistaken if you think that Peter Blayne is a wealthy man. He isn't. If you're asking a huge ransom for my return you won't get it."

"*Señora*, we do not want money. Money, bah, what is that? A man wants money, it is easy. He works for it."

A new fear settled over her; they didn't want money! Then...

Julio suddenly pounded his heart. "Freedom! You will be our ticket to freedom!"

"But..."

Her feet were free. Miguel was standing above her again, taking her hands.

"Let me go! I can stand by myself."

He looked as if he were going to argue with her, but he didn't. He released her, and she swung her long bare legs over the bunk and attempted to stand in a huff.

She keeled over instantly, right into his arms. And she felt those hated hands encircle her waist, holding her steady.

"Damn you!" She tried to slap him, but he ducked, and she cried out when he caught her wrists. They were so sore!

Julio laughed. "You and Miguel had better make up, *señora*. Oh, you needn't worry—or pretend. We will say nothing to the senator about your affair. He might not think an unfaithful wife worth much."

"I'm not—"

"You said you had to go to the head!" Miguel snapped, his English heavily accented again.

She was certain that this ordeal had cost her her mind.

He muttered something to Julio in Spanish, then reached for her arm and wrenched her to her feet. Julio moved out of the way, and Miguel led her roughly

through the little door and three feet down a narrow
hallway to another door.

"The head!" he snapped, shoving her in.

Face flaming, she slammed the door.

And then she didn't even have to go anymore. She
pressed her palms to her temples, dizzy, nauseated—
and scared. He'd said she should trust him. How the
hell could she, and who was he, anyway?

She tried to take deep breaths, and at last she felt
that at least she wasn't going to be sick. She noticed
then that the facilities were quite clean, and managed
to use them. The water that ran into the sink was spo-
radic, but clear and clean, and she splashed a lot of it
over her face, thinking how good it was to rinse the
salty stickiness away. She stared into the mirror over
the sink and saw that her eyes were as wide as gold
doubloons; her cheeks appeared far too pale beneath
her tan.

Feeling dizzy again, she gripped the small sink. At
last she opened her eyes and stared longingly out the
circular porthole. The sailboat's outer rail hid any view
of the water, but she could see the sky, and it was a
beautiful blue, with just a few puffs of cottonlike
clouds.

What a glorious day! Monday. She should have been
at work by now, joining her colleagues at the site.
White-smocked and gloved, she should have been up
to her wrists in dirt, seeking the treasures beneath it.

Where was help? The whole dock had been chaos.
Surely the police had been called. Surely someone—
everyone!—knew that she was missing by now. They
would have known it as soon as she had been taken;
there had been witnesses all over the place!

"*Señora Blayne!*"

Her name, snapped out in a feminine voice, was followed by a rough pounding at the door.

"What?" she yelled back.

"Open the door! I will give you a robe, and you can take a shower."

Mandy gazed instantly at the tiny shower cubicle; the longing to feel clean was a strong one. She didn't know how many hours they had been at sea. She had no idea of where she was, or what the chances were that she would ever get back to civilization alive. It just didn't make any sense to turn down a shower.

Mandy threw open the door to find a young woman standing before her, a very young woman, somewhere between eighteen and twenty-one.

What she lacked in age, though, she made up for in manner. She was beautiful in an exotic way, with flashing dark eyes and a voluptuous figure, well defined in tight jeans and a red sweater, and with a head of richly curling, near-black hair.

She was shorter than Mandy's five-feet-eight inches, which for some odd reason—she was clutching at straws!—made Mandy feel just a little bit better.

The Latin girl lifted her chin, eyeing Mandy regally, then stuffed something made of dull gray terry into Mandy's hands.

"I am Maria. Here, take this. The bathing suit is not much covering, eh?" the girl said, and once again swept Mandy with a disdainful glare. She chuckled, displaying a fine set of small white teeth beneath her generous rose-tinted lips. "Not that you have much to cover!" She shook her head. "What Miguel sees in you . . . but then, maybe he has not had enough to distract him!"

Mandy was about to tell her that she really didn't give a damn what Miguel saw in anyone. All she wanted to do was get away from the whole stinking lot of them. She decided to keep silent, though she wasn't sure why, because she certainly didn't trust Miguel.

"Thanks for the robe," she said flatly, and closed the door, smiling bitterly as she heard the girl burst into an outraged spate of Spanish. Maria was no part of the power here, that much was obvious. She was nothing more than a young girl—uncertain, insecure, and perhaps idolizing the handsome well-built Miguel.

Mandy turned on the water; it came out cold, but she hadn't been expecting anything better. Stepping beneath the weak spray even as she peeled away her bathing suit, she started shivering vehemently—and not from the cold. Fear swept through her again as she wondered just what was going on. Who was Miguel? Who was Julio? And, for that matter, just who the hell was Maria? And if they were after "freedom" instead of money, just how did they think she could supply it?

She swallowed convulsively and found a fairly new bar of soap. She let the water run over it as she stood there behind the strangely new pink plastic curtain in a state of something akin to numbness. She didn't want to use anything of theirs, but she decided that the soap would be okay if she let the water rinse away layer after layer in a pool of suds.

And then suddenly she began to feel better—angrier, but better. She really did have to fight them; she couldn't allow herself to be so victimized. Fight them . . . and use any means that she had. Maria's very childlike insecurity was a weapon she must remember and use.

She would get to the bottom of this! She would find out exactly what they wanted—and see that they never got it! There would be a chance for escape somewhere along the line. There would have to be!

She closed her eyes and ducked her head beneath the trickling water to rinse her hair, shaking and shivering still, but now just a bit calmer, a bit more in control. It was amazing what a cold shower could do.

But just then—just when she had convinced herself that she could survive!—she heard her name spoken again, and spoken much too close!

"Mrs. Blayne..."

She let out a shriek of horror, aware that the husky, low-timbred, unaccented tone belonged to green-eyed Miguel.

"Damn you!" he swore next, and she shrieked again, because his arms were suddenly around her, wrapping her in the pink plastic curtain. She dragged in a breath to scream again, but that massive tanned hand of his was suddenly over her mouth, and to her absolute horror he was standing behind her, touching her, in the tiny confines of the shower stall.

He pulled her hard against him. All the naked length of her back was against his chest and hips; he wore only a pair of cutoffs, and she could feel with painful clarity all the rippling muscle that composed his shoulders and arms, all the short dark hair that ran riot over his chest. She squirmed, near hysteria, but she managed only to wedge her bare buttocks more intimately against him.

"Stop it, please, will you?" he begged her in a whisper, dipping his mouth near her ear. "I'll explain if you'll just—"

His hold had loosened. With a burst of strength she wriggled away from him and opened her mouth to inhale again for a frenzied scream, too frightened to realize that her scream could do nothing but bring her other captors running.

"Damn it, you're worse than a greased pig!" he rasped out, and then his hands were on her again, but far worse. Because this time, in his attempt to restrain her, his fingers closed over her breast before finding a hold against her ribs again, and he'd already regained a smothering hold over her mouth.

Still swearing beneath his breath, he manipulated her around to face him, and that, too, was far worse, because then her breasts were pressed against his chest and her hips were horribly level with his, and she had never been forced to realize so staggeringly that a man was a man, and this one was made of iron. She almost passed out, but the water, cold and beating against her back, revived her, and she found herself tilting her head to stare into those incredibly green eyes. She realized a little belatedly that he was angry and aggravated, but intense and serious and not—apparently—about to molest her. Not any more than he already had, that was!

"Listen! I'm not going to hurt you! I had to come in here because I had to talk to you without the others hearing. Mrs. Blayne, please, promise me that you won't scream again and I'll move my hand."

Promise that she wouldn't scream....

She wasn't sure that she could. The screams just kept building inside of her. She was standing naked in a two-by-two cubicle, crushed against a near-naked stranger with the muscled build of a prizefighter. Screaming was instinctive!

"Please!" he urged her again.

She didn't know why she nodded at last. Perhaps because she didn't have any choice. And perhaps because she wanted to believe him, because she wanted to trust someone. Perhaps it was something in his eyes that promised pride and integrity and sincerity. Perhaps it was because she would pass out and pitch helplessly against him, if she didn't breathe soon....

Slowly he eased his hand from her mouth. His eyes slipped from hers for just a moment, traveling downward, then upward once again, locking with hers.

"Mrs. Blayne," he whispered, "I'm a cop. If you want to come out of this, play along with me. I'm all that can stand between you and—"

"A cop!" she gasped incredulously. A cop? The hell he was! Where was his badge? Where was his gun? Cops didn't help kidnappers. They didn't assault the victims!

"Mrs. Blayne, I'm with—"

"If you're a cop," she demanded, shaking, realizing all over again that she was naked with him in a tiny space, "where's your badge?"

"I dumped it. I lost my gun coming after—"

"Get out of here!" she snapped suddenly, aware that hysteria was rising in her again. "Cops don't crawl into the shower with kidnap victims! They don't—"

She hadn't realized how her voice was rising until his hand fell over her face again, shutting her up.

"*Shh!* Are you trying to get us both killed? If they even get a whiff of who I am, I'll become shark bait, lady. And I'll be damned if I think you're worth it!"

Her eyes widened. Could it possibly be true? His Spanish had been perfect; his English, when he spoke to her alone, had no accent whatsoever. Yet when he spoke to Julio, he sounded as if he was barely comfortable with the language. Like a chameleon, he could change in the wink of an eye. . . .

"Eh? Miguel?"

They both froze as someone rapped on the door again and called out to Miguel. A barrage of Spanish followed. Miguel held still for a moment, then called something back, something that she didn't understand a single word of.

Footsteps moved away from the door. Mandy was crushed so tightly to his chest that she felt the expulsion of his breath and the rapid beating of his heart.

He stared down at her then with absolute dislike and fury. Still holding her to him, he reached around and turned off the water; it seemed that his striking eyes became razors that sliced right through her.

"Listen to me, lady. Listen good. I'm a cop—whether you believe it or not. Go along with me. I'm only going to warn you once, because, honey, I can bail out of this thing real easy by myself. I spent all night talking my heart out to convince them that I'm a refugee, too, that I was your gardener, that you're married to a man twice your age, and therefore became involved with me hot and heavy. They didn't take you to kill you or rape you. Julio Garcia is a desperate man, but fairly ethical, for a kidnapper. I don't trust his companions all that far, however. Julio decided to keep me around because he thinks I can keep you under control. Blow that, and we could both be dead. Pull one more stunt against me and I swear I'll jump overboard and swim out of this thing. I don't mind sticking around to fulfill my job, but I'll be damned if I'll keep worrying about getting killed *because of* you instead of *for* you!"

She stared at him, shaken by his anger, shaken by the intensity of his words. Was he really a cop? Or was he one of *them*, just a little more educated, a far better actor? What a way to control a captive, to convince her that a cop was with her and on her side!

He shook her suddenly. "Do you understand?"

She lowered her eyes, then closed them quickly. All she saw when she looked down was his muscled and hairy male chest, slick and hard against her breasts. And of all things, she felt her nipples harden against him.

"Yes!" She gasped, trying to escape him, but he held her against him, and she shook in sudden horror and confusion. "Yes! No! I don't understand any of this. I—"

"Just go along with me now! Julio just said to get the hell out, lunch is ready. I don't have time to try to convince you any further."

He released her completely and stepped out of the shower stall, finding a towel to dry his slick shoulders and chest. He didn't look back at Mandy but stuffed the towel toward her, then found the gray terry robe and shoved that to her over his shoulder.

Quivering and confused, Mandy hurriedly accepted the towel, though she didn't bother to dry herself thoroughly, and fumbled into the robe. It was worn and fell to her feet, but it didn't make her feel especially secure. She wrapped it around herself as tightly as she could, then knotted the belt.

His back was still to her, but just inches away. Beneath his tan she noted a smattering of freckles across his shoulder and thought them curious, considering his coloring.

Oh, God! Who the hell was he really?

"Are you decent?" he asked her.

She started to laugh, but caught herself quickly, afraid that if she got started, she would never quit. "You didn't worry whether I was 'decent' or not when you charged into the shower!" she accused him.

"Shh! Damn you!" he said in a vehement whisper, whirling around, hands on hips, to face her.

Her lip started to tremble, but she didn't intend to let it. She tossed back her head and stared at him dubiously. "Do cops always run around in the pursuit of duty with no weapons, no ID and no shoes?"

He groaned impatiently. "I told you—"

"Oh, I know what you told me," she said. "I'm just not sure I believe a word of it."

He closed his eyes and sighed, then stared at her in exasperation. "Gamble, then. You're with me, or you're not. But if you're against me, remember, I'm gone."

"Gone? From where?" she demanded.

"From wherever we are. Near Cat Cay, I think. I'm a hell of a good swimmer. A dive overboard, that's all it would take. They don't watch me like they're going to watch you."

"And why the hell should they trust you?"

"Because I know how to play this game, lady," he said grimly.

"Either that, or you're one of them."

He smiled with a certain malicious humor and advanced those few inches to her, rounding his fingers over her shoulders so that she almost screamed again from the pure electricity of that touch.

Never had she seen anything as intense, as compelling, as frightening—as dangerous!—as the kelly green blaze of his eyes. She couldn't speak; she couldn't have screamed even if it had been her most ardent desire. She could only stare at him in silence.

"Lady, place your bet quickly. We've got to go now, unless you want Julio in this head along with the two of us! If I were you, though, I'd change my tune—quickly. I'd admit to this ignoble affair and cling to me as if we'd been passionately involved for ages! Hey—" he cocked his head, daring her "—you might not like your other options. Julio is fairly ethical, but those other two have been talking about your *senos* all day."

"My—my what?" Mandy swallowed.

"Breasts, Mrs. Blayne. They're quite entranced with . . . them."

She started to jerk away, and he laughed without a trace of amusement. "Like I said, there's only so far I'll go for you if you won't cooperate. So have it your way. I'm a fugitive like the others, probably a murdering rapist. Take me—or leave me."

She swallowed again, lowering her eyes, desperately trying to decide whether to trust him or not. She didn't. . . . But what were her options?

He'd kissed her, struck her, abused her! But not done half of what he might have, she reminded herself.

He was already reaching for the door. She clutched his arm, and he turned back to her, arching a dark brow.

"If you're really a cop, why can't you overpower them? Why can't you arrest them?"

"Oh, God help me!" he breathed, looking heavenward. "Mrs. Blayne, should I really introduce myself as a police officer? And arrest them? Now that's a laugh. I'll say, 'Hey, let's go to jail.' I haven't got a weapon on me, but they'll just say, 'Sure, let's go, you want to put us in jail, fine.' "

Mandy flushed. "But you should be trying...."

"I *am* trying!" He swore heatedly. "I'm trying to keep you alive—and I'm trying to stay on top of you myself to keep these guys from deciding that, hey, they have you, so what the hell... if you catch my meaning, Mrs. Blayne. Although God knows you seem to be strange enough! Maybe you'd enjoy their attentions. Did you marry Peter Blayne for his money? Yeah, I could be way off. Maybe you'd enjoy the excitement."

"What?" Stunned, outraged, she shrieked the word.

She should have learned not to shriek by now. He slapped a hand over her mouth before she could blink and drew her against his hard length in a frightening manner, staring down at her with danger sparking from his eyes.

"Shut up!"

Shut up? She had no choice. So she blinked, realizing that this man—this cop?—thought she was the senator's wife, just as the others had assumed. He actually assumed that she'd married an older man for money. Oh, how dare he!

His hand moved from her mouth. She smiled very sweetly, narrowing her eyes. "No, Miguel. I married Peter Blayne because he's fabulous in bed, and I don't need any excitement! So lead on. Just keep your hands off me and I'll be as quiet as a mouse."

He grinned crookedly, and she was startled at the effect of his expression on her. He was a handsome man, really handsome. Dark, tall, broad, muscled, sexy and very physical. And fascinating, with those strange bright eyes. And when he looked at her in that dry, insinuating fashion she felt an involuntary sizzle sweep through her. One she instantly denied, vehemently denied. She was still in love with a memory, still convinced that only a deep and rich emotion could ever create such steaming awareness....

She closed her eyes, dizzy. What if he wasn't a cop? And what if he was?

It was insane. Was she cracking already? So weak that she was willing to cling to anyone—especially anyone male and muscled—because she was scared? She wasn't. She wasn't!

His scent was all around her, the roughness of his touch, that feel of steel in his arms. She wanted to trust him.

"Mrs. Blayne," he said softly, with a touch of amusement, "I won't touch you, but I suggest that you *do* touch me now and then. You were having a passionate affair with me, remember?"

"Why...why," she whispered, head lowered, "would they believe that? Why would they believe that you would risk your life to be with me?"

He chuckled dryly. "Because Latins are a passionate people, Mrs. Blayne. They usually love deeply, hate deeply—and possess their women as loyally and heatedly as they do their pride."

She stared at him, searching his features, seeking an answer, and she prayed that she wasn't a victim more of his arresting features and eyes than she was of the circumstances.

"Are you Latin?" she asked him.

"Half," he answered curtly.

"Miguel!"

The call came from very near the door. Had they been overheard? Mandy started to shiver all over again. If he *was* here to help her and she caused him to be murdered, she would never forgive herself in a thousand years—even if he was an SOB.

Damn him! She wouldn't tell him that she wasn't Peter's wife, either!

"Let's go!" he hissed.

She nodded. He took her hand, and she didn't resist him, but just before he opened the door he twisted his handsome head ruefully toward her and mouthed out a quick query.

"I almost forgot. What's your name?"

"Blayne! You know—"

"Your first name, stupid!"

"Amanda!"

"Mandy?"

"Only to friends," she said pointedly.

He smiled. "And lovers, Mrs. Blayne? Mandy, let's go!"

4

Lunch consisted of a salad and *arroz con pollo*, chicken and rice, served belligerently to Mandy and charmingly to Miguel by Maria and another woman, up on deck.

Mandy had tried her hardest to assimilate the layout of the craft during her quick walk through the hall to the steps leading topside. There hadn't been much to assimilate. The vessel was old, at least forty years, worn, but well-kept. There were another two sets of sleeping quarters past the head, then a shabby salon and a galley, and to the extreme aft, the captain's cabin.

The older woman had stared at Mandy with extreme disapproval as they moved through the galley. Mandy had ignored her, but she hadn't been able to ignore the smell of the food; the aroma was captivating, and she was forced to realize that she was starving.

The deck of the motorized two-masted sailboat was lined with old wooden seats, and that was where Miguel led her. Mandy kept her mouth shut for several minutes while she perused her surroundings and her curious party of abductors.

There was Julio, called Garcia by the others; the young woman, Maria; the older woman; and two more men, one a heavyset fellow with a swirling mustache, the other gaunt and hungry-looking. Mean, Mandy thought, and far different from Julio Garcia, who, strangely, had the look of a poet.

They all laughed and chatted in rapid Spanish, drinking Michelob out of bottles and eating off paper plates as if they were simply out for a picnic at sea.

Including Miguel. He laughed and chatted along with the others, tensing only slightly beside her when some apparently ribald comment was made about her by either the man with the mustache—Juan, she thought his name was—or Roberto, the gaunt man with the lascivious eyes.

If Miguel was on her side, he certainly knew how to enjoy himself in the interim. He ate with a hearty appetite, complimenting the two women on their cooking. So far Mandy hadn't been able to pick up more than a word or two of the conversation, but mannerisms were universal, and it was easy to tell that Miguel was managing to fit right in. There was only one difference between him and the other men: they were carrying large guns in shoulder holsters.

Miguel had none. He was still barefoot, bare chested, clad in his wet cutoffs, assuring her that he could not be hiding a weapon anywhere on his person.

She turned her gaze to the ocean surrounding them, wondering how far they had come, and in what direction. Miguel had told her that he thought they were near Cat Cay, which meant the Bahamas. She saw nothing around them right now but the sea and sky, and her heart sank in desolation. She might never be found, never be rescued! There might well be hundreds of uninhabited islands in this stretch of the ocean. She'd been taken away in a little speedboat, and now she was on an old sailboat. The police—if they could even look for her now that they were out of American waters!—wouldn't even know what they were looking for.

The police!

She twisted her head slightly and stared at Miguel, seated so casually beside her, idly holding his beer and laughing at one of Roberto's jokes. Was he really a cop? It was hard to believe at the moment! He was taller, stronger, tougher than the other men, muscled but trim, lean and mean-looking. If he was a cop, why the hell hadn't he done something?

She told herself that no amount of muscle could combat a bullet, that maybe he was doing his best just to keep them both alive. It was hard, though, even if she realized that half her problem was that she resented him heartily for assuming that she was Peter's wife and that, being younger, she had latched on to him for material reasons.

And maybe she also resented him out of sheer frustration. By God, he was physically beautiful. His stomach was taut, his legs long and hard, his shoulders those of an Atlas.

That dark hair; those flashing eyes, emerald in the sun; that handsome face, high boned with arching dark brows, teeth pearly white against the full sensual curve of his mouth.... Not even the thick shadow of beard detracted from his looks. He seemed like a bulwark of character and strength—and he wasn't doing a damn thing for her! Just chatting away in Spanish and drinking his *cerveza*!

Maria collected his empty plate, and he stretched his free arm around Mandy. She tried not to stiffen; it was a casual gesture, and she decided she would rather trust him than be left vulnerable to Roberto's naked ogling.

Maria took Mandy's plate less than graciously, eyeing her maliciously, and to Mandy's own surprise she returned that nasty glare and inched closer to Miguel.

"Mandy." He spoke softly and she jumped, turning to look up at him. "You want something to drink?"

The accent was back in his words.

"Ah, yes. A diet Pepsi, please."

He started to laugh. "What do you think this is? They've got beer, water, guava juice and Coca-Cola. 'Classic', I believe."

She recognized his dry humor and just barely held her temper in check. "A Coke!" she snapped.

He started to translate her request to Maria, but Maria snapped, "I heard her," then disappeared below.

Maria returned with the soda and sat staring pointedly at Mandy. The older woman said something to her, which she ignored; then Julio grated out something impatiently and the two women—along with Roberto, Mandy noticed gratefully—went below deck. Mandy sipped her Coke, thinking that a soda had never tasted so delicious before. She stared around again, tensing as she realized that there was a small island on the horizon, and that a pleasure boat was anchored just beyond its beach.

How far away was it? she wondered yearningly. Three miles—or five? And did it really matter? If she had to, she could manage a five-mile swim....

"So, Señora Blayne, you are resigned to our company, sí?"

She started, forced into an awareness that the oddly genteel Julio Garcia was watching her.

"Resigned?" she queried regally, ignoring the pinch of Miguel's fingers suddenly tightening around her shoulders. "Not in the least. Perhaps," she added sarcastically, "You'd be so kind as to explain to me just what you're after so that I may become . . . resigned!"

Julio gazed curiously at Miguel then returned his dark soulful eyes to hers. "Miguel has not explained it to you?"

"She gave me no chance, this one!" Miguel pulled her closer against him, irritating her beyond belief by playfully fluffing her hair. She stiffened against him, but his hold was a powerful one for all its casual appearance, and she had no recourse except to smile grimly at Julio Garcia.

"I haven't the faintest idea of what is going on."

Julio shrugged and grimaced. "Your husband betrayed me, Mrs. Blayne. He swore to have my father freed. Empty promises."

My husband is dead, she thought with fleeting pain, and he never betrayed anyone in his life.

"My fath—my husband," she amended quickly, "is a senator, not a warden! What are you talking about?

"He is still in prison! Jorge Garcia—statesman, poet, one of the finest, most courageous freedom fighters ever to live!—still rots in prison! Peter Blayne promised to have something done. He said to trust in the law! Well, I have tried his laws for years! Ever since the Mariel boatlift—"

"Wait a minute!" Mandy interrupted in a burst of passion. "Are you trying to tell me that your father was a prisoner—a criminal—in Cuba, but that we should let him roam free in the United States?"

"*Idiota!*" Julio shouted, then went on in an irate shouting spree.

"Julio, Julio! She does not understand!" Miguel said, trying to soothe him.

Mandy was more furious than ever. She couldn't believe that this whole thing was over another criminal! "Don't swear at me in Spanish! Say it in English. *No hablo español!* This is the United States of America—"

Suddenly that long-fingered sun-bronzed hand was over her mouth again, and brilliant green eyes were boring into hers. "*Quieta! Cerra la boca,* Amanda!" Miguel snapped. "You want English? Shut your mouth. You don't understand! Julio, I will take her forward and explain, eh?"

Julio exploded into rapid speech again, pulling his gun from his holster and waving it around. Mandy inhaled deeply in shock as Miguel dragged her to her feet, his hand still over her mouth, and half led, half dragged her to the few clear feet of space that surrounded the main mast.

"Damn you!" he grated out tensely, releasing her mouth at last, but only to grip her shoulders and stare down at her like the wrath of God while he spoke. "Are you trying to get us both killed?"

She tossed her hair back. "He's crazy! I won't—"

"Yes, he's crazy! And that's exactly why you'd better start paying a little heed. Don't you know this story? Doesn't your husband ever talk to you about his work?"

Her husband? Oh, Peter...

Yes, Peter talked to her. But she'd been so involved with her own work lately that she hadn't really seen him in a while. She shook her head stiffly. "I don't know anything about any of this! Except that if Peter has refused to let some murderer roam the streets, then—"

He took a deep breath, a bitter breath. "For your information, Mrs. Blayne—Mrs. Bigot!—not everyone who came in on the Mariel boatlift was a murderer!"

"I am not a bigot! But don't you dare try to tell me that Castro didn't empty his prisons on the U.S.!"

"Oh, great! So everyone who is Cuban—"

"I didn't say that!"

"But you meant it!"

"The hell I did!"

"What are you, the head of the DAR, Mrs. Blayne? Your impeccable bloodlines go back to the *Mayflower*, I take it!"

"As a matter of fact," Mandy lied coolly, "they do!" She suddenly felt as if she was going to burst into tears. She hadn't meant to offend him, but she'd be damned if she would be responsible for putting a criminal—be he Irish, German, Spanish or all-American—back on the streets.

Her lashes fell over her eyes; she didn't understand why this terrible antagonism had suddenly erupted between them. He was her lifeline, however tenuous. She was simply terrified, and trying not to be.

Frightened, but determined to be strong. And there were so many chinks in her armor!

He was still angry, but was holding his temper in check. He spoke flatly to her, still holding her shoulders, his voice very distant.

"Jorge Garcia was not a murderer, a rapist, or even a thief. He was a political prisoner, but the charges trumped up against him could have sent him before a firing squad. He was, once upon a time, a brilliant man. Rich and a philanthropist, a lawyer, a scientist. He still had a few friends in the Castro regime, but even so his enemies managed to have him labeled as dangerously insane. He was sent out on the Mariel boat-lift and consequently wound up with dozens of other cases, waiting to be reviewed by the immigration board.''

"You're trying to tell me that Julio's father is not just a good man but a great one?"

"From all I've heard, yes."

She shook her head, her temper growing. "So we're at fault! The Americans are at fault, and it's okay for Julio to attempt to assassinate Peter and kidnap me."

"I didn't say it was all right! Julio has obviously snapped. Yes, gone mad, in a way. Apparently he's been frustrated half to death. It doesn't make him right. It just explains his behavior. You can't do any-thing—your husband probably couldn't even have done anything, no matter how hard he tried, except speed up some paperwork."

"Then why are you yelling at me?"

"I'm not yelling!"

"You sure as hell are!"

He released her shoulders abruptly. "Excuse me, Madame DAR. It's my Latin temper, you know."

"You're stereotyping yourself—not me!" Mandy snapped.

"I'm not trying to do anything except get us both out of this. I'm a cop, not a lawmaker, and not a politi-cian. I don't even know what I'm doing here myself! But, Mrs. Blayne, please, if you're at all interested in living, please don't get into moral fights with Julio Garcia!"

She stared at him, then tossed her head. From the corner of her eye she glimpsed the island she had seen before—and the massive pleasure craft anchored right before it.

"I, uh, won't argue with Garcia anymore," Mandy said absently.

"Good. I don't think he wants to harm anyone. I—"

He broke off, frowning, as excited shouts suddenly came from the aft deck.

"Let's see what's up," Miguel murmured, and he started back. Mandy didn't follow him. She stood dead still where she was, feeling the ocean breeze, feeling the sun on her face.

The boat wasn't far away. No more than three miles, she was certain. And she really was a good swimmer. Her captors were so excited about whatever was happening off their own craft that she could probably be halfway to that other vessel before anyone even noticed that she was gone.

She hesitated just a second longer, thinking of Miguel. She didn't want to worry about him, yet she did. She had the sneaking suspicion that his presence had saved her from sexual abuse by the leering Roberto, and she didn't want him harmed on her behalf.

But he had managed to make himself one of them. They wouldn't kill him. At least, she convinced herself in those moments that they wouldn't. And if he was a cop, he would know how to take care of himself. She had a chance to escape, she didn't dare risk losing it.

She moved at last, staring forward. They were all there now: the two women, Roberto, Juan, Julio—and Miguel.

"A bloodbath!" she thought she heard someone say. But she wasn't really listening—or thinking.

Quietly she moved portside, stepped to the rail and dove into the water.

It was a good clean dive. The gray robe bulked around her somewhat, but to obtain her water safety certification every three years she'd had to swim a mile in her clothes—shoes, too—so the robe shouldn't be that bad. And of course she could always ditch it. And arrive at a strange boat stark naked. What a thing to think of at a time like this! Swim...

She broke the surface and took a breath, stroking smoothly, aware that she would have to pace herself to make the distance. Stroke, breathe, stroke, breathe. The sun was high in the sky, warm; the water was almost as warm as that sun, and very blue here, where it was deep. It felt good to swim, to feel the salt against her face, to feel the promise of freedom....

She cocked her head, inhaling, stroking, and heard shouts distantly from behind her. She clenched her teeth in dismay, having hoped to gain more distance before they discovered her absence.

She paused for a second, treading the water, to see what was happening. She was shocked to see that they were all watching her—not angry, but pale as a troop of ghosts.

"Stop, Amanda! Stop!"

It was Miguel shouting, and as she turned to begin swimming again with stronger strokes, she swore inwardly. Damn him! He'd said he was on her side, but he was the one standing on the rail, ready to dive after her and recapture her.

The salt stung her eyes; she felt like crying as she heard the splash of his body entering the water. He was coming after her. She renewed her strokes, still hoping she could outdistance him. She was good, she reminded herself. She really was a good swimmer....

But so was he. And he was stronger. In a matter of seconds he was almost at her feet.

"Amanda! Get back!"

His hand slid around her ankle, a vise that jerked her under water, then into his arms. She choked and gagged and came up against his chest, gasping.

"Damn you! Damn you!" she shrieked, furious and ready to cry. She could have done it except for him. "I hope you rot in hell for all eternity. Liar! You son of a bitch. You—"

He still looked white and grim. He shook her. "Get back. *Now!*"

He gave her a strong shove back toward the boat. The terry robe seemed to be locked all around her now, hampering her movements. She couldn't seem to swim at all anymore; she couldn't untangle her arms.

And Juan and Julio had already climbed into a little dinghy with no motor. They reached furiously, desperately, for the oars, then began coming toward her.

Miguel gave her another shove.

"I can't!"

He jerked at her robe; she tried to hold the sodden material while struggling to stay afloat.

"Take it off!"

She'd never heard such a fervent command. The robe was suddenly gone. "Swim!" he bellowed, shoving her.

She didn't have to swim; the dinghy was right behind her, and Julio and Juan were bending over, grasping her arms. Naked and humiliated she was lifted from the water and cast to the rotting floorboards of the tiny dinghy.

Instinctively she brought her knees to her chest and locked her arms around them, and only then did she realize that they weren't paying her the least attention—they were pulling Miguel into the dinghy after her. He landed half on top of her, dripping wet. There was nowhere to move, and when she tried to shrink closer within herself, he opened his eyes and stared at her with such grim fury that it was as if his eyes had become a glittering inferno that meant to consume her.

He was still gasping for breath, but he threw the robe over her as he shook his head in disgust. "Stupid woman!" he muttered.

Julio muttered a few words to Juan, gesticulating with a sharp intake of breath, and it was then that she realized the awful danger she had almost encountered. Surrounding the little dinghy was an assortment of at least five fins. Shark fins...

And the creatures were still swimming about, thrashing, nearly upsetting the tiny dinghy.

"Sit!" Miguel snapped, and the other two men instantly obeyed.

Mandy shivered miserably beside him as he fumbled for the oars and slowly, carefully, rowed the dinghy toward the sailboat.

Oh, God! She'd nearly swum into the middle of a school of sharks! She would rather be shot ten times over than die such a gruesome death. This man had actually dived after her, pitting himself against the same danger....

"Up, and carefully!" he told her tensely when they reached the boat. Julio and Juan went up the rope ladder first. Julio looked very gray, and she thought that he might be a kidnapper, but he hadn't wanted to see her die—not that way! "Up!"

Somehow she was touching the wet rope ladder. Clinging to it. She didn't feel as if she had any strength at all.

He was behind her, using the force of his body to protect hers against its own weakness. She closed her eyes, fighting dizziness.

She could still hear the sharks thrashing in the water. She turned back and froze in renewed fear. The water was red now. Blood red. The others had turned on one of their own kind and were ripping it apart with their huge jaws and razor teeth. . . .

"Amanda, go."

One foot after the other. Again and again. Julio was there to drag her over the rail. She pulled the robe about her shivering body and lay on the deck, spent, exhausted, and still in shock.

She saw the sun above her, slowly sinking into the west. She felt the chill of a night breeze coming on. The sky was becoming pink and crimson and beautifully gold, and the moon, pale but full, had risen even before the sun could set.

Twenty-four hours . . . it had been a full day, she thought numbly. A full day since she had been taken, and suddenly none of it mattered except for those last few minutes. She had always thought that she would never really be afraid to die, but she was. And she would have died. In her furious quest for escape she would have stirred up the water to such an extent that the mindless beasts would have found her—except for him.

She was dimly aware that he had come aboard the boat, dimly aware that tense Spanish was being spoken in bursts all around her.

She opened her eyes. Maria, her huge almond eyes ablaze, was staring down at her. She spat on the deck, then began speaking again.

Puta. That was one word Mandy recognized. Maria was screaming because Miguel had almost died to save his Anglo whore. She was trash; she was not worth it.

Julio said something curtly; Maria started to speak again, but he slapped her.

Mandy knew she had acquired a serious enemy. She couldn't even care about that. She felt totally exhausted and numb, and she shivered with spasms she could not halt.

She opened her eyes once again in startled surprise when someone leaned down to her, wrapping strong arms around her.

She met glowing orbs of green: Miguel's eyes. She was too entangled in the robe to fight him, nor did she even think that she should. She stared at him, unable to find the words for an apology, unable even to form a "thank you" on her trembling lips.

Spanish broke out all around her again, but she didn't worry about it. In absolute exhaustion she laid her head against his chest and closed her eyes again.

"I am taking her below," Miguel said determinedly, breaking into English.

"*Sí.* Do it then, *amigo,*" Julio agreed.

"*Madre de Dios!*" Juan swore, but Julio interrupted him.

"She will do us no good dying of pneumonia!"

Miguel walked past them with Mandy in his arms. She opened her eyes just before they came to the steps.

Night had almost fallen. It seemed to come so quickly out here on the water. Only a few stretches of gold and crimson lay against the eternal sea and sky.

And then, as if they had been a delusion, those colors faded to black.

They moved through the galley, through the salon, down the hall. He used his foot to kick open the door, then laid her on the narrow bunk, swathing her in the blanket, holding her, his eyes enigmatic, only the pulse in his throat displaying any emotion.

"I—I'm sorry—" Mandy began.

"I swear to you," he interrupted her, "I *am* a cop! If you trust me, I'll get you out of this!"

He had every right to be furious, she knew. He'd put his own life on the line—for her. She shivered all over again, knowing she would never have had the nerve to dive into the water if she had known about all those sharks.

Suddenly there was a rapping at the door. Miguel stood quickly and opened it.

The older, gray-haired woman was there, a wooden tray in her hand. She spoke Spanish softly and gazed down at Mandy with the closest thing to sympathy that she had yet seen.

The woman lifted the tray, offering it to Miguel.

"Gracias, gracias," he told her, then she asked him something, and he answered her, stepping aside to allow her to enter the room. She sat down by Mandy's side, touched her forehead and cheeks, offered a weak smile, then wagged a finger beneath Mandy's nose, giving her a motherly scolding. She touched Mandy's cheek once again, shivered and then left.

"What...?" Mandy began, struggling to sit.

Miguel stuffed a shot glass of amber liquid into her fingers. "Drink it—it's rum. It will stop the chill."

She couldn't drink it. "Miguel..."

"Señora Garcia," he told her, wrapping his fingers around a second shot glass and setting the tray on the opposite bunk, "is not at all happy that her son took you. They meant to take your husband. Drink that!"

"Miguel..."

"Mrs. Blayne, by tomorrow they plan to reach some remote and private island where they have a little cottage. Juan will then return to Miami with the ransom note. Obviously your husband won't have any real power to give the Garcias what they want, but negotiations will start. At that time they will also be one man short. They don't want to hurt you. If you would have just one bit of faith in me and give me a little time, I could manage to settle this thing without risking your life."

"Miguel..."

"Drink that!"

She brought the shot glass to her lips with still-trembling hands, then gasped at the potency of the liquor, choked and coughed. He sat beside her and patted her back, but with little mercy. He tilted the glass toward her lips again.

"All of it!"

On her next try she drained the glass. He took it from her hands as she wheezed for breath once again. He swallowed his own without a grimace, haphazardly returned both glasses to the tray, then turned back to her.

He touched her lip, her cheek. "Good," he said. "You've got a little color back."

She lowered her head, her fingers plucking at the blanket. "I'm sorry. I had to do it." She moistened her lips and stared at him again. "Thank you," she whispered stiffly. "You saved my life."

"Line of duty," he told her, his eyes narrowing peculiarly on her hand. He clutched it, looking at the raw marks that still surrounded her wrists. "Do they hurt?" he asked, staring into her eyes again.

She shook her head. It was only a little lie.

The door suddenly burst open to reveal Julio Garcia. He gave a curt order to Miguel. Miguel shook his head vehemently. Chills of fear crept over Mandy again; she knew that they were arguing about her. Her wrist was suddenly shoved up toward Julio's face. He hesitated, then said something back to Miguel. Miguel glanced her way curiously then nodded to Julio. Then Julio, too, was gone, snapping out the cabin light as he went.

Darkness fell all around them. Mandy knew that she was still shivering, that he was still staring at her in the darkness.

"What...what was that all about?" she asked faintly.

"He wanted me to tie you up again."

"You tied those knots?"

"Yes. I had to make them good."

She sniffed in the darkness. "They *were*."

He didn't reply at first. Then he merely said, "Move over."

"What?"

"Move over. I can tie you up, or sleep next to you."

Something rebelled inside her. She wanted to tell him to tie her up, that she would rather suffer through that again than have him sleep beside her.

But she didn't. She didn't ever want to experience that panicky feeling of being so helplessly bound again. She didn't want the rope chafing her flesh until it was raw. And she felt so horribly tired and exhausted.

She moved as close as she could to the paneling that rimmed the bunk, painfully aware of his length and heat as he crawled in beside her. He didn't say a word. In time her eyes adjusted to the darkness and she realized that he was lying there very stiffly, hair still damp from his dive into the water, his profile clean and fascinating as he stared upward into the night.

"Miguel?" she whispered softly.

"What?"

"I really am sorry. I felt that I had to try.... It isn't that I distrust you so much, it's just that the opportunity was there. Thank you. I mean it. And I'm terribly sorry about putting you in danger."

She felt him shrug. The narrow bunk was barely wide enough for one person; two would necessarily feel each other's slightest movement.

"It's okay," he returned in the darkness. And then he was silent again.

"I know you're angry—"

"I'm not angry." He rolled toward her and touched her cheek in the darkness, lightly, for the briefest moment. Then he jerked his hand away from her, as if remembering something.

"I know what it's like to run for freedom, Mrs. Blayne. To seek escape at any cost. Go to sleep. You'll need rest and awareness, should another opportunity come along."

She swallowed and nodded, but knew she would never sleep. Escape... freedom. They seemed like hollow empty echoes now. He knew what it was like. That was what he had said.

She wished fervently that he was not beside her. And yet she was fervently glad of him, too. Of the feel of heat and strength.

She might detest him for some of the things he had said and done, but he was on her side; she had to believe that. And even if she feared him just a little in the deepest recesses of her heart, she could not help but admire him and believe in him.

Only a fool—or a very brave man—would dive into water teeming with sharks to save a woman who had done nothing to deserve it of him.

Sleep was impossible. She lay there miserably for hours and hours, not daring to move, not daring to get any closer to him.

Memories drifted in and out of her mind, good ones, bad ones, some from the distant past, some more recent. She couldn't tell if the man beside her slept, or if he continued to stare into the darkness, lost in the recesses of his own mind.

Somewhere in the night exhaustion and nerves overwhelmed her and she fell into a restless sleep. But even there the memories plagued her. Her son's tiny coffin seemed to float in space, and then the larger one, Paul's. Then the coffins began to change. Darkness and shadow became red, dripping red, blood red, and she could hear and see the terrible gnashing teeth of the sharks. . . .

"Shh, shh! It's over! I'm beside you . . . you're all right!"

She stiffened, unaware that she had cried out, biting her lip.

"Mandy, go back to sleep. Easy . . ."

His hand was on her hair; his body was like a heat lamp next to hers. His voice was like the soothing whisper of an ocean breeze.

And maybe because she was still half-lost in a shadow land herself, she allowed herself to listen to that whisper, to be soothed by that strong masculine touch.

She sighed softly.

"You're all right," he whispered again. "It was just a dream."

The tension fell away from her body, and she slept. And this time no dreams came to plague her, just the pleasant sensation of being held safely in strong arms.

5

In the morning she came awake with a curious sense of peace, followed by a haunting disillusionment.

The senses could play such tricks upon the mind! She'd awakened to so many brilliant mornings feeling the lapping of waves, the movement of the ocean beneath her, the coolness of the dawn, and salt-flavored air all around her. Awakened smiling, warm, secure, content, her husband's arm wrapped around her, the lazy tempo of a night's anchorage away from the bustle of the city like a blissful balm.

All the things that went with it came back to her: laughter from above; calls that the "sleepyheads" should awaken; the smell of sizzling bacon—and then whispers. Whispers because Peter would be telling Miranda that the kids should be up, and Miranda would be hushing him, lowering her voice still further, and reminding him that the "kids" were still newlyweds, and newlyweds didn't spring right up from bed; they liked to stay there a while.

And of course by then Mandy and Paul would both be awake, staring at each other, giggling and trying very hard to shush each other so that his concerned parents wouldn't hear them. Then they would shoot out of bed anyway, because Jonathan would have awakened by then, and they were both still so overawed at being parents that they sprang to attention the second he opened his tiny mouth and let out his ear-splitting cry.

Then they would be grabbing for robes, because the older Blaynes would come bursting in, so overawed at being grandparents that they too sprang to instant attention.

And then the bacon would burn, and it would have to be started all over. But it wouldn't matter, because they would have all weekend to dive and snorkel and swim and fish and play, and the real world would be miles away. The *Flash Point* would be their fantasy-land until they all returned to their responsibilities.

Mandy opened her eyes and felt a nearly over-whelming hopelessness sweep through her. Those times were gone, Miranda was gone, Jonathan was gone and Paul was gone. She blinked against the sudden agony of reality. She hadn't felt this way in ages; she'd learned to insulate herself, to remember the good times, to find other things in life. She could even laugh aboard the *Flash Point*, bring flowers to the cemetery and smile as she remembered her infant son's beautiful smile.

It was this boat; it was this stinking boat. It was so much the opposite of all that had been beautiful. She was a prisoner, not a beloved wife, not an adored daughter-in-law, doted upon by her husband's happy parents. This was a rotting hulk, not the graceful *Flash Point*. It was all a mockery. There wasn't a grain of truth in any of the sensations.

Except that, rotting hulk or not, this vessel rolled on the sea just like any ship. The sea, the sky, the salt air—they were never ending. No matter what came and went in life, they would remain the same. But the warmth...

Mandy rolled over quickly. Miguel had taken the sodden robe off her when he put her on the bunk. Now she was barely covered by the worn blanket he had bundled around her. She was still warm, still warm from his body heat, gone now, but haunting her as thoroughly as the dream.

Mandy pulled the blanket back to her chin, wondering at the anguished stream of emotions he could elicit from her. She felt drawn like the proverbial moth to the candle, but she felt a little ashamed, too. He'd dragged her around half-naked—completely naked actually—bound her, knocked her out, reviled her—and saved her life. She knew exactly what he thought of her; he had said it in so many words. He'd prejudged her as a mercenary bigot, and he deserved to pay for that. Yet in his absurd way he was going above and beyond the call of duty, and he was certainly the most extraordinary man she had ever met.

And that was the main reason she resented him, Mandy thought. In the past three years she had become very independent. She'd been friends with Peter; she hadn't leaned on him. They both had their own work, and work had kept them sane.

But last night...last night had taught her something that she hadn't wanted to learn. Paul was gone; love was gone. Oh, every minute hadn't been perfect. They'd fought; they'd yelled. Any two people did that. Neither one of them had been able to cook worth a whit; she'd wanted a puppy; he'd thought one child was enough. Little things, big things. That was life. You just couldn't zoom through agreeing on everything. But through all those things there had been love. She'd barely known two years of it, but it had been good and solid and real. She had known when she buried her heart and very nearly her existence with her husband and son that she could never settle for anything less— and also that she didn't ever want to know that kind of love again. The pain of loss was so unbearable, so like a set of knives that whittled and whittled away at the insides....

She closed her eyes, inhaling and exhaling.

No, she didn't want to love again. And she certainly wasn't in danger of falling in love with this stranger. But it was dismaying to learn that sensation remained; just like the endless sea and sky, the basic need remained. A need to be held, to feel strength when one was failing, security when all was darkness. To admire, to respect a man, to like the feel of rippling muscle beneath her fingers, the tangy scent of sea and man, the gentle touch of fingers against her cheek.

She gave herself a furious shake, hoping to clear her mind of fantasy. She had to learn to get through these days one by one. She needed some good common sense. If only she had paid attention yesterday she would have known that the sharks were in the water and she would have never made that ridiculous attempt to escape. She had to learn to be wary and alert—and to try to remember that this was a team effort.

She started suddenly, aware not of sound but of a presence at the door. It was open, and Miguel was standing there, watching her with a strange dark expression. She frowned, and the expression faded. He was once again the same enigmatic man she was coming to know.

"I was trying to let you sleep," he said, sauntering in. His hair was damp, and he smelled like soap, and though he was still clad in cutoffs, they were different ones, undoubtedly borrowed from one of the other men. He carried a towel-wrapped bundle, which he gave her, tossing it over the blanket to land in the vicinity of her middle.

"Clothes. They're Maria's. She wasn't very happy about lending them, but Señora Garcia told her that you couldn't run around naked."

Mandy couldn't keep a rueful smile from creeping across her lips as her lashes fell over her cheeks. "Thanks," she said softly. "And thank Señora Garcia. Is there any chance of coming up with a toothbrush?"

"Yes, as a matter of fact, there is. Check below the sink in the head, there's a nice supply. Seems Julio is a tooth fanatic. He told me his teeth were riddled with cavities when he first came to the States. He's been trying to preserve the rest ever since."

"What about you?" she murmured.

"What?"

She kept her lashes downcast, wondering why she was so curious about him. "When you left Cuba..."

"I wasn't born in Cuba."

"But you said—"

"Oh, I am Cuban. Half. I just wasn't born there."

"Here?" She gazed up at him.

He grinned at her, sudden amusement in his eyes. "Here? Was I born in a boat? No. I wasn't born in the water, or in the Bahamas, which is where I'm pretty sure we are."

"I meant—"

"I was born in Dublin, Mrs. Blayne."

"Dublin! Ireland?"

He quickly brought his finger to his lips. "Would you please shush! Are you that determined to hang me?"

"No! Really, I'm sorry!"

She sat up as she spoke, and the blanket dropped to her waist.

She reached for it again quickly, embarrassed, and dragged it back around her before looking at Miguel again.

That strange expression was back...dark, tense. And hungry. Suddenly she was aware of exactly what it meant. He might be a cop, but he was a man, too, a man who found her appealing. He might think very little of her as a human being, but as a woman he found her appealing. Sexually appealing.

And that fact was not something he realized with any great fondness.

She tossed her hair back, a little bit indignant, and a little bit shaken.

She suddenly felt like teasing him! It would provide revenge that seemed very sweet. After all, he thought she was a mercenary woman who had married an old man for his wealth and position. And he was thoroughly convinced that she was a complete bigot. He deserved any torture she could dish out, even if he had dived into the sharks.

"Oh!" she murmured, sweetly distressed, holding the blanket to her breasts but allowing it to fall from her back. Then she had to lower her head and smile discreetly, because she had drawn exactly the response she wanted from him. He had stiffened like a poker. His jaw had squared, and she had heard the grating of his teeth.

She cleared her throat. "Really!" she whispered softly. "I wouldn't want to hang you at all. I appreciate everything that you've done for me!"

"For you and your husband, right?" he asked her softly.

"Peter? Ah . . . yes, of course."

She lowered her eyes again, very aware that he was doing his best to keep his distance from her because she was—in his mind—a married woman. His own assumption! Poor baby! Compelled by a sense of duty to dive into sharks after her. Compelled to sleep beside her to keep her from being bound and tied.

A part of her appreciated that sense of duty. But she didn't at all appreciate his continual jumping to conclusions about her, nor any number of his macho techniques. She'd suffered at his hands; he could damn well suffer at hers. He had taken his own sweet time to inform her that he was a cop, and he'd grabbed her in the shower to do it.

She gave him another wide-eyed innocent stare. "Do you know what the island will be like? I mean, what will the, uh, sleeping arrangements be?"

"You're stuck with me again, Mrs. Blayne. They'd set up a room for your husband. It will be yours—and mine—now."

"Oh."

"Don't worry, Mandy, love. I'll be as safe to be with as a teddy bear. Married women aren't my style. Especially—"

"Bigots?" she inquired sweetly. "A young bigot married to an old man for his money?"

"Your words."

"Ah, but Miguel! Doesn't that scare you to pieces? What if the story were close to the truth? Poor young me, married to poor old Peter! I mean, after all, think about the situation! You half attacked me at first, but then I discovered that you're my savior." Dragging the blanket with her, she came up to him, still smiling sweetly. "And here you are...young...muscled like a panther. I could just lose my mind!" she told him, lightly stroking his cheek with the tips of her nails.

He didn't move. Not a muscle. Not until he grinned slowly and snaked an arm around her so swiftly that she wasn't even aware of his intent until it was complete. She was pulled against him, while his fingers brushed tantalizingly over the small of her back and her buttocks.

"Mrs. Blayne—Mandy, darling!" he drawled in a soft and perfect parody. "Aren't you forgetting that your husband is a wonderful, wonderful lover?"

"Let me go!" she snapped. He'd meant to call her bluff! He did, pushing her from him. "Like I said, *Mrs.* Blayne, I'll be as safe as a teddy bear."

She recovered somewhat and smiled coolly again. "Good." But she was bluffing again. Touching him had been dangerous. Coming too near him would always be like tempting fire. She had realized it too late.

"Dublin!" she muttered beneath her breath. "Like hell! Cop—I wonder."

"I am a cop."

"*Miami Vice*, I take it." She sighed elaborately. "Humph. Where is Sonny Crockett when you need him?"

"Metro Miami. Investigator, homicide. Homicide gets kidnappings and death threats. And I'm sorry about not being Sonny Crockett. Luck of the draw, what can I tell you?"

"The truth is always nice."

"That is the truth."

"You're a half-Cuban detective who was born in Dublin?"

He laughed. "I think I fascinate you, Mrs. Blayne."

"Egos like yours always fascinate." The words were out quickly; she suddenly regretted them, along with her foolish actions. "I'm sorry," she said for what felt like the thousandth time. "Really, I am. I'm alive. I'm grateful." She couldn't help looking back up at him and shrugging. "And you're a teddy bear, if you say so."

"I am."

He was still grinning, aware that he intrigued her. And if he was bitter about what he considered her bigotry, he was also amused. It was a mixture of feelings she didn't particularly appreciate, but what did it matter? They had been cast into this situation together, she by no choice at all, and he simply because he had become a little overinvolved in his job. Besides, he could laugh at her all he wanted. She had one on him, too. She wasn't Senator Peter Blayne's wife.

His smile faded suddenly as he watched her, and he sounded tense when he spoke next. "You can, uh, take a shower and get dressed now if you want. Breakfast is on, and then we're going on to the island."

Mandy nodded wearily, reminded that she was still a captive. She whispered her next words. "Do you really know where we are?"

"Yes, I think I do."

He stiffened suddenly, and she realized that someone had come up behind him in the hall. His next words carried the heavy Spanish accent again. "Now, my love! In the shower. We eat, we go!"

The door closed. She wrapped herself in the still-damp robe, collected the clothing he had given her and slipped from the cabin to the head.

She was delighted to find a stack of new tooth-brushes beneath the sink, so pleased that she issued a little cry of sublime happiness. Then she paused, shivering to discover that joy could be found in such a little thing under these strange circumstances. But, she told herself wryly, it seemed that as long as she was breathing and alive there could be elation in little things, and she might do well to seek it out.

She was uninterrupted in the shower this time, though she didn't close the curtain completely but kept a wary eye on the door, determined to be prepared if someone did burst in on her. That thought made her shiver and burn all over again, and she wondered once more at the contradictory range of emotions Miguel could elicit from her. She clenched her teeth as she rinsed her face, reminding herself again that he was just a cop doing his duty as he saw it and that his opinion of her was a harsh one.

This wouldn't last long! It couldn't! If they'd met at a cocktail party she would have coolly accepted his hostile notions, shrugged, then forgotten him. It was nothing more than the situation and her fear that were creating this horrible tendency to lean on him, to care what he thought. She didn't know anything about him. Not even his whole name. Not whether he was married or not, maybe a father of four or five. Maybe...

She turned the water off and dried herself quickly, then dug into the clothing that Maria had so grudgingly lent to her. Well, pooh to Maria—Mandy didn't like the clothes. The shirt was some kind of a ridiculous halter top in bright red that should have been worn in the early seventies. The cutoff jeans had been tie-dyed with a total lack of artistry and were too big, but at least they came with a ribbon belt. The whole effect was ridiculous, and Mandy thought wryly that Maria had planned it that way. For God's sake, what was the girl jealous of? Mandy wondered irritably. Then she decided she was glad she wasn't eighteen anymore; it was a hard age, when it seemed that women, especially, struggled to find security.

And then she wondered why she cared what she wore as long as she was wearing something, and why she cared one way or another about Maria's psyche, when the girl was doing everything in her limited power to be miserable.

Chin up, kiddo, she told herself. This whole thing boiled down to attitude. The sharks had stripped away her courage yesterday; she was going to dredge it back up for today. She was caught in a nightmare vortex, but even nightmares came to an end. This, like all things, would pass.

Thus determined, she swung open the door—only to have her head-high attitude quickly lowered a peg in confusion, because it wasn't Miguel waiting for her when she emerged, but Roberto. She didn't like the way he looked at her, and she didn't like the way he reached for her arm, sliding his hand along her ribs. She jerked away from him, saying that she was quite able to walk by herself, and hurried topside with him at her heels.

The first thing Mandy saw was the island—if one could call it that. It was really nothing more than a large growth of mangroves with a few handfuls of sand creating a spit of beach. Straining her eyes against the sun and the foliage, she could see some sort of ramshackle structure.

Roberto shoved her in the back. "Move."

She did so, quickly taking a place beside Miguel, who was already eating. The food smelled wonderful. It appeared that they were eating omelets. Even the coffee smelled rich and strong.

Maria, pouring more coffee for Julio, lowered her rich dark lashes and gave Mandy a narrow glance, sniffing delicately at her appearance. Julio barked out something to her, which brought on an immediate argument, with Maria stamping her foot and sullenly shouting and gesticulating. Julio gestured back, totally infuriated, and to her own irritation Mandy found herself inching closer to Miguel, barely aware of the arm that came around her shoulders, except that it gave her a sense of safety and security.

She didn't have the faintest idea what the argument was about, except that she was involved, and if Maria had been in control of the weapons Mandy would surely have been shot on the spot.

Señora Garcia stood up suddenly, clapping her hands over her ears and snapped out a single word. Julio and Maria both ceased their fighting instantly; Maria tossed her head in silence and stalked off below deck, while Julio slipped an arm around his mother's shoulder and spoke to her softly, apologetically.

Miguel took that opportunity to whisper to her, "Maria resents waiting on you. She thinks that you should be made to work. Julio says that you cannot be blamed for your husband's incompetence."

"Peter is not incompetent!" Mandy snapped indignantly.

He gave her a strange gaze, then looked away. "That's rather beside the point right now, isn't it? Here comes Maria. Take your food."

Maria, still sullen, was approaching Mandy, balancing a mug of coffee and a plate at the same time. Mandy accepted the coffee and set it down with a stiff, *"Gracias,"* then held up her hands to accept the plate.

Maria—purposely, Mandy was certain—let go of the plate just short of Mandy's hands.

The hot eggs spilled over her bare legs, burning. Mandy jumped to her feet to get the scorching food off her, while Maria jumped back, ostensibly in a startled fit of apology.

It was suddenly too much for Mandy to handle; she took two furious steps forward and caught the startled Maria by the shoulders and shook her.

"You little brat! Grow up! I didn't ask to be here, you idiot! You hurt me again and I'll find a way to hurt you back!"

Maria instantly started screaming as if Mandy had been trying to throttle her. Miguel leaped between the two, wrenching Mandy hard against his chest. Julio was shouting again in disgust, and Mandy suddenly realized with a little swallow that he was the only one who hadn't pulled out his gun. Both Roberto and a nervous Juan had their weapons aimed right at her.

She was wide-eyed with fright for a second, then she tossed her arms into the air. "You want me to behave? I'll behave! But keep that spoiled brat away from me!"

She spun around with such vengeance that she took even Miguel by surprise, returned to her seat and sipped her coffee while she wiped off her legs, looking for damage.

There was absolute silence for a moment. Then Mandy heard Julio say in English, "Clean it up, Maria."

"Me! The American whore dropped it. Julio, she half strangled me. *Me*—your cousin!—and you take her side!"

Mandy glanced up just in time to see Maria's huge almond eyes filling with tears. "Oh, for God's sake!" she snapped, and stood, doing her best to scoop up the eggs that lay on the deck onto the fallen plate. She shoved them at Miguel with a viciousness that caused him to raise one brow, but he gave her an amused grin and a little thumbs-up sign, then turned to give the plate to Maria.

Maria looked as if she would not accept it. She opened her mouth and closed it again, then finally snatched the debris and flounced away to discard it below.

Mandy hadn't seen Señora Garcia moving, but suddenly the dignified lady was standing before her, holding another plate. Mandy hesitated; Miguel sat down beside her. "Take it," he advised softly.

She did, thanking Julio's mother with another *"Gracias."* Señora Garcia smiled grimly in return and started into a soft monologue that left Mandy staring at her, quite lost.

"The *señora* apologizes to you for Maria's behavior," Miguel told her. "The girl is her niece, and not her daughter. If she had raised her, she would not be so rude. She would be much more a lady."

Mandy didn't know what to say; she merely nodded. She liked Mrs. Garcia, but she didn't know what she thought of her as a mother. After all, she had raised Julio, and Julio was definitely a kidnapper.

"Eat," Miguel warned her. "We are going to the island."

Mandy was startled to discover that she could eat with such an appetite; she was hungry, and the food was excellent. She finished one cup of coffee, then Señora Garcia came back over and offered her more. She asked Miguel something, and Miguel laughed.

"What?" Mandy asked.

"She asked if you wouldn't prefer Cuban coffee. I told her no."

"Did you?" Mandy asked him a little coolly. "As a matter of fact, I like Cuban coffee."

"Now and then, eh? Patronizing the locals?"

"Oh, God!" she muttered. "You're as bad as the rest of them! *You're* the damn bigot!"

"Shut up!" he told her suddenly.

"I will not—"

His fingers closed around her arm and he bent down to whisper to her tensely. "Mandy darling, we do not sound like a sweet pair of illicit lovers sitting here arguing about coffee!"

She glanced at Julio quickly and saw that he was gazing at the two of them suspiciously. She lowered her head quickly, then made a point of arguing back in a whisper that could be overheard.

"I'm sorry, Miguel, really!" She ran a finger delicately down his chest. "I'm just so afraid of everything! And Peter will certainly find out about the two of us now...." She let her voice trail away.

Miguel's eyes were on her in amazement—an amazement he quickly hid as he slipped an arm around her shoulders again. "You could always tell him the truth. You could get a divorce."

"Oh, but Miguel! I just love the money! Think what it does for us! I love making love in the Jacuzzi. I love the silk sheets, the champagne we sip—just touching one another—in the sunken garden. . . .''

She heard him swallow sharply and, despite everything, she had to lower her head with a little shiver. What was wrong with her? She should be ashamed, but all she could think was that there were certain triumphs to be gleaned in any situation!

When she raised her head again she discovered that all the men were staring at her, and that she didn't like the look in their eyes at all.

She inched closer to Miguel again and heard him swallow sharply. This time she didn't take any great pleasure in the effect she had caused.

''Well,'' Julio said stiffly, rising. ''Juan—supplies. Roberto—get the dinghy ready. Juan—you and I will take Señora Blayne first. You will come back for the others. Move quickly now. You'll need the day to get back.'' Juan rose, following orders like a trained puppy.

Mandy discovered then that she didn't want to leave Miguel's side; she was nervous, but also grateful that she would be with Juan and Julio, not Roberto. Small comfort, but all she had.

''Señora Blayne—come!'' Julio had a hand extended to her; she hesitated, so Miguel prodded her slightly. She stood, but didn't take Julio's hand. He shrugged. ''Starboard, Mrs. Blayne. The dinghy is ready. Mama, you come, too.''

Mandy preceded him to the rope ladder and climbed over without looking back. Juan was there, ready to help her into the dinghy. She cringed at the feel of his hands on her waist, but he released her quickly, and once again she was grateful that he was not Roberto.

Señora Garcia followed her down; Juan helped her, too, with the greatest respect. Julio came next, then the dinghy moved away from the ship.

Mandy stared straight ahead, toward the island.

Sean couldn't believe his good fortune—just Roberto and Maria left aboard with him. If he could only assure himself that the two of them were occupied he could take a chance at the ship's old radio. He'd found it easily that first night, when he sat around with the three men drinking beer and telling them his woeful tale of being madly, passionately in love with a married woman, a rich American bitch, but oh, so sweet!

"Hey, Miguel, help me!" Roberto told him. He was pulling boxes of food from the galley cabinets to the deck.

"*Sí, sí,*" Sean said agreeably and ambled down to the galley.

Maria was there. She turned and leaned against the counter, giving him a broad, welcoming grin.

"Hello," she said in a soft, sultry voice.

He smiled, because she was such a pretty kid—with such a lot of growing up to do. Circumstances, though, hadn't been in her favor. Maria had grown up in a household of political protesters. Her father and mother had died; her uncle had been jailed in the old country and then the new.

Sean felt that he could understand her, and even Julio Garcia, in a way that Mrs. Peter Blayne never would. Julio didn't know that he was wrong; in his own way he had been at war all his life. Involved in a dying protest that knew no rules, all was fair. He was too young to remember the revolution when Castro had overthrown Batista. He only knew that suppression had given way to new suppression.

He wanted to be an American. He just didn't know how. Just like Maria. She wanted to be a woman. She wanted to be free and liberated. She didn't know how to go about fulfilling her wishes, either.

"Hi," he answered casually.

Julio had given her a little pistol, too. She had it tucked into the waistband of her very American designer blue jeans.

He was very tempted to reach for it. Maria would be incredibly easy to seduce and overpower.

But the timing was wrong. Julio and Juan had Amanda Blayne on the shore, and though Sean instinctively believed that Julio would never kill her on purpose, he just might panic and become dangerous because of his very nervousness. He hadn't quailed at all when he had riddled the dock with bullets.

Maria sauntered up to Sean and drew a bloodred nail over his naked chest. "You are stupid!" she told him huskily. "She is not for you. You will grow tired of her, yet you risk so much for her!"

He had to think about that one. *She is not for you....*

No, she wasn't. She was a married woman. And though he had acquired a reputation for his nightlife and the chain of broken hearts in his wake, he'd always stopped short when it came to married women.

He was supposed to be distant, professional. Yet she—far beyond the situation—was making him crazy. At the moment he wished with all his heart that he'd never lost his mind and gone diving after the speedboat. He wished he'd never thought of his story....

He wished that he'd never seen her face. Her perfect, beautiful, delicate Anglo face. Tawny eyes, tawny hair, tawny...flesh. Sun golden, sleek, curved, sensual. He wished he'd never seen her, touched her, known her, watched her, listened to her....

It made professionalism damn near impossible. He even hated the fact that he liked her. Liked her brand of determination, so wholehearted that she'd been ready to swim miles in the dusk for freedom. So heated that she refused to bow to anyone—not even with a trio of guns aimed at her.

He gave himself a shake, took both Maria's hands, smiled and placed them back by her sides. "*Chica*, I walk here by a slender thread already. You want your cousin to kill me for your honor?"

"Julio?" She sniffed indelicately. "If Julio were a real man we would not be in this fix. He would have taken the right man, not some *puta*."

"Maria! Bring the food!" Roberto ordered from above.

She grimaced, but decided not to disobey the order. It seemed that everyone knew Roberto had a streak of meanness in him.

Maria disappeared above deck. Sean reached beneath the cabinet and started gathering up supplies with one hand while he reached across to the radio with the other, keeping his eyes trained on the ladder and the hatch above it.

At first he could get nothing. He had to forget the supplies and give his entire attention to the ancient radio. Finally a voice came in—and to Sean's vast relief and amazement he realized that he'd reached the Coast Guard.

Quietly he tried to give his location and discovered
with little surprise that search parties had been out
since they disappeared. He warned the voice over the
radio that he might have to cut out quickly. He advised the man as to the number of kidnappers and said
that Juan would be coming back in to make their demands, then assured the man that the senator's wife
was fine.

He was surprised by the silence that followed.

"Lieutenant Ramiro, the senator's wife has been
dead over a year."

"What?" Sean shouted, then realized what he had
done. He lowered his voice quickly. "She's here, with
me. They nabbed her, and I came after her!"

"Oh, you've got a Mrs. Blayne all right, but she's
not his wife. She's his son's widow. But he's tearing his
heart out over her just the same. Just keep calm, lieutenant. It may take us some time to find you."

"I am calm," Sean retorted dryly. "I'm a ten-year
vet with the force. Don't you come barging in. Garcia
is as nervous as a cat."

"We'll tell the FBI. You keep a lookout. You're out
of the U.S., but I'm sure they'll get complete cooperation from the Bahamian authorities. We'll advise the
senator that his daughter-in-law is doing—"

Sean heard Roberto yelling at Maria as he approached the ladder. He flicked the radio off and
turned back to stacking cans.

"That's enough!" Roberto snapped, holding his gun
on Sean. Sean knew that Roberto didn't trust him. The
man just wasn't the trusting sort. They were a strange
alliance, Roberto and Julio. Julio the idealist; Roberto the thug.

Sean stood up, shrugging. Roberto waved the gun at him. "Go up. The boat is back."

Sean obediently went up to the deck. Juan was back with the dinghy, and Maria was handing the supplies over the rail to him.

"I'll help," Sean told her.

"*Gracias*, Miguel," she purred softly.

He took over her work, moving mechanically and grinning despite himself.

So she wasn't the senator's wife. He'd been torturing himself for nothing. She'd been intentionally driving him up a wall, but now...now it was his turn.

"Miguel! Come aboard!" Roberto ordered.

Juan was staying on the sailboat so he could return to Miami. He waved to Sean, who crawled down to the dinghy.

Sean looked at the island before him. It would still be dangerous getting out of this mess; Roberto was a danger all by himself.

And he was still a cop, and she was still one of the citizens he was sworn to protect. He just couldn't stop that damn grin.

Because she was going to pay.

6

It might have been a paradise, one of those quaint little outer islands where only those with their own boats might venture, a little piece of heavenly unaltered nature.

The island was beautiful, Mandy thought wryly, feeling the pressure of Julio's hand on her back as he urged her along. There was a stretch of beach so miraculously white it might have been snow rather than sand; to the left of the beach was an outcrop of coral and rock, fantastically entwined with the mangrove roots. To the right a stretch of rock and mangroves jutted out into the sea, creating a natural harbor. It was too small a spit of land to hold a hotel, just a dot on the ocean, but it was one of the loveliest little islands Mandy had ever seen.

"Señora Blayne, *por favor!*"

Julio prodded her once again, and she realized that she was stopping every few feet to look around. He was ushering her toward the structure she had seen between the trees, and she wondered why he should be so insistent. There was nowhere for her to go, and he certainly couldn't think that she intended to overpower him—especially since he was carrying a gun.

She shrugged wearily and continued walking. Señora Garcia had already entered the ramshackle place through a screen door; Mandy followed her, curiously surveying her surroundings.

It was an old frame house, with a kitchen being the first room, and something like a parlor behind it, and two doors at the rear of that parlor. Someone had cleaned the place, and Mandy could only assume that that someone had been Señora Garcia. Even clean, though, it was dismal. There was a double-sided fireplace between the kitchen and the parlor, a rickety old table in the kitchen, and an even more rickety sofa in the parlor. There were two mattresses on the floor lined up against the wall by the left rear door. And there were three pickle-barrel end tables, one by the sofa, one between the mattresses and one near the fireplace. There were no electrical wires—what had she been expecting?—and the only concession to contemporary standards seemed to be a battery-powered icebox next to the counter in the kitchen.

"Go through," Julio told her. His mother glanced at her unhappily and started to say something, but Julio interrupted her.

"She can be trouble! You have seen so!"

Mandy kept walking. Julio indicated the left door, and she opened it.

It was a bedroom, or at least it resembled a bedroom. There was a mattress on the floor. And there was another door at the rear.

"Is that a bathroom? Or am I allowed to ask?" Mandy asked bitterly.

Julio compressed his lips and nodded. Mandy found herself studying him curiously. He was a young man, handsome, with curling dark hair and a slim, sinewy build. But his dark eyes were full of such a feverish tension! She couldn't believe that he would really harm her; he seemed such a different type from Roberto.

A trickling of unease sped along her spine, and for all that she was usually ready to strangle Miguel, she suddenly wished desperately that he was with her.

"Yes, it is a bathroom. Old and faulty—and the water is brackish. Do not drink it. You understand?"

She nodded.

He smiled peculiarly, a little sadly. "This is it, Mrs. Blayne. Make yourself at home. I'm afraid it will take some time to reach your husband and have my demands met."

He turned to leave her.

"Wait a minute!" Mandy cried, not at all sure what she meant to do, but suddenly determined to make the young man with the nice mother go straight.

"Julio! Señor Garcia! Listen to me. You haven't harmed me. Not really. I feel that this is all a great misunderstanding. If you were to bring me back now— well, I wouldn't press charges. I guess you wouldn't get off scot-free, because you did fire bullets all over the docks. But I don't think you hit anyone, did you? Really, Julio, you don't want to be a criminal! You could go for an insanity plea—temporary insanity. Mental duress. Julio, they will straighten your father's situation out. It just takes time. You don't want him to be free while you're forced to be in jail, do you? You can't get away with this. Think about it. What good is it going to do when you do get hold of Peter? Julio, if we stop this whole thing right now, I'll do my best to help you. Peter will—"

"Mrs. Blayne," Julio interrupted laconically.

"Yes, Julio?"

"Shut up."

From sheer surprise, she did so. He gave her a rueful smile, turned and left her. When he closed the door she heard the sharp final sound of a bolt sliding home.

"Damn you!" Mandy muttered, threading her fingers through her hair in frustration. "Damn you, you idiot!"

Exasperated and desolate, she sank onto the mattress. For several moments she just sat there, pressing her temples between her palms. Then she lay back on the bed and stared around. There was nothing to see. Nothing but four walls and the door to her primitive bathroom. There was only one window in the room, and that had been boarded over. There was nothing but gloom.

She wished she could sleep. She wished that they had left her just a square inch of window to look through. Time hung so heavily! Each second seemed like an hour, and her imprisonment had only begun. All she could do was lie there in the gloom with her own thoughts—which were not particularly good company.

Every once in a while she heard voices from beyond the door. They were faint, and she couldn't make out a thing, because they were speaking in Spanish.

Where the hell was Miguel?

To her irritation, she was longing to see him. Longing desperately to see him, just because she couldn't stand the shadowed gloom and her own company anymore.

She tried to think about her work; she tried to think of all the little tedious things she had to do when she got back. She tried to think about the sea, serene and calm. She even tried to imagine sheep jumping over a fence so she could sleep and keep her mind from going a million frustrated miles an hour. Nothing worked. She had never imagined that simple confinement could be so frightening, so wearing. She thought that soon she would go mad; she would race for that bolted door and scream and cry and beat her head against it.

Just when she felt that she had reached that point, the door suddenly swung open. Mandy blinked against the sudden light, shielding her eyes.

For a moment she froze; it was Roberto. Roberto, giving her his lascivious white-toothed smile. She shivered inside, going as cold as ice. She was alone in this room with nothing but a white-sheeted mattress, no avenue of escape. No strength, no hope—and fully aware of the man's feelings regarding her.

No, no, Julio wouldn't allow it. Miguel wouldn't allow it. But where the hell *was* Miguel?

"Amanda?"

She took a deep breath and felt the blood move through her veins once again.

Miguel stepped past Roberto and stared at her, offering her his hand.

She didn't think anything then. She bolted from the mattress, straight toward him, grasping that hand and pressing herself against the strength of his naked chest, her head lowered.

She felt his free hand on her hair, hesitant, then soothing. He wrapped an arm around her and led her through the tacky parlor, Roberto at their heels.

Julio sat at the kitchen table, playing cards with Maria. Señora Garcia was standing over a frying pan set on a Sterno stove on the counter. She was cooking hamburgers; it might have been the great American barbecue.

Miguel started to move away from Mandy; she inched toward him with a little gasp, drawing a snicker from Maria. Mandy stiffened, while Miguel accepted two plates of food from Señora Garcia. He shoved them at Mandy with a curious expression, then turned back to accept two cans of Old Milwaukee.

"Two hours, no more," Julio warned Miguel without looking up from his game.

"Dos horas," Miguel agreed, and Julio did look up then, but not at them. He stared at Roberto, who insisted on keeping his gun out and trained on Miguel.

"I'll spell you soon, amigo," he said.

Roberto leered at Mandy and shrugged to Julio. Mandy thought she saw Julio shudder slightly, and she wondered again how these two had come together, an idealist and a . . . vulture.

"Come on," Miguel urged her with his Spanish accent. *"Dos horas!"*

She had no idea what he was talking about, but she eagerly followed him outdoors.

It was late afternoon again. The sea stretched out eternally before them, touched by the reflection of the dying sun, sparkling and rippling like something magical. Even the white beach seemed to shimmer with the colors of the coming evening, gold and pink, delicate mauve and diamond glitter.

Miguel walked beside her; Roberto followed at a distance. "This way," Miguel advised, walking toward the part of the beach where the rock and mangroves formed a secretive little haven, shadowed now in dusk.

She looked back. Roberto had paused. He was sitting on the beach, watching them, but giving them a certain distance. Mandy expelled a long sigh, which drew a sharp gaze from Miguel.

"He makes me nervous," she muttered.

If she'd expected reassurance, she didn't get it. "He doesn't thrill me, either," Miguel agreed. "But forget him for now. I spent hours arguing to get Julio to agree that you would go mad and be far more difficult to handle if you didn't get out a little."

He led her as far away from Roberto as possible, to the place where the roots met the rocks.

"Have a seat, Mrs. Blayne," he told her with a grin.

She sat on a stump, balancing both plates of hamburgers until he settled himself on the sand beside her. He opened both cans of beer, then handed her one as he took his own plate.

"Thanks," Mandy muttered, then lowered her head, because she was thinking about him, and she didn't want him to guess. She was on the stump; he was at her side, the breadth of his bare shoulders and back at her knee, his dark head angled toward her, his rich green eyes looking out to the sea.

She found herself liking everything about him; his height, his build, those eyes—even his scruffy jaw, strong beneath the beard. He was attractive—and she was attracted. She despised herself for it, because she considered herself sane and mature, and thought she knew enough about the human psyche to keep herself under control. She'd barely known him for forty-eight hours, yet she was desperately glad of his presence, ready to race to the sound of his voice, more than willing to trust herself to him.

Naturally. She sensed that he was all that stood between her and Roberto. But he was a cop—that was his job. There was no reason she should feel so ... quiveringly grateful. Especially when she knew what he really thought of her!

"Eat," he told her, and she saw that he was looking at her then, rather than the sea. And that there was a peculiar glint of amusement in his eyes.

Mechanically and a little warily, she brought her hamburger to her mouth. It seemed to stick against the dryness of her throat, and she sipped the beer to force it down.

Miguel seemed to have no such problems. He ate his hamburger with a hearty appetite, then leaned back against her legs, very relaxed—like an idle beach bum—while he sipped his beer.

She stiffened, ready to jerk her legs away. She stopped herself only because she knew that Roberto watched them, not fifty feet away.

The water, stretching out before them, was magically beautiful, as were the white purity of the sand, the wild and primitive tangle of mangrove and coral, the eternal sky, the twilight....

And the two of them. He was touching her, relaxed and lazy, as if they were the only two people on earth, a man and a woman.

She set her half-eaten hamburger down and sipped the beer. She was so glad to be out of that room, away from her own thoughts.

Yet she was so nervous, so horribly aware of him: of his tanned flesh, so sleek over the rippling muscles of his back and shoulders; his hair, ebony with the coming of the night; his scent, as fresh and salty as the night air, and here, in this wild splendor, so masculine that she felt nearly consumed just by his presence....

It was all because she had to rely on him, she told herself furiously. Circumstance! At a cocktail party she would have walked away from him.

But here she couldn't walk away. Being with him was playing dangerous havoc with her emotions and her senses, and she knew it.

But what was she afraid of? He assumed that she was married to Peter, and he steered clear of married women; he had told her so with indisputable passion.

Maybe she should be glad, grateful to learn that her instincts and emotions still functioned. She worked, she laughed, she enjoyed people, but she hadn't really felt anything in so long. Maybe even the fear and the fury were good; she was reacting, and there had been times when she had felt that anything would be better than the horrible numbness. But this . . .

Even Peter had tried to introduce her to a string of young men. She'd never felt the least interest, just the numbness. And now she felt like a traitor, to Paul and—far worse—to herself. How could she possibly be attracted to a man who treated her so poorly?

He was there; he was a buffer. That was all, absolutely all. And she wasn't only attracted to him. She was also indignant and outraged by his methods. To top it all off, she still didn't even know if she should really believe him or not, because he was a fabulous actor, slipping from accent to accent with barely a thought.

"You really are absolutely beautiful, you know."

Mandy started, choking on her beer, staring involuntarily into the heavy-lidded sparkling green eyes that were now resting on her in the most sensual fashion. She swallowed warily. "Thank you," she muttered. Then she asked, "You really are a cop?"

He chuckled softly. "Yeah, I really am."

Mandy stared out to sea again while confusion overwhelmed her. His voice... the huskiness in his voice. What had happened to him suddenly? The cut-and-dried manner was gone—as was the hard and passionate man who had vowed he didn't touch married women, who despised her for marrying an old man.

"Uh..." She cleared her throat, searching for a safe topic of conversation. "What is Julio doing with Roberto? They don't seem a bit alike."

He shrugged. "They're not. Juan is with him because they're second cousins or something. I think Roberto is merely in it for the money."

"The money?"

"Mmm. The Garcias still have family in Spain, and a number of wealthy Colombian connections. If I've gotten things right, Roberto is a mercenary. He's been hired for his expertise. That's why I don't trust him. God, you're beautiful."

"Would you stop that!" Mandy snapped after a moment. He'd changed his tone so quickly that it had taken her time to catch up, and now she knew that she was nearly as red as the twilight.

"I can't seem to help myself," he said, swallowing the last of his beer, then crushing the can in one hand while he continued to stare at her.

She swallowed the last of her beer, compelled to return his stare, fascinated, horrified.

He took her can from her hand, brushing her fingers with his own, rising to his knees, a breath away from her.

"You hate married women. Especially me. I married old Peter Blayne for his wealth and possessions, remember?'' she told him quickly. Too quickly. Breathlessly...

"I know,'' he told her softly, his arm moving around her. His face wasn't an inch from hers. She felt the power of his chest and shoulders, saw the smoldering green fire in his eyes. "I know all that. But don't you feel it? The sea and the breeze and the night, you—and me?''

"No! No!'' Mandy told him hastily. "I don't feel anything. Just that you hate me. Remember?''

He shook his head. "I don't hate you, Mandy, though I keep thinking of all the reasons why I should. I think and think of all the reasons why I should stay completely away from you. I tell myself over and over again that you're married. That I'm a cop. That you're completely off limits. But, Mandy... I tell you, I can't help myself. No matter what I think, I see you. I see those golden eyes of yours, that tawny lion's mane. I see your body—oh, God! Do I see your body! Naked and gold and glistening, lithe and curved—''

"Stop it!'' Mandy shrieked, trying to edge away as his knuckles brushed over her cheek. She lost her balance instead and toppled over into the sand.

He was right behind her, stretching over her, bracing his weight on his hands, his palms beside her head. He seemed to cover her, his legs entangled with hers.

"Get up—'' she began in panic.

"Oh, Mandy! I can't!'' he vowed passionately, and she felt all the sexual quality of him, the power in his thighs, the brush of his hairy chest against her skin, the ridiculously sweet pressure of his hips on hers.

"Roberto! Roberto is watching us!'' she protested.

"And I must convince him that we are lovers,'' Miguel whispered softly, shifting, bringing himself halfway to her side, cupping her jaw in his hand to bring her face to his.

"Amanda, I can't bear this. Being with you, night and day. Sleeping beside you. I'd sell my soul for you. I can't care that you're a married woman, I can't think of anything. I have to have you!"

Heat like liquid fire exploded through her—right along with a raging sense of panic. He was way too much male. She didn't know what to do with him; she didn't know how to escape him. She felt lost and overwhelmed and desperate!

"Wait. Wait!"

"Hold me, Mandy. Just hold me!"

Hold him? His arms were vise clamps around her, his body an inferno of steel. She was quivering like a cornered rabbit, straining against him with all her might—futilely.

"Miguel..."

"Oh, Lord, I was in agony, listening to you! I envisioned the two of us in a Jacuzzi, sipping champagne, just barely touching, coming nearer and nearer, until you were mine."

He shifted, touching her. Lightly. Fingertips against her cheek, stroking her throat, running over her collarbone, so near the neckline of her halter top. Fingertips...dancing dangerously over the mounds of her breasts, fascinated with the naked flesh of her midriff. Gentle, tender, erotic in their motion, in their very being. And she was powerless. Shivering and aware and powerless, and so keenly touched by the vibrant heat of his body, his weight, the rough feel of his legs.

"Champagne...you and me. The warm waters rushing around us. Mandy, you've got the most beautiful breasts I've ever seen."

"Miguel, don't you—"

"God, you're glorious...splendid. Champagne and pizza. Completely naked...us...together."

"Damn you! I'll strangle you once we're free."

"Remember when you touched me? This morning? Oh, Mandy, I felt desire in that touch. I know that Peter Blayne's an old man. I know that you're young and sensual and I can't see any reason why we shouldn't—"

"There are a million reasons!"

He smiled, totally disbelieving her. And then his fingertips were moving again. Just gently stroking her ribs...then moving higher, brushing her breasts. Her nipples were hard, and he could feel it, and that was making him grin even more widely.

"I'll report you. If we live I'll report you to all your superiors. Every one of them! They'll fire you."

"You're just saying that, Mandy. I can feel you. I knew this morning that you wanted me."

"I do not!"

"I don't care about anything! Report me. I'd give my job—my life—for one night with you."

Oh, no! What had she done this morning? Threats weren't working; they didn't mean a thing to him!

"Please..." she whispered, but even that did nothing.

"You've cast a spell on me," he told her huskily. "I can't let you go. It's all that I can think about—you, me, tangled together, hot, sweating, straining."

"Miguel, you're a cop! I'm a married woman!"

Suddenly he was laughing, staring down at her and laughing. Then he rolled away from her and sat up, wrapping his arms around his knees and staring out at the sea once again.

"Mrs. Blayne, you're the most ridiculous liar I've ever met," he told her with curt amusement.

"What?" Stunned, she scrambled to her feet and stared down at him, her hands on her hips. She felt relieved, furious—and bereft.

He gazed up at her, still smiling. "Amanda Blayne, you're Peter Blayne's daughter-in-law, not his wife."

"How do you know?"

"Because I managed to get through to the Coast Guard on the radio."

"What?"

"I keep telling you—I'm a cop. Sworn to protect and all that jazz. I'm sorry I haven't tried to stop a bullet for you yet, but I did get to the radio."

Her temper flared out of all proportion. She should be jumping up and down with joy that someone had been advised of the situation, but he'd just made such a fool of her! Without thought she suddenly leapt at him, pummeling his chest and shoulders.

"You bastard! You didn't bother to tell me! Instead you pulled this little act. I'll kill you! I'll wring your stupid neck!"

"Whoa!" he protested, stunned by her vehemence, falling backward into the sand at her assault. He collected himself quickly and caught her flailing fists, then rolled and cast a knee over her hips and stretched her arms over her head, where he held them while he leaned against her, panting.

"Don't touch me! I swear, I *will* report you! How dare you?"

"Roberto is looking!"

"I don't give a damn!"

"You'd better—unless you want Roberto in this position!"

"What diff—"

"A lot, Mrs. Blayne. I'm not going to rape you, but Roberto would give his eyeteeth to do just that!"

Mandy went dead still, clenching her teeth and staring up at him, trying to regain her breath.

"You son of—"

"Hey! You lied to me! I risked my neck to let you know that I was a police officer. You lied—"

"I did not! You assumed that I was Peter's wife! You judged me without a—"

"You could have corrected me!"

"And why should I have bothered?"

"Courtesy, Mrs. Blayne. Common courtesy. Especially in this situation!"

"Courtesy! Oh—"

"Shush!"

She grated her teeth together again. He was staring down at her with an emerald spark in his eyes. He was amused.

And she was far too aware of him all over again. His fingers, curled within hers. His thigh, cast over her hips. His warmth. Everything about him that was male, that called to something inside her despite herself. She was quivering from the effect of his touch....

"Let me go, please, Miguel," she whispered.

He stared at her a moment longer, his eyes growing dark, tension suddenly lining his face. He sighed and released her, but still lay at her side.

"You asked for it, you know," he told her.

"Men!" she snapped. "They say you're all alike, and I believe it! You came at me with all kinds of insinuations and I just played along because *you* were the one who deserved it!"

He laughed again, and she was aware once more that she liked his smile, liked it very much.

"The champagne in the Jacuzzi was a killer," he told her.

She stiffened. "I was acting for the benefit of our captors, and you know it."

He shrugged. "You're just such a good little actress!"

"Oh, stop, please." And don't stay so close, please don't stay so close! she added silently, cast into an agony of confusion. It was just the circumstances, she told herself.

She closed her eyes. "Thank God you got to the radio! When is help coming?"

"I don't know."

Her eyes flew open again, and she edged up on her elbows to frown at him. "What do you mean you don't know? You just told me—"

"I mean I don't know! I tried to tell them where we were, but I'm not positive. It only takes a day to reach Cat Cay—we were on that old scow for two nights. I think that they motored in circles, backtracking on purpose. I still think that we're somewhere near Cat Cay. But there must be hundreds of these little swamp islands around. It may take time. And this has to be handled carefully. The Coast Guard can't just zoom up. That's not the way you handle a hostage situation You could—"

"Get shot?"

He shrugged. "That's not going to happen, Mandy." Distracted, he called her by her given name, not by the acid "Mrs. Blayne."

She looked from his profile to the ocean, picking up a handful of sand, letting it fall through her fingers.

He stood up abruptly and reached a hand down to her. "Let's walk on the beach. Our two hours are almost up."

"How can you tell?" she asked him despondently.

"Because," he said softly, "I can read the sky. And Julio has come out to take Roberto's place as watchdog."

Mandy glanced over her shoulder. It was true; Julio was sitting where Roberto had been.

She looked back to the strong hand being offered to her. She hesitated a moment longer, then took it. He pulled her to her feet, cast an arm around her and started walking idly down the beach.

Mandy went along because she felt she had little choice. It did feel good to move; it felt wonderful to be outside, rather than in that dim stuffy room. It felt good to have his arm around her. To know that he was with her, even if she still wanted to strangle him. Yet at the same time she knew that she needed him. He was her security, her buffer against fear and madness. This would end; all things ended. But for now . . . the evening sky was beautiful; the breeze was delightful. He was at her side—far better than facing Roberto's leers alone.

They walked through the surf, and the cool water bathed her feet. If she closed her eyes she could pretend that she was just on an outing, away for the day, taken to a primitive paradise on the winged sails of the *Flash Point.*

She sniffed suddenly and managed to cast Miguel a wry smile. "I don't even know your last name."

He gazed at her, hesitated a minute, then said, "Ramiro."

"Miguel Ramiro," she said. Strangely, he hesitated once again.

"Not exactly."

"Not exactly?"

"Well, don't tell these guys. My name is Sean. Sean Michael Ramiro."

"What?" Mandy started laughing. Maybe it was hysteria. She stared at him incredulously.

"Sean Michael Ramiro?" She moved away from him, almost doubled over with laughter, so incredible did she find it all. "Now I know you're a liar!"

"I told you I was born in Dublin!" he retorted.

"You said you were Cuban—"

"I said *half*-Cuban! My father was Cuban, my mother is Irish."

She was still laughing. "What a combination!"

"Oh, yeah! I forgot! You're Miss DAR! Daughter of the old *Mayflower*!"

She was still laughing so hard she couldn't even take offense.

"Sean?"

"Yeah. Want to make something of it?"

"No, no!" She held out a defensive hand, but too late. He splashed over to her, gripped her hands, slid a foot behind her ankle and sent her crashing into the surf, then dropped down beside her.

"I'm sorry! I'm sorry!" she shrieked when he made a move to dunk her.

But he didn't dunk her. He touched her cheek, his weight and warmth against her again, while the cool surf raced delicately around them both. She felt the power of his arms on either side of her, saw the tension in his eyes, and she might well have been spellbound.

His head lowered. His lips brushed hers.... Just brushed them. And then his eyes were on hers again. Like the sea around them, reflected by the sinking sun, touched by the coming moon. They quested and they sought...and she must have answered.

Because his lips met hers again, with a coercive hungry pressure. His kiss filled her with that same hunger, captured her with fascination. She tasted sea and salt and passion and heat, felt the sweep of his tongue over her teeth...deep into her mouth. Filling her, entering her with a spiraling heat that sent a searing wonder rippling through her. He wasn't really touching her, just his mouth. Just the tickle of that growth of beard against her flesh, the fire of his lips, the fever of his mouth...

"Hey! Your two hours are up! She goes back to her room!"

Startled, they broke apart at Julio's announcement, shaken from the moment.

Mandy stared at Sean Michael Ramiro in absolute horror. She didn't accept his hand, nor did she even notice Julio, standing on the beach.

She raced back toward the house, eager now for her prison, desperate to be alone.

7

When darkness came to her shuttered prison, it came completely.

Mandy was absolutely convinced that she would go mad. She couldn't see her own hand in front of her face. She hadn't known that she was afraid of the dark, but then, she'd never seen darkness so complete.

For hours she lay on the mattress, still soaked from the surf, shivering, then going deathly still before shivering all over again. Sometimes it seemed that her mind was blank; sometimes it was as if a cacophony of thoughts and ideas raced within it.

And always it came back to two things. The darkness. Haunting, suffocating, ebony darkness. And Miguel. No, not Miguel. Sean Michael Ramiro.

Her feelings, his touch. The strident need she was beginning to feel for him. The moral horror that she could be so vulnerable, so dependent . . .

And so hungry. To be held, touched, loved. To laugh, to play and enjoy the play.

She yearned for him now in a terrible aching way. She thought that she could endure the darkness, if only he was next to her. Here, in this hell within paradise, he had become her salvation, and more. It seemed ridiculously complex; the emotional and the physical; the desire, the need. It seemed so incredibly basic and primitive. She simply wanted to fit against him, as nature had intended, without thought, without words.

There was no way to escape her sense of disloyalty, no way to lie in this utter darkness and not think of Paul, not think of the baby. No way to do anything other than lie there in anguish and agony, suffering the ceaseless gnawing of a fear that came not just from circumstances now, but, like desire, from instinct.

She went still when the door opened at last. The streak of light that entered was painful, as blinding as the darkness. Mandy closed her eyes against it, casting her arm over her face.

The light was quickly gone. Her whole existence suddenly centered around her other senses.

Someone was in the room.

She could feel that presence so strongly! Logic warned her that it could be Julio or Maria or Señora Garcia. A trembling within warned that it could too easily be Roberto.

But her world now knew no logic. She didn't need to be afraid; it was Sean. She knew from the presence that filled the room; she knew from his salty scent, the sound of his breath.

He stood just within the doorway for several moments, his eyes adjusting to the darkness. Then, very slowly, he came toward the mattress. He reached it and fumbled along the edge, then smoothed his hand over the sheet.

She shifted, giving him room. He started suddenly, aware of her movement.

"You're awake?"

"I'm awake."

"My God, it's darker than a coal mine in here."

"I couldn't find the light switch," she said, trying to joke, but she had no idea what his reaction was, since she couldn't see his face.

He didn't answer as he stretched out beside her. She didn't dare touch him, but she knew his position. Hands laced behind his head, ankles crossed, feet probably dangling over the edge.

"You okay?" he whispered after a while.

"Of course. Why wouldn't I be?"

She imagined that he might have grinned. "I guess you're not afraid of the dark."

"Terrified. But what could I possibly do about it?"

"Ask for a lantern."

"Would I get one?"

"Probably." He hesitated. "I don't think Julio means to be cruel. He just doesn't know that it's as black as Hades in here. Not that it matters if you're sleeping, but you've been in here quite a while. I'll get a lantern tomorrow."

She didn't answer him. She wasn't sure what to say. She was excruciatingly glad of his presence; he was like a lantern against the darkness.

She was also excruciatingly aware of him—and the last moments they had shared. She was frightened, not of him, but of herself, and so keyed up that she would never sleep, so miserable that she longed for nothing except oblivion.

The silence seemed to grow in the darkness and become a black cloud above them, filled with the portent of wind and rain. They did not touch, though they were no more than an inch apart. Then suddenly Mandy sneezed, and that sneeze ended the silence.

"Bless you," he muttered, turning toward her. His hand brushed her arm, and suddenly she knew that he was above her, that his dark brows were furrowed with concern, and that his handsome features had hardened into a scowl. "You're shivering like a leaf, and you feel like an ice cube!"

"Do I?" Mandy murmured.

"Yes, you do." He quickly stood, pulling at the mattress, fumbling and swearing when he stubbed his toe against it.

"Get up—can you?"

"Of course I can," she murmured, confused. "But why?"

"There's a top sheet on this thing, and you need to get under it. Take your clothes off."

"What?"

"Oh, come on! I can't see a damn thing in here. Besides, I've already seen you. Your clothes are still all wet from the beach, and you'll get pneumonia if you sleep in them. And then, should the time come when you need to move quickly, you won't be able to. Take your clothes off."

"I think I'd rather risk pneumonia!"

"Than me?"

How could a voice do so much? Reach out through the air and darkness like a velvet brush, teasing, warming.

"Umm."

"Still don't trust me?"

"Not in the least."

"Well, that's okay. I don't trust *you*, either."

"I'm not asking you to take your clothes off."

"Not yet. You'll get to it, though. Women are all alike."

She rolled off the mattress, laughing, perplexed. Somehow he had brought light and warmth into the room. And also that sense of security that was so very easy to rely on, so very easy to need—and so very dangerous. More dangerous, perhaps, than Julio and his accomplices.

"Laugh at me, will you, Mrs. Blayne?" he charged softly, and she knew that he was walking around to her. He hunched down in front of her and felt for her. She didn't know what he was looking for, but he found her breast.

"Hey! And you're asking me to take my clothes off?"

"Sorry, I thought it was your face."

"Umm. You'll get yours one day."

"Promises, promises. Off with 'em, lady."

"I don't think this is proper police procedure."

"Off!"

"Well, move, then!"

He did. Feeling like a stripper in broad daylight, Mandy shed her soggy cutoffs and top, then groped with a fair amount of panic for the sheet.

It was there, in his hands, ready to be wrapped around her. She sensed that he was laughing at her.

"I've already slept with the...real...you, you know."

"Oh, shut up!"

She was still shivering, but she did feel much better; she hadn't realized how chilling her wet clothing had been. But even now, with the dry sheet wrapped around her, she was cold.

"Lie down now," he said huskily.

"What wonderful relationships you must have, Mr. Ramiro! Take off your clothes. Lie down."

He laughed softly in the darkness, and once again she felt touched by the sound, brushed by velvet.

"When it works, do it. Lie down."

Gritting her teeth, she did so, cocooning herself in the sheet. Then she tensed as he crawled over to her. He didn't keep his distance this time; he brought his chest to her back and wrapped an arm around her waist, pulling her close to absorb his heat.

She must have been as stiff and unyielding as concrete, though she made no protest, because he chuckled softly again. "Ease up. I'm just trying to make you warm."

She didn't know that she had held her breath until she released it in a long sigh.

"I'm not the big bad wolf."

"Are you sure?"

"Positive. Why do I make you so nervous?"

"I'm not nervous."

"You are."

"Well, I have a right to be! Since I've met you, you've knocked me down, thrown me around...."

"What's a lover for?" he teased. "Mandy—Mrs. Blayne—I do apologize for my rougher methods."

"And your gentler ones?" she murmured without thought.

His arm tightened slightly around her midriff. "Meaning?"

"Nothing!" she said quickly. What had caused her to say such a thing?

And even as she asked herself the question, she knew the answer. The kiss. The real one, in the salty foam of the surf, interrupted by Julio's appearance.

In the darkness she felt his every breath, knew his every movement, no matter how slight. Knew him, living and breathing beside her.

Silence spread again, total in the darkness. And in that silence she thought it would be the easiest thing in the world to turn to him, to give in to temptation under cover of darkness.

She'd always known that she was young, that she would make love again one day. But one day had always meant some indeterminate future. It was something she hadn't dwelled upon, had not imagined easily. It would be awkward and difficult, and she would be nervous and afraid and, certainly, making comparisons. She had even begun to imagine how difficult it would be to remove her clothing, or watch a man disrobe, knowing his intent.

She wore no clothing now, but it was dark. And in the darkness she would not have to see a man's face. Not have to know if she brought pleasure or ennui, nor bear visible witness that she found it not thrilling in the least, but actually distasteful....

But it *would* be thrilling. With him. For her. She knew from his eyes, from his laughter, from his words, from the hands that touched her so well, from the hard length of his body, taut and warm against hers.

It was easy to forget because of circumstance. Easy to imagine that the darkness could cover her, and she could hide from truth and light and thought. Easy...

She would never do it; not even the darkness could take away her memories. And it wasn't just Paul; it was Paul and the baby. If one of them had made it—just one of them—she wouldn't have felt as if she had been stripped of everything. Everything that mattered. She wouldn't have been so afraid of emotion, of reaching out. But she had learned that pleasure brought pain.

She hadn't known that she was crying; her tears were as silent as the night. Then suddenly she felt a thumb against her cheek, wiping away the moisture there.

"How long?" he asked her very softly.

And she knew exactly what he meant. "Three years ago."

"What happened?"

She had to breathe very deeply before she could whisper out her answer. "A drunk driver," she said flatly. "The baby was killed instantly. Paul lingered a few hours."

"And the driver?"

"He died, too. There wasn't even anybody left to hate."

He didn't say anything else to her; he just ran his fingers gently, idly against her cheek, then over her hair. And he stayed there, beside her, his warmth all around her.

And in time she slept.

She awoke to find his glittering green eyes upon her.

The absolute darkness was gone; hazy light filtered in, like a gray fog. She could see him now, and herself, too well.

In the night she had turned to him. Turned and twisted and left half of her sheet behind. Their legs were completely entangled, her left one beneath his, her right one thrown across his thigh. She'd made a pillow of his arm—which he couldn't possibly move without tearing out a handful of her hair. Thus his patient and amused stare as she opened her eyes wider and wider with the realization of her position.

"Oh! Get off me, you—"

"Hey, you're the one on top of me, Mrs. Blayne."

And of course she was. Clenching her teeth and emitting a soft oath, Mandy moved her legs away from his and wrenched furiously at the sheet. It wouldn't give, not until he laughed and shifted his weight. Groaning, she wrapped it around herself and stared disgustedly at the ceiling, drawing another soft chuckle from him.

"Can't you go somewhere, do something—get out of here? You're never around when I—" She broke off abruptly.

Naturally he pounced on her words, leaning on one elbow to watch her closely. "When you what?"

"I have no idea. I was just talking."

"You were not. You were about to say 'when I need you!'"

"I do not need you." She paused, lowering her lashes. "You're just better than some of the alternatives around here."

"Wow! What an endorsement!"

"Will you please go do whatever it is you do when you're not around?"

"Ah, jealousy becomes you."

Mandy sighed with exaggerated patience. "I'm not jealous." Then she turned suddenly, holding the sheet tightly to her breasts, surprised that it really did seem nice to wake up and find him there, smiling at her— even if she had been definitely disturbed at first.

"I'm curious," she murmured, remembering what she had intended to say. "Here I am, entirely harmless, and they keep me under lock and key. And there you are—at least two hundred pounds of you—and they let you run around. Why?"

"Because I'm madly in love with you. I'm allowed to be here to keep a lid on you. I'm a kindred spirit, a refugee, too, or so they believe. I'm one of them—a gardener—pulled into the bedroom. And you, Mrs. Blayne, are the farthest thing from harmless that I've ever come across.''

"What?"

"You half killed me the other night."

"*I* half killed *you*?"

"Umm. Scratching, flailing, slapping—you're about as harmless as a basketful of vipers.''

"Oh, really? Funny, you don't look much worse for wear!"

"But I am. You might well have cost me months of normal sexual activity."

"What?" she shrieked, astounded at his accusation.

"You must have learned your kicks from Bruce Lee. Honestly, I felt mortally wounded. My mother would never forgive you. She's expecting grandchildren one of these days."

She saw the grin he couldn't keep hidden then. "Oh, will you please get out of here? Go join your fellow refugees!"

The humor instantly fled from his eyes. "A refugee, Mrs. Blayne," he said, "is one who seeks refuge. I was born in Dublin, but both my parents were American citizens. Therefore I never had any need to seek refuge."

He rolled away from her and rose, leaving her feeling a strange remorse; she had been teasing him, and she wasn't sure what she had said to make him draw away from her with such disgust.

His back was to her, his hands on his hips. "It isn't a dirty word, you know," he said.

"What?"

"Refugee, Mrs. Blayne. Little Miss Mayflower Princess. This country was established because people sought a better life. The Irish have come, the English, Italians, Germans and so on forever. That's part of the reason we're so unique, Mrs. Blayne. What do I do out there? I talk with them—in Spanish. I try to watch which way the wind is blowing, I try to read people. For your safety, Mrs. Blayne. If you had bothered to learn some Spanish—"

"Why should I have?" she snapped, simply because she needed some defense; he was definitely attacking. "It's an English-speaking country!"

He swung around then, and to her surprise he was suddenly on his knees on the mattress, green fire in his eyes and radiating enough tension to make her shiver. "Yes, Mrs. Blayne, yes! It's definitely an English-speaking country. And you're right—those who seek its shelter should learn its language! But what kind of an isolationist are you? Nine out of ten Europeans learn at least two languages. They have to. They have to be able to talk to their neighbors. Haven't you ever wanted to learn for the simple joy of learning. Relating? Are you so smug, so satisfied with what you are, that you feel no need to give?"

"What the hell is this?" Mandy retorted. "A soapbox? I took another language, Mr. Ramiro—it just happens to have been German, not Spanish. And I'm not a linguistics whiz. I'm ever so sorry. And if you think that I'm a bigot, I'm sorry about that, too, but it's certainly your prerogative." Mandy was gaining steam as she continued her argument. Gripping the sheet, she rose to her knees to face him, as angry as he was. "You'd better face a few facts, Mr. Ramiro! We had a lot of real criminals dumped on us! As a police officer, you should know that! And I don't care if a murderer is German, French, English, Japanese or all-American mongrel—he shouldn't be walking the streets!"

"So what are you saying? The Cubans are all murderers?"

"I didn't say that and you damn well know it!"

His hands suddenly clamped down on her bare shoulders; she felt their leashed force and the blaze of emotion that seemed to leap from him to her. And then, just when she was certain that he would either shake her or scream at her again or both, he released her with an oath of disgust and scrambled back to his feet.

He strode straight toward the door without a backward look, opened it and slammed it behind himself.

"Oh, you stupid son of a bitch!" Mandy muttered after him. But then she realized that tears were stinging her eyes, and she didn't know why.

She hurried up, stumbling to grasp her clothing, racing for the bathroom. Brackish water, a little yellowed from rusting pipes, spewed from the spigot. She closed her eyes to ignore the color and splashed her face. Why did they keep getting into all this? Why didn't he understand...? And why the hell was she worrying about him when she was still a kidnap victim?

She sighed and realized that she wasn't really frightened. Not anymore. Julio seemed more like a misguided child than a menace. Except that he did know how to use a gun.

But she didn't believe that he would really hurt her. The only person she was afraid of—bone deep!—was Roberto, but she didn't have to worry about Roberto, because Julio seemed determined that no harm would come to her.

"This is insane!" she whispered aloud.

She had faith that this would end, and it was strange what that feeling did for her morale. Strange, but even her arguments with Sean made her feel stronger—impatient, but optimistic.

"Pain in the . . ."

Her cutoffs and top were still damp, but since she had no other choice, she took a brackish and slightly yellow shower, then donned them again. When she had finished, she noticed that a delicious aroma was reaching her from beyond the door of her prison.

Sean had simply walked out. Why shouldn't she do the same?

She stalked over to the door and wrenched at the knob. It didn't give; since Sean had left, someone had come to bolt the door.

"Probably did it himself!" she muttered.

"Hey!" She slammed a fist against the wood. To her surprise, the door opened. Julio was standing there, clean shaven, attractively dressed in a clean cotton shirt and jeans.

He looked just like a nice kid—except that he was still carrying the gun tucked into his boy-next-door blue jeans.

"Good morning, Señora Blayne. We expect to hear something from your husband by tonight."

He smiled at her as if Western Union was simply sending the money to get her out of a rather sorry jam.

"Great," she muttered.

"Coffee?"

"Please," she accepted, with just a trace of irony. He indicated that she should precede him into the kitchen.

His mother was there, smiling at Mandy with her usual sympathetic apology as soon as she saw her. Eggs and bacon were cooking in a skillet, and two kinds of coffee were brewing: the thick sweet Cuban blend and what was—according to the nearby can—Maxwell House.

Julio noticed the direction of her gaze. "Mama brewed it specially just for you."

Marvelous, she thought. Cater to your kidnap victim. Except that that wasn't really true, and she knew it. Señora Garcia was very upset that Mandy had been taken; she had made both kinds of coffee in a sincere effort to do anything in her power for Mandy.

She went up to accept the cup the woman offered her, telling her thank you. Señora Garcia smiled, and Mandy glanced out the kitchen window to the beach beyond.

Maria, Roberto and Sean—Miguel! She had to remember that, no matter how mad she got!—were all sitting around, paper plates discarded, laughing and chatting while they drank coffee.

Maria, it seemed, was growing quite fond of Sean. She kept placing her red polished fingertips on his bare bronzed arms as she spoke to him, her dark eyes beautiful with laughter.

And Sean . . . well, he was laughing back.

Oh, nuts to you! Mandy decided belligerently.

"Señora, por favor . . ."

She turned around. Señora Garcia had pulled out a chair for her at the table, where she had set down a plate filled with bacon and eggs. Mandy thanked her again and sat down.

Julio was sipping his coffee by her side. She picked up her fork because she was hungry, but after a few minutes she turned to her captor and spoke to him. "You know, don't you, that what you're doing is very wrong?"

He gazed at her sharply. Then he lifted his hands and let them fall. "My father is getting old, and he is very ill. Too many years in a dank prison. He will not live long. Using any means that I can manage, I will see to it that he knows freedom before he dies."

"But—"

"Señora Blayne," he interrupted very softly, "I was three years old when Batista was overthrown. He was certainly not a prize, but we went from one dictator to another. In the States the exiles pray for another revolution. In Cuba, those who have not been indoctrinated into the new regime work for the next revolution. When I was a child gunfire raged, people bled, and people died. The needs create the means, don't they? Spying is fine—when it is for your country. A spy must be hanged when he is from the other side. This is life. Violence is an ugly thing, but it can also be a way of life. Secrets, trial and error, violence, abduction. They are all means to an end. I will see my father free. It is that simple."

"Not here it isn't!" Amanda protested, frustrated. "Julio, this is a huge country! Peter Blayne doesn't run it, he just plays his part. The courts can be slow, justice slower, but they're the best shot we've got! Julio..."

"I cannot go back," he said flatly, rising. "If you want some time away from your room, now is it. The day is beautiful, the surf is warm. Come out to the beach."

She rose along with him, ready to take her plate to the counter. Señora Garcia took it from her hands, smiling.

Mandy stepped outside with Julio. The others fell silent as they passed by. Mandy caught Sean's eyes on her, but they were filled with the sun's reflection, and she couldn't read their expression.

She gazed at him just as blandly, then walked on toward the surf with Julio.

"What happens," she asked softly, "if Peter Blayne doesn't respond to you? I'm telling you right now, he doesn't have the power to walk up to a federal penitentiary and demand that your father be released."

Julio stared at her. "He'd best find that power."

"You'd kill me?"

He sat down on the sand, letting the water rush over his bare toes. Mandy did the same. "I would have to send him a piece of you next."

"A...piece of me?"

"A finger, Mrs. Blayne."

She thought that she would keel over into the water. It wouldn't happen; the Coast Guard were on their way. Sean ...

Sean was laughing away with the charmingly voluptuous Maria up at the house.

She lowered her head, thinking that no matter what he thought of her, Sean would never allow her to be...dismembered.

"I would not wish to harm you," Julio added.

"Thanks," Mandy breathed bitterly. She turned around, looking back to the house. Sean, with his guarded gaze, was still watching her.

And so was Roberto, in that fashion that sent horrible chills down her spine. There was something about his grim look that was like a rabid dog's. She felt that she could almost hear his teeth gnashing, as if he would devour her like a shark.

Shivering, she looked back to the water. To the sea. It stretched out endlessly, as if they were alone in the world. With nothing better to do and a yearning to move, Mandy stood and started walking out into the waves.

"Where are you going?" Julio demanded sharply.

She turned and stared back at him, laughing with real humor. "Where could I go, Señor Garcia? I'm going to swim, nothing more. I certainly don't expect to swim back to Miami, if that's what you're afraid of."

He had the grace to laugh sheepishly in return, and Mandy kept walking until the water came to her chest, then she began to swim.

The sharks were still fresh in her mind, so she didn't venture too far, but it felt so good to be moving. She swam against the current; she swam with the current. She floated on her back and felt the sun on her face.

When she got back to the beach, Julio was gone. He was sitting with the others nearer the house. They had switched from coffee to beer to cool them against the heat of the sun.

Mandy lay back in the sand for a while, resting, then headed for the water once again. She knew the physical exertion would help her to sleep, to keep from thinking.

When she came out again, she faltered. The others had gone into the house; only Roberto waited for her.

Roberto, who liked to keep his gun out, smoothing it with his fingers while he stared at her. He stroked that gun like . . . like a man would stroke a woman.

Mandy kept her distance from him, tossing her hair back, squeezing the water from it. She realized from the direction of his eyes that the soaked shirt was tight and see-through against her breasts.

Sucking in her breath, she crossed her arms over her chest and strode past him, heading for the house. He didn't follow her—except with his eyes.

In the house she discovered that Maria was loudly playing a portable radio. The girl was sitting in the parlor, idly dangling one long leg over the arm of the sofa, listening to the music. She looked Mandy up and down and smirked at her. Mandy ignored her, aware that she was damp and that her hair looked like a mop. What did it matter?

In an annoying way, though, something did matter. Mandy was still itching to slap Maria. She didn't like having that scornful laughter directed her way, nor did she like the way the girl watched Sean. Exactly what Maria wanted was written all over her lovely face, expressed soundlessly in her sensual pouting lips.

Poor kid, the teenage years were rough. Poor kid hell!

Mandy returned Maria's stare with a shrug, then looked around the kitchen. Lunch was on the table. Julio and Sean were eating; Maria had apparently already finished.

Señora Garcia laid out a plate for her. It was fish, deliciously spiced. Mandy sat and ate; Sean and Julio both glanced at her, then resumed their conversation.

She grew irritated again that Sean Ramiro—policeman *extraordinaire*—still did nothing. Then she noticed that even while he was eating, Julio carried his gun, one hand in his lap, ready to make a grab for it.

When Julio finished eating he went up to his mother, encircling her waist with his arms to say something. Sean leaned across the table to her. "Want to go back outside?"

She would never understand what possessed her to snap back at him, but she did. "No, thanks. We bigots like to be alone!"

He sat back, lashes shielding his eyes, his mouth tightened in a grim line.

Mandy stood up and waltzed past Maria and her radio, surprised to hear a voice with a beautiful Bahamian accent announce that it was almost four o'clock.

Swimming had done one thing for her; it had caused time to pass. But, like an idiot, she had resigned herself to a locked room when she might have known freedom.

With a sigh she sank down on her mattress, then realized with a bit of a start that there was a kerosene lantern on the floor, and a book of matches.

Sean had kept his word.

With shaking fingers she lit the lantern. It occurred to her that she could probably light a fire and burn down the entire place. It also occurred to her that they might let her burn to death, and she wasn't desperate enough—yet—to risk that.

She frowned suddenly as a little pool of light fell around her. There was a book beside the lantern. She picked it up and read the title; it was on Caribbean fish. It might not be compelling, but it was certainly better than nothing. It had probably been the only thing that Sean could find in the place.

Smiling slightly, she began to leaf through it. Then she began to yawn, and to her amazement she found that she was drifting off. She blew out the lantern and let sleep come.

Later, probably much later, because it had become dark, she awakened with a start. Puzzled, she rose up on her elbows, keenly attuned to the darkness, frightened to the core, but not sure why.

And then she knew. There was no sound, no movement—but she knew. Someone was in the room.

And it wasn't Sean.

Someone was in the room and moving swiftly. She opened her mouth to scream, but a hand came down over it. A heavy sinewy weight fell against her, and she heard a terse whisper in Spanish.

Madness catapulted through her. She couldn't scream, so she tried to bite. She tried to kick and flail and fight, but that wiry arm remained around her, firm and unrelenting.

She could feel his breath. She could see again that image of gnashing teeth, of brutal hunger.

She tried everything, but she couldn't dislodge the hand over her mouth nor the weight bearing down on her.

She heard the sudden tearing of fabric and realized that his free hand was on her halter top. She felt his palm on her flesh, hot, urgent.

That was when she managed to twist her mouth free at last in a spurt of desperate energy. She gasped for breath, then screamed as loud as she could, and long.

His open palm crashed against her cheek, and the world seemed to spin. But it didn't matter, not at all. Because the door had burst open, bringing help.

She needed no light, no sound, no movement. She recognized the presence filling the doorway, filling the room.

Sean.

8

One moment Roberto was above her; the next he was not.

Light streamed surreally into the room from the parlor beyond. Gasping for breath, Mandy clutched the torn halter top to her, scrambling to her feet.

The still ebony night was immediately shattered. She was suddenly surrounded by shadows and shouts, and between those bursts of staccato noise she heard the heavy sounds of fists landing against flesh.

There was a loud crash. Roberto and Sean had gone flying through the doorway together to land on the parlor floor, both grim, both bloodied—both still at it. Shaken, Mandy followed them. Julio was yelling; Maria was screaming; and Señora Garcia was watching the proceedings, white-faced.

Just then a gun went off. Mandy screamed again, but no one heard her that time. Sean and Roberto had both ceased fighting at that shot, twisting to stare at Julio.

Mandy didn't understand what followed. Everyone was speaking in Spanish. Roberto was obviously swearing vehemently and trying to make some point. Every bit as vehemently, Sean was arguing his side. Señora Garcia tried to say something, and Maria started up again, staring at Mandy, then spitting in her direction.

Julio shouted out a command, which everyone ignored, so he shot another bullet into the ceiling—which finally brought the silence he desired.

With everyone quiet once again he started to talk to Roberto, and then to Sean. Finally he paused to stare at Mandy who was standing, wide-eyed and ashen, in the doorway. He cocked his head with interest, then shrugged and spoke to the two men again. Roberto protested; Julio swore.

And then, whatever the argument had been, it was decided. Sean and Roberto both stood and walked grimly out the front door. Señora Garcia crossed herself and stepped into the second bedroom, slamming the door. Julio followed the two men outside.

"What is going on!" Mandy finally screamed, clenching her fists at her side.

Maria, elegantly decked out in a long gauzy nightgown that nicely displayed her attributes, gave Mandy another of her scornful looks and spoke disdainfully. "You—you are the problem! You will get him killed!"

"What?" Mandy demanded, startled and alarmed.

"It is all your fault."

She'd had it with Maria, and no one else was around. Mandy strode to her in a sudden fury and grabbed a handful of dark glistening hair. "You tell me this instant what is going on!"

"Oww! Let go!" Maria screeched, trying to free her hair. "Julio says they are welcome to fight it out over you! And Roberto is a killer, you stupid *puta*! You will get Miguel killed!"

"Julio is not going to let them kill one another!" Mandy snapped.

"Roberto will break Miguel's neck! And all because of you!"

"He tried to rape me, you stupid little witch!"

"You should have enjoyed him—"

"Enjoyed? Rape? If you like him so much, sweetie, you're welcome to him! Now get out of my way!"

Mandy shoved Maria aside, wondering just how much of a killer Roberto was. Any man could look tough with a gun, and that seemed to be the source of Roberto's strength. She tried to assure herself that he was nothing but hot air, and that Sean could take care of himself.

But she was frightened. Very frightened. If something did happen to him, she wouldn't be able to live with herself.

If she lived at all, she thought grimly, because she would fight Roberto herself until she had no breath left in her body.

Mandy swung open the front door. The natural coolness of the ocean breeze touched her cheeks soothingly, but she felt no ease as she paused and stared into the star-studded night. She could see the three of them down near the surf.

Julio's gun was in his hand; Sean and Roberto were wrestling on the sand, coming together, drawing apart, falling to roll on the beach together.

Mandy ran down to where Julio stood. He was watching the action with no apparent emotion.

"Why are you letting them do this!" she screamed at him. "You can make them stop."

"I cannot. No one can."

"You've got the gun—"

"Miguel says that you are his, only his. Robert says that you are no virgin to be returned untouched. If you've had one lover, he should have rights, too."

"You didn't kidnap me for that vulture's amusement, Julio! Come on, think! You're in charge of this thing, aren't you? Julio, you're wrong in what you're doing, but you're a man with morals and ideals. You—"

"I am not in this alone now! If Roberto loses, he loses!"

"And if he doesn't? Julio! I can't believe this of you!" She paused, swallowing, because there was a set expression on his handsome face. "Julio! I am a person, not the spoils of war! And you know that!"

"Roberto cannot shoot Miguel. They are evenly matched, no weapons. That is fair—and it's all that I can do."

"Fair..." Mandy paused in horror, because beyond Julio, the two men were on their feet once again, carefully circling each other.

Mandy caught her breath. There was a scratch on Sean's shoulder, and a smear of blood at the right corner of his mouth, but he looked all right otherwise. The shimmering fury of the fight was in his narrowed eyes; he appeared more than ready to keep up the battle.

Roberto was the one looking the worse for wear. He was wiry and strong, but he simply didn't have Sean's powerful shoulders or arms. Roberto had already accrued one black eye—which was puffing and turning an ugly green color right now—and his jaw was swollen, too. But he still had a look of blood lust about him, as if he was playing right now. As if he would win when he was ready.

Sean suddenly ducked his head and made a lunge for Roberto, throwing him to the ground. They rolled together, then split apart. Roberto didn't look so self-assured this time, but he smiled slowly at his opponent and reached into his pocket, drawing out a switch-blade.

"Look out!" Mandy screamed.

Sean saw the blade. It made a rushing sound as Roberto brought it slicing through the night, and Sean ducked. Roberto struck nothing but air. The pattern was repeated. Sean was a second ahead of it every time.

Mandy spun on Julio. "You told me he had no weapons! You said that it would be fair. You said—"

"I cannot intercede! Don't you understand? He must beat Roberto, or Roberto will not respect him."

Mandy didn't think that Roberto would ever respect anyone. No matter how this ended, he would try to stab Sean—or anyone—in the back whenever it suited his purpose.

She started walking across the sand, but Julio caught her shoulders. "What are you doing?"

"Roberto has a knife. Miguel will have me!"

"Get back here! Do you want to wind up cut?"

"I'd rather be cut," Mandy retorted vehemently, "than handed over like a trophy!"

"No!" Julio said, but she wrenched herself away from him, ignoring his gun as if it didn't exist. She didn't believe that he would shoot her.

Sean saw her coming. "Get out of here, Mandy!"

Roberto laughed, thinking to take advantage of the distraction. He lunged; Sean escaped in the nick of time. Mandy instinctively reached down for a handful of sand to throw in Roberto's eyes.

She did throw the sand, but it didn't matter. In that split second Sean had kicked Roberto's wrist, sending the switchblade flying out into the night.

Then Sean was flying, too. He threw himself against Roberto, sending the man down on his back, with Sean on top of him. He rolled Roberto over, wrenched the man's arm behind his back, then straddled him.

Mandy gasped with relief and sank onto the sand herself. She watched as Julio walked over to the two men and spoke to them, clipping out orders in a soft but furious rush of Spanish.

Mandy's fingers dug into the sand. She realized suddenly that she was touching something metallic. Her eyes fell to her fingers, and she saw that she had the knife. Her fingers curled completely around it. While the men were occupied with one another she slipped it into the pocket of her cutoffs.

Sean got back to his feet then; Julio was still talking to Roberto in scathing tones as Sean walked over to Mandy. He threaded his fingers through his hair, grinning at her, and reached down to help her to her feet.

She accepted his assistance, staring at him. "Are you—are you okay?"

His grin deepened and he shrugged. "Yeah, Ma, you should see the other guy."

She lowered her head, smiling, then allowed him to pull her to her feet. He slipped an arm around her, and they returned to the house together.

Maria was waiting in the kitchen. When she saw Sean, she gave a little cry of ecstasy and raced toward him, ignoring Mandy. Maria leaned on his free shoulder, kissing the cut there between bursts of excited concern.

Amanda eyed her with tolerant patience, raising a brow to Sean and moving away.

He set Maria away from him, speaking softly but firmly. She touched his shoulder again. "I will take care of it—"

"There is no need, Maria. It is nothing. I..." He paused, pulling Mandy back to his side. "We are going to bed."

He started walking, leading Mandy with him. She glanced back to see Maria standing there, and despite everything she felt sorry for the girl.

She and Sean seemed to share an opinion of Maria: that she was still a child, a child trying to play in a grown-up's world, no matter how lovely her face or figure.

I could be jealous, Mandy thought, and it was a disturbing idea. It was...the circumstances, she told herself. But it was more, and she knew it. Their time together had been limited, but it had also been very intense. She felt that she knew him better than people she had known for years and years. He angered her; he intrigued her. He absolutely fascinated her.

The other bedroom door opened before they reached their own. Señora Garcia, still ashen, came out. She spoke softly to Sean, and he replied in kind. She smiled at last, nodded, then returned to the bedroom she apparently shared with Maria.

Mandy glanced back once again. Julio and Roberto still had not come in. Maria remained where she had been, though, watching them. Watching them just as tragically as Scarlett O'Hara had watched Ashley Wilkes walk into a bedroom with his Melanie.

Then she couldn't see Maria, because Sean prodded her into the bedroom. He lit the lantern before shutting the door.

Mandy stood still, feeling a little rueful, a little shy— and more than a little confused.

Sean placed the lantern by the bed, then noticed her standing there. He frowned curiously. "What's with you?"

"Thank you."

"For what?"

"You saved my life."

He shrugged, casting himself back on the mattress, locking his fingers behind his head, then gazing at her with an amused grin. "I didn't save your life. He had no intention of killing you."

"But I'd have rather died," she said softly. "And— and he might have killed you."

"I should hope not!" Sean snorted.

She walked over to the mattress and sank down beside him on her knees, then lightly ran a finger over the red scratch on his shoulder. "Shouldn't you clean it?"

He gritted his teeth and caught her hand. "It's no big deal. Just leave it alone."

She snatched her hand away, reddening. But he didn't notice; he was suddenly sitting up, playing with her torn shirt, trying to find a way to make it stay completely where it belonged.

"It's all right. Just leave it!" she snapped.

He drew his hand away, scowling. "If you walk around like that tomorrow we'll be in trouble all over again. In fact, if you hadn't flounced around today, all this might not have happened!"

"What are you talking about?" Mandy demanded furiously.

"You—in the water! Making that stupid outfit look like something from a centerfold."

"It's not *my* stupid outfit! Nobody warned me to dress for a kidnapping. And Maria didn't exactly give me the best stuff she had!"

"You could have stayed out of the water!"

"Oh, yeah? I'd like to see you locked up for hours and hours on end without going completely mad!"

He didn't have a ready answer for that one. He closed his eyes and lay back down, sighing. "I am going mad, I think," he mumbled. He kept talking in a flat monotone. "If I'd stayed locked up with you, I would be mad. And I wouldn't know anything."

Mandy hesitated a second. "What do you know?"

"Not too much," he admitted. "Juan was supposed to be back by now, but he isn't."

"Is Julio worried?"

"Not yet. He will be by tomorrow night, though. But if we're lucky, by tomorrow night we may be able to spot the Coast Guard."

Mandy moistened her lips. "What happens if Juan never makes it back? What will Julio do then?"

"Nothing," he told her.

"Nothing?"

"Stop worrying, will you? Things will break soon."

She didn't answer.

"For God's sake, lie down, will you please? Get some rest. If things do move, you'll want to be alert."

She lay down beside him, not touching him, but all too aware that he was there. He didn't speak.

"He threatened to chop off one of my fingers," Mandy murmured at last. "Julio did. To send to Peter."

There was a soft sigh from beside her. "That was a threat, nothing more."

"It sounded real."

"What good is a threat if it doesn't sound real?" He sat up, leaning over to blow out the lantern.

"But—"

"Mandy, quit it! Trust me. Everything is going to work out all right. Please, go to sleep."

He flopped back down on the mattress, and the ebony darkness surrounded them once again.

There had been exasperation in his voice, and the harsh sound of his temper rising. Cast once again into a vortex of confusion, Mandy lay still and concentrated on each breath she took.

It wasn't fair; he was blaming her for things that were beyond her control. She'd tried to thank him for risking his life, but even that had annoyed him.

"I didn't ask to be here!" she snapped suddenly, whirling to face him, though she couldn't see him at all.

"I didn't say you did."

"You have an attitude about this whole thing! In fact, you're one great mass of attitudes! I have to thank you, because I couldn't have dealt with that weasel myself. But it's not my fault he's such scum, and it's not my fault I've been given such ridiculous clothes to wear."

"I—"

"You just shut up for a minute! Don't you dare blame me for anything! I didn't make you come along—that was your choice."

Silence followed her last emphatic words. He didn't move, and she wondered what his reaction would be to her sudden show of temper.

"Sean?"

He chuckled softly, and the sound touched her like a caress in the night. "Are you quite through?" he asked.

"Quite!"

"Good. I'm not blaming you for anything—except for the sleep I'm missing right now."

"Sorry," she said stiffly.

"Lie down."

"You're at it again."

"I'm not." She couldn't see his grin, but she could feel it. "I didn't tell you to take your clothes off, I just said to lie down."

"You—"

"You—" His movement was swift, startling, as he gently shushed her with a hand over her mouth. "*Querida*, go to sleep!"

Meekly she sank back onto the mattress, his touch, his voice, reducing her to quivers.

Querida . . .

He'd said it so softly. *Querida* . . . darling, loved one . . . sweetheart. It wasn't just the word; it was the way he had said it, in Spanish, as if there wasn't an English word that would do justice to his meaning.

He curled up beside her, his back to her. She tried breathing again, deeply, counting each breath. She was no longer irritated, or even hurt, but she was still confused, both by him and by her own feelings. And also by the yearnings she felt in the darkness.

She tried to sleep, but she felt as if she was in the center of a maelstrom. It was of her own making, but it was there nevertheless. She heard the beat of her heart, each breath she took. And each breath that he took. She imagined that despite the space he had left between them she could hear the beat of his heart.

She couldn't sleep; she couldn't even keep her eyes closed. She felt a restless energy that defied the night, and if she closed her eyes too long, she thought of Roberto. She remembered waking up, not being able to see, yet knowing he was the one above her. She remembered feeling his hands, knew again the horror of failing in her fight against him....

She took a deep breath, then exhaled. Sean wanted to sleep, but maybe she could sit with the lantern on the other side of the room. Maybe he wouldn't mind.

Sean. She felt awareness ripple through her again, and she couldn't begin to understand herself. She should have been thinking of the million reasons why she didn't want anything to do with him. She should have been burying herself in guilt—even in pain. But none of that mattered, not tonight.

She didn't even really want the light; she wanted *him*, awake. Whispering to her, talking to her, reassuring her. She wanted to run her fingers over the sun-browned sleekness of his chest, press soft kisses against his skin, taste the salt of the sea on his flesh....

It was dark, but she knew that she burned crimson. How could she be thinking this way? Feeling this way?

She sat up abruptly, determined to reach carefully across him for the lantern and matches. She would take the light to a corner of the room and read her book. That might distract her from the thoughts that were playing such havoc with her mind.

But when she groped her way over him the rounded curve of her breast fell against his arm, and her bare midriff collided with his naked chest. The short crisp hairs there seemed to tease her mercilessly, just as the contact of their bodies, hot despite the coolness of the night, seemed to create a kinetic energy so startling that she drew in her breath.

He caught her arm, holding her where she lay. "Mrs. Blayne, just what are you doing?"

"I was ... just ... I was—"

"Mrs. Blayne, please don't touch me unless you mean it."

He said it jokingly, lightly, but she knew that he wasn't teasing.

"I won't . . ." she began, but the words froze on her lips. "Don't touch me unless you mean it," he had said. And she had meant it with all her heart and soul and being . . . this night.

The midnight blackness left no room for reason or thought, for a past or for a future. All she knew was that she wanted him. Wanted to touch him. To be touched. To go wherever touching might lead them.

She leaned over him, pressing her lips against the hollow of his shoulder, holding them there for a fervent moment, then pushing the tip of her tongue between them, tasting his flesh, closing her eyes at the sleek salt sensation, savoring the elusive liquid quivering that burst and streaked through her like dancing stars. Savoring his gasp, the catch of his breath, the shudder that racked him.

"Hey!" He clutched her shoulders harshly, wrenching her high above him. Even in the night she could see the glitter of his eyes. His muscles were taut, his whisper harsh.

"I said—" he swallowed sharply and continued through clenched teeth "—not to touch me unless—"

"I mean it," she interrupted him abruptly, her voice as harsh as his. She didn't want to talk about it; she didn't want to be warned. She wanted to be held. She wanted to make love. To feel the world spiraling around her, to arch and writhe and roll in sensual splendor and temptation.

Still he only held her.

She tried to whisper to him, but sound eluded her.

And then it didn't really matter, because he lowered her against him, slowly, until their bodies touched completely, her length on his, legs tangling, her breasts hard against his chest, their mouths not an inch apart.

Then touching.

Perhaps he was still distrustful; perhaps he had a reason to be so. He held her shoulders when he first kissed her, just touching her lips, then pulling away. Then he touched them once again, curiously, questingly. He tasted them next, his tongue an exotic paintbrush that swirled across them like sable. He traced the shape of her mouth, then pressed his lips against her shoulder.

And then it was as if he gave up all thought of reason. Of sanity. Of the past. Of the future.

His arms wrapped strongly around her; his lips were hard against hers, almost bruising in their sudden passion. His tongue made an intimate invasion, demanding total entrance, total surrender, bending the night magic of her body solely to his will, throwing her heart to the four winds of chance.

He held her in his arms and rolled with her, sweeping her beneath him, and the magic continued. His body against hers felt incredibly good, right, as if they had been made not just as man and woman, but as this man meant specifically for this woman, this woman meant just for this man. His body seemed to meld to hers, a fusion of heat, of fire. Like flint to stone they sparked, drew away, then sparked again...and ignited. It was a blaze she never wanted to put out....

He drove his fingers through her hair, holding her still to meet his kiss. He cupped and massaged her skull, cherished the richness of her hair. She stroked his nape and then his back, skimming lightly over his spine with her nails. And she thrilled to the pressure of his hips against hers, his desire evident.

He broke the kiss, easing away from her, longing with all his heart to see her. To see the color of her hair. To watch her as he touched her, stripped her...slowly, relishing each new bit of golden flesh revealed to his gaze.

Rolling closer to her, he ran his fingers over her cheek, then kissed her again with slow fascination and let his hands roam, exploring the roundness of her breast, soft and yet firm, the nipples taut beneath the thin cotton material. Just thinking of them, he felt an inner combustion. Now. He had to have her now....

But he forced himself to stay under control. He stroked her naked ribs before seeking out the tie of the halter top, gently undoing it, letting the material fall aside. Urgency claimed him again, hot and strident, as her naked breasts fell freely into his hands, taunted his palms. He lowered his head to her, drawing a pattern with his tongue in the deep valley between her breasts, then feeling the splendor of imagination obliterated in the magic of truth as he savored her with his lips, the gentle tender grazing of his teeth.

He felt dizzy with desire. He moved his hands against her, fingers slipping beneath the waistband of her cutoffs, dipping low upon her abdomen, then nearly yanking at the snap and zipper. She issued a soft little cry, and he kissed her to silence her, the motion of his hands edging the cutoffs lower and lower.

And then it was he who cried out, an oath of impatience, and he moved away from her, grasping the tattered hems of the cutoffs, easing them down the wickedly lovely length of her legs.

He wanted the light. He wanted to see her: the glorious fan of sunlight and wheaten hair; the shimmering desire in her eyes; her features taut with passion. The rise of her breasts; the dip of her belly. Her back; the curves of her buttocks. He wanted to see all of her.

He started to move off the mattress, and she realized his intent. Crying out softly, she rose to meet him, grasping his shoulders, burying her head against his neck and seductively pressing her breasts against him.

"No! Please."

"I was just going to light the lamp."

"No. No light. Let it be darkness. Let it be magic."

He should refuse. He should tell her that there could be magic in the light. He should not allow her to make love in the darkness.

Done in the darkness, in the ebony night, it would not be real. It would not exist in the morning's light.

"Please, Sean. Please."

Her whisper, her breath against his flesh, stirred the blaze of his near-desperate passion once again. He couldn't refuse her anything.

Kneeling, they moved together. Kneeling, he felt the exquisite femininity of her body, touched so thoroughly by his own. He kissed her, explored her and forced her back at last, pressing her down upon her stomach.

He couldn't see her; he had to know her. He pressed his mouth against the small of her back, against her spine. Lust burned raw inside of him. It was torture; it was delicious.

All along her spine he kissed her, moving his hands down over her buttocks, down her legs, knowing their shape. Down to her feet, and even there he played, kissing her toes, stroking the soles of her feet, massaging them. She arched; she moaned softly; she made little inarticulate sounds. Dear God, he wanted to see her! He smiled a little grimly, even a little maliciously, for the movements of her body cried to his, though she choked back her cries of arousal, of readiness.

He had no intention of being had so easily.

When his fingers left her feet they stroked, slowly, excruciatingly slowly, to her inner thighs, urging them apart, finding she had no strength for denial.

He rolled her over. She was as pliable as a kitten, as passionate as a tigress as she reached for him, whispering incoherently for him to stop, to come to her.

"Not yet," he whispered against her lips. He waited there, above her, as his fingers played between her legs, as she gasped and arched against him, holding him, pushing him away, trying to touch him in turn.

Her nails scratched lightly over his chest, explored his back, tried to dip beneath the waistband of his cutoffs and met with frustration. She tugged at the button and the zipper with trembling fingers and found frustration again. They would not give for her. And again for him it was agony... and it was ecstasy.

He kissed her, his tongue delving deeply into her mouth. And then he whispered of the wonder of her body, and what it was doing, whispered with his lips just half an inch from her mouth until she thought she would go mad.

"Sean!"

"What?"

"Take—take your clothes off."

"Aha! I told you that you would get to it eventually. All women are alike!"

"Sean..."

"Mandy, I'd strip for you anytime. In private, of course."

She half giggled, half sobbed.

And he thought that if he waited any longer he would explode, and they would have to pick up the pieces of what had once been a man. In seconds he had obliged her, tossing his cutoffs somewhere into the magical black arena surrounding them, returning to her with the full strength of his desire evident.

She touched him, and his impatience soared. He held her face with his hands, spread her thighs with his knees, kissed her deeply and entered her deeply.

The black magic of the night swirled around them. At first the tempo of their loving was slow, then frenetic. Kisses, caresses and the spiraling maelstrom of desire set them apart from the world. This was passion, born in the darkness, bred by fear and sensation, gratitude and natural hunger. And something more....

He had to be mad. He was lost within her. Lost in the welcoming embrace of her body, shuddering with sensation, volatile, ecstatic, as he had never been before. Touching her inside and out, knowing her, caressing her, reaching the pinnacle together, holding each other, drifting.

It was passion only, he told himself.

Strange. When he touched her damp brow, when she curled against him, when the curve of her breast so comfortably touched his chest and her slender leg was cast so trustingly over his...

It was passion.

Yet it felt ridiculously as if he were falling in love.

9

When Sean awoke, it was barely dawn with just the palest filtering of pink light entering the room. He could make out Mandy's huddled form, curled so trustingly against him, lips slightly parted as she breathed, her lashes falling against her cheeks, her hair falling over her shoulders—and his own.

He eased away from her and carefully pulled the covers to her shoulders. He wanted to hold her, to glory in her all over again, but the shield of darkness was gone, and he knew innately that she had been his only because of that darkness.

Sean rose silently and donned his cutoffs. He needed to be alone. He crept quietly from the room, closing the door tightly behind him.

Julio, on a mat outside the door, was awake, watching him, the ever-present Magnum at his side.

"I'm just going down to the beach," Sean said.

Julio nodded and lay back down on the mat. Sean continued on out the kitchen door. No one was really awake yet. No one but him.

He was glad. There was no time here like the breaking of the dawn. No time when the heavens appeared more magenta, no time when the coming sun kissed the sand more gently. A breeze stirred the trees and the rippling water.

He walked over the soft dunes and neared the water, listening to the soft rush of the tide, gazing at the glittering droplets caught and dazzled by the coming sun. Again the irony of it all struck him. Here, in this incredible Eden, they were prisoners. It should have been a place of freedom. No crime should touch this shore, only laughter and tenderness and . . . passion.

They should have made love beneath the stars, not on a shabby mattress inside a primitive cabin in the dark. This was a place of exquisite loveliness; it should have remained unsoiled.

Sean sat down and wrapped his arms around his knees.

So many things in his life had been beautiful, he thought.

Havana had been beautiful. Once upon a time it had been a fantastic city, a playground for the rich and famous. There had been dancing and music, beautiful women, poets and musicians, artisans and scholars. The warm Caribbean breezes had touched the patios of homes and nightclubs; the palms had swayed; the air had been touched by perfume.

Once upon a time . . .

He had been only six the last time he had seen Havana, but as long as he lived he would never forget that night.

Revolution had been brewing for a long time. The old men at the cafés had talked about it; the young men had shouted about it. Batista had been a dictator, and it was very true that the poor had suffered beneath him. Yes, revolution had been brewing. His father simply had not seen it clearly enough.

As a six-year-old Sean had adored both his parents. They'd met in New York City, where his mother had been a model and his father had been selling superior Havana cigars. They had fiery tempers, but totally different cultural backgrounds. Love had always been the tie that bound the two of them. It had been imperative that they learn about each other's cultures to appreciate and understand each other. Consequently, Sean had been born in Dublin, beneath the benign eyes of his maternal grandparents.

And consequently they had been in Havana on the night the gunfire began.

He could remember it all so clearly. December, but a hot night. His father had been downstairs on the patio, talking with a few cronies. His mother had been in the kitchen, humming, fixing rum punches for their company. Sean had been sitting at the kitchen table, laboriously practicing his handwriting.

And then it had started, a rat-tat-tatting somewhere down the street, so soft that they had ignored it at first. But then there had been screams, and his father, such a handsome man with his flashing dark eyes and lean whipcord physique, had come dashing up the stairs.

He'd shouted that they must go, that they must get to the airport. Sean could remember his mother bursting into tears when it became clear that his father was not going to join them.

"You're an American, too! You're an American citizen! This is not your—"

"I am an American, but I am also Cuban. Siobhan, go, now, for my son's sake! I will meet you in the States. I will meet you!"

And so they ran. His father's friend, Xavier, got them through the streets. Streets littered here and there with bodies. With soldiers, with revolutionaries. With the injured, with the dying. Streets that seemed alive with screaming.

At one point, they'd been stopped—by a looter, of all things on such a night. His mother had been held while he, a child, had struggled ineffectually. That had been when he decided he would never be helpless again.

With the pure fury of a child he had escaped the man holding him and bitten the man attacking his mother, giving Xavier the chance to wrest the gun from the man. Xavier had killed him, and their mad dash for freedom had continued.

They'd reached the embassy—and they'd gotten out.

But he'd never seen his father again, nor Xavier. They'd settled in Miami, where his mother had spent the next ten years of her life waiting for news of his father. When it came, it was bad. He had been shot that night. He had died with the revolution.

Adjusting to life in Miami had been hard. Sean spoke Spanish fluently, but his English had an Irish accent, and all the kids had made fun of him. Nobody had cared much what you sounded like in New York, because New York had been full of all kinds of people. But not Miami—not then.

Cubans began entering the city in droves, escaping to freedom. The federal government helped them, which led to resentment. Sean's life became ever harder. No one could understand a Cuban boy named Sean who had an Irish mother.

Somewhere along the line—the third grade?—he'd created a new world for himself. He started telling his schoolmates that Ramiro was Castilian, that his mother had married his father in Madrid.

Then his mother found out about the story. She'd gone as white as paste and started to cry in a way that tore his insides all to pieces. "Sean! How could you? How could you deny your father?"

That had been the last time he had ever done so. He had gone to his mother, and they had cried together. When he went to bed that night all he could think about was his father, his laughter, his temper, his total devotion to his wife—and to his son. His love for the world at large and for his own heritage.

From that moment on he was proud of what he was. Irish, Cuban—and American. American all the way.

And naturally, as time passed, things evened out. In high school half his classmates were various forms of Anglo, half were various forms of Latino. He played football with a natural ability, and by his junior year that made him incredibly popular.

He went to college in Nebraska on a football scholarship. He liked Nebraska, but not as much as home. And though he earned a law degree, he didn't want to practice. He wanted to be a cop. He'd wanted to be one ever since that night in Havana, when he had learned that law and order were precious commodities.

Then, when he'd first come home, he'd fallen in love. Her name was Sandra Johnson, and she had been beautiful. Blond and blue-eyed and blue-blooded all the way. They'd met at a nightclub and fallen in love to a John Denver tune, slow dancing beneath the colored lights. All he'd really known about her was that she worked in her family's business as a receptionist. That seemed to be all he needed to know at the time. They met every night. They made love on what seemed like every beach in the state.

She was passionate, lovely, and everything he had ever desired.

But on a cool September night, when he was twenty-four and thought that he owned the world, he had received a blow that nearly destroyed him.

She met him that night, tremendously nervous, teary-eyed, anxious and excited. She blurted out instantly that she was pregnant, then awaited his reaction.

He was thrilled. A home and a family. He was ready for them both. A child, his father's grandchild, to hold and love and nurture—and to whom to give the world, just as his parents had given it to him. America, with all its merging fascinating cultures.

He'd held her tenderly, and they'd planned their life. They would look into the nice new town houses on Miller Road, and they would be married in St. Theresa's. His pay wasn't great, but it was sufficient.

Sandra had been starry-eyed then, as happy as a lark. They had to meet each other's parents, of course. Sean knew that his mother would love Sandra. And by this time in his life he could see no reason why the Johnsons wouldn't like him.

He arrived at their house neatly suited. He was somewhat stunned by the mansion on the water, but he hadn't come from poverty. His mother had done well modeling, and his father's investments had all been in the U.S. His mom had a wonderful old home in Miami Shores. And if anyone was "class," it was Siobhan Ramiro.

But not to the Johnsons.

When the maid led him into the elegant receiving room Sandra was nowhere in sight. Only her mother and father were there, greeting him politely but informing him that Sandra was gone.

Where? he had demanded, confused.

And then it had all come out. They were terribly sorry, but didn't he understand that they were "the" Lockwood Johnsons; they couldn't possibly allow their daughter to marry a—a refugee.

Lockwood Johnson went on to say coolly that the baby had already been aborted.

Well, he—a cop—had gotten arrested that night. His temper—Irish, Cuban or all-American—had soared to a point where he had seen nothing but red, and he'd charged Lockwood Johnson with all the fury he had learned on the football field.

Johnson had probably expected something along those lines. He'd whistled, and four bodyguards had come rushing in. Even then, it had taken them fifteen minutes to wrestle him down.

He could still remember Mrs. Johnson murmuring something about the behavior of "riffraff," but all he really knew was that he had woken up in a jail cell.

All he could think at the time was that the Johnsons were the ones who deserved to be in jail. They'd murdered his child; they'd taken a piece of his heart.

Logically, he had known that they represented an extreme. His friends, his best friends, his co-workers, all came in mixed nationalities. Half the Cuban girls he knew had married Anglo men, and vice versa. Of course there were still cultural differences. Some people resented those who spoke Spanish; some thought it was good to know two languages. Things didn't change that quickly. But people were people, and friendships formed where they would, as did love—when it was allowed.

He had decided then that he wouldn't fall in love again. Especially not with a blonde.

So what the hell was he doing now? It was ridiculous; it was impossible. He should be staying as far away as he could from Mrs. Amanda—Anglo—Blayne.

He closed his eyes tightly then opened them to the lightening sky. He realized that he was clenching his fists so tightly that his nails were cutting into his palms.

He wasn't in love, he told himself dully. This whole thing was nothing more than circumstance. He had known her only a few days, and she'd turned to him only because she was frightened and lonely. She'd turned to him in the dark, hiding.

He straightened his shoulders. God! If they could just get off of this damned island!

He tried to bring himself under control, but anger filled him. He reminded himself that under no circumstances could he risk her life, yet he was ready to run headfirst into Roberto, just to end it all. Last night had been ecstasy; this morning was hell.

"Sean?"

He turned around and saw her standing there. All blonde and all beautiful. Thin and lithe and curved, and yet suddenly so Anglo that he wanted to scream. Her face was so perfect: tawny eyes alive above the high Anglo cheekbones. He couldn't read her expression; she seemed a little pale beneath her tan. She carried two cups of coffee and pressed one toward him.

He accepted, and found himself staring at her legs. Long legs, slimly muscled. He thought about the way they had wrapped around him, and he felt dizzy once again.

Good God, he wanted her. With all the heat and tempest and passion inside him, he wanted her. Right here, on the beach. He wanted Julio and Roberto and even Mama Garcia and Maria to drop dead, to fall into a hole. He wanted her naked beneath him on the white sand, far away from society. Far from a nightmare that he had forgotten, far from a place where an unborn child could be killed because of his heritage.

She laughed softly, just a little bit nervously. "Aren't you going to ask me to sit down?"

"No. Thanks for the coffee. Go away. What are you doing out here, anyway?" He scowled, staring back toward the water. He felt her stiffen and knew it was for the best. He didn't have any difficulty being friends with beautiful Anglos, or with dating them, or with going to bed with them, for that matter.

Just falling in love with them.

"I just walked out with the coffee. No one stopped me."

"Well, walk somewhere else."

She told him exactly what he should do with himself and turned on her heel.

Where the hell was the damned FBI? he wondered. One lousy little kidnapping and they hadn't appeared yet! They had a lot of nerve calling the cops yokels!

She walked away, not back to the house, but down the beach. He felt as if part of him had frozen over.

He turned slightly. Roberto was outside now, sitting near the door, training his damn Magnum on Amanda.

Sean looked back in her direction. She had finished her coffee and thrown herself into the surf.

For a long while he just sat there, watching her swim. Then she stood, wringing her hair out. Her ribs were bare, gleaming with water. The torn halter she had somehow mended was clinging to her breasts like a second skin. The cutoffs were doing little better at her hips.

Sean twisted slightly to see Roberto watching her, leering. Sean stood and marched down the beach. With no thought whatsoever, his temper soaring toward red again, he strode through the shallows to reach her, then grasped her shoulders, shaking her.

"Let me go, you animal!" she snapped. Her beautiful tawny eyes were red-rimmed. From the salt water? Or had she been crying?

He started to soften.

"I mean it! Get your filthy hands off me!"

He released her. Just like that.

"You liked my filthy hands well enough last night," he sneered.

"That was last night," she said coolly.

"Good. Because if you keep on the way you're going, it's not going to be my filthy hands on you—it will be Roberto's. And if you think I'll battle it out for you again, lady, you'd better think again."

He turned around and walked away from her.

By the time he reached the house Señora Garcia and Maria were outside. Maria had on a cute-little-nothing bikini. Accomplice to a kidnapping or not, Maria knew how to dress. She headed down to the water.

And at that moment Sean felt like speaking Spanish. He noticed that Amanda had stretched out facedown on the sand, a good distance away from them all. He strode back into the surf. Maria was just a kid, but right now he felt like nothing so much as playing kids' games in the water with her.

It was the longest day Mandy had ever experienced in her life.

When she awoke she was glad of the solitude he had given her. Though she was bundled in the covers, she felt her nudity acutely. Her nudity, and her body. Muscles that had been unused for a long time were delightfully sore. She felt guilt and she felt shame, yet she felt like a cat at the same time, wonderfully stroked and petted and loved.

Tears came to her eyes because it had been so good. Because he had been so tender and gentle and so wonderfully savage at just the right moment. Because she couldn't remember lovemaking being such a vivid experience, and because that made her feel guilty all over again, because she had loved her husband so much.

Yet even then, amid the guilt and shame, she had been all too aware of the forbidden knowledge that he had the power to ease the past, if not erase it. He was so powerful and fascinating that she savored the thought of him, just as her body savored the memory of his. His scent was still with her, as were the memories of his arms, of the way he felt inside her.

They were captives on an island, forced together, she reminded herself. It was a nightmare, and please God, it would end, and they would go their separate ways, back to the lives they had led before this one. And yet...

She had to see him. To talk to him. To admit that she was afraid of the light, but that she wasn't denying anything. She needed to touch him again, to know that his arms were still there—for now, at least. She needed to tell him how much she cared about him, how much she appreciated him, how much... she was fascinated by him.

It was almost like falling in love.

And so she had dressed, only to find her halter still ripped. She had stepped out of the room holding the shirt in place. Señora Garcia had clucked disapprovingly, then given her a needle and thread, and she had mended the halter. Then Señora Garcia had given her coffee, and she had hurried out to the beach, anxious to see Sean again.

She had received only the most horrible slap in the face, and it had hurt so badly that she had found herself awash with pain and confusion. The only way to rid herself of them had been to dive into the water.

Then he had touched her again, and she had felt such waves of shimmering heat, of anger, wash over her that she had been stunned all over again.

What had she done but make love with him?

She spent the morning lying in the sun; he spent it playing with Maria. Damn him. Cradle robber. What the hell did she care? She had been an idiot, and that was that.

So why in God's name was it tearing her to pieces? She should be worrying about her physical well-being. Juan wasn't back yet. When was Julio going to start snipping off her fingers?

A feminine voice started to chide her in Spanish. Mandy rolled over to find Señora Garcia standing beside her with a plate of food. She shook her head; she wasn't hungry.

Señora Garcia sighed, unhappily plumped her full figure down on the sand and pressed the plate into Mandy's hands.

Mandy ate resignedly. Lunch was a thin steak with rice and black beans, deliciously cooked. She ate everything on the plate, while Señora Garcia smiled at her.

At one point the older woman disappeared, then returned with a Coca-Cola. Mandy thanked her again and enjoyed the soda. The next time Señora Garcia left her, she didn't return.

Bored, and increasingly anxious and upset despite her determination not to be, Mandy took off for the water again. She swam and swam—and suddenly bumped into another body. Hands righted her, and she found herself staring into Roberto's dark eyes.

He laughed and gave her a mocking sneer. She kicked away from him swimming strenuously in the opposite direction, only to collide with another body.

Sean.

He pulled her back against his chest, but he didn't look at her. Instead he stared over her head at Roberto, who shrugged, then swam away.

Still Sean didn't release her shoulders. The water was cool, but she could feel his body heat like an inferno. She could feel his body, every part of it, pressed against her.

She was furious; she wanted to jerk away from him. At the same time she felt as if all his heat was seeping into her, turning her muscles to liquid. Making her wish ridiculously that they were longtime friends and lovers. That they could laugh like guilty children, that under the cover of water they could shed their cutoffs and fit together....

Roberto swam toward Maria. Señora Garcia had gone back into the house. Only Julio was on the shore, leaning against the house.

It might have been a scene from a resort brochure—except for the Magnum that Julio was holding.

Mandy wanted to break the silence, to tell Sean that she hated him, that she wanted him to get away from her—now! But his whisper touched her ear, soft, silky, sensual. So raspy and exciting that her mind might have been swept completely clear of all thought, except for... except for that all-encompassing excitement. It raced through her; it took control of her.

"Don't move," he implored raggedly. "Don't move at all."

His arms tightened around her as he started backing into deeper water. She was weightless; her feet didn't touch the sand. She just drifted along with him, his arms around her keeping her hips level with his.

And then they were in deeper water. So cool, when they were so hot. She didn't move; she didn't try to speak. His hands moved slightly, cupping her breasts, his thumbs grazing her nipples. A sound caught in her throat as he pressed his lips against her neck.

Then he moved so deftly that she was filled all over again with a quaking desire that was so physical it overrode even the sensation of the sun. She felt his hand near her midriff, and then his fingers were sweeping beneath the waistband of her cutoffs before sliding the zipper down. The pressure of his palm against her abdomen made her breath come too quickly, made her heart race. She thought that she was mad, then she felt that she had reached the clouds, because his mind held the same thought as hers. That simple touch, body to body, had brought this. The need... the desire... despite all else... It seemed somehow illicit, and therefore all the more fascinating. She should have been shocked; she should have hated him; she should have turned him away—she should have been screaming bloody murder.

And instead she couldn't wait to feel him inside her.

Her cutoffs fell, but he caught them. Beneath the water she was nude. He wrapped one arm around her waist and let his free hand play over her buttocks.

Then, swiftly, he lifted her until her legs locked around his hips.

She couldn't stare into his eyes, so she rested her head against his shoulder. She stifled the cry that rose to her lips when he thrust into her, pressing her teeth lightly into his flesh.

"Look at me!" he warned her harshly. "Laugh, as if we're talking."

"I—I can't!" she gasped.

He was filling her. She burned; she ached; she needed more.

"Mandy . . . do it. Oh, Mandy."

He jerked, forcing her head back, forcing her to lace her fingers behind his neck and stare into his eyes. His smile was so wicked that once again it was as if the fact that they could get caught made every motion more thrilling. The friction of the water, the wonder of him, the pulsing of tension rose in her swiftly. Wonderfully. Suddenly she knew that she was going to burst, and that she would scream with the joy of it all.

But she didn't. He caught her lips in a kiss, and her animal cry of awe and shuddering satiation was caught between them. He held her tight, moving hard against her one last time, a part of her. She went lax, incapable of movement in the aftermath. Thank God he held her. Thank God that he groaned softly, crushing her against him. She couldn't have stood; she might well have drowned in reality, rather than just drowning in his arms.

The water rippled around them and actually began to grow cold.

"You've got to get these back on," he told her huskily.

"I can't move."

suggestion that Mandy might want a shower seemed casual, the older woman was very upset.

It also frightened her that Sean had seemed upset by the argument. He hadn't protested at all when Señora Garcia led Mandy out. He had remained at the table, listening tensely.

Mandy ambled restlessly around the room for a while as the argument went on. Finally she decided that she would take a shower; it would kill time.

When she came back into the bedroom Sean was there, lying under the blanket on the mattress, eyes open, staring up at the ceiling. He turned to her quickly, though, and flashed her a smile in the lantern light.

"What—?" she began.

But he didn't let her finish. He sprang up and she saw that he was naked. He walked quickly to her, then began unwinding the towel from her body. And then he began to kiss her shoulders, breasts, ribs.

She caught his shoulders. "Sean, wait. What—what was that all about? What's going on?"

"Later," he murmured.

His hands were on her hips, his lips pressed to her belly. His breath was against her flesh, and her flesh was responding.

She dug her fingers into his hair. "Sean . . ."

He nudged her legs farther apart, and his mouth rubbed over her until she thought she would fall.

She forgot the question she had asked. She forgot everything. She gasped and hung on to his hair, because she had to remain standing.

She came near to weeping, so vital was the sensation. She twisted and whimpered and gave herself gloriously to him. And only then did he stand to collect her weak form, carry her to the m[...] own reward.

The wonderful heat of the ni[...] around Mandy so completely that [...] truth have been their own. Yet fina[...] lain quietly together for some time, [...] smoothing back her still-damp hair.

"We have to do something—tom[...]

Her heart pitched and thudded; re[...] knife. "Why? What happened?"

"Juan hasn't returned. Roberto thi[...] caught. He wants to take the skiff [...] go back."

In the darkness Mandy frowned. [...] stand."

Sean hesitated for a long time.

"He wants to take one of your fir[...] called Julio a coward with no convic[...] that his father will die in prison."

"Oh, God!" Mandy gasped.

Sean's fingers grabbed painfully [...] are to do nothing! Do you under[...] when you find me gone. Don't m[...] won't be able to follow through w[...] to worry about you, too. I mean [...]

"Go to sleep?"

"Yes!"

She would never sleep. And t[...]

Sean [...]
plan.

The [...]
tain th[...]
were s[...]
day-to[...]
ment r[...]

The [...]
see tha[...]
If this [...]
been st[...]
cop, he[...]
gate wo[...]
ping wa[...]
any of t[...]
No hour[...]
ments w[...]

But th[...]
gotten t[...]
bombshe[...]
God, wo[...]
envy?

Yeah, [...]
he'd gone[...]

couldn't be. He and Miss DAR just weren't cut out to make a go of things.

But face it, he had a chip on his shoulder. And she didn't deserve his anger. So until she was taken away from him, for more reasons than one, she was his, and they would touch one hair on her head only over his dead body.

No joke there, he warned himself. So far he'd played the lackey because every fool knew what one bullet from a .357 Magnum could do to the human body. If one entered his body, there wouldn't be a prayer in hell that he could ever do anything for her again. But now...

Damn the FBI! They should have been here by now.

Divide and conquer—the saying was as old as time, but as true. He had to surprise one of them, get the gun and, if necessary, shoot the other.

Despite it all, he didn't hate Julio Garcia. Julio was just a dreamer, out of sync with the times, believing that he could change the world. This wasn't the way to do it, but Julio was no desperado. Sean just didn't know how far he would go.

Still, Julio would be the one he had to disarm. It would be risky, but it had to be done. Roberto was a hard-core criminal. He would slice off Mandy's finger without a second thought. Given half an opportunity, he would have raped her until she was half-dead—with no thought whatsoever.

Sean didn't think that Señora Garcia would interfere. She seemed to know that her son was diving straight for jail. She would just wait stoically for him.

And Maria? Maria was the long shot. Given a chance, she might well be dangerous. But then, she wouldn't want any of her precious beauty destroyed, either.

"Sean?"

Mandy whispered his name softly with the coming of morning, touching his arm, well aware that he was awake.

He shook her hand off. The last thing he wanted now was her touch. He couldn't waver; he couldn't think of her. He touched a finger to her lips in the darkness. "No words, no movement, no sound! Do you hear me?"

"Hey, it's my finger they're after!"

"Shut up. I mean it! Do you want to get me killed?" he asked angrily.

He thought he saw her eyes flash, even in the darkness. "No! I'd rather kill you myself!"

He chuckled softly, squeezed her hand and groped for his cutoffs. Then he stood quickly before she could say anything else and headed for the door.

As he'd expected, both Julio and Roberto were sleeping on mats outside the door. Roberto stirred slightly, gazing at Sean with wary contempt. Then Julio roused himself, so Roberto went back to sleep.

It was curious that Julio followed Sean so quickly, but it was to his advantage, and Sean was glad. He didn't look back, just hunched his shoulders instinctively and walked out the kitchen door and toward the beach. He paused just before the surf.

"You're upset, my friend?" Julio inquired from behind.

Sean shrugged, needing to get him to come closer.

"She won't be hurt, not really. She'll survive. What is one little finger, eh? They must know that I mean business."

Sean kept looking out to sea. "One little finger? Julio, I ask you, what is one little finger to you? And think about this—what if they catch you? So far you haven't hurt her. Perhaps she'll testify in your defense. She likes you."

Julio made an ugly sound. "The Americana testify for me? No, I do not think so. Her husband will not let an innocent man go free. Why should she bother with a guilty one?"

"Don't maim her, Julio."

"What? Maim?" Julio asked with annoyance, moving closer. "Will I touch her eyes? Her hair? Her legs? The things you cherish? I will leave plenty to love. It will one day be a brand of her courage for her."

"She'll probably die out here!" Sean replied bitterly. "Your dirty knives will give her tetanus. She'll bleed to death."

"Men have survived far worse things."

Julio was there—right where Sean wanted him. He never got a chance to say anything more. Sean smashed his elbow into Julio's ribs with such force that the man doubled over, unable to do more than gasp for breath.

Sean couldn't afford to show him any mercy. He brought his knee up into Julio's chin, sending him keeling over backward.

The Magnum fell into the sand without a shot being fired, nothing but harmless metal.

Sean scooped it up and tucked it into his pants, then reached down to Julio. "Sorry, *amigo*, but you're not touching her finger."

Julio, his mouth bloodied, still unable to stand without clutching his middle, grasped Sean's hand and stared at him heatedly. "Roberto was right!" he gasped. "I should have killed you at the very beginning."

"I think you've got a few broken ribs," Sean said flatly.

"I will scream. I will shout that Roberto should kill her."

"You don't want her dead, and you know it. Nor do you want to face a murder charge. Besides, I don't think you could shout that loud right now."

Julio winced, and Sean knew that his ribs were hurting him. "Let's go," he said. "To the door. You will call to Roberto to come outside. You will not sound alarmed, or I will put a bullet through your eyes. Got it?"

Morosely, Julio let himself be dragged back to the door of the shack.

"Do it!" Sean demanded, shaking him.

"All right! All right!" He hesitated just a second longer, then called, "Roberto! Roberto! *Ven aquí!*"

They waited, Sean using Julio as his shield. He listened, and he heard footsteps. The door opened, and though Julio had not sounded alarmed, Roberto was wary. He looked around the corner of the door—and instantly took a shot at Sean.

Sean ducked his head without a second to spare. He fired a quick shot back; he had no other choice.

He winced as he heard Roberto scream. That was followed by another scream, then another. Maria was up, along with Señora Garcia, and everyone was screaming.

Sean shoved Julio ahead of him once again and entered the cabin, searching for Roberto.

The man was on the ground, slumped against the wall, a trail of blood trickling down the wood. Sean saw that only his arm had been hit, but blood was spouting everywhere.

Roberto was keening with pain. Maria was standing by the back door, arms up, shaking and screaming hysterically. Señora Garcia just stood there, white-faced.

Sean inclined his head toward the wounded man. "Tend to him," he said briefly, then he carefully reached over Roberto to retrieve the other gun.

He barely noticed when Maria disappeared back into her room. He ordered Julio to sit beside his wounded friend.

"You've killed him," Julio said reproachfully.

"I have not. He'll live."

"What are you?" Julio demanded, narrowing his eyes. "You're no gardener."

Sean sighed. "I'm Lieutenant Ramiro, Homicide Division."

"Eh, Roberto, his name was real at least, eh?" Julio tried to joke to the still-suffering man. Señora Garcia was bending over him by then, trying to do something with the wound.

"Drop it—*cop!*"

His eyes shot immediately to Maria, who was holding a small Smith & Wesson with a pearl handle. He trained the Magnum on her in return. "Sweetie, you're not going to use that. Drop it."

Maria smiled and raised the muzzle just above his head, letting off a shot that splintered wood.

"Don't bet on that, lieutenant," she said calmly, adding a very explicit threat in Spanish.

He was just about to call her bluff and fire back when the other bedroom door suddenly flew open, and there was Amanda Blayne, in all her blond glory and rage. To Sean's astonishment she was wielding a switchblade, which she instantly pressed into the small of Maria's back.

"You drop it, brat. I've just about had it with you!"

As meekly as a lamb, Maria dropped her gun.

"Get it!" Sean warned Amanda, and she instantly did so. "You two—Julio, Maria—into the bedroom. *Señora*, can you help Roberto?"

Señora Garcia looked imploringly at Sean. "He needs treatment. He needs medicine," she begged in Spanish.

"I'm sorry. He should have thought of that before he shot at me."

When they had all been hustled into the bedroom that he had shared with Mandy—Mrs. Blayne, he had to start thinking of her that way again—he stood in the doorway and formally placed them all under arrest, reciting their rights. Although, if this was the Bahamas, they would have to go through it all over again, since he didn't have any jurisdiction here. Still, he wanted to play it safe.

Just as he was locking and bolting the door, Amanda started speaking excitedly. "Sean! The boat—Julio's boat—it's returning!"

Sean raced back to her and stared out the window. He turned to look at her. "I thought I told you to stay in the bedroom and not make a sound?"

Her huge tawny eyes met his. "You needed me!"

"I had the situation under control."

"Hmph!" Amanda sniffed indelicately. "She wanted to shoot...a certain part of your anatomy off! I rather thought you might miss it."

"I thought you didn't understand Spanish?"

"I've picked up a few words here and there."

"All the good ones, huh?"

"Sean, the boat!"

"Ah, yes."

"Well?"

He shrugged. "It could be Juan. Or it could be Juan and the Bahamian authorities and the FBI." He stared at her thoughtfully for a minute. "One way or the other, Mrs. Blayne, you'll be able to go home. Aren't you glad?"

"Of course. Aren't you?"

"Absolutely. I've got tons of paperwork waiting for me." He watched her speculatively a second longer, then stared back out the window. "As I said, it could be Juan. Or it could be Juan and the authorities. We have to find out. I'm going out. He won't be surprised to see me on the beach. You stay here. If anyone puts their face out that door—though the bolt should hold—shoot. Don't ask questions—shoot. Got it?"

"Sean—"

"Got it?"

"Oh, yes, sir! Yes, sir, Lieutenant Ramiro!"

"Damn WASP!" he muttered, pulling open the kitchen door.

"Excuse me, lieutenant!"

"What?" he asked, pausing. He felt empty. Already a gulf was opening up between them.

"I'm Catholic."

He frowned, shaking his head in confusion. "Good for you, Mrs. Blayne. What in hell does that have to do with anything?"

She smiled bitterly. "You just called me a WASP. It stands for white Anglo-Saxon Protestant. You'll have to think of something else to call me."

"Oh, Lord!" he groaned softly and slipped through the door.

He sat on the beach and watched as the boat moved closer. He sat stiffly, the gun concealed in his lap, feeling a niggling apprehension. Actually, it had gone easily. Far better than he had ever expected. No one was dead. And among the ones who were not dead were himself and the victim, Mrs. Amanda Blayne. They hadn't even been scratched.

But he was worried now that this might just be Juan, or Juan with a few reinforcements. He felt excitement and anxiety—and, strangely, that same overwhelming emptiness.

He'd wanted it to be over, right? Sure, right. It had been a kidnapping; a woman had been in danger. The fantasy had never been real. Never. It had all occurred in the midst of a nightmare.

But now it was over, and he felt empty.

He kept his eyes trained on the boat. It was about to anchor, and he saw Juan on the deck.

And then—moving so quickly he almost missed him—he saw another man. A tall black man in a uniform.

He stood up without thinking, hailing the boat, rushing down to the shoreline. "Hey! It's all right! Come on in!"

The figure stopped trying to disappear and stood, then brought a megaphone to his mouth. "Lieutenant Ramiro?"

"Yeah, yeah! Come on in!"

"Where is Mrs. Blayne?"

"Inside! She's—she's fine!"

The old boat was suddenly teeming with people. Juan was cuffed and disappeared with someone. The dinghy was lowered, and five men boarded it. Two Bahamian officials, a man in a three-piece suit—and an older, dignified looking man with a sad gaunt face and salt-and-pepper hair. Sean recognized him from his pictures. Senator Peter Blayne.

Sean just stood there as the dinghy came in. He was barely aware that Amanda came out of the house, that she stood slightly behind him. He wasn't aware of anything but the breeze and the sand beneath his bare feet.

"Mandy! Mandy!" The older man didn't wait for the dinghy to reach the shore. He stepped out while it was still in shallow water, soaking his shoes and his pant legs. "Mandy!"

In seconds she was racing down to meet him, and then she was in his arms. It was almost painfully apparent that they meant the world to each other.

Sean suddenly found it difficult to breathe. The older man was speaking, barely coherently, saying how frightened he had been, and what a fool, and how he'd never, never risk her again.

Sean had been as irritated as hell when Blayne had turned up his nose at police protection, but as he watched the scene and the man's agony he felt as if he should insist that this mess wasn't Blayne's fault at all. And, as it happened, if he'd accepted protection, the Miami PD wouldn't have been at the dock when Amanda Blayne was taken by the kidnappers.

Blayne wouldn't want any assurances from him, though; Sean knew that. The older man was staring at his daughter-in-law as if he could devour her, and Mandy was lightly trying to tell him that it hadn't been so bad, that she was fine, that he certainly wasn't at fault, that she was so glad to see him.

Then Sean couldn't give the tender scene his undivided attention anymore; one of the men in the three-piece suits was approaching him.

"Ramiro? Farkel, FBI. What's the situation here?"

What was it about cops and the FBI? Farkel had only introduced himself, but Sean disliked him already. He was a thin reedy sort of man, with a narrow nose, brown eyes, brown hair and a colorless complexion. When he smiled it looked more like a grimace.

Sean indicated the shack. "Two men, two women. They're in the back left bedroom. One has a gunshot wound to his shoulder, he probably needs medical attention as soon as possible."

The FBI man frowned. "You had a gun battle here? You were probably out of line, Lieutenant. You should have waited for us to come in. You could have caused injury to a civilian."

Sean curled his lip stiffly. "Sorry, Farkel. You see, they were going to start hacking off her fingers this morning, and it just didn't sound real nice to me."

"A finger would have been better than her life," Farkel said stiffly.

"They're in the back, Mr. Farkel. And I believe they're your responsibility now. Hey, go gentle on the old lady. She wasn't too happy about having anything to do with this."

The FBI agent walked past him; his associate—a younger blond man—glanced apologetically at Sean, who grinned in return. Some of the federal guys were okay. In fact, he was willing to bet that this one shared his opinion of Farkel.

"Damn yokel cops," Farkel was muttering. "They all think they're TV heroes."

"What's his first name?" Sean asked the young guy curiously. The man chuckled. "Fred. His name is Fred Farkel."

"He looks like a Fred Farkel," Sean muttered.

The blonde extended a hand. "Bill Duffy, Lieutenant. Sorry, he's my superior, but I'll try to be the liaison on the case in the future."

Sean nodded. Then the two Bahamian policemen walked up and introduced themselves, questioning him about the situation, too. They didn't seem to be any fonder of Fred Farkel than anyone else, and Sean had a feeling the man had made a few attempts to usurp their authority as well.

It didn't matter; it was all over for him now. All over but the paperwork.

The taller Bahamian, a guy named Matt Haines, told Sean quietly that a cutter would be coming in to take them back to Miami. Sean thanked him, then he and Bill Duffy went inside to deal with the fugitives in the house.

He was able to glance back at Mandy at last. For a moment her eyes met his. And for just a moment he thought that he saw something in them. Something warm. Something caring. Something that went beyond circumstances.

Then it disappeared. Her father-in-law's arm was around her shoulder, and he was suddenly pulling her enthusiastically forward, determined to reach Sean.

The senator's hand was extended, his smile deep and warm and real, and Sean thought in that moment that he knew why the man was elected over and over again.

"Lieutenant Ramiro! If I had a hundred lifetimes, I could never thank you enough!"

Sean returned his handshake, trying to keep his eyes off Mandy. "Senator, my pleasure. I mean, I didn't do anything out of the ordinary. I mean—"

She was turning bright, bright red. He didn't seem to be able to say anything that came out right.

"Didn't do anything out of the ordinary!" Peter Blayne exclaimed. "Why, son, you were seen! Jumping off that dock, trying to board a moving motorboat. Sir, I call that above and beyond the call of duty. You're too modest."

"Oh, yes, he's modest! Terribly modest!" Mandy said—and she felt the same confusion she knew he was feeling, because they both knew, even if Peter didn't, that neither of them had been modest at all.

And this was her father-in-law! Paul's father! Oh, God, if he found out, what would he think?

She stiffened miserably. There were so many things that she wanted to say to Sean; but none of them could be said. Not here. Not now.

She stared into his eyes and felt as if her insides congealed as he stared back.

His eyes were bright, as green as emeralds, as hard as diamonds. She must have been insane to think that there had ever been anything gentle about him. Or tender. He wasn't the man she had known, not the man with whom she had made love. With whom she had lain, afraid, in the night. With whom she had triumphed in the end.

His stare reduced the warmth of the Caribbean day to winter's chill. He was once again the stranger who had ordered her away from him on the beach, the man who had loved her—then hated her.

She lifted her chin, feeling her eyes well with tears, willing herself not to shed them. She didn't know what went on inside this man, and she decided then that she didn't want to know, that she didn't give a damn.

Circumstances . . . were over. Peter was standing beside her. She must consider the past few days a dream, a fantasy, a nightmare.

She extended her hand to Sean then, as cool as the waves that washed the beach. "Lieutenant, I want to thank you, too."

With a wry smile he took her hand. He remembered how it had felt on his body. It seemed so slim and soft and elegant—and now so remote. "No problem, Mrs. Blayne," he drawled. "Anytime."

"Oh, you'll be seeing more of us!" Peter Blayne assured him. "I'll see to it!"

Sean smiled. That was life as a cop. People you arrested wanted to kill you. People you got out of a jam wanted to be your friend for life. Peter Blayne would forget his promise. People always did.

"Sure," he said agreeably.

"Sean—Lieutenant, what will happen now?" Mandy asked him stiffly.

Sean shrugged. "The feds will press a number of charges. I assume they'll want you to testify in court." He gave her a slightly malicious grin, then laughed. "Fred Farkel will answer all your questions now. It's his ball game, as they say."

Mandy nodded. A silence fell over the three of them that seemed to puzzle Peter Blayne. It didn't matter. Two cutters had appeared on the horizon.

Matt Haines came out of the house and walked toward them. "Lieutenant, Mrs. Blayne, we'll have to invite you for a brief stay in Nassau. I hope you won't mind. We just have to clear up a few things and arrange our extradition procedures. It will just be for to-night. I'm sorry. I know you're anxious to get home.''

Then everyone was on the beach—Julio, in hand-cuffs, Roberto, Maria, Señora Garcia, the FBI men and the Bahamians. Julio stopped in front of Mandy and Peter.

''Señor Blayne, I never wished to hurt her. But now perhaps you will understand. I wish for my father's freedom, just as you wished for hers.''

Peter Blayne smiled sadly. ''Julio, I told you I was doing my best. Your father will be out in a matter of weeks. But now *you* will go to prison.''

''That does not matter, if my father is free.''

''C'mon, Garcia,'' Farkel said roughly.

They passed by. Mandy was glad to see that they would not be on the same boat. She felt sorry for Se-ñora Garcia; she even felt sorry for Julio. But she didn't ever want to see Roberto again, not as long as she lived.

She had to sit next to Sean in the dinghy that took them out to the cutter. She had to feel his bare leg, feathered with the short dark hairs, next to her own. To feel his breath, inhale his scent.

She didn't look at him; she stared straight ahead.

The cutter provided some relief; she was given a small cabin where she could bathe, and a soft terry robe that was totally decent and comfortable.

Mandy showered forever, loathe to leave the clean water. And loathe to reappear on deck, although she knew that Peter was waiting anxiously for her. Natu-rally Peter would quiz her. And naturally Sean would be there. And . . . oh, God!

Eventually she went out on deck. To her vast sur-prise and relief Sean was nowhere in sight.

She was given a delicious rum drink and an equally good meal, and Peter sat next to her, as if he never wanted to leave her side. He told her that her parents had been wired about her safety, that he'd had a student feed her cat. He chattered like a magpie, totally out of character. Then he asked her at last, "Oh, Amanda! Are you really all right? My dear, you're all I have left!"

Guilt churned in her stomach. "I'm fine, Peter, honest."

"But how—"

She took a deep breath. "Sean—Lieutenant Ramiro—pretended to be your gardener."

"My gardener?"

She grimaced and lowered her lashes, staring at her drink. "His Spanish is perfect. He's, uh, half Cuban. He convinced them that he was your downtrodden gardener, and my... my lover, and that he could convince me to be a well-behaved hostage. Julio really isn't a murderer, although I think his associate—Roberto—might have been. Thanks to the lieutenant I, well, I was as safe as possible the entire time. And Señora Garcia really shouldn't be punished, Peter, if there's a way around it. She was against what happened, and she was good to me."

He patted her hand. "We'll see, dear. We'll see what can be done. I'm sure you'll be able to speak in her defense at the trial."

She nodded, and then she wondered where Sean was.

Peter's thoughts must have been running along the same lines. "Where is that young man?" he wondered aloud. "What an interesting fellow. I'd quite enjoy getting to know him. He seems fascinating, don't you think?"

"Uh . . . fascinating," Mandy agreed, swallowing.

She didn't see him again, though, not on the boat. They docked in Nassau harbor and were given rooms in a hotel at the end of Market Street. Mandy had barely entered her own before Peter returned to her with a suitcase of her clothing, packed for her as soon as he'd received permission to come with the authorities to take her home.

She barely had time to dress before she was taken to the Bahamian police station. The authorities were charming, though. They asked her a million questions, which she answered to the best of her abilities.

Then she was free—or she thought she was. The FBI man, Farkel, was there, warning her that once she returned to the States she would be called upon once again.

She had a pounding headache by then, and Farkel felt like the last straw. She thought she was about to explode and then he was interrupted by Sean.

He, too, had changed. He was wearing a lightweight three-piece gray suit, austere, but very handsome on him. He stepped out from one of the little cubicles and spoke not to her, but to Farkel. "Fred, lighten up, will you? You'd think that Mrs. Blayne was the criminal. She's had enough for today, don't you think?"

Farkel stiffened. "I was just—"

"Every dog has his day, Farkel. You'll get yours. She's free for tonight. Our plane leaves in the morning, and once she's on U.S. soil you get to give her the whole third degree."

"And tonight?" Mandy heard herself whisper.

Peter answered for her. "Tonight we're going out on the town! That nice young Bahamian officer suggested Paradise Island for dinner, a show, even gambling." He chuckled, encircling Mandy's shoulder, pulling her close to him. "Mandy, I think we owe Lieutenant Ramiro the best dinner we can find. You, me, the lieutenant—and Paradise Island."

No, paradise is lost! Mandy thought a little frantically. But what could she do? Her father-in-law was on one side of her; the man with whom she had betrayed his deceased son was on the other.

Sean bowed whimsically, watching her in a strange way. He didn't want to go, she thought. No, he wanted to, and he didn't want to. Again she wondered if he hated her... or cared about her?

"A night on the town sounds good, senator," he told Peter. "Mrs. Blayne?" He offered her his arm.

Farkel snorted derisively and turned away. "Damned if they don't all think they're Sonny Crockett these days."

"Damn!" Sean snapped his fingers. "I just wish I could afford his wardrobe, Farkel."

"Your suit's not so bad."

"Thanks—your partner lent it to me."

"Gentlemen . . ." Peter began, distressed.

But he needn't have bothered. Sean didn't wait for Mandy to take his arm; he took hers. And the cool Bahamian breeze touched her heated face as they moved out into the night. . . .

11

Mandy didn't know why Sean had decided to come to dinner with them. The place was lovely, the food was wonderful, but he seemed stiff and uncomfortable. She wondered if she looked as rigid as he did.

Only Peter seemed to be having a good time. He delighted in the story that the kidnappers had assumed that Mandy was his wife, telling Sean, "Good Lord! What flattery, that I should have such a child bride!"

Then he and Sean went on to discuss the situation with the elder Garcia.

Mandy concentrated on her shrimp cocktail. It was amazing. Last night she had been in absolute terror, wondering how Sean would ever stand up to two guns. Staring at her fingers, she shivered. She glanced up and found Sean's eyes on her. He smiled. She looked down again quickly, hoping that Peter hadn't caught the exchange.

"Oh, Mandy! I forgot to tell you! The team from Colorado called the school. You've been invited to be a part of the new dig."

"Really? How wonderful," she murmured.

"Dig?" Sean inquired.

"Yes," Peter said proudly. "Mandy is a paleontologist."

Sean arched one dark brow. "Dinosaurs?"

Despite herself, she grinned. "Their bones, actually, lieutenant."

"She teaches at the state college these days, but this sounds like the perfect time for a leave of absence. You could still manage some skiing out in Colorado."

"Yes, I suppose I could."

Skiing. She loved to ski. But at the moment the prospect meant nothing to her. She closed her eyes briefly. The dig, though, the dig would be good. The painstaking exploration, the wonder of discovery. The piecing together of ancient puzzles. It would be far away and remote, and she could forget all about Julio and Roberto—and Sean Ramiro.

Their main course came, pompano, broiled and garnished and savory, but Mandy couldn't taste it. She could only feel Sean's eyes on her from across the table. She wanted to scream. She wanted to demand to know what he was trying to do to her, here, in front of Paul's father.

"Do you have a family, lieutenant?" Peter asked Sean.

Sean grinned, swallowed a piece of fish, then replied. "Well, sir, everyone has some kind of family. But am I married? No. No children. My father is deceased, my mother lives in Miami Shores, and I've got no brothers or sisters."

"Divorced?" Peter asked him, and Mandy was stunned. Peter was never this rude.

"No, sir. I've never been married."

"Never came close?"

"Oh, yeah. I came close. Once."

Peter's curiosity was quelled by the tone of that reply. No further questions in that direction would be answered.

They bypassed dessert and ordered liqueurs. Mandy found herself feeling amazed. Last night she had been wearing old dirty clothing and sleeping in a hovel. Tonight she was surrounded by opulence: plush velvet, twinkling chandeliers, marble and silver. How quickly the world could change.

As quickly as Sean Ramiro.

They left the restaurant and went into the casino. Peter chose a roulette table; Sean sat down to play blackjack. Nervous and wishing that the evening would end, Mandy restlessly decided to play the slots.

Her little buzzer went off instantly to announce a two hundred dollar jackpot, and two hundred silver coins came spilling out into the catch tray.

She just stared at the coins, then started. Sean wasn't playing blackjack anymore. He was leaning casually against her machine, staring at her mockingly, lashes low over his eyes, looking sensual and handsome despite his negligent stance.

He touched a trailing lock of her hair. "Everything you touch turns to gold, huh?"

She jerked away from his touch. "Silver dollars, Mr. Ramiro. And my hair is dirty blond."

"Oh, I don't think anything about you touches . . . dirt."

"I work in the dirt. I dig up bones, remember?"

"I wonder why that never cropped up in casual conversation."

"We've never had a casual conversation."

"That's right. We were always pretty intense, weren't we? Need some help with your money?"

"No thanks. I'll just play it back."

He moved closer to her, his dark head bending. "Mind if I watch."

"Yes, I do. What are you trying to do to me?"

"What are you talking about?"

"Peter is here!"

He arched a cynical brow at her. "Peter is here?" he repeated. "And now that Peter is here you have to pretend that you don't know me? Funny, I don't see the senator as a snob."

"He's not—I'm not. Just go away, will you, please? Look, it's over. I never understood you, you never understood me. You've got a chip on your shoulder the size of a cement block. And I've got a few—"

"Prejudices?"

"No! Damn you. Problems of my own!"

"And what are they, Mrs. Blayne?"

How dare he? she wondered furiously. Confusion joined the tempest in her heart, and she was afraid that she would burst into tears right there.

She didn't. She just inhaled deeply and spoke with a voice as sharp as a razor. "No one, Ramiro, will ever need to tell me that life can be rough. I don't care what's happened to you, there is nothing—*nothing* in life like losing a child!"

She turned around in a whirl, leaving her coins in the machine, fleeing the room.

Peter would be upset, of course. He would wonder what had sent her flying out. But she couldn't even care about Peter just then; she had to leave.

Mandy had no problem getting a taxi to take her back over the bridge to Nassau and her hotel. Once she got there she knew she had to leave a message for Peter. She did so, then started forlornly for the elevator. She didn't know why she felt so lost, so miserable. It was as if the past and the present had collided to bring her agony just when she should have been eternally grateful that she had been rescued and given a future.

She should have sensed that something was wrong the moment she entered the room, but she didn't. She didn't even bother to turn on the light; moonlight was drifting in through the parted curtains anyway. She just closed and bolted the door, tossed her handbag on the dresser and fell back on the plush double bed.

It was then that she heard the rustle of movement and saw the silhouette moving in the darkness.

She tensed and opened her mouth to scream, but a hand clamped tightly over it.

"Shut up. It's just me."

"Just you!" Furiously she twisted away from him, sitting up, wishing she could see him clearly enough to belt him a good one. "You scared me half to death! What are you doing in here? I'm getting so sick of your strong-arm tactics."

"Take your clothes off, Mandy."

"What?"

"Take your clothes off. It seems to be the only way we can communicate."

"Get out of here! I'll call the co—"

"Cops? Honey, you've got one already."

"Sean . . ."

"Mandy?"

His fingers slid into the hair at her nape, his palm cradling her skull. He held her there while he came ever closer, his lips meeting hers at last, hesitating for just a breath, then coming alive. For an instant, she clenched her teeth against him, but the warm pressure of his tongue dissolved her resistance, and with a little sigh she fell into his arms.

Circumstances changed. People did not. And darkness had come again.

In seconds he was stretched out beside her. They were both fully clothed, but she felt as if she was touching him, all of him.

But it was not passion that goaded him, not that night. He brushed her cheek, and she felt his eyes, emerald flames that defied the darkness.

"I'm sorry, Mandy."

She couldn't answer him. She shrugged.

"I can't forget what happened."

"No one has asked you to forget."

"Mandy..."

"You're strange, Sean. I thought I was, but you're stranger. We make love at night, and in the morning you behave as if I'm a bee with a particularly annoying buzz. One second you're as charming as a prince, and then the next—"

"I had a few raw deals. I took it out on you."

"I can't help the color of my hair, or who my ancestors were."

"Wait a minute! Wait a minute! Get off my case. You were the one who didn't want to touch me with a ten-foot pole the second other people appeared on the scene!"

"You don't—oh, never mind. You just—"

"Mandy!"

"What?"

"Did you smell this bed? Did you touch it? Feel it. So soft, so fresh."

She didn't know why she obeyed the command, but she did, inhaling deeply. And it was true, of course. The bedding smelled wonderful.

"It's so clean," she murmured.

He ran his knuckles tenderly over her hair. "And you're so clean."

"I beg your pardon. I was always clean."

"Well, I wasn't so great."

"Really? For shame, Lieutenant Ramiro." She couldn't stop herself from grinning in the darkness. "I'd never thought your confidence could be so low. I always thought you were at least okay."

"I was . . . okay?"

"Oh, definitely."

"Hmm. Well . . ."

"Well?"

"I'm great now. Want to try me? Clean as a whistle. I even shaved, and you didn't even notice."

"Oh, but I did. I think. You looked so great in that suit."

"Aha! I told you I was great!"

"Bragging will get you nowhere."

"Okay. Take your clothes off. We'll go back to brute force."

"Sean . . ."

He stopped her words with a kiss that seemed the most natural thing in the world. It always seemed to be like that; the taunts and the bitterness, but then somehow the laughter, and the irresistible urge to touch.

She would probably never know which was real, the laughter or the pain. But in the darkness, even darkness kissed by moonlight, it didn't seem to matter. When she was with him she always felt as if she had a driving thirst, as if his touch was water that cascaded over her, a fountain that sparkled and rippled, soothing and delighting, sweeping her away to new heights.

His hands moved over her, frustrated by her dress. He groaned softly. "Take your clothes off."

"Is that the only line you know?" she whispered.

"It's a damn good one," he assured her. And she laughed, laughed until his fingers rode along her bare legs to her bikini panties and teased her flesh through the silky fabric. Then her breath caught and she could laugh no more, and she was suddenly thinking that surely this would be the last time that she had to drink in all of him; the bronze flesh and muscle and sinew; the dark hair that dusted his legs and chest; the powerful line of his profile....

"You take *your* clothes off," she told him huskily. "On second thought..."

She started working on the tiny pearl buttons of his vest. He took a deep breath, watching her, watching the tiny frown that furrowed her brow. He held his breath as she undid the vest and then his shirt, and then he expelled it with a heady groan as she brought her mouth against him, delicately touching him with the tip of her tongue. Then she grew bolder, grazing his skin with gentle teeth that sent streams of lavalike desire rippling through his body. She moved sinuously against him, her hands moving over his back, his chest, then to his shoulders to shove the annoying material from the form she was so eager to know.

There was nothing like this, she thought. Nothing like feeling his reactions to her kiss, her touch. He trembled beneath her, yet he was taut, and with each ragged breath he took she felt bolder, more feminine, more vibrantly aroused herself. He was right: he was clean; he was great; the fresh masculine scent of his body was an aphrodisiac in itself, and she wondered at the beauty of him as her head reeled. She slipped her fingers along the waistband of his pants, teasing his belly, finding his belt buckle and leisurely working it free.

Too leisurely, perhaps. His groan resounded like thunder, and he set her aside, destroying her illusion of power. He left her to feverishly shed the remainder of his clothing, then lay back beside her.

"What's this?" he whispered huskily.

"My dress."

"Get rid of it!"

She giggled breathlessly. "I thought you were going to do a striptease and then dance."

"I intend to dance, all right." He swore softly in Spanish, having a miserable time with the tiny hook at her nape. He paused, shrugged and snapped it, and she didn't care in the least. She was suddenly as anxious as he was to feel their bodies together.

As soon as her clothes were gone she stepped back to him, remembering their first time. She knelt down and let her hair fall over his feet as she massaged them, then dusted them with kisses. Her body was liquid as she moved against him, using the tip of her tongue at the backs of his knees and all along his thighs.

He held his breath again, as taut as wire. She waited, drawing out the moment, her hair spilling over him.

And then she took him with her touch, with her kiss.

She heard his words, sweet and reverent, in English and in Spanish, and they all meant the same thing. His fingers were tempered steel when they closed around her arms as he drew her to him, moving swiftly, stunning her with the electric force of his entry. The moment was so fulfilling that she cried out softly, only to have her words stolen once again by a kiss.

They moved together in the moonlight, until finally she lay panting in sweet splendor. She was so tired, so spent, yet each new touch awakened her anew, until she moaned softly, curling into his chest with the sweetest sigh.

He held her there for what seemed like forever.

She didn't know when the change came, only that he suddenly stiffened and then rose before padding naked to the window to stare out at the Bahamian night.

She was too drowsy to rouse herself, and she wondered bitterly why he had decided to do so at such a time.

"What's the matter?" she asked softly.

He whipped around, like a lethal predator, and moved back to the bed, perching at the foot of it.

"What are we going to do now?" he asked her harshly.

"Sleep," she responded.

"That's not what I mean, and you know it."

"Sean, don't..." She lifted an imploring hand to him, but he ignored it.

"I asked you a question."

"Sean, I'm so tired."

"Then wake up. What are we going to do?"

"We're—we're going to fly back to the U.S. in the morning!" she snapped at last. "I have to go back to work. I assume that you do, too."

"And?"

"And what?"

"What about us?"

She held her breath, wondering what he was so upset about. Was he afraid that she would think she had some kind of hold on him? What was it with him? She didn't understand him, and when he was like this he actually frightened her.

She cared too much. Way too much. And she had promised herself that she wouldn't risk caring that much ever again. Her career, her love of the past, would be her life. Nice safe dinosaurs that had been extinct for years and years and years....

"You don't have a thing in the world to worry about, lieutenant," she whispered wearily. "I have no intention of becoming involved with you. You're as free as a lark."

"Oh?" he said coldly.

Chills raced along her spine; she wanted to touch him and erase the tension from his face. But she had already reached out to him, and he had ignored her.

"So," he murmured, "it all came true in a way, didn't it? I might as well have been your gardener, dragged in when the odd occasion warranted it, huh?"

She was instantly furious with him—and with herself, for always falling prey to him so easily. "You stupid bastard!"

"Yeah, you're kind of right there, too, aren't you?"

He prowled over to the window once again. "I've got just one more question for you, Mrs. Blayne."

"Do ask, lieutenant."

"I'm curious as to what precautions you've been taking."

"Precautions?" Mandy echoed hollowly.

He turned so suddenly that she thought he was about to take the drapes with him. "I'll be blunt, Mrs. Blayne. I'm talking about birth control."

"Don't you dare stand there and yell at me! I wasn't planning on having an affair! I was kidnapped! I usually don't worry about birth control when maniacs are abducting me! There's an old saying that it takes two to tango, and I'm here to tell you that it's true!"

"That's irrelevant."

"The hell it is!"

"It's irrelevant," he repeated, bending over her so that his arms surrounded her like a cage. "Because any precautions I might have taken would have been evident. So we know that wasn't the case."

She felt that she really did hate him at that moment. He stood over her like some superior god, the epitome of masculine force, beautiful still, and more hateful for it.

She stiffened her spine, as heedless of her nudity as he was of his. "You have no problems whatsoever, lieutenant. I will never again have a child. Does that satisfy you?"

For an instant she thought that he was going to hurt her, he looked so fierce. He didn't. He pushed himself away from the bed in a fury, muttering something she didn't understand. She shivered because without his warmth the night had grown cold.

She closed her eyes tightly. "Sean," she said miserably, "get out of here. Please, go!"

Once more he came back to her. He took a strand of her hair, curling it around in his fingers. She'd never seen him quite like this, and it was all she could do to keep from tearing away from him, to keep from screaming out.

"Not again, Mrs. Blayne," he said softly. "Not again. Here's another expression for you—those who play sometimes pay. And if you're given a price, my love, you will pay it."

"What—?"

"You can expect to see me again. Quite frequently. For the next few months, at least."

A new wave of trembling swept over her, along with a rush of conflicting emotions. She understood him now; at least, she thought she did. She'd assumed at first that he had no desire to be saddled with a child from their affair; now she knew it was the opposite. And with that knowledge she experienced a blank and cold dread, terrifying, horrible. It was if she had gone back in time, gone back to the time when the young highway patrolman had stood on her doorstep, telling her that not only her husband but her infant had been killed in the collision, the baby mercifully quickly....

But for her there had been no mercy. There had been her breasts, filled with milk for a tiny life that could never draw from them again. There had been the emptiness in her arms, the rage, the despair....

"Get out of here," she repeated dully.

He reached for her cheek, but she pushed his hand away. "I'll be around, Mandy."

"No," she pleaded.

And then she knew that he had misunderstood her entirely, because he swore again, then said, "What is it, Amanda? You couldn't handle a child named Ramiro? Too ethnic for your ears?"

She pressed her palms over her eyes tightly. "Yes! Yes! That's it! I'm planning to move to Boca Raton, too. Away from Miami. Haven't you heard that saying? 'Will the last American out please remember to bring the flag?' Please! Get out of here."

But he didn't. Not then. He straddled her and pulled her hands away from her face, then stared into her eyes with a gaze that burned into her soul. "No!" he thundered harshly. "You can't run away. Not this time!"

And then, miraculously, he released her.

She closed her eyes. She heard him dress swiftly, and then she heard him leave even more swiftly.

For at least an hour after that she didn't move. Not a muscle. She just lay there, trying to breathe.

And praying that she wasn't pregnant.

In the morning she felt awful.

The flight back took less than an hour. Peter's car met them, and they reached her home in another thirty minutes.

Peter was worried and solicitous. She could only be grateful that Sean hadn't been on their plane. He must have altered his arrangements.

Peter had arranged for the police and the FBI to come to her; she spent the afternoon with a pleasant blond man and a sergeant from the Miami PD. Things weren't really difficult; all she had to do was repeat what had happened over and over again. It was a cut-and-dried situation, but the culprits still had to be prosecuted.

A twinge of conscience touched her, and Mandy remembered to tell them that in her opinion Mrs. Garcia had been an unhappy bystander. She hesitated, then even spoke up for Julio, saying that she didn't believe he was malicious, just misguided. She was told that if she would say so at the trial, she might lessen their sentences.

"But kidnapping is a federal offense, Mrs. Blayne. No one can walk away from it," the FBI man told her.

"I know." She paused, shivering. "And Roberto should be locked up, with the key thrown away." She lowered her lashes. She had told them, of course, that he had attempted to rape her. She told them, too, about Sean's fight to save her from him.

She hadn't mentioned what had happened after that, though.

They left her, and she was alone with Peter. He wanted to stay with her; he wanted her to drink warm milk and go to bed and get better, since her shadowed eyes and pale cheeks had convinced him that she was sick.

He was supposed to be in Washington, and she knew it. With a dozen assurances she finally got him to go home, convincing him that she was determined to get a good night's sleep and go back to work in the morning. "All I want is Koala," she told Peter lightly.

Koala was her cat, so named not because he was cute, but because he was so ugly. He'd come to her door one day and moved in without giving her much choice.

Peter hugged her, then turned to leave at last, a haggard-looking man. She loved him so much. "Peter."

"Yes?"

"Promise me that you'll get a good night's sleep, okay?"

He grimaced. "Promise."

She thought that now her day was over. She thought that she could sink into a warm bath and try to think about about the new dig. She wanted to do everything she could to create distance between herself and Sean, the things he had said to her—and the horrible things she had said to him.

But she couldn't forget him; all she could do was miss him.

She couldn't even get comfortable. She ran her bath, but before she could step into the water, the phone rang.

It was her mother, sobbing over the phone, and once again Mandy was cast into the depths of guilt, aware that any decent daughter would have called her own parents by then. She talked to her mother for half an hour, then to her father for another twenty minutes.

They both wanted to fly in immediately, but her father was just recovering from bypass surgery, and Mandy didn't think he should be traveling yet. She managed to persuade them to wait a few weeks, telling them that she was absolutely fine and planning on a trip to Colorado anyway. She talked about the dig with forced enthusiasm, and at last they seemed to believe that it would be all right to wait to see her until the end of the month.

Hanging up from her parents brought no relief. The phone rang again instantly, and this time it was a reporter. She spoke politely to him, but then the doorbell rang. Another reporter. She spoke politely to him, too.

But when a third reporter reached her over the phone she was ready to scream. She had a pounding headache; all she wanted to do was hide.

She got through the third interview, then hurried through her small house, pulling all the drapes shut. She finally got into the freshly filled bathtub, where she strenuously ignored the phone every time it rang.

She sat in the tub for a long time, feeling the heat ease some of her tension away. Again she tried to think about work, to plan for the trip.

The water began to cool, and suddenly she jumped out of it as if she had been scalded. It had suddenly reminded her... of Sean. Of a day in the surf when she had surfaced to face Roberto, when she had backed away from him, when Sean had been there—and their minds had functioned as one.

She grabbed a towel and wrapped it around herself, shaking. She closed her eyes.

She couldn't stop thinking about him. Everything, every little thing, was a reminder.

After a few seconds she groped blindly in the medicine chest for one of the tranquilizers the doctor had given her just after the accident. She swallowed it quickly.

She paused for a minute, breathing deeply. Then she walked into the living room and resolutely did the one thing that would convince her that she had been right not to try. That it was better, much better, to have him hate her than... than anything else.

She picked up the picture on the mantle. The picture of a happy family. Herself, Paul and the baby.

As she stared at the tears welled in her eyes, and the immediate past dimmed slowly away.

12

Sean was back in his cubicle on the fifth floor, sipping his coffee and reviewing his file on the McKinley murder case, when Harvey Anderson sauntered in, leaning against the divider, the daily paper in one hand, his styrofoam cup of coffee in the other.

There was such a grin on his face that Sean sat back, crossing his arms over his chest and arching a wary brow.

"Whew!" Harvey whistled. "Nice, man, nice! Damned if you don't get all the luck."

"All right, Harvey, what luck? So far the situation looks like hell to me. I'm gone for a week, and what did you guys do? You let the paperwork on my desk grow like the stinking yellow pages.

"Hey...!" Harvey lifted his shoulders innocently. "We missed you—what can I say?"

"Thanks. Thanks a lot."

The grin left Harvey's face. He indicated the top file on Sean's desk. "We just got the report back from ballistics. The murder weapon was a Smith & Wesson, fifteen shots. One bullet fired, the one that killed him."

"The same gun found in the house?"

Harvey nodded. "Looks like the wife to me, beyond doubt."

"We can't use 'looks like' with the D.A.'s office, Harvey. You know that. I think it was his wife, too. We're going to need a motive—especially since she's still claiming that it was a break-in. And we can't get anyone except her stepchildren to say that there might have been trouble in the marriage. Let's work on it from that angle."

"His money was motive enough," Harvey snorted.

"Yeah, well..."

"Viable proof in court, yeah, yeah. We'll get it. I've got a hunch on this one." He grinned once again, "They can't all be neat and clean and wrapped up in a bundle for the feds, with glowing praise and the word 'hero' in all the papers."

Sean's eyes narrowed. "Okay, Harvey, out with it."

"Out with what?" His face was all innocence beneath his shaggy brown hair. "What's with you? When did you stop reading the paper?"

"I overslept. Hand it over."

"Man, you get all the luck. A week in the Bahamas and the blonde to boot."

"The paper, Harvey!"

Sean snatched it from him. It was true. His name and the word 'hero' were splattered all over the front page—along with a picture of Amanda Blayne in her doorway.

It shouldn't have been a flattering picture; it was a grainy black-and-white snapshot, and she was in the process of trying to close the door. Even so, she looked beautiful. Distressed, her hair tumbling about her face. Even in black-and-white, you could almost see the color, feel it...smell its fragrance.

Sean glanced over the article and gritted his teeth. The article was mainly about him; she couldn't have commended him more highly.

"Damn her," he muttered, the world suddenly turning a shade of red. What was she trying to do? Buy him off?

He slammed the paper down on the desk.

"Hey! What's with you?" Harvey protested. "If she were gushing all over me, I'd be halfway to heaven. And the big boys down at city hall are thrilled. What with so much corruption going on in the police force these days, they're thrilled to have gotten some favorable publicity for a change."

Sean just shook his head. "If the PR is good for the department, great. I just don't like being all over the paper, that's all."

Harvey didn't leave. He sat down on the edge of Sean's desk. "What was she like, huh?"

"Polite," Sean said curtly. Then he softened. Harvey wasn't actually his partner; Todd Bridges was. But homicide worked in teams, usually on several cases at a time, and the three of them, along with Harvey's partner, Jill Santini, had worked together many times.

They were friends, and Harvey's tone had been more curious than anything else.

"She's a . . . nice lady. Lots of spunk, lots of spirit. Hey, you can be the liaison between the PD and the FBI. You'll probably get to meet her that way."

"Naw, Sean. You're the man on this one."

"We're a team, right? You take it."

"Really?"

"Really."

"Wow!"

Harvey walked away, leaving his newspaper behind. Sean stared at it for a moment longer, threw it down, then picked it back up. He drummed his fingers on his desk, then picked up the phone and dialed information. He glanced at his watch. It was just after seven.

The hell with it. He dialed her number.

A soft, sleepy, too-sultry voice said, "Hello?"

"What the hell did you think you were doing?"

"I beg your pardon? Oh—Sean."

"Yeah, Sean."

"I don't know what you're talking about."

"Don't you get the paper?"

"I don't read it until I'm awake. Why?" she asked, suddenly defensive. "What did I do? Insult you?"

"No, no, you were glowing."

"Then what's your problem?"

"Too glowing, Mrs. Blayne. It isn't going to change the way I feel about anything."

She was silent, then she laughed bitterly. "Actually, I don't begin to understand how you do feel about anything. If anything I said offended you, I'm sorry. It wasn't intended. Excuse me. If you're done yelling, I have a class in an hour."

She didn't give him a chance to say anything else. She hung up.

He was left staring at the phone.

Harvey came back into his cubicle, his jacket slung over his shoulder. "Ready?"

"For what?"

The other man sighed. "You called me last night— at midnight, I might add—to say you wanted to go over to forensics first thing this morning."

"Oh, yeah. Give me just a second, will you?"

Harvey nodded and disappeared.

Sean stared at the phone again. He picked it up, not at all sure what he really intended to do.

"Hello?" She sounded more alert this time.

"Want to go to a party Friday night?"

"Sean?" she inquired skeptically.

"Yeah, it's me."

"And you're calling to see if I want to go to a party?"

"Yeah, well, it might be a little dull. It's just a... ethnic sort of thing. You're, uh, welcome to invite Peter, too."

"He's out of the state," she answered, and then dead silence came over the wire. "I don't believe you," she said at last.

"Will you come?"

"I..."

"Please."

"You're crazy."

"Probably."

"I..."

"I'll pick you up at seven."

He hung up quickly. He didn't want to give her a chance to refuse him.

"Sean?" Harvey called. Todd was standing there, too, now.

Sean grabbed his jacket, grinning as he joined them. He hadn't slept a wink all night, but suddenly he felt as if he could work three shifts straight.

Todd commented dismally on the weather as they went down in the elevator.

Sean cut him off. "You all coming to the annual bash this Friday?"

"Wouldn't miss it," Todd said, perking up.

Sean grinned. "Good. Harvey, you'll get to meet her after all."

"The blonde? She's coming?"

"Uh, yeah, I think so."

Harvey grinned suddenly, rolling his eyes. "I think there's a whole lot more to this story than the papers know!"

"And it's going to stay that way," Sean declared warningly.

"Sure. Sure it will," Harvey vowed solemnly.

Harvey stared speculatively at Sean's back as they walked out to the parking lot. Sean had sounded serious, and Harvey was surprised.

He and Sean had gone through the academy together. He'd been around when...well, he'd been with Sean's lawyer when they pulled a few strings to get Sean out of jail. It just...didn't seem possible.

He wondered who was in for the worse time, the beautiful blonde, or Sean Ramiro.

Amanda was still partially in shock when she reached the campus. In shock because he had called her, yelling, when she had given him every compliment she could, though she had been ready to scream at the mere mention of his name. And in shock because he had called her back and asked her to a party—just like that.

And also because she hadn't said no.

After a few minutes she roused herself somewhat from her stupor; it was wonderful to be back. There was a giant coffee cake waiting in her office, along with a score of her students and half the faculty. Everybody wanted to hug her, to tell her how grateful they were that she was fine, and how happy they were to see her back.

It was nice to feel so loved, but in time the furor died down.

She had an introductory class that morning, and a second, more advanced class after that. Teaching was fun. She loved it as much as she loved the subject, and it was good to back at work. It was so... normal.

But when her classes were over her mind returned to Sean—and to her own idiocy. Why in God's name hadn't she just told him that he was crazy, that he was absolutely insane, and that no, she wouldn't go anywhere with him? She didn't want to get involved with anyone, and especially a man who was like Dr. Jekyll and Mr. Hyde!

She had barely sat down behind the desk in her office when Valerie Gonzales, one of the associate professors, came by. "How about lunch?" the other woman asked.

"I'm not really hungry," Mandy told her ruefully.

Valerie wrinkled her nose. "I'm not, either, but Ed Taylor came in with a decaying alligator that he's determined to preserve, and the smell of formaldehyde is driving me nuts. Let's get out of here."

Mandy leaned back and grinned. "All you want is the inside scoop."

"That's right. Are you going to give it to me?"

"No."

Valerie shrugged. "I'll buy you a Mai Tai. That ought to do it."

"Think so, huh?"

They went to one of the nearby malls, where one of the restaurants specialized in appetizers. They ordered two apiece. Amanda refused the Mai Tai that Valerie had been sure would make her open up, but she decided that a glass of Burgundy was just what she needed.

And though she certainly didn't open up, she found herself admitting that she was going out that Friday with the "way-out cop," as Valerie referred to Sean. Mandy decided that she needed a little advice, and that Valerie might be able to help her. "Val, all he said was that it's some ethnic thing. What do you think I should wear? Is there some kind of Cuban holiday coming up?"

Valerie sipped her beer and pondered the question. "Not that I know of, so go for something casual. If they're celebrating, they might roast a pig."

"So. . . ?"

"Well, you roast them whole, in a pit in the ground. It's an all-day event. By night it's ready to eat."

"Can you teach me some Spanish? I think I'm going to feel like a fish out of water."

Valerie laughed. "I know you know some Spanish. I swear all the time and you always know what I'm saying."

"Yeah, well, I don't think that's party conversation."

"Okay." Valerie hesitated. *"Buenas noches."*

"Good evening? Good night?"

"Yeah, both. *Como está usted?* How are you? *Bien, gracias*—fine, thank you. Umm...*dónde está el baño?* That one is very important to every woman."

"Why?"

"It means, where is the bathroom." She chuckled softly. "Then there's *te amo*."

"Which means?"

"I love you."

"Valerie!"

"Aren't you in love with him? Just a little bit?"

"No. I'm not in love with anyone."

"Then it's just sex."

"Of course it's not just sex."

"Wow! Then you have made love, huh?"

"Valerie, stuff some more food into your mouth, will you, please?"

"Sure, but I can't teach you much Spanish that way!"

Friday seemed to roll around very slowly. Mandy fluctuated between longing to see him so badly that she hurt and dreading it so thoroughly that she almost called to cancel.

He didn't call her. She even began to wonder whether he had been serious. He hadn't asked for her address, but then, she was certain he could get it easily enough.

At some point she realized that although he might be crazy, she was the one suffering a terrible illness. She didn't want an involvement, yet she was involved. And that made her dilemma all the worse. She knew that she shouldn't see him. Seeing him would only bring more arguments, more disaster. She still couldn't tell whether he liked her or hated her—or if he was using her.

But none of it mattered. She had to see him. And not even the memory of her tragic past could intrude on that basic desire.

The week was a slow one on campus, too. They were almost at spring break. She made her arrangements to leave for the dig in Colorado on the Monday when the vacation began. She wouldn't really be able to get too involved in the work—she wouldn't have the time—but it would be fascinating just to be a part of it.

As much as she was looking forward with dread and fascination to seeing Sean again, she was glad that she could hop aboard a plane and leave—run away—the Monday after.

Friday night did come, as things inevitably did. He had said seven; at five she was in the shower, shampooing her hair, taking a long luxurious bath. She couldn't help reminding herself that he had usually seen her at her grubbiest, and she wanted to be perfect—as perfect as she could be.

If he was really coming for her . . .

She had never experienced anything in her life like the emotions and physical agitation that came to her unbidden that night, growing worse and worse as seven o'clock approached. She was anxious and scared and nervous—and her fingers shook so badly that her first application of mascara was applied to her cheeks rather than her eyelashes. Her stomach felt as if fifty jugglers were tossing eight balls apiece inside it. Her palms were damp; her body felt on fire. And to her eternal shame, she seemed incapable of remembering what he looked like dressed, recalling instead every nuance of his naked body. She was trying to pour herself a glass of wine when the doorbell rang.

She dropped the glass and stupidly watched it shatter all over the tile floor. She swept it up in a mad rush, raced to the door—then stopped herself, smoothing back her hair before throwing open the door.

At her first sight of him all the nervous heat and energy and anticipation churned through her anew. He was tan and clean shaven, his hair still damp from the shower. He was wearing a light suit, tailored to fit his physique, enhancing the breadth of his shoulders and the trimness of his waistline. The most noticeable thing about him, as always, was his eyes. So green, so shocking, against the strong planes of his face. The look of character in them gave him his rugged appeal, raised him above such an undistinguished word as "handsome."

Then she realized with dismay that he was in a suit—and she was in jeans. "Oh," she said softly.

"Does that mean come in?" he asked.

"Yes, yes, of course. Come in." She backed away from the door awkwardly. He followed her. For several seconds he stared at nothing but her, then he looked around her house.

There wasn't much on the first floor, just a living room that led to the kitchen on the left, the sun porch in the rear and the staircase to the right. It was pretty, though, she thought. The carpeting was deep cream, the furniture French provincial. The screen that separated the dining area from the rest of the room was Oriental.

"Nice," he said. He meant "rich."

She shrugged. "Thank you. Uh, would you like a drink? I think I need to change."

He acted as if he was just noticing her clothing. Then he frowned. "Where did you think I was taking you?"

"A friend of mine suggested . . . never mind. Why don't you help yourself. The kitchen is all yours. I'll be right down."

She fled up the stairs, tripping on the last one, and hoped he hadn't noticed. She changed into a kelly green cocktail dress, almost ripping it in her haste to reclothe herself. It seemed very illicit, suddenly, just to be in the same house with him, half-clad. Especially half-clad, and trembling, and thinking that she would just as easily, just as gladly, crawl into a bed, onto a floor—anywhere—with him as she ever had.

Unwilling to consider such thoughts for long, she raced hurriedly and breathlessly back down the stairs.

He was sipping wine and had poured a glass for her. He handed it to her, watching her. She thanked him, then they fell silent.

"How, was, uh, getting back to work?" she asked at last.

"Fine. How about you?"

"Fine."

Silence again.

"I've got great students," she offered.

He nodded. Eventually he said, "We should get going."

"Yes."

She was somewhat surprised to discover that his car was a lemon-yellow Ferrari. He smiled at her look, leaning over her shoulder as he opened the door to whisper tauntingly, "No, I'm not on the take. My father was a cigar king once upon a time, and he left a trust fund, which I managed to invest rather decently."

"Did I say anything?"

"Your eyes did."

She didn't even know where they were going; he drove in silence. When they got onto the Dolphin Expressway, and then onto I-95, she finally asked him.

"Miami Shores," he said simply then lapsed back into silence again.

She decided to break it. "I've been taking a few Spanish lessons."

His eyes met hers briefly in the mirror. "Oh? Why?"

"I thought I should be able to say a few things tonight."

He smiled. "That's nice."

There was something about that smile she didn't like.

He flicked on the radio. Mandy gave up, closed her eyes and leaned back in the seat. It was better than watching his hands on the steering wheel and remembering other places where they had been.

Eventually they turned off the highway and drove through a series of side streets until they pulled into a circular drive fronting a beautiful old Deco residence. Mandy wanted to ask him whose house it was, but he didn't give her a chance. He helped her out, then hurried to the door so quickly that she nearly tripped as she followed him.

He didn't ring the bell; he just walked in. And then Mandy understood that smile.

It was a party all right. It was even ethnic. Half the people there were dressed in green, and on a beautiful rich oak bar at the back of the living room was a massive glass keg of green beer.

"St. Patrick's Day!" she gasped.

"It is the seventeenth," Sean murmured.

"You rat!" It was all she could think of.

"Sean! You made it! Come in, dear, and introduce me to Mrs. Blayne!"

She didn't need to be introduced to his mother; Mrs. Ramiro had apparently given her son the emerald green of her eyes. She was a tiny creature, no more than five-two, slim and graceful, with marvelous silver hair and a smile that could melt a glacier.

Mrs. Ramiro was charming. She had a soft brogue and an equally soft voice, and she was entirely entrancing. "I'm Siobhan, Mrs. Blayne. You come with me!'' She winked and tucked Mandy's arm into her own. Then she walked her guest around, introducing her to various people—who seemed to come in all nationalities. Spanish was spoken by some of them, but it was always broken off politely when Mandy appeared, and she was impressed with the sincere interest shown by those who met her.

At last Mrs. Ramiro brought her to the bar, where she was given a green beer.

''You look shell-shocked, child. What's the matter?'' Siobhan asked her.

Mandy found herself being perfectly honest. ''I thought I was going to have roast pig,'' she admitted finally, and Siobhan laughed. ''I spent all week practicing my Spanish.''

''Well, I daresay you'll get to use it. A number of my guests are Cuban and Colombian.''

''On St. Patrick's Day,'' Mandy murmured.

''Oh, everyone's Irish on St. Patrick's Day.'' Siobhan laughed. ''Aren't you, just a smidgen?''

Over the rim of her glass, Mandy saw Sean coming toward them, and she said very clearly for his benefit, ''Oh, honestly, I don't know, Siobhan. As far as I know I'm just an American mongrel. No one ever seemed to be able to trace my family.''

Siobhan laughed softly again. ''I'll warrant there's some Irish in you somewhere!''

Sean smiled down at his mother, helping himself to the green beer. ''Maybe there is, Mother. I tried to call her WASP once, and she told me that she was Catholic. Could mean a good Irish priest was nestled in the family somewhere.''

''You called her what? Sean!''

''Dreadful of me, wasn't it?''

"Certainly. I don't know how you stood him for all that time, Amanda!" Siobhan shook her head. "I must get back to my other guests. Please, Amanda, have a wonderful time. I'm so glad to meet you. And I promise," she added, her eyes sparkling, "we'll roast you a pig next time!"

Mandy was left to face Sean again. She sipped her beer, staring steadily at him. "You really are a rat."

"Why?"

"You knew what I assumed."

"I'm sorry about the lack of a pig. Well, actually, we do have a pig. Cabbage and bacon."

"Umm."

He set his beer down on the bar and swept hers from her hand, then looped his arms around her and brought her against him. She stiffened, but he seemed not to notice. "There's music out on the patio. People are dancing. Dance with me, Mandy."

She didn't really have a chance to refuse. He simply led her out to the back, where a trio was playing and people were indeed dancing beneath soft colored lights.

The music was slow, and she found herself in his arms. Dancing with him came as easily as making love.

"Why did you come with me tonight?" he asked her at length.

Her face was against his shoulder; her hand was clasped in his. She could feel all the rhythms of his body, and the softness of his dark hair brushing her forehead as he bent his head.

"I—I don't know."

"Are you glad you did?"

"I don't know."

"Do you hate me?"

"I . . . no."

"You smell great."

"Thank you."

"You feel great."

"Thank you."

"Do you know what I'm thinking?"

"Do I want to know?"

"I don't know." He waited a moment, then continued. "I was thinking that I wish a leprechaun would suddenly whisk all these people away so I could ravish you this very second."

She wondered how just his words could affect her so deeply, but they could. She was glad that she was clinging to him; she needed the balance.

She closed her eyes before she spoke. "I didn't mean what I said, you know," she told him, then hesitated. "About Latins. You know. The, uh, last American remembering the flag."

His arms tightened around her as they swayed.

"You'd marry a Ramiro?"

"That wasn't the question. You never mentioned marriage."

"I suppose I didn't. But if I had—hypothetically, of course—what would your hypothetical answer have been?"

"I—I don't think that I—"

His interruption was a whisper that swept her ear like velvet. "But you can handle an affair?"

She didn't answer him.

"You'll sleep with me, but that's it, huh?"

Suddenly she wasn't leaning on his shoulder any longer; she was being held away from him, and his eyes were searching hers.

And she was desperately wondering why she was here. Dr. Jekyll always turned into Mr. Hyde.

He started to say something, but before he could a slim dark-haired young man tapped his shoulder apologetically, smiled with rueful fascination at Mandy, then cleared his throat as he remembered his mission. "Sean, we've got an emergency call. And you promised to introduce me."

"Harvey Anderson, Amanda Blayne. What's the call?" he inquired, annoyed.

"Mrs. McKinley's being treated at Jackson. Suicide attempt. Sorry, Mrs. Blayne. They want us. Pronto."

Sean's shoulders fell as he stared at Amanda. She knew that he was really aggravated, he had wanted the discussion to go further.

So had she. He never understood her, and it was largely her fault. Still, maybe this was for the best.

"I've got to go," he said. "Mom will see that you get home. I'm sorry."

"It's all right."

"I'll call you."

She nodded, knowing that he wouldn't reach her. She was going to change her flight and leave for Colorado in the morning.

He looked as if he was going to say something else, as if he longed to. As if he longed to touch her one more time.

But he didn't. He just closed his eyes briefly, shook his head and left her.

And perhaps it *was* for the best. Because although Mandy insisted again and again that she could call a cab, Siobhan Ramiro was determined to drive her home. She kept up a pleasant stream of chatter from the north of the city to the south and, surprisingly enough, agreed to come in for coffee before driving home.

Mandy soon discovered why.

As Siobhan sipped her coffee she dropped all pretense of casual interest and stared at Mandy with her clear green eyes. "I think my son is in love with you."

Mandy couldn't pull her eyes away from that green stare. Nor could she give anything but a bitter, honest answer. "Sometimes I think he hates me."

Siobhan lowered her eyes, smiling slightly. "No, he just doesn't always handle himself very well. You see . . ." She hesitated briefly, then shrugged and continued. "I came here to tell you something. I hope I can trust you. I'm not supposed to know this. A friend of his told me about it, because I was beside myself, worrying about him. There was a spell a few years ago when he had a different woman every week. He almost seemed to—to delight in starting an affair. And ending it. And they were all . . . blond."

Siobhan sat back in her chair with a sigh. "He grew out of it quickly, though he never became really involved again. Cruelty really isn't a part of his nature. I should have known all along. You see, there was this particular girl . . . well, he'd been madly in love with her. He wanted to marry her. He was going to meet her parents, she was going to come and meet me. All of a sudden it was off. I found out later that she had been pregnant—and that her parents had forced her into an overseas boarding school after a quick abortion."

"Why?" Mandy gasped, stunned by the story.

Siobhan smiled with a trace of her son's bitterness. "They were very rich. And totally bigoted. The name Ramiro just didn't fit in with their idea of their daughter's future."

"Oh," Mandy said weakly.

Siobhan rose. "Well, that's it. I—I hope I've helped. I noticed the sparks flying at the bar tonight, and knowing him, well, I thought maybe you deserved an explanation."

Mandy bit her lip, rising to escort her visitor to the door. "Siobhan," she said impulsively, "It *has* helped. And I hope you believe that I would never feel that way. Sean ... Sean thinks that I do, though. I've got a few problems that he doesn't understand."

"I know," Siobhan said softly. "I know about your husband and your child. And I'm so sorry. But you've got a long life ahead of you. Neither of them would have wished you to spend it in misery."

"I'm afraid," Mandy told her.

"To care again? We all are."

"Siobhan," Mandy said again impulsively, "I'm going away for a while. To work."

"And more than that, to think?"

"Yes."

"Well, whatever you decide, I wish you the best."

"Thank you."

Siobhan kissed her cheek, smiled encouragingly, then hurried down the walk to her car.

Mandy watched the taillights until they disappeared in the night, then thoughtfully closed her door.

13

The dig was a recent one; the site had only been discovered about a year before. A camper had found a piece of bone sticking out of the ground in a field near the mountains. Curious, he had asked another friend to look at it, and luckily, the professionals had been called in before anything could be destroyed.

Mandy's time had just about expired, and she wasn't sure if she was sad—or grateful. There was a yearning in her to go home. She had desperately wanted to get away to think, but she hadn't really thought at all. By day she had chiseled and wrapped and plastered; by night she had lain alone and wished that she was not alone. What frightened her was that, though Sean hadn't actually said so, she knew that he wanted a wholehearted commitment, and she cringed like a child from that thought.

But then, she had thought she couldn't possibly make love with him, and that had occurred easily, beautifully. Maybe all things would follow suit. Maybe all she had to do was take the plunge.

As the afternoon fell she was sitting in her little spot in front of the phalanges of a Tyrannosaurus rex, carefully dusting the last of the sand from them with a sable brush so that they could be prepared for removal.

There was gigantic oak behind her, and a pile of rocks before her, so although the site was filled with workers, she was virtually alone. The find had been magnificent: a dozen of these particular beasts, and then any number of other creatures they had fed upon. She was glad to be alone, yet when she did try to think she panicked and wished that she was in the middle of a crowd.

A shadow suddenly fell across her work. Instinctively she looked up.

She was so surprised that the breath was swept cleanly from her.

Sean was standing there, in a standard three-piece suit. Tall and dark and handsome, a stray lock of hair falling over his forehead, his eyes as green as the spring fields. He stood there silently, then smiled slowly.

"Hello, Mandy."

She eased back at last, just staring for several moments. She lowered her head, thinking that this wasn't exactly how she had wanted to see him. She was in overalls and a dusty lab coat, and half the dirt that had been on the bones was smudging her face.

She shook her head, frowning, before she managed to speak. "What—what are you doing here?"

"I have a paper that needs your signature."

She frowned again. She'd heard from the FBI sporadically throughout the week, and no one had mentioned anything that required her signature.

"You're here on business?"

He hesitated a second too long. "Yes."

She smiled, looking back to the bones, delighted to see him, but wishing she'd had just a little more time.

He reached into his coat pocket for an envelope, then crouched down across from her. "This is it. You said you wanted to testify for Señora Garcia. This is a document compiled from your conversations with the FBI and the Miami PD. I need to get it back to the D.A.'s office. They've set a trial date for late September."

"Oh," Mandy murmured.

She read the document over. It had been accurately compiled and said exactly what she thought. She started to scrawl her name on it. "Is Señora Garcia in jail?"

"No. She's out on bond." He hesitated, then shrugged. "Julio's father is out, too. Peter had been pulling strings for him."

"What about Julio?"

Sean shook his head. "He's in jail. It's probably for the best. He'll definitely get time, and this will count toward it."

Mandy nodded. "Roberto?" she asked.

Sean's mouth twitched grimly. "I don't know what the courts will decide. But he's been connected to everything—drugs, robberies, murder. If they manage the case correctly, he'll end up with a dozen life sentences."

She lowered her head, shivering a bit. She still couldn't help but feel that Roberto deserved whatever he got.

"I, uh, got a telegram from Peter."

She raised her head quickly, frowning. "You did? Why?"

He smiled and reached into his pocket again, then passed her the paper. There were only two words on it, other than the address and the signature: MARRY HER.

Her hand started to shake; she clasped it with the other one and pursed her lips. Finally she said, "I guess he knew something was going on."

"So it seems."

"And you were wrong. He doesn't mind."

"I'm sure he minds." He paused, then asked, "Do you mind what I do?"

She stared at him, then shrugged. "Police work isn't the safest profession."

"But I'm in homicide. I deal with people who are dead—and harmless."

"But the people who made them dead aren't harmless."

He sighed softly. "Mandy, narcotics is a little scary. Not homicide. The last time I pulled a gun before I was on those docks—except on a shooting range—was four years ago. You watch too many cop shows."

She grinned. "Actually, I don't watch any."

"Oh."

"Aren't you forgetting something?"

"What?"

She tilted her head back, determined that, no matter what followed, she would not be punished for anyone else's sins. "I'm a blonde. Daughter of the American Revolution all the way. Rich bitch."

"Yeah, I know. I'm willing to overlook that."

"Are you? And what made you decide that I might not be a bigot?"

He lowered his head. Lowered his head, and lifted his shoulders and hands a little helplessly. "Mandy—"

"Oh!" she cried suddenly.

"What?"

"You're on his hip!"

"What?"

"Move back! Move back quickly. You're on my bone!"

"Oh." Red-faced, Sean scrambled to his feet, quickly moving away. Mandy hurried back to the slightly protruding bone, checking it quickly for damage.

She sighed with relief.

"Er, uh, what is he?"

"Tyrannosaurus rex," she answered absently.

"The big bad guy? The one in all the Japanese horror films?"

"Uh-huh. Except that he wasn't really so bad. See, look."

She stood, skirting the area to show him the complete layout of the skeleton. "Look at his arms—there. See how tiny they were in comparison to his bulk? He couldn't really grab and rip and tear. He could barely get things to his mouth. We think now that he was a scavenger—a carnivore, but one who went in *after* the kill had already been made."

She glanced up and blushed, surprised by the softness in his eyes as he stared at her. "You like your work, don't you?"

"Yes, very much."

"I like it, too. You could teach—me."

She didn't know what to say. As the breeze lifted her hair and wafted it around her face, she knew she should say something but, at that moment, she couldn't.

And then the moment was gone, because Dr. Theo Winter, who was in charge, came around the oak tree with a group of workers behind him, ready to start the plastering process. Mandy introduced Sean, but Dr. Winter was understandably unimpressed with anything but the cache of bones. All he wanted was for Sean to get off the site.

It was a good thing Dr. Winter hadn't seen Sean standing on the protruding skeleton, she thought wryly.

"I guess I'd better go," he told her, surprising her. She wasn't sure whether she was relieved or disappointed.

One of the assistants was asking a question, and she knew she had no right to be standing there talking while everyone else was working. But she didn't seem to be able to move any more than she could talk.

Sean solved that dilemma. He saluted her with a rueful grin, then walked away. She simply stood there, feeling the breeze in her hair, watching him leave.

Why hadn't he asked her to dinner or something? she wondered over and over again as the day wore on. But it wasn't a question that took much pondering on her part. It was going to be all or nothing. They weren't going to date. They weren't going to go for dinner or cocktails, or to the movies, or for a picnic in the park.

They were either going to get married or not—and only if she did marry him would she get to go to dinner and the movies and for walks on the beach. Maybe after the way they had begun it would be impossible to date.

She was beginning to understand him now; maybe he even understood her. She didn't think he was insensitive to her reasons for holding back; he just felt that they could be overcome—and should be.

Mandy thought she might hear from him the next day, but she didn't. He didn't contact her hotel, and he didn't appear on the site. She wondered if he had returned to Miami already and was startled to find herself annoyed at the thought. So much for hot pursuit!

On her last night there was a dinner party for her, which she made it through by rote. She realized that she had actually been doing all of her living by rote—until she met Sean.

There were a million good reasons why she should marry him, two that were extremely important. One, she loved him. Two, if the test she had bought at the drugstore worked, she was expecting his child.

The only thing that stood against her was the panic she felt at the prospect of loving so deeply again.

And the problem, which Sean didn't understand, was that it wasn't just an emotional reaction. It was physical. Her hands would sweat, her heart would beat too loudly. Confusion overwhelmed her at the thought.

Thought... Once upon a time she had assumed that she would simply never have another child, because the horror of loss was so deep. Of course, if not for circumstances, she would have been responsible enough never to let such a thing happen.

And now... now she knew that nothing would keep her from having this child.

Her thoughts would not leave her alone, not even for an instant. Not even while she said her goodbyes, lingered over breakfast to thank everyone—and nearly missed her plane because she seemed so incapable of doing anything right. She groaned while she raced through the airport terminal and decided that she was either going to marry Sean—he *was* serious, wasn't he?—or move to an isolated village in Alaska.

She settled into the sparsely populated first-class section of her plane and picked up a magazine. She had been staring at the picture of an elegant dining-room set for several seconds before she realized that it looked odd because it was upside down. She sighed, then froze.

Because Sean was on the plane, blocking those trying to board behind him, staring down at her in dismay.

"You're in first class?"

"What?"

"Oh, damn!"

He moved on by to let the others pass. Mandy just stared at the seat ahead of her. In a few minutes the passengers were all boarded and belted. The stewardess made her speech on safety, and then they were airborne.

At last Mandy kicked off her shoes and curled her feet beneath her, determined to get comfortable for the duration of the trip, despite the fact that her heart refused to slow its frantic beat. She didn't know if she wanted to laugh or cry. He really meant to force the issue.

The stewardess offered her champagne; she took it, intending to sip it. Instead, she swallowed the contents with a toss of her head.

The stewardess, of course, came right back, thinly concealing a shocked expression—and offered her more champagne.

"There's really nothing to be afraid of," the attractive young blonde told her. "Honestly. Captain Hodges has been flying for twenty years. He's wonderful. You won't feel a bump the entire way."

Mandy shook her head, smiling. "I'm not afraid of flying. I love to fly."

"Oh." Confused, the woman smiled, then quickly walked away.

Mandy stared out the window. They were already high above the clouds. It seemed that they were standing still above a sea of pure white cotton. If only she could concentrate. If only she could think about anything besides the fact that Sean was on the plane.

Her stomach lurched. What was the matter with her? He really did care. He had to care, or he would never have gone so far.

She took a deep breath, shivering. Did she really want to spend the rest of her life alone? Life was full of risks, and, yes, loving was a risk. But what was life except for a lonely expanse of years without the loving?

And now that Sean had touched her life, it seem absurdly bleak without him.

But could she love again? Worry about him, day after day? Pray that he came home each night? And what about children? Could she hold a child again, always knowing how quickly that life could be snuffed out?

"Move your feet."

Mandy started at the sound of his voice, then gasped, spilled her champagne and stared up at him guiltily.

"C'mon, move your feet!"

She did so, and he slid in beside her.

"What are doing up here? You're supposed to be in economy class!" she demanded.

"I bribed the stewardess."

"Stewardesses don't take bribes."

"Everyone takes bribes."

As if on cue, the stewardess walked by, watching them with a curiously knowing eye.

"What did you tell her?" Mandy asked suddenly.

He shrugged.

"Sean?"

"Nothing major." He smiled. "I just said that you were a deranged criminal whom I was trailing from Miami. I said I didn't want to put cuffs on you and frighten the other passengers—I just wanted to keep an eye on you." He smiled pleasantly, reached for a magazine, and gazed idly around the first-class cabin. "Nice."

"Sean, you didn't—"

"I did."

"I'll kill you!" Mandy snapped angrily just as the stewardess walked by again. The woman's eyes, cornflower blue and already big, seemed to grow as wide as saucers.

"Now, now, calm down, Mrs. Blayne," he said in a professional soothing voice. He winked at the stewardess, giving her a thumbs-up sign of assurance.

"Sean Ramiro—"

"Maybe you can plea bargain, Mrs. Blayne. Just stay calm, and I'll be at your side."

"I'm not a criminal!"

"Tsk, tsk, Mrs. Blayne. I'm afraid the State believes that lacing your great-uncle's coffee with that arsenic was a criminal offense."

The stewardess, barely a row ahead of them, stiffened and swallowed, and almost poured champagne on a businessman's lap.

"Sean, I *will* kill you!"

"Please, Mrs. Blayne. I really don't want to have to use the handcuffs."

"Oh, Lord!" Mandy groaned, sinking back into her seat and giving up. "There's definitely Irish blood in you—I've never heard so much blarney in my life!"

"Behave," he said wickedly, "and I'll get us more champagne. I do like this," he observed casually. "First class. It's a pity the department is so cheap."

"You really got the department to send you out to Denver?"

"Of course. I had to talk to you about the trial."

Mandy groaned again and turned to face the window. She didn't see the clouds anymore; only the reflection of his face. And for all his dry humor, she thought she saw pain mirrored there.

Her heart began to beat faster. It was the strangest thing, the most awful emotion. There he was, and there it was, all the laughter, all the love. All she had to do was reach for it, but she was unable to, taking two steps backward for every step forward.

She closed her eyes, then jumped when she heard him call the stewardess back.

"Could we get some more champagne, please?" He lowered his voice to a whisper. "I can control her much more easily if I keep her a bit sloshed, you know?"

"Oh, yes, of course!"

"Ohh!" Mandy groaned. "Couldn't you just have paid the difference for a first-class ticket?"

He started to answer her, then paused, thanking the stewardess gravely as she poured Mandy more champagne and offered a glass to Sean.

"Cheers!" he said, clinking his glass against hers.

She pursed her lips stubbornly, refusing to respond.

"Come on, where's the Mandy I used to know?"

A twitch tugged at her lips. "Damned if I know. Last I heard, you were taking a criminal back to Miami."

He started to smile wryly at her, but the stewardess returned with their lunch trays. And then, to Mandy's surprise, he didn't pay any attention to her at all. He was watching the stewardess.

The pretty woman seemed exceptionally nervous, which Mandy thought was Sean's fault, since he had convinced her that Mandy was a criminal.

The stewardess almost dropped the trays, but recovered her poise. Sean continued to watch her as she moved down the aisle, then sat back in his seat, perplexed.

"What's wrong?"

"Hmm?"

"What's wrong?"

She didn't like the way he looked. She really did love to fly, but suddenly she thought of all sorts of disasters. Someone had forgotten a little pin or something, and their jumbo jet was about to fall apart in midair.

Except that the flight wasn't even bumpy. It was so incredibly smooth that it felt as if they were standing still.

She gripped his arm tensely. "Sean," she whispered, "do you think there's something wrong with the plane?"

He stared at her. "The plane? Something wrong?" He shook his head. "I've never felt a smoother flight."

"Then what—?"

"Are you going to eat that steak?"

"What?"

"Eat, will you?"

He didn't pay any attention to his own food. He ate it, but he was giving all his attention to the stewardess.

The woman still seemed a little shaky when she returned. She had poise, though. She smiled; she chattered. It was just that her manner was slightly different, and not only with the two of them.

Mandy tried to quiz Sean again as soon as they trays were removed, but he interrupted her first word, murmuring, "Excuse me for a minute, please."

"Sean!"

But he was already gone. He disappeared into the little kitchen area—right behind the stewardess. And he seemed to stay there a long, long time.

When he emerged, he returned to his seat beside her like a sleepwalker, totally remote.

"Sean . . ."

"I don't believe it," he murmured distractedly.

"You don't believe what?"

"Shh. You didn't finish your champagne. Drink it."

Drink it. As if she would need it.

"Sean!" She slammed a fist against his shoulder.

"Shh!"

"You said there wasn't anything wrong with the plane."

"There isn't. I swear it."

The stewardess came hurriedly toward them once again, then bent to speak softly in Sean's ear. "We need you now, lieutenant."

He nodded and stood, ready to follow her again. She paused suddenly, looking back at Mandy with dismay.

"Will she be all right?"

"What? Oh, yes, of course. As long as you don't have any arsenic on board."

They disappeared together toward the cockpit. Mandy was ready to scream.

It seemed an eternity before he returned, though it was only about twenty minutes.

"Sean, what the hell is going on?"

"Hey!" someone complained loudly from behind them. "I take this flight constantly. What's going on?

They should have announced landing by now. And we should be over land—not water!"

"Damn you, Sean Ramiro!" Mandy whispered, alarmed. "What's going on?"

He turned to her at last. "I didn't want to alarm you—"

"You didn't want to alarm me?"

"Shh! There's nothing wrong with the plane. Honest. In fact, there's really nothing wrong at all. We're just taking a little side trip."

"Side trip?"

"Er, yes."

Just then the pilot came over the loudspeaker. He sounded marvelously, wonderfully calm. He started by explaining that obviously their seasoned passengers would realize that they were not flying their usual route. He assured them that nothing was wrong. It was just that they had a "gentleman" aboard who was insisting that they fly on to José Marti airport—in Havana.

Mandy gasped and stared at Sean. "We're being hijacked to Cuba!"

"Yes, I know," he said uncomfortably. "I tried to talk him out of it."

The pilot then turned the microphone over to the "gentleman" in question, who told the passengers in broken English that he didn't want to hurt anybody, certainly not Captain Hodges, but that he had been away from his homeland now for eight years and was determined to go back.

"I don't believe this!" Mandy breathed. She stared at Sean again. "Can't you do something?"

"I'm afraid not. He's got a Bowie knife at the captain's back and a hand grenade to boot."

"How'd he ever get on the plane?"

"How the hell should I know?"

Their conversation ended at that point, because the stewardess began calmly putting them through a crash-landing procedure just in case they had difficulty landing. There was no panic on plane, possibly because the pilot came on again, assuring them that they had been cleared to land at José Marti.

"I really don't believe this!" Mandy whispered nervously as she prepared for landing.

"I am sorry, Mandy. Really."

"You're sorry?"

"Yeah. I'm trying to convince you that we're a great people, and all you get to meet are the kidnappers and the hijackers."

She gripped his hand tightly. "That's not true. I got to meet one really great cop."

The plane jolted as the landing gear came down.

"Hey, you're admitting it at last. I told you I was really great."

The wheels touched the ground and the brakes came on with a little screech. Mandy prayed that the runway was long enough for the jet.

It was.

In seconds the plane came to a complete stop. And then, seconds later, it began filling with the Cuban military.

Mandy quickly lost Sean. The stewardess came back for him, desperate for a translator.

It seemed to Mandy that she sat there by herself forever. Nothing happened to her; nothing happened to anyone, but it seemed like absolute chaos. There were just too many people on the plane, and at some point, the air conditioning went out.

The heat was sweltering, and just when she thought she couldn't take it anymore an announcement was made that buses would be coming to take the passengers to the terminal, where they were welcome to exchange their money and buy food and souvenirs.

Mandy craned her neck to find Sean, but she couldn't see him. Unhappily, she started to leave along with the others.

She was stopped at the steps by a trim officer with a Clark Gable mustache. She couldn't understand him, and he couldn't understand her. All she could tell was that he was insisting she stay behind, and a case of the jitters assailed her again. Why her? Oh, God! Maybe *they* though she was a murderess, too!

But she merely found herself escorted back to the center of the plane, where Sean was in earnest conversation with several more mustachioed officers. The talking went on and on, with everyone gesticulating.

Finally the man who looked to be the ranking officer shrugged, and the others laughed, then stared at her, smirking.

Sean turned to her then and gripped her arm. "Quick!" he whispered into her ear. "Let's go. There will be a car at the foot of the steps. Get right into it, and act as if you love me to death!"

"What?"

"Shh! Just do it!"

"I—"

"Mandy! Please!"

He didn't give her any choice. He shoved her down the aisle, then hurried her down the stairs.

The car was there, just as he had said, a black stretch limo. She climbed into the back with Sean, and was surprised when the official with the Clark Gable mustache followed.

At last they reached an impressive building with emblems all over beautiful wrought-iron gates. She managed to whisper to Sean, "Where the hell are we, and what the hell is going on?"

"The Swiss embassy," he whispered back. "The pilot is around here somewhere, too. He has to make special arrangements for fuel to get home."

The car stopped. The Cuban official was greeted by a tall blond man, but though this might have been the Swiss embassy, they were still speaking Spanish, and she was lost.

"Sean, I don't care about the pilot. What are *we* doing here?"

"They're, uh, trying to keep me here," he said.

"What?"

He took both her hands earnestly. "Just help me, Mandy. Go along with me. They know who I am."

"Who are you?"

"Oh, it all goes way back. You wouldn't want me to be stuck here forever, would you?"

She gazed at him warily. "Go on."

"Marry me. If I marry an American citizen—"

"You are an American citizen."

"Ah, but I told you, they know me! My father was involved in some things that—"

"Uh-uh! This guy is acting like your long-lost friend."

"Actually, he is. I was in school with him until the night I fled the country."

"I thought you were born in Ireland."

"I was. It's a long story." He put his hands on her shoulders and pulled her anxiously to him. "Well? They've given me a chance. The Swiss will give us a license and a minister. Mandy! Come on! You've got to get me out of this one."

She stared at him for a long, long time. At the sun above them, at the flowers, at the sky, at the beautiful mountains in the distance.

This wasn't how she had expected things to go at all. The other passengers were busy buying trinkets as mementos of their incredible day, while she was here with Sean, listening to the most outrageous cock-and-bull story she had ever heard in her life.

She lowered her head, smiling slowly, and just a little painfully. After all these years, he had come back to his Cuban heritage, and it was his Irish blarney that was showing!

Her past flashed before her eyes. And she knew that although it would always be there, the time had come to gently close the door on it.

"If I don't do this, they'll keep you here, huh?"

"They could put me in prison."

"Oh."

"Well?"

"I don't suppose I could let that happen to you, could I?"

"It would be terribly mean, considering all I've done for you."

She was silent. He gazed at his watch impatiently. "Mandy! We have to do this before they make the fuel arrangements!"

She shrugged. "Then let's do it."

The Swiss were charming. Papers were secured, and they were ushered into a little chapel that adjoined the building. The ceremony was in French, and amazingly quick, because everyone was rushing.

Mandy smiled through it all, wondering how Sean had ever convinced the Cuban military authorities to let him get away with this nonsense.

But when her "I do" was followed by a very passionate kiss, she assumed it would be something they could talk about for ages.

They were whisked very quickly back to the airport. The fuel had been secured, and all the passengers had reboarded with the rum, cigars, and so forth.

They were in the air before Sean turned to her sheepishly at last. "I have a confession to make. I asked Captain Rotello for special permission to marry you. I lied, though I really did go to school with him. And he did know about my father. Our dads had been friends."

"Oh," Mandy said simply.

"Well, do you hate me?"

She looked at him regally, a superior smile playing on her lips. She saw the tension and passion in his wonderful green eyes.

"Actually, no, I have a confession to make myself."

"Oh, really?"

"I knew you were lying all along. I may not speak Spanish, but I'm not a fool."

"Oh," he said blankly.

"I did intend to learn the language, of course. Completely. I mean, I'll be damned if I'll have you and our son talking about me when I don't understand a single word you're saying!"

"Our son?"

"Or daughter."

"We're—we're having one?"

"In December. Maybe November."

He swallowed then, a little stiffly. "You married me . . . because you're pregnant?"

"I swear I'll hit you! I married you because I love you! Not because of your ridiculous story, and not because I'm pregnant. Come to think of it, you did threaten me about that! But—"

He smiled, his arm coming around her as he interrupted her. "You love me, huh?"

"Yes, and you know it."

"Yeah, well, it just sounds real nice to hear the words now and then. You'd better start practicing, because I'd like to hear them more frequently from now on."

"Hey, what's good for the goose—"

"I love you, Mrs. Ramiro. Desperately. Passionately. I love you, I love you, I love you—"

Unfortunately, the stewardess made an appearance just then.

"She loves me! She married me!" Sean told the woman.

"But I thought she was—you just married a murderess?"

"Oh, well, that—"

"Lieutenant Ramiro, what a line you gave me! Get back where you're supposed to be—in economy!"

But she wasn't serious. After all, it had been a most unusual flight. She merely arranged for more champagne.

Mandy laughed with him while they sipped champagne, then sobered slightly. "Is this real?"

"It's real."

"Sean . . . I may need help sometimes."

"We all need help sometimes."

"I do love you. So much. I guess I did, even on the island. I wanted to be rescued, but I didn't want to go back. Not to a life without you."

"Mandy..."

His champagne glass clinked down on his tray. His arms swept around her, his fingers curling into her hair. And when his lips touched hers she was hungry for him, so hungry that it was easy to become swept up in his embrace and to forget that they were on a populated plane.

He broke away from her, groaning softly, excitingly, against her cheek. "Mrs. Ramiro, watch your hands."

"No one can see me."

"Well, they might see me! Oh, God, I can't wait till we get off this plane. Your place or mine?"

"Mine. I think we should sell yours."

"I think we should sell *yours*." He smiled. "Oh, hell! I don't care where we go—as long as we get there!"

It took them another two hours to get anywhere; in the end he went to her house, because it was closer to the airport. And though Mandy would have thought that such a feat was impossible, he managed to disrobe them both while climbing the stairs, strewing fabric down the length of the steps, then landing them on her bed in what was surely record time.

She was so happy. So amazed that she was his wife, that they were making love on the evening of their marriage. That they were both totally, completely committed.

It was fast; it was feverish—it had to be at first.

But the night stretched before them. Time for her to warn him that she owned one of the ugliest cats in the world, time for him to warn her that his partners could be a pain in the neck. Time to discuss things that hurt; time to talk about the past, and time to put it to rest.

And then time to make love all over again.

"*Te amo*," Mandy told him carefully, practicing the Spanish she had learned.

He smiled, tenderness blazing in his eyes, and she murmured the strange words again, "*Te amo*—here," she said, meeting his eyes, then kissing his chest. "And *te amo*—here."

With each repetition she moved against him, finding more and more deliciously erogenous zones.

"And *te amo*—here."

He gripped her hair, breathless, ablaze. He groaned, and at last swept her beneath him, pausing just an instant to whisper, "Mrs. Ramiro. I have never, never heard Spanish more eloquently spoken."

"*Querido!*" she whispered, and contentedly locked her arms about him.

He found life in her arms. And he gave her a new life, all she would ever ask in the world.

"*Querida!* My love, my love."

He kissed her abdomen and smiled as she arched to him.

She knew that she could love again.

Love a child, love a husband.

Even if he was rather manipulating and most certainly strange—and, oh, passionate!—and...

"Sean..."

She simply couldn't ponder it any longer.

It was the...circumstances.

Epilogue

Sean hesitated momentarily after he opened the door, wondering what Mandy's reaction would be to the visitor he was bringing home.

"Amanda?"

He stepped into the entryway of the big old frame house they had bought and stared through the living room to the office. As he had expected, she was at her desk, her reading glasses at the tip of her nose as she pored over term papers.

Katie—a toddling and mischievous two now—was playing sedately with her locking plastic blocks, probably trying to recreate a dinosaur like the one her mother had made her the night before, Sean thought wryly.

"Mandy?" he called again.

She looked up, saw him, threw her glasses down and scooped Katie into her arms before coming to meet him excitedly, her words rushing out.

"Sean, believe it or not, I had the best time in the world today! I went into the market on Flagler because they have the best ham in the world. I have to admit I always resented going there before, because everyone spoke Spanish, but mine has gotten so good, and I got into this wonderful conversation with the clerk and I started to teach her English! I—oh!"

Her spiel came to an abrupt halt when she saw that her husband was not alone, and she stared at her visitor in dead surprise.

Sean slipped an arm around her. "Julio stepped into my office just when I was getting off for the day. He was just paroled, and he was anxious to see you."

"Oh," Mandy murmured.

Julio Garcia, gaunt-looking in a too-big suit, smiled hesitantly and offered his hand.

She took it, balancing her daughter in her other arm.

"I had to come," he told her softly. "The government has released me. But that is nothing. I must ask you to forgive me. I must hope that you understand and can believe that I did not ever wish to harm you. That—that I know now how wrong I was." His eyes were totally in earnest.

Mandy smiled at last, feeling the assurance of her husband's arm around her shoulders. "I forgive you, Julio. How... how are your parents?"

He gave her a smile that seemed to light up the room. "They are well. Even my father is well. The United States gave him a doctor who is good. And Mama, Mama is Mama."

Mandy nodded, then asked curiously, "And Maria?"

Julio laughed. "Mama married Maria off to a man with a will like iron. She is like you—one babe in her arms, one to come."

Mandy didn't ask about Juan or Roberto. Sean had assured her at the trial that Roberto faced so many charges that even if he lived to be an old, old man, he would probably never leave prison again.

Juan, too, would not come up for parole. He had been involved in a narcotics case before the kidnapping, and the judge hadn't shown him one bit of leniency.

"I am very happy for you, Mrs. Ramiro," Julio said. "Congratulations. Your daughter is beautiful."

Mandy discovered that she was able to laugh proudly. "Yes, she is. Thank you."

Katie was staring at Julio with her knuckles shoved into her mouth, but she really was beautiful. She had Sean's green eyes and a headful of ebony curls.

"You wish a son now, yes?" Julio asked.

It was Sean, lightly massaging his wife's nape, who answered. "Not necessarily. I'm awfully fond of girls. A son, a daughter, it doesn't matter. Mandy and I were both only children, and we both wished that we'd had a brother or a sister, so..."

He shrugged, and Mandy flushed, because though they'd both been quite happy about it, this baby was as completely unplanned as Katie had been.

"Well..." Julio cleared his throat and shifted his weight from foot to foot. "I must go now, I did not wish to impose. I just wanted you to know that I appreciate how you told them at the trial that you did not think I was cruel, but needed help. And that I wished so much for your forgiveness. I have a good job already, too. I am a mechanic. One day I will own my own garage."

"I'm sure you will," Mandy said softly.

"Goodbye, then, *señora*. I wish you and your husband and your lovely family all the best."

Sean walked him to the door. Mandy watched them, hugging Katie to her.

When Sean returned she was still smiling, so he arched one of his dark brows curiously. "Okay, out with it. What are you thinking?"

She laughed, managing to hug him and Katie at the same time. "I was just thinking that I really do forgive him with all my heart. Without him, I'd have never met this weird cop who stuck by me through thick and thin—and then married me, to boot."

"Hey, duty called. And you were such a marvelous blond bombshell."

"Yeah?"

"Yeah."

He grinned, then kissed her warmly and deeply until Kate let out an outraged squawk that Mommy and Daddy were crushing her.

They laughed together again, and their eyes touched, full of promises.

New York Times Bestselling Author

NORA ROBERTS

This November, lose yourself to the pulsing rhythms of

Dance to the Piper

She was in perfect harmony to the music that ruled her life, both onstage and off. Music was his business and he was *all* business until she lit up the stage.

An instant attraction. An impossible dream. Did they dare defy the odds and make the impossible... possible? And would her dreams be big enough for both of them?

Reach for the brightest star in women's fiction with

MIRA™ ™

MNR1

"You have to."

"You got them off, you get them back on."

She was so drowsy; his answering chuckle was so husky. She wanted to forget everything. She wanted to remain against his shoulder and fall asleep.

"All right," he said agreeably.

And then he let her go and dove beneath the water. But what he did to her there had nothing to do with getting her pants back on, and everything to do with getting her excited again. She started to protest, swallowed water, then wrenched the cutoffs back from him and struggled back into them.

When she finished, he was still laughing. "Not fair!" she cried.

Suddenly he wasn't laughing anymore. He pulled her close to him, against his heart. His whisper touched her ear. "I'm sorry. Do you forgive me?"

"I guess I just did."

"No, that was sex, not forgiveness. Do you forgive me?"

She couldn't say anything. She didn't know if she did or didn't; she just knew that she didn't want him to let her go.

"Damn it, Julio is waving that stinking gun of his around. Come on. We've got to go in. Night must be coming."

It was. And with the night came a horrendous argument between Julio and Roberto.

Mandy didn't understand any of it; it was all in Spanish. She was in the kitchen when it began, eating a sausage sandwich for dinner. Señora Garcia decided that Mandy shouldn't be a part of it. She hurried Mandy into her room, made her wait, then returned with shampoo and soap. Mandy knew that though her

her weak form, carry her to the mattress and find his own reward.

The wonderful heat of the night wrapped itself around Mandy so completely that the island might in truth have been their own. Yet finally, when they had lain quietly together for some time, Sean turned to her, smoothing back her still-damp hair.

"We have to do something—tomorrow morning."

Her heart pitched and thudded; reality cut her like a knife. "Why? What happened?"

"Juan hasn't returned. Roberto thinks that he's been caught. He wants to take the skiff out tomorrow and go back."

In the darkness Mandy frowned. "I don't understand."

Sean hesitated for a long time.

"He wants to take one of your fingers with him. He called Julio a coward with no convictions and told him that his father will die in prison."

"Oh, God!" Mandy gasped.

Sean's fingers grabbed painfully at her hair. "You are to do nothing! Do you understand? Stay in here when you find me gone. Don't move, and I mean it. I won't be able to follow through with my plan if I have to worry about you, too. I mean it! Now go to sleep."

"Go to sleep?"

"Yes!"

She would never sleep. And that night she didn't.